RURAL POLICIES AND EMPLOYMENT

TransAtlantic Experiences

Titles of Interest

Agriculture & Food Systems to 2050: Global Trends, Challenges and Opportunities
edited by Rachid Serraj and Prabhu Pingali
ISBN: 978-981-3278-34-9

The Economies of China and India: Cooperation and Conflict (In 3 Volumes)
Volume 1: China and India: The International Context and Economic Growth, Manufacturing Performance and Rural Development
Volume 2: Competitiveness, External Cooperation Strategy and Income Distribution: Changes in China
Volume 3: Economic Growth, Employment and Inclusivity: The International Environment
editor-in-chief: John Whalley
edited by Manmohan Agarwal, Jing Wang and John Whalley
ISBN: 978-981-3100-39-8 (Set)
ISBN: 978-981-3100-51-0 (Vol. 1)
ISBN: 978-981-3100-52-7 (Vol. 2)
ISBN: 978-981-3100-53-4 (Vol. 3)

Global Challenges for Future Food and Agricultural Policies
editor-in-chief: Tim Josling
edited by David Blandford and Katharine Hassapoyannes
ISBN: 978-981-3235-39-7

RURAL POLICIES AND EMPLOYMENT

TransAtlantic Experiences

editors

Sophia M. Davidova
University of Kent, UK

Kenneth J. Thomson
University of Aberdeen, UK

Ashok K. Mishra
Arizona State University, W. P. Carey School of Business, Morrison School of Agribusiness, USA

World Scientific

NEW JERSEY • LONDON • SINGAPORE • BEIJING • SHANGHAI • HONG KONG • TAIPEI • CHENNAI

Published by

World Scientific Publishing Europe Ltd.

57 Shelton Street, Covent Garden, London WC2H 9HE

Head office: 5 Toh Tuck Link, Singapore 596224

USA office: 27 Warren Street, Suite 401-402, Hackensack, NJ 07601

Library of Congress Cataloging-in-Publication Data

Names: Davidova, S. (Sofiia) editor. | Thomson, Ken, 1946– editor. | Mishra, Ashok K. (Ashok Kumar), 1967– editor.

Title: Rural policies and employment : transatlantic experiences / edited by Sophia Davidova (University of Kent, UK), Ken Thomson (University of Aberdeen, UK) and Ashok Mishra (Morrison School of Agribusiness, USA).

Description: New Jersey : World Scientific, [2019] | Includes bibliographical references and index.

Identifiers: LCCN 2019008592 | ISBN 9781786347084 (hc : alk. paper)

Subjects: LCSH: Rural development--Government policy--United States. | Rural development--Government policy--European Union countries. | Manpower policy, Rural--United States. | Manpower policy, Rural--European Union countries. | Agriculture and state--United States. | Agriculture and state--European Union countries.

Classification: LCC HN90.C6 D38 2019 | DDC 307.1/412--dc23

LC record available at https://lccn.loc.gov/2019008592

British Library Cataloguing-in-Publication Data

A catalogue record for this book is available from the British Library.

For any available supplementary material, please visit
https://www.worldscientific.com/worldscibooks/10.1142/Q0210#t=suppl

Desk Editors: Aanand Jayaraman/Jennifer Brough/Shi Ying Koe

Typeset by Stallion Press
Email: enquiries@stallionpress.com

About the Editors

Sophia M. Davidova is a Professor of European Agricultural Policy and Honorary Director of the Center for European Agri-Environmental Studies (CEAS) at the School of Economics, University of Kent, UK. Her main research interests lie in the area of the effects of CAP reforms on producer performance and income diversification in the EU, rural labor market, and in particular on policy impact on small farms. She is a former President of the UK Agricultural Economics Society.

Kenneth J. Thomson is a Professor of Agricultural Economics at the University of Aberdeen and Honorary Research Associate at the James Hutton Institute, Aberdeen, Scotland, UK. His main expertise and interests are in European agricultural and rural policies, including various countries in Central Europe, as well as within the UK and Scotland. He also has interests in economic modeling, regional economics, and policies for forestry, fishing and rural tourism. He is a former President of the UK Agricultural Economics Society.

Ashok K. Mishra holds the Kemper and Ethel Marley Foundation Chair in Food Management, Morrison School of Agribusiness, W. P. Carey School of Business, at the Arizona State University, USA. He previously held positions at Louisiana State University and the Economic Research Service of the USDA. He conducts research and teaching activities in public policy, finance, agri-business, food security. He currently serves as the Co-Editor of *Agricultural Economics: An International Journal* and Editor of *Journal of Agribusiness in Developing and Emerging Economies*.

About the Contributors

Mary Ahearn was formerly a Senior Agricultural Economist with the Economic Research Service of the US Department of Agriculture. Her primary areas of expertise were the economic well-being of farm operators and their households, the structure and the performance of the agricultural sector, and policies affecting structure and well-being.

Alastair Bailey is a Reader in Agricultural Economics and Head of the School of Economics at the University of Kent, UK. His research interests lie principally in agriculture and agriculture's impact on the environment, including the study of small farmer market engagement, rural-to-urban migration, the valuation of consumer concerns for pesticide use in food production systems, and technology adoption.

William J. Bamka is an Associate Professor and County Agricultural Agent with Rutgers University, New Jersey Agricultural Experiment Station. He is involved in the Agritourism Working Group and provides extension programming and educational outreach on agri-tourism and direct marketing to farmers and agricultural service providers.

David Blandford is a Professor Emeritus, Agricultural and Environmental Economics in the Department of Agricultural Economics, Sociology and Education, Penn State University, USA. His research interests lie in policy development for agriculture and food, environment and natural resources, and community, regional and international development. He is a former President of the UK Agricultural Economics Society.

Tessa Conroy is an Economic Development Specialist with the University of Wisconsin, Extension Center for Community and Economic Development, and a Professor at the University of Wisconsin–Madison, US in the Department of Agriculture and Applied Economics. Her research is focused on community economic growth and development, small business dynamics, and women entrepreneurs.

Steven C. Deller is a Professor in the Department of Agricultural and Applied Economics, University of Wisconsin–Madison, US. His research areas include modeling community and small regional economies to better understand the changing dynamics of the economy, assess the impact of those changes, and identify local economic strengths, weaknesses, opportunities and threats.

Charles B. Dodson is a Senior Agricultural Economist within the Economic and Policy Analysis staff of the Farm Service Agency of the US Department of Agriculture. He serves as the primary advisor on farm credit programs and is responsible for conducting economic analysis of direct guaranteed loan programs, including assessing program effectiveness, anticipating problems, and making appropriate recommendations for change.

Trevor Donnellan is a Principal Research Officer and Head of the Agricultural Economics and Farm Surveys Department at Teagasc, the Agriculture and Food Development Authority of the Republic of Ireland. His research involves the economic analysis of agricultural input and output markets in Irish and European agriculture, and of policy issues affecting the agri-food sector.

Liesbeth Dries is an Associate Professor at the Agricultural Economics and Rural Policy Group of Wageningen University, the Netherlands. Her research interests are in structural adjustment, and in particular issues of organization and governance in EU agri-food chains, with specific focus on vertical and horizontal coordination and the use of contracts in the agri-food sector.

Janet Dwyer is a Professor of Rural Policy and Director of the Countryside and Community Research Institute (CCRI) at the University of Gloucestershire, UK. Her research expertise centers on European and UK rural development policy and practice, with particular interest in integrated approaches, environmental sustainability and institutional adaptation.

Michelle Haefele is a Research Scientist with the Department of Agricultural and Resource Economics at Colorado State University, USA. She studies the economic benefits of public lands, while working at the US Forest Service and the Wilderness Society.

Kevin Hanrahan is a Research Officer in the Agricultural Economics and Farm Surveys Department at Teagasc, the Agriculture and Food Development Authority of the Republic of Ireland. His research interests are the economic analysis of agricultural factor markets, of agricultural and trade policy reform, and of Irish beef production.

J. Michael Harris was formerly an Economist in the Rural Economy Branch of the Resource and Rural Economics Division, Economic Research Service, US Department of Agriculture. His research included agri-business, farm finance, farm financial analysis, farm household economics, developing and enhancing measures of farm stress and insolvency, and analyzing data from the Agricultural Resource and Management Survey and other data sources.

David R. Harvey is an Emeritus Professor of Agricultural Economics at the University of Newcastle upon Tyne, England. He is the Editor-in-Chief of the *Journal of Agricultural Economics*. His research interests are centered on the analysis of agricultural policy, particularly the EU's Common Agricultural Policy, and its effects on trade and land use. He is a former President of the UK Agricultural Economics Society.

Thomas Hertz is an Economist in the Rural Economy Branch of the Resource and Rural Economics Division, Economic Research Service, US Department of Agriculture. Prior to coming to ERS he taught at American University and the International University College in Turin, and was a visiting scholar at the Food and Agriculture Organization (FAO) in Rome. Tom studies immigration policy, and rural and farm labor-market trends.

Berkeley Hill is an Emeritus Professor in the Center for Environmental Policy, at Imperial College, London. His specialism is the interface between economic statistics and policy, particularly the measurement of income and wealth of farm businesses and farm households. He has been a specialist advisor to the House of Lords (UK) for two of its Inquiries into the future of rural society, and the problems of instability and resilience in farming. He is a former President of the UK Agricultural Economics Society.

Rebecca Hill is a Research Scientist with the Department of Agricultural and Resource Economics at Colorado State University, USA. She specializes in research related to agri-tourism, outdoor recreation, water resources and economic impact analysis.

Michelle L. Infante-Casella is an Associate Professor and Agricultural Agent, Rutgers University, New Jersey Agricultural Experiment Station. She is involved in the Agritourism Working Group, and provides extension programming and educational outreach on agri-tourism and direct marketing to farmers and agricultural service providers.

Thomas G. Johnson is a Professor Emeritus at the University of Missouri, USA. He was formerly the Frank Miller Professor of Agricultural and Applied Economics, and Professor in the Harry S Truman School of Public Affairs. His recent research areas include the process of wealth creation and distribution in rural communities, fiscal and economic impact analysis, local government finance, renewable energy, rural entrepreneurship, broadband, land use and rural transportation.

Mathias Kloss is a Head of Risk Management at the University Hospital Halle (Saale) and a former staff member at the Leibniz Institute of Agricultural Development in Transition Economies (IAMO), Halle, Germany. His fields of expertise include the analysis of agricultural factor markets and applied micro-econometrics.

Stephen J. Komar is an Associate Professor and County Agricultural Agent with Rutgers University, New Jersey Agricultural Experiment Station. He is involved in the Agritourism Working Group and provides extension programming and educational outreach on agri-tourism and direct marketing to farmers and agricultural service providers.

Matthew Kures is a Community Development Specialist with the University of Wisconsin, Extension Center for Community and Economic Development. Working in partnership with Extension's statewide network of Community Resource Development (CRD) educators, he assists communities and organizations in the areas of regional economic analysis, labor force research, socio-economic impact analysis and industry sector competitiveness.

Sarah Low is an Associate Professor, Heinkel Chair in Agriculture, and State Extension Specialist, at the University of Missouri, USA. She previously worked in the USDA Economic Research Service where she conducted research on rural economic development strategies, including local food marketing, entrepreneurship, labor, land use, amenities and spatial analysis.

Francesco Mantino is a Senior Researcher at the Council for Agricultural Research and Analysis of Agricultural Economics-Policies and Bio-economy (CREA-PB) in Rome, Italy. He has worked on research projects in the broad field of rural and regional development: structural changes, policy analysis, rural development strategies at local level, development of lagging regions and peripheral/mountain areas, evaluation of EU programmes.

Jack Peerlings is an Associate Professor at the Agricultural Economics and Rural Policy Group of Wageningen University, the Netherlands. He has research experience on topics related to agricultural policy, land use and the relation between farming, and the environment in the Netherlands and the EU. Specific topics of interest include the provision of green services, landscape valuation, rural policy modeling and land use analysis. He acts as editor of the *European Review of Agricultural Economics*.

Martin Petrick is a Professor of Agricultural, Food and Environmental Policy at Justus Liebig University Giessen, Germany, and a Visiting Research Fellow at the Leibniz Institute of Agricultural Development in Transition Economies (IAMO), Halle, Germany. His fields of expertise include structural change in agriculture, agricultural transition in former Soviet countries, the evaluation of agricultural policy measures and public action in rural development.

John Powell is a Senior Research Fellow at the Countryside and Community Research Institute (CCRI) at the University of Gloucestershire, UK. His current research includes the governance and management of commons resources, and the development of techniques for valuing ecosystems services and cultural heritage within an ecosystems service framework in two areas of the UK, and in Norway.

Marian Rizov is a Professor of Economics at the Business School of the University of Lincoln, UK. His research interests concern applied microeconomics and finance, covering economic development and productivity, food economics and agri-business, labor economics and industrial relations. He has been involved in research on the EU New Member States of Central and Eastern Europe.

Brian Schilling is the Director of Cooperative Extension and Associate Professor of Agricultural, Food and Resource Economics at Rutgers, the State University of New Jersey. His research interests include agricultural viability and policy in urbanizing areas, agri-tourism enterprise development, farmland preservation/farm retention and development, and economic performance, trends, and public policies in the food industry.

Bill Slee is an Honorary Fellow at the James Hutton Institute, Aberdeen, Scotland, UK. His research is focused on interrelationships between the farming and forestry sectors and the other component parts of the rural economy, and the exploration of the environmental externalities associated with rural land use.

Martha Sullins is an Extension Specialist at Colorado State University where she works with agricultural producers around the state to improve business viability through value-added enterprises, such as agri-tourism, and teaches business planning, marketing and overall risk management strategies.

David Swenson is a Community and Regional economist in the Department of Economics at Iowa State University and a lecturer in the School of Urban and Regional Planning at the University of Iowa, USA. His areas of research include state and local fiscal policy, rural economic transformations and the demographic consequences of regional economic change. He has studied a wide range of value-added production in agriculture, including ethanol, animal processing, local food systems, and alternative energy opportunities.

Dawn Thilmany is a Professor and Outreach Coordinator, Department of Agricultural and Resource Economics, Colorado State University, Fort Collin, USA. Her specialization is in the area of agri-business management, agricultural marketing and regional economics. She conducts research on food system issues, from analysis of consumer behavior and market trends to assessment of economic implications of new agricultural and food system innovations.

Catherine C. Thomas is an economist with the Fort Collins Science Center Social and Economic Analysis Branch. Catherine specializes in regional economic impact modeling, data collection, survey analysis and data visualization. Since joining the US Geological Survey in 2010, she has built models to estimate the jobs and business activity associated with National Park visitation, Fish and Wildlife Service Wildlife Refuge management, and ecological restoration projects.

Leon van de Pol was involved as a Research Associate in the project on strengthening European food chain sustainability by quality and procurement policy. He currently works as a policy officer at the European Commission, Directorate General on Agriculture (DG AGRI).

Anders van Sandt is a Postdoctoral Extension Associate in the College of Agricultural Sciences, Texas A&M University, where he conducts research on rural economic development, such as spatial and visitor heterogeneity in the agri-tourism industry.

Davide Viaggi is an Associate Professor in the Department of Agricultural and Food Sciences, University of Bologna, Italy. His research includes the evaluation of the effects of the EU's Common Agricultural Policy in rural areas, water management in agriculture and broadly the economics of agri-environmental policies. He has also analyzed farm investment behavior, and innovation in farms and agri-food small- and medium-sized enterprises.

Mauro Vigani is a Senior Research Fellow at the Countryside and Community Research Institute (CCRI) at the University of Gloucestershire, UK. His current research interests concern the impact of sustainable innovation and risk management practices on farm productivity, the effects of adoption of agricultural technologies on farms' sustainability and household food security, and the role of mass media in influencing policy outcomes.

Katarzyna Zawalińska is a Head of Economic Modeling Department at the Institute of Rural and Agricultural Development, Polish Academy of Sciences, Poland. Her expertise is in policy evaluations based on advanced quantitative methods. Her specific interests are in regional Computable General Equilibrium modeling, econometric analyses and applied policy evaluation techniques.

Contents

List of Abbreviations

ACS	American Community Survey
AEMs	Agro-Environmental Measures
AFF	Agriculture, Forestry and Fishing
ARMS	Agricultural Resource Management Survey
CAP	Common Agricultural Policy
CEE	Central and Eastern Europe
CEECs	Central and Eastern European Countries
CMEF	Common Monitoring and Evaluation Framework
CMO	Common Market Organization
DEFRA	Department for Environment, Food and Rural Affairs
DG Agri	Directorate-General for Agriculture and Rural Development of the European Commission
DPs	Direct Payments
EAFRD	European Agricultural Fund for Rural Development
EAGGF	European Agricultural Guidance and Guarantee Fund
EEC	European Economic Community
EMFF	European Maritime and Fisheries Fund
ERDF	European Regional Development Fund
ERS	Economic Research Service
ESF	European Social Fund
ESIFs	European Structural and Investment Funds

EU	European Union (EU-15, EU-27, EU-28 the number of EU members)
Eurostat	The Statistical Office of the EU
FAME	Financial Analysis Made Easy
FEOGA	French acronym for EAGGF
FCA/FCS	Farm Credit Administration/System
FLS	Farm Labor Survey
FPBT	Food Processing, Beverages and Tobacco
FSA	Farm Service Agency
FSS	Farm Structure Survey
FY	Financial (or Fiscal) Year
GAEC	Good Agricultural and Environmental Conditions
GAP	Gross Agricultural Product
GDP	Gross Domestic Product
GNI	Gross National Income
GSE	Government Sponsored Enterprise
GVA	Gross Value Added
IBP	Iowa Beef Processors
IDP	Integrated Development Programs
I–O	Input–Output
ISTAT	National Institute of Statistics
KBBE	Knowledge-Based Bio-Economy
LAU	Local Administrative Unit
LEADER	Links between Actions for the Development of the Rural Economy
MFF	Multiannual Financial Framework
NASS	National Agricultural Statistics Service
NAWS	National Agricultural Workers Survey
NEET(s)	Person(s) not in Education, Employment or Training
NMS(s)	New Member State(s) of the EU

NUTS	Nomenclature of Territorial Units for Statistics
OECD	Organization for Economic Cooperation and Development
OGA	Other Gainful Activity
OMB	Office of Management and Budget
PDO	Protected Designation of Origin
PGI	Protected Geographical Indication
RDP	Rural Development Program (or Plan)
RDR	Rural Development Regulation
SAPARD	Special Accession Program for Agriculture and Rural Development
SAPS	Single Area Payment Scheme
SFP	Single Farm Payment
SIC	Standard Industrial Classification
SMEs	Small- and Medium-sized Enterprises
SNAP	Supplemental Nutritional Assistance Program
TSG	Traditional Speciality Guaranteed
UAA	Utilized Agricultural Area
UK	United Kingdom
US/USA	United States of America
USDA	United States Department of Agriculture

List of Figures

List of Tables

Chapter 1

Introduction and Key Conclusions

Sophia M. Davidova*,§, Ashok K. Mishra†,¶
and Kenneth J. Thomson‡,||

**School of Economics, University of Kent, Canterbury, UK*
†Morrison School of Agribusiness, W. P. Carey School of Business, Arizona State University, USA
‡University of Aberdeen and James Hutton Institute, UK
§s.m.davidova@kent.ac.uk
¶ashok.k.mishra@asu.edu
||k.j.thomson@abdn.ac.uk

1.1 Introduction

Rural areas are a vital part of the geography and economy of almost every country. They are places of residence, work and recreation for many or even most of the national population, and very often the location of long-standing cultural traditions. One of their most important features is that agricultural land, almost in its totality, is managed in rural space. However, this does not mean that the terms "rural" and "agricultural" are synonymous, particularly in developed countries, where rural areas have a complex economic structure. Apart from agriculture and forestry, these rural areas contain many non-agricultural activities, such as manufacturing and services, in particular recreation and tourism, which have increased greatly in recent years.

To focus a study on rural areas is a complex task due to their heterogeneity in terms of local biophysical, economic, demographic and cultural characteristics. It is no less complex to study rural policies, which often derive from a range of supranational, national, regional and local competences. In the European Union (EU), the measures of the Common Agricultural Policy (CAP) combine with an array of national and regional policies, specific to each EU Member State (MS), both for agriculture as an economic sector and rural development. In the United States (US), rural areas are affected by federal, state and local policies, and, compared to the EU, there is much less policy emphasis on rural as opposed to urban. Major policy instruments, e.g. tax and public welfare, are not targeted specifically at rural areas, although they may have different outcomes there due to the structural, economic and demographic characteristics of rural space. It is even a more complex task to compare policies and their outcome for rural labor market in the EU and USA — the main subject of this book.

Although rural policy variations between the EU and the USA may, on many occasions, hamper direct comparison, employment in view of rural job creation and/or job retention is a commonly stated or implicit policy objective in both the EU and the USA. The issue of the availability of local jobs is exacerbated in more remote rural areas where commuting to towns and cities is difficult, and thus the rural population is not able to exploit the growth of urban economies to find employment.

The relationship between rural policies and employment is a multifaceted one. For this reason, the book is divided in several sections dealing with different aspects of this relationship in both the EU and the USA, along with some special studies based on targeted geographical analyses. In sequence, the book covers the following: the general policy context; rural trends; farm policies; agricultural entry and exit; post-farm agri-food processing; household and rural diversification; and rural recreation. Each section and the chapter is focused on the link to the number and nature of jobs in the relevant sectors.

Although the range of topics included has been carefully selected, the book does not pretend to be comprehensive. Various aspects of relevance are missing, e.g. health and safety in agricultural and rural work, gross job number gains and losses, and the balance and status of rural jobs by gender; a few topics of these are discussed briefly in Section 1.3. The importance of these issues is not underestimated, but a more concise book was thought to be more attractive to the readership.

1.2 Main Issues

The lack of a unified definition of what constitutes "rural" leads to different estimates of the share of rural areas in the economy of both the EU and the USA, and of their populations. In the EU, the problem is compounded by the change in 2010 from the use of Organization for Economic Cooperation and Development (OECD) criterion of population density to a system based on a 1-km^2 grid, i.e. "rural" cells are those with fewer than 300 inhabitants and outside contiguous grid cells of at least 5,000 inhabitants [Eurostat, 2017]. In the USA, more than 20 definitions of rurality are used by federal agencies. For example, the United States Department of Agriculture (USDA) defines rurality as any place with fewer than 50,000 inhabitants and not located adjacent to an urban area. Similarly, the Census Bureau defines rurality as any place outside a town, city or "urban cluster" with more than 2,500 residents. Finally, the Department of Veterans Affairs defines rurality as areas with a population density between seven and 1,000 people per square mile. Data are usually differentiated according to metropolitan (metro) urban areas and non-metro (rural areas) on the basis of county units.

In the EU, apart from the CAP and its European Agricultural Fund for Rural Development (EAFRD), and national and regional policies, there are four Structural and Investment Funds (SIFs) with direct implications for rural employment: the European Regional Development Fund (ERDF), the European Social Fund (ESF), the Cohesion Fund, and the European Maritime and Fisheries Fund (EMFF). Although in popular perception, the CAP is targeted at rural development via a wide range of measures, including those for farm modernization, knowledge transfer and innovation, agri-environment, and social inclusion, the SIFs budgets are larger and more focused on employment.

In the USA, rural policies aimed at employment mainly promote infrastructure development, but, as mentioned previously, it is not common to have different policies for rural and urban space. Still, 10 states have taken actions to promote development of rural areas, e.g. providing information on rural issues and making recommendations at the state level for rural policy. But the most targeted at rural areas are federal rural development programs, mainly the so-called "discretionary programs" with a budget annually approved by the Congress. Some of these programs are quite different from the EU rural development measures and focus on assistance for utility services, housing and public safety.

At the core of the book is the rural labor market, which operates alongside those for land (natural resources) and capital (physical or financial resources). Each of these markets can be affected by policy intervention, with effects on the amount and types of labor supplied to, or demanded by, farming and other rural sectors. The supply of labor depends on the size and nature (e.g. age, sex, skills) of the available "economically active" population, while labor is sought by employers by offering wages or salaries, and sometimes also housing, etc., to potential workers. The resultant market often has specific features of local oligopoly (few sellers) or oligopsony (few buyers), imperfect information about possible jobs or wage levels, and policy intervention, e.g. hiring and safety regulations. In rural areas, some of these features are emphasized, while others are less clear-cut. Much farming is undertaken as a family business — a type of enterprise often favored by fiscal and other policies — in which personal relationships may be as important as financial considerations, especially when household income is shared between spouses, their parents or children, and perhaps other relations, and where the farm itself is an asset whose management and future are of concern to all.

Again, the physical location of rural businesses, often with few nearby alternatives on either side of the market relationship, affects how labor is acquired and retained. While better physical and electronic communications — mostly arising from direct or indirect policy activity — have reduced the isolation of rural families and communities, there are still relatively few easy opportunities for employers to acquire additional or replacement workers when desired, or for workers to look for and try out new positions.

In both the EU and the USA, although agriculture is important for rural jobs (mainly through self-employment), it is not the principal employer. In the EU, rural economies do not heavily rely on the primary sector, i.e. agriculture, forestry, fishing and mining, although it is relatively more important in a few of the EU New Member States (NMSs), in fact the poorest ones, Bulgaria and Romania. Instead, it is the tertiary (service) sector that is crucial for rural employment. For example, the primary sector accounts for 13.5% of rural employment, secondary for 26.8% and tertiary 59.7%. The importance of tertiary sector is even larger in the "old" MSs — the EU-15. The Great Recession of 2008 onwards hit rural employment more strongly than the urban one, but by 2016, the average employment rate was similar across all types of regions, with the usual big variations across the MSs.

Employment in rural USA also does not rely mainly on farming, but depends crucially on manufacturing and public services. This structure of employment led to substantial job losses following deep cuts in government spending during the Great Recession and subsequently to a lower rate of employment recovery in rural areas in comparison to urban areas. Until 2016, job losses were not fully recovered, although the self-employed sector has been somewhat more dynamic. This may be a sign of a stagnating rural labor market as people have been discouraged to look for wage or salaried jobs.

The fact that both in the USA and the EU rural jobs are not predominantly in agriculture clearly emphasizes the importance of non-farm job creation, which in turn depends on the degree of economic diversification. It should be borne in mind that such diversification develops at different levels: at the farm level when farm assets are used for activities outside farming, e.g. rural tourism or renewable energy, and at the level of rural economy, where economic activity and employment in rural space are spread amongst more sectors. Apart from creating non-farm jobs, rural diversification increases the resilience of the economy to negative supply or demand shocks in a particular sector.

In the EU, farm and rural diversification has been an explicit policy objective, and diversification into non-agricultural activities has been supported by a measure in Pillar 2 of the CAP. A special study in this book on Poland indicates that, for the period 2007–2013, 5.4% of rural development funds was spent on diversification into non-agricultural activities and on support for the establishment and development of micro-enterprises. The latter measure generated 26.2 thousand rural jobs at a public expenditure cost of over €23,000 per job. In the USA, the rising importance of off-farm income to smooth total household income of farmers and to provide benefits to the local communities is driven by private initiatives. One can conclude that US agricultural and rural policy is highly motivated by the economic conditions in the farm sector rather than conditions — rural and non-rural — more generally.

1.3 Special Issues

1.3.1 *Health and safety in farm and rural work*

Agriculture is widely known as an unsafe and sometimes unhealthy sector of employment, with high rates of illnesses, accidents and deaths, although other rural occupations, such as forestry and small-scale mining, are even more dangerous. On the other hand, outdoor activity is widely considered — especially by higher-income groups — as healthy, with beneficial effects on "wellness", and farming as a satisfying "way of life", with important socio-economic roles. A mixture of physical and mental health issues, coupled with remote locations and often lone working, produce a complex picture in which government action is sometimes seen as desirable in trying to reduce the incidence of harmful events, as well as promoting more general participation in healthy activities.

About 500 people per year die while working in EU agriculture, forestry and fishing, and there are about 150,000 non-fatal accidents at such work, as well as work-related physical and mental health problems. Numbers in the USA — though the recording system is different and incomplete — are similar [NIOSH, 2018]. Accident and illness incidence rates are also generally higher than in other sectors. Moreover, on-farm accidents happen to a very wide range of ages, from the very young to the relatively old. There is no clear pattern of incidence rates across EU MSs, for a number of possible reasons, such as different systems of official reporting or farming (e.g. crops *vs.* livestock, large *vs.* small), and different national health patterns. Policy action can take a number of forms, but must take into account changes in farming technology, and the need to reach a wide range of potential casualties.

Occupational health and safety is a field well recognized in legislative, institutional and professional terms, with nearly all countries having specialized arrangements for defining, enforcing and monitoring dangers to workers in most sectors of the economy. However, agriculture sometimes has specialized legal and organizational arrangements, and in any case farming conditions often include a number of factors, such as self-employment, family-working, remoteness, and multiple and season-varying work tasks, which make it harder to apply policy to the industry.

1.3.2 *Employment and gender*

There is a considerable, though sometimes geographically patchy, literature on gender in developed-country farm occupations, though much less on gender aspects of rural employment generally. However, with the rising importance of gender equality, policy interest in this area, though still limited, has become noticeable [European Commission, 2012, 2016; European Parliament, 2016; USDA, undated]. In both the EU and the USA, about 30% of farm holders are registered as female, but this proportion almost certainly overestimates their decision-making influence on land-based production and economic activity, or (even more so) their role in policy-making. This is not to underplay women's contribution to farming — and probably other rural occupations — in terms of labor time, especially when "invisible work" such as book-keeping and office management is taken into account.

Policy intervention to increase and enhance female employment can take a number of forms, both to support women's initiatives and skills, and to remove barriers — both formal and cultural — to their fuller participation. In the former category, specialist training courses for women, or on topics likely to interest women, or at least extra encouragement to women joining standard courses can be provided, taking into account likely problems in attendance during times of family responsibilities. Amongst the latter, a major factor is the tendency — sometimes reinforced by inheritance law — to pass on farms (especially large farms) to sons rather than daughters [Shortall, 2010].

As a case study, a current initiative in one part of Europe [Scottish Government, 2018] has revealed a number of barriers to women taking a more important economic role in rural life. A taskforce, involving farmers, academics, government officials and others, has been set up to tackle inequality in Scottish agriculture and to ensure that the potential of women in farming is realized. It will seek ways to implement a set of 27 recommendations based on research. These involve training in skills and safety, rebalancing financial assistance, changing farm succession practices, and institutional reform — the latter focusing on representation within farmer unions and similar organizations, which are crucial to policymaking.

In the United States, women principal operators tend to be older than principal operators overall: in 2012,[a] the average age of women principal operators was 60.1 years, nearly 2 years more than the average age overall. However, such operators had increased their Internet access to match the access rate of all principal operators. Women operators were less likely to report farming as their primary occupation and more likely to work off the farm. Off-farm work is most common among the women operators of farms with sales less than $10,000 [Hoppe and Korb, 2013]. Farms with women operators tend to be smaller than farms overall, with fewer acres and lower sales, and about a fourth of women farmers specialize in combination crop farming (including hay production), followed by beef cattle farming, ranching, and combination livestock farming [USDA-NASS, 2014]. Women farmers in America have a strong conservation and stewardship ethic, committed to healthy farmland, farm families, and farm communities.

1.3.3 *Canada*

With the exception of the chapter on agri-tourism by Thilmany *et al.* (Chapter 22), little mention is made in this book of the important other country in North America, i.e. Canada.[b] In many ways, the picture is similar to that in parts of the United States, especially considering the regions

[a]At time of writing, the 2012 Census of Agriculture was the most recent with results available.

[b]Mexico, although an OECD member, is excluded from consideration here due to its relatively undeveloped agricultural and rural sectors.

on either side of the common land border between the two countries.[c] In Canada, an OECD [2009] report observes that:

> The rural economy, both farm and non-farm, is closely tied to nearby urban centers.
>
> Farming is neither the main source of farmers' employment nor their main source of income. In 2005 less than 50% of farmers reported working more than 40 hours per week in farming activities. On the other hand, almost half of them reported off-farm work in the year previous to the last 2006 census of agriculture.

Moreover, primary agriculture (farming) represents only 15% of the employment generated by the total agri-food sector in Canada, while:

> remote rural communities are struggling to retain a critical mass of residents, particularly young residents, the trend in rural agriculture and manufacturing is towards more capital intensive technologies, providing little new employment for rural residents.... [W]ith advances in technology, reductions in the cost of transportation of goods and improvements in communication systems, many communities in Canada have become more competitive in manufacturing. Niche marketing for specialty and value-added products, including biofuels, nutriceutical products as well as recreational and environmental services represent strategies that entrepreneurial communities are adopting to improve their economies.

Thus, in Canada, "agricultural policy would appear to have a weak demographic overlap with 'rural' and rural development policy". However, it may be observed that Canada has a stronger federal structure in terms of provincial powers and budgets for several relevant policy areas than amongst the States south of the border.

1.4 Key Conclusions

1.4.1 *Policy context*

On both sides of the Atlantic, the political, macro-economic, demographic, and to some extent, the cultural context is an important determinant of the

---

[c]About 87% of the Canadian population lives within 100 miles (161 km) of the border. There has been little change in Canadian metro:non-metro proportions of about 69:31%.

types of rural employment policies which are adopted and implemented. Islam [2014] points out that employment is a cross-cutting issue, with both horizontal (i.e. between relevant government agencies and other institutions) and vertical (i.e. between various levels of implementation, central and local) components, and that, to be effective, responsibility for policy coordination has to be at a sufficiently high and influential level. In rural areas, this involves various ministries, including those for agriculture, labor, environment, and economic and business development. Apart from the "normal" business cycles which dominate economic activity and thus employment, trends — which may be accelerating — in consumer tastes and technological possibilities also affect how governments perceive, and tackle, the maintenance and improvement of work opportunities and practices.

In the EU, MSs have different attitudes to the need to support employment in general through government intervention. In France, Italy and other MSs, "social dialogue" [Government of France, 2017] has led to consistently high unemployment over several decades, accompanied by employment legislation defending worker rights and pension provisions. In the Netherlands, Germany and the UK, policies have focused on creating a more flexible job market, along with support for training, and have resulted in generally lower rates of unemployment, though with some years of crisis and a more stringent attitude to worker availability and entitlement to state benefits. The NMSs in Central and Eastern Europe (CEE) experienced the loss of central planning in the 1990s, with massive job losses in previously state-supported enterprises. These patterns and developments have been to some extent reflected in farm and rural employment policies, though overlaid by the CAP which has tried — not always successfully — to adopt a similar approach across the MSs. Thus the CAP's Pillar 1, for market and income support, has sustained farm employment only indirectly through payments linked originally to production levels and more recently to land area, while its Pillar 2, for rural development, has included both an element for farm modernization and development, with ambiguous implications for farm job levels, and another element for innovative farm-based rural diversification, with explicit job targets. MSs have been allowed to apply Pillar 2 in different ways, with different emphases on these and other elements, such as environmental payments, and consequently assessment of the policy effects has been difficult [ÖIR *et al.*, 2012].

In the USA, with its more disengaged attitude to government intervention, O'Leary and Straits [2000] have suggested that labor market support initiatives have usually been forged at federal level in difficult economic times, with contributions and compromise from the full political spectrum. Individual states have been inhibited from greater policy action by fear of disadvantaging local industries, and perhaps by urban–rural tensions [US Chamber of Commerce, 2011].

On both sides of the Atlantic, the potential effects of general employment policies, as they affect farms and other small-scale rural enterprises, are often reduced by the fact that a large proportion of such employment is self or family employment. Thus, formal job contracts and wage regulations have been less important than personal relationships and expectations, e.g. of succession to farm ownership and management. Moreover, physical distance from other employment opportunities (and routes to these, such as retraining centers) has probably limited the sensitivity of rural employment levels to market and policy conditions, though this is lessening with improved internet links and social media.

Comparison of the European and North American situations suggests that farm and rural employment is of lesser policy concern in the USA, where personal responsibility and greater socio-economic diversity are more notable features than in Europe, where the CAP has been a "cornerstone" of the EU, and is seen as at least partly responsible for labor and other conditions in the countryside, alongside longstanding political views at the national level. In the general discussion concerning rural development in Europe, the role of Structural and Investment Funds is often underestimated, although these funds, though lacking a focus on rural areas, may be better placed to facilitate employment than the CAP. The undergoing policy process for closer integration of the CAP and the Structural and Investment Funds may be an effective way to enable diversified rural employment.

1.4.2 *Trends in rural employment*

Rural areas in the EU and the USA face several challenges which affect employment and may justify government intervention, e.g. a growing educational gap between the rural and the urbanized areas, generally declining and aging populations, and pockets of poverty. However, depending on the specific characteristics of rurality in Europe and the USA, policy objectives and interventions differ. The large average size of rural counties in the USA puts the maintenance of local infrastructure, transport and communication at the forefront of the policy agenda. In the EU, the large variations in the development of rural regions amongst the EU-28 brought about a drive toward cohesion policy and support to lagging behind regions. However, one of the main conclusions from the analysis presented in this book on both sides of the Atlantic is that employment trends seem only modestly affected by policies.

The transatlantic comparison shows that agriculture is no longer a dominant sector in rural areas either in the EU or USA. Instead, growth (or lack of it) in non-agricultural industries is more essential for jobs. Despite this, farming is still important, providing some occupational stability, particularly in periods of general economic downturn. This may justify the use of agricultural policies to retain jobs in agriculture, and in upstream and downstream industries. However, expectations as to the ability of agricultural policies to contribute to rural employment are often overestimated. As mentioned before, in the EU, rural development is associated with the CAP's Pillar 2, which may create jobs but at a high price in public expenditure, as evidenced by the study on Poland. Moreover, not only the number of jobs matters, but also the quality of these jobs and rewards they bring to labor. Often, farm employment is in low-productivity activity, which leads to low incomes and maintains a large rural–urban income gap, as evidenced in some of the EU NMSs. In the USA, there is less emphasis on the direct use of agricultural policy for rural job creation, and policy funding is mainly targeted at rural infrastructure. There, private entrepreneurship, and particularly self-employment, has been more effective in addressing the issue of rural unemployment. On both sides of the Atlantic, the growing importance of internet access, online sales, and physical services, such as custom (contract) farming, are affecting how farm and rural people are spending their work and leisure time.

1.4.3 *Job entry and exit in agriculture*

Over the years, agricultural sectors in the US and the EU have gone through structural changes, including increasing size of operation, aging farming populations and fewer new farming entrepreneurs. These structural changes have significant impacts regarding product competitiveness, and labor supply and demand.

The EU agricultural sector, and logically policy, is concerned with the entry and exit of farmers. While in the past, the EU policy was more focused on retirement of old farmers in order to free resources for new entrants through succession or otherwise, currently the CAP is mainly targeting young farmers, since entry problems exist for younger people interested in taking up farming as a business. A study for the Agriculture Committee of the European Parliament identified access to land as the major barrier to entry, but equally new entrants have more limited non-land resources than the established farmers and it is often difficult for them to compete [Zagata *et al.*, 2017]. In order to reduce the impact of these problems, CAP includes various measures both in Pillar 1 and Pillar 2, and age-differentiated support, discussed by Viaggi (Chapter 12). Successors of the existing farms are the main beneficiaries of this support. Young farmers in the EU have substantial lobbying power as they are organized at national and European levels.

In the US, policy is less oriented to influence entry and exit. However, in 2017, the National Young Farmers Coalition (NYFC) organized a survey, in partnership with the Executive Director of Sustainability at George Washington University, to better understand the challenges and opportunities faced by existing and aspiring young farmers [NYFC, 2017]. Similarly, to the EU, the main challenge to young farmers appeared to be access to land, followed by student loan debt, labor availability and access to credit. Young farmers are often outbid for purchase of land by established farmers or non-farmers who have easier access to credit. The report based on the survey results has many policy recommendations for the next Farm Bill aiming to mitigate some of the barriers to new farmers.

Many young aspiring farmers choose to work in an off-farm job before entering farming. In fact, the role of off-farm employment is becoming prominent in the US farming households in order to stabilize family income. Off-farm jobs provide income that can be used as capital to buy additional real estate holdings. As younger people work more off the farm, the US has experienced labor shortages, especially in California and Florida, due to the decreasing supply of immigrant labor coming from Mexico. Thus, the US immigration policies affect farm and rural labor supply, demand and wages. In order to address these changes, the US farmers have adopted labor-saving technologies and are hiring temporary foreign laborers through the H-2A visa scheme.[d]

1.4.4 *Farm policies and rural jobs*

Farm policy usually has several objectives, including food security and safety, farm income support, and environmental conservation and enhancement. Amongst these, the maintenance of farm and rural employment may loom large, weak or hardly at all in the statement and implementation of different measures. The various EU and US authors of chapters in this book illustrate the variety of policy approaches taken on either side of the Atlantic.

In their review of recent EU literature on the effectiveness of the CAP in supporting employment, Vigani *et al.* (Chapter 7) find that the influence of the policy measures on agricultural and rural jobs increases with the amount of support received. However, the overall effect of CAP Pillar 1 support has been to slow or halt the decline in agricultural jobs (and incomes) rather than to create new jobs. The impact of Pillar 2 schemes on employment is more difficult to estimate, but there is little indication of the permanence of jobs beyond the funding period, and influence seems to depend a good deal on how policies are implemented at national/regional levels.

Mantino finds that structural and context variables contribute to territorially differentiated changes in farm employment more than policy measures. Indeed, Pillar 1 payments to farmers appear to have affected

[d]The H-2A temporary agricultural program establishes a means for agricultural employers who anticipate a shortage of domestic workers to bring non-immigrant foreign workers to the US to perform agricultural labor or services of a temporary or seasonal nature.

farm employment negatively in most areas, perhaps due to the introduction of activities requiring lower labor input, or to risk-averse behavior by farmers. The Pillar 2 Rural Development Program (RDP) measures all showed positive, but not always statistically significant, effects, which differ according to measure type: farm and agro-industrial investment support generates higher employment effects than other environmental or "rural" types. However, in some cases, investment in rural diversification also contributes to farm employment. Beyond the farmgate, Rizov *et al.* (Chapter 9) find positive though small net spillovers of CAP payments to non-farm employment in the UK. In general, Pillar 1 has a stronger positive employment effect than Pillar 2, but Pillar 2 payments have a stronger positive effect per Euro spent in rural areas and within the agricultural supply chain.

For the USA, Ahearn in this book finds that the longstanding Farm Bill approach of funding an assortment of supports for basic inputs into development has some advantages for communities with leaders able to access and integrate these and other programs. However, major shifts in US rural development policy have been driven by differing visions for the appropriate development role of government in a market economy. There has been a shared view of the important role of investing in people, e.g. in education and training, and in local infrastructure (roads, broadband), but little agreement on the total levels of funding, or on responsibilities for funding among levels of government.

Dodson analyzes how the US Farm Credit System addresses broad-based credit availability issues related to informational asymmetries and non-competitive markets. The USDA credit programs are designed specifically to serve creditworthy farm businesses that are of higher risk, while direct loan programs, which are costlier to administer, have become directed toward groups and purposes where the net social benefit is greater. This includes encouraging new entrants into farming, especially members of young, small, beginning farmers, socially disadvantaged groups, and, more recently, promoting organic and farm-to-table types of agriculture. Government-guaranteed lending[e] has

[e]In 2011, the Farm Credit System made nearly $10 billion in new farm loans to beginning farmers. The 2014 legislation continues the Beginning Farmer and Rancher

evolved as a cost-efficient method to serve middle- and large-size family farms suffering temporary financial hardships and thus to safeguard core agricultural jobs and businesses.

1.4.5 *Agri-food*

The agri-food and processing sectors in the EU and the USA have evolved through the years due to changing consumer preferences. The EU has implemented different food quality schemes in order to stimulate rural development, while the US has promoted food and related industry transformation in order to gain market power.

Different trends are observed in agri-food and processing industries and its impact on labor in the EU and the US. In the EU, despite the growth in the Food Processing Beverage and Tobacco (FPBT) sector, there is still a decline in employment in the overall agri-food sector. As illustrated by Donnellan and Hanrahan, among the EU MSs, one sees differential growth rates for Gross Value in Agriculture (GVA) in FPBT and in Agriculture, Forestry and Fishing (AFF). On the other hand, the food quality schemes such as Protected Designation of Origin (PDO) and Protected Geographical Indication (PGI) in the EU have created rural employment in general, although the impact is heterogeneous across EU. For instance, in the Mediterranean region and in Germany, the policy has decreased unemployment. On the other hand, in the EU's "less favored" and remote areas, food quality policy has been ineffective in increasing employment but has led to differential employment levels.

The US processing sector has witnessed structural changes due to changes in consumer preferences and demographics. For example, there has been a sharp rise in chicken demand and hence food processing employment growth in rural poultry processing plants. Linking to an issue discussed above, worker safety and labor supply are two concerns that agri-food employers face in the USA. Food and feed processing plants rely greatly on foreign-born workers, and workers in meat and

---

Development Programs, but increased mandatory funding from $75 million to $100 million over the 2014–2018 period.

seafood processing have higher turnover rates than those in other food and feed producing industries.

1.4.6 *Rural and farm household diversification*

With falling agricultural labor needs, economic diversification by farm and rural businesses — sometimes involving pluriactivity by farm household members — offers promise of alternative job creation to maintain populations and incomes in rural areas. Diversification is perhaps the most direct way to create non-farm rural jobs and to use existing agricultural assets for non-farming activities, which can increase and/or smooth the incomes of farming households, and thus secure or even increase rural job numbers. In this book, Johnson reports that 80.2% of the incomes of US farm households come from off-farm activities. In the EU, the proportions amongst MSs appear lower, but increased after the 1980s [OECD, 2003], and almost certainly has continued more recently.

In the USA, policy is aimed at supporting firms with employers, e.g. relocation of some businesses from urban to rural areas, instead of targeting "non-employer" activities which might be more important for jobs in the long run and might have a more important contribution to local communities. In the EU, the CAP is more directly dedicated to farm and rural diversification though its success seems rather modest, with farm diversification levels being very low in some Southern and East European countries. In 2013, only 5.2% of all EU farms were diversified in terms of having income from "other gainful activities", such as agri-tourism, food processing or forestry, although those holdings generated 18.9% of all EU agricultural standard output, indicating that larger farms found this to be an easier route to follow. Overall, the effect of CAP support for diversification is mixed and more successful where location, natural capital and agricultural landscape can be attractive to consumers.

1.4.7 *Rural tourism and recreation*

As developed and prosperous economic blocs, both the EU and the USA show relatively high and increasing use of rural areas for direct enjoyment (i.e. consumption by residents and non-residents) rather than production of food. This is not only common in areas where cultural landscapes are juxtaposed with low-intensity farming and strong local food cultures, but also takes place around cities, along coastlines, and in "wilderness" areas with little or no agriculture. The range of activities is enormous, from mass-tourism accommodation, food and entertainment facilities, through farm-based bed-and-breakfast and craftwork, to individual or small-group hunting and sighting of wildlife.

The employment and policy aspects of this phenomenon are therefore highly variable, depending as they do on regional conditions, including local farm and rural community structures, and natural landscapes. They also depend on the demand for governmental intervention in order to support rural jobs, as well as on changing consumer demands, such as concerns for the environment and the growing importance of recreation for older people.

Policy to support these activities, with their employment, can take a number of directions, including improvement of rural infrastructure, assistance in training employees, and support for the marketing of regional tourism. Most of these policy measures have their roots in pre-existing governmental structures, such as departments for transport, employment and environment. However, as the basic and widespread economic sector, agriculture is often used as the basis for intervention by encouraging farm diversification (see above) and by regulating change in land use, management, e.g. to preserve public goods, and sometimes land tenure, i.e. to determine eligibility for loans or grants. The nature of employment in rural tourism and recreation also needs to be taken into account: it is often highly seasonal, and often low paid, whether due to the lack of other local job opportunities, or to intense competition between enterprise and/or workers.

Comparison of Europe and North America in this subject area shows reflections of the wider political and policy context. In the EU, the CAP has been adapted — though perhaps not always enthusiastically — to include measures to encourage farm- and food-based tourism, while the USA, with its stronger culture of land-owning privacy, and low-level support for the more extensive forms of farming found in many of its recreational regions, has relied more on a mix of simple infrastructure (roads, power, water) and private initiative. In both cases, fiscal policy seems important, in particular whether rural recreational enterprises can benefit from the tax and grant support provided to "agriculture".

1.4.8 *Final thoughts*

With rising general concerns over future employment as the next "robot" and information technology (IT) revolution looms in many industrial and service processes, agriculture and other rural sectors exhibit several special characteristics which affect how government policies might, or should, support jobs in these sectors.

On the one hand, these technological developments promise to move as fast, if not faster, on farms and elsewhere in rural areas, as more generally. They include genomics applied to both plants and livestock, satellite-based and local sensors for soils, crops, livestock and pests, and machine learning by robots employed both on and off the farm. These are all likely to reduce rural labor requirements, continuing a longstanding trend initiated by the first crop machinery 200 years ago. Similarly, many household and business services can increasingly be supplied by better physical and electronic communications which reduce the need for traditional local, i.e. rural, or small-town jobs. Almost everywhere, economies of scale point in the same direction, with capital replacing labor whether for fieldwork, farm product processing, or office-based services.

On the other hand, changing consumer demands, whether for food, residence or other services, are becoming more sophisticated and specific, with rising household incomes able to support relatively high-cost sectors such as local or organic food production, the maintenance of houses, gardens and the countryside, and outdoor leisure services. The socio-economic aspects of these developments, e.g. in terms of income disparities between families and between regions, are yet to become apparent, but in any case, policy support for existing or even past employment patterns seems pointless.

The analyses in this book almost uniformly suggest that "horizontal" policy support for farm and other rural incomes is largely ineffective, or possibly even counterproductive, in protecting jobs against the technological, economic and social forces. It is also expensive in terms of public funds, and in terms of foregone efficiency, especially as important agricultural and rural interest groups defend longstanding payments and regulations which work in their favor.

More targeted and transformational support is therefore indicated, where public funds and opinion allow, in order to help more disadvantaged groups to adapt to the changing employment situation, usually by means of different skills, but sometimes by the provision of start-up capital and public infrastructure. However, targeting involves higher administrative costs, e.g. to determine eligibility and to monitor compliance and progress, and to provide organizers or *animateurs*[f] who can help and encourage persons and businesses, whether individuals or groups, to take advantage of available support which has to be tailored to specific local and temporal conditions. This is work in progress, but the need for more targeted policies is apparent.

References

European Commission (2012). *Women in EU Agriculture and Rural Areas: Hard Work, Low Profile*. EU Agricultural Economic Brief No. 7. Brussels. https://ec.europa.eu/agriculture/sites/agriculture/files/rural-area-economics/briefs/pdf/07_en.pdf (accessed 26 August 2018).

European Commission (2016). EU Policies to Promote Women and Youth in Agriculture. Presentation to G7 International Forum for *Empowering Women and Youth in Agriculture and Food Systems*, Japan, 12–13 December. http://www.maff.go.jp/e/g7_niigata.files/attach/pdf/161222-2.pdf (accessed 26 August 2018).

European Parliament (2016). Women and their Roles in Rural Areas. Report no. 2016/2204(INI) to Committees on *Agriculture and Rural Development Committee and on Women's Rights and Gender Equality*. http://www.europarl.europa.eu/committees/en/agri/home.html (accessed 26 August 2018).

Eurostat (2017). *Urban-Rural Typology*. https://ec.europa.eu/eurostat/statistics-explained/index.php?title=Archive:Urban-rural_typology&oldid=335872 (accessed 7 September 2018).

[f]A French term in rural development: A person who enlivens or encourages something, especially a promoter of projects.

Government of France (2017). *Boosting Employment in France*. http://www.strategie.gouv.fr/sites/strategie.gouv.fr/files/atoms/files/17-27_boosting_employment.pdf (accessed 20 August 2018).

Hoppe, Robert, A. and Korb, P. (2013). *Characteristics of Women Farm Operators and Their Farms*. EIB-111, U.S. Department of Agriculture, Economic Research Service, Washington DC.

Islam, R. (2014). *Employment Policy Implementation Mechanisms: A Synthesis Based on Country Studies*, Employment Policy Department Working Paper No. 161. International Labour Organization, Geneva. https://www.ilo.org/wcmsp5/groups/public/---ed_emp/documents/publication/wcms_251002.pdf (accessed 20 August 2018).

National Institute for Occupational Safety and Health (NIOSH) (2018). *Agricultural Safety* https://www.cdc.gov/niosh/topics/aginjury/default.html (accessed 26 August 2018).

National Young Farmers Coalition (2017). *Building a Future with Farming: Results and Recommendations from the National Young Farmers Survey*, November 2017. https://www.youngfarmers.org/wp-content/uploads/2018/02/NYFC-Report-2017.pdf (accessed 23 September 2018).

Organization for Economic Cooperation and Development (OECD) (2003). *Farm Household Income: Issues and Policy Responses*. http://www.oecd.org/tad/agricultural-policies/farmhouseholdincomeissuesandpolicyresponses.htm (accessed 7 September 2018).

Organization for Economic Cooperation and Development (OECD) (2009). The Role of Agriculture and Farm Household Diversification in the Rural Economy of Canada, Report to *OECD Trade and Agriculture Directorate*. http://www.oecd.org/agriculture/agricultural-policies/43245349.pdf (accessed 26 August 2018).

Österreichisches Institut für Raumplanung (ÖIR), ÖAR-Regionalberatung, Polish Academy of Sciences, University of Gloucestershire and ECORYS (2012). Synthesis of Mid-Term Evaluations of Rural Development Programmes 2007–2013. Final Report to *European Commission DG Agriculture and Rural Development*. https://ec.europa.eu/agriculture/sites/agriculture/files/evaluation/rural-development-reports/2012/synthesis-mte-2007-2013/full-text_en.pdf (accessed 26 August 2018).

O'Leary, C. J. and Straits, R. A. (2000). *Intergovernmental Relations in Employment Policy: The United States Experience*, Upjohn Institute Working Paper No. 00-60. Kalamazoo, MI: W.E. Upjohn Institute for Employment Research. https://doi.org/10.17848/wp00-60 (accessed 20 August 2018).

Scottish Government (2018). *Women in Agriculture*, https://www.gov.scot/Topics/farmingrural/Agriculture/Women-in-Agriculture (accessed 26 August 2018).

Shortall, S. (2010). *Women Working on the Farm: How to Promote their Contribution to the Development of Agriculture and Rural Areas in Europe.* Note to European Parliament, Brussels. IP/B/AGRI/IC/2010_090. http://eige.europa.eu/docs/2026_IPOL-AGRI_NT(2010)438609_EN.pdf (accessed 29 August 2018).

United States Department of Agriculture (USDA) (Undated). *Women in Agriculture.* https://www.usda.gov/our-agency/initiatives/women-agriculture (accessed 26 August 2018).

US Chamber of Commerce (2011). *The Impact of State Employment Policies on Job Growth: A 50-State Review.* https://www.uschamber.com/sites/default/files/legacy/reports/201103WFI_StateBook.pdf (accessed 20 August 2018).

US Department of Agriculture, National Agricultural Statistics Service (USDA, NASS) (2014). *2012 Census of Agriculture*, Vol. 1: Geographic Area Series, Part 51: United States Summary and State Data.

Zagata, L., Hrabák, J., Lošt'ák, M., Bavorová, M., Ratinger, T., Sutherland, L.-A. and McKee, A. (2017). Young Farmers — Policy Implementation after the 2013 CAP reform, report to *AGRI Committee, European Parliament, Policy Department for Structural and Cohesion Policies*, Brussels. http://www.europarl.europa.eu/RegData/etudes/STUD/2017/602006/IPOL_STU(2017)602006_EN.pdf (accessed 23 September 2018).

Part A
General Policy Context

Chapter 2

EU Policies and Rural Employment

Berkeley Hill

Imperial College London, Kensington, London, UK
b.hill@imperial.ac.uk

This chapter outlines the diverse picture of employment and incomes in the EU's rural regions, the general problems they face, and trends in their key variables. Policies to provide employment are a mixture of national- and EU-level interventions, including assistance from the EU's Structural and Investment Funds to regions that are lagging economically, many of which also happen to be rural. Rural development has traditionally been seen in the EU, not as an aspect of regional policy but rather as part of the Common Agricultural Policy (CAP) and funded from the European Agricultural Fund for Rural Development. In creating jobs, there has been a focus on the role of primary agriculture and forestry. Arguably, this has been misplaced in that agriculture is, in most rural regions, a minor part of the economy and incapable of correcting general unemployment. Increasingly, the EU is requiring its major Structural and Investment Funds to function together, including in the evaluation of their impact on the problems of rural regions. This is a work in progress, and the success of an integrated approach is by no means assured.

2.1 Introduction

In a chapter that aims to consider EU policies and rural employment, it is necessary to clarify what is meant by each of these terms. One way of interpreting rural employment is to relate it to the occupations of people who reside in rural areas — a regional approach. Another is to link the term to working in the agriculture and forestry sectors, land uses that in the popular European mind help determine what is a rural area — a sectoral approach. It would be impossible to think of such areas without these activities dominating land use there. However, as will become clear, what is classified as a rural area in the EU does not depend on the presence of these activities. Neither should it be assumed that farmers and foresters dominate the pattern of employment found in rural areas, nor that rural-type activities are confined to regions classed as rural; both could lead to expensive errors in policymaking.

A similar ambiguity surrounds what can be meant by EU policies. Employment levels, and associated incomes and living standards, will be determined by complex factors that are often outside the control of governments, though they may try to influence them. EU Member States (MSs) have national policies on issues such as, the level of public spending, personal and business taxation, general education and social mobility. When taken together, these are likely to outweigh the influence of interventions that can be traced back to the common policies (such as those for agriculture, regional and social development etc., discussed later) which have been adopted by the EU and are funded by its general budget. Nevertheless, it is these common policies that are usually implied when the term "EU policies" are applied.

It is helpful to start with reviewing the historic role that agriculture plays in the national economy. Evidence shows that, with the passing of time, the turning of the treadmill of technological advance results in a relative decline in the importance of primary agriculture to generating a country's income and to engaging its available workforce. Typically, despite a loss of people from agriculture, increased productivity enables the volume of agricultural production to be at least maintained. Structural change occurs among farms as labor leaves, with the larger farms accounting for an increasing share of total production and land area, and the minimum farm size from which a viable living can be made from agriculture alone rising.

By 2016, the number of people employed in EU-28 agriculture had shrunk to 3.9% of total employment (forestry a further 0.2%), forming a rather smaller share in the older MSs (EU-15) (2.5%) than in the newer ones (EU-13)[a] (9.6%) [Eurostat, 2017]. In line with the trend, within the period 2011–2016, numbers of persons in agriculture fell by an annual average of −2.8% in the EU-28, rather more slowly in the EU-15 (−1.1%) and faster in the EU-13 (−4.0%). This was after substantial public support to agriculture through the Common Agricultural Policy (CAP). However, it is also necessary to acknowledge that short-term shocks, such as from the impact of unusual weather or disruption caused by historical events like trade disputes, may nudge the trend and precipitate change in the adjustment process that is part of economic development.

2.2 The Complex Reality of Rural Areas and Rural Regions

The economic changes affecting agriculture will almost by definition impact on rural areas as this is where most of the affected households live. However, it would be misleading to assume that agriculture is the sole, or even the main, activity taking place in rural areas. Agriculture, in the sense of the production of goods and services that are conventionally listed by Eurostat statisticians as being agricultural, accounts for typically only a minor, and declining, proportion of economic activity in rural areas [European Commission, 2018].

Before going further, it is necessary to consider the definitions of what a rural area is. Until relatively recently, the EU relied on the OECD classification based on population density. However, from 2010, a sophisticated system has been employed based on grid cells of 1 km^2 [Eurostat, 2010]. Rural grid cells are, by definition, those that are not part of urban clusters, which are contiguous grid cells with a density of at least 300 inhabitants per km^2 and a minimum population of 5,000. The rural grid cells can be overlaid with Local Administrative Units (LAUs)[b] that correspond to the lower levels of the Nomenclature for Territorial Units for

[a] Bulgaria, Cyprus (phasing out support), Czech Republic, Estonia, Greece, Croatia, Latvia, Lithuania, Hungary, Malta, Poland, Portugal, Romania, Slovenia and the Slovak Republic.

[b] A distinction formerly made between LAU1 and LAU2 levels was dropped in 2017.

Statistics (NUTS) system and typically represent single municipalities (local authorities). There are almost 100,000 LAUs in the EU-28 (the number will change as local government evolves). If more than 50% of the population in the LAU live in rural grid cells, the LAU is classified as a *rural area*. Rural area dominates the geography of the EU, and even in the relatively densely populated countries, there is more than a sprinkling of rural area between the cities, towns and suburbs.

On the same basis (50% of the population living in rural grid cells), this classification can also be extended up to NUTS 3 level, described as *predominantly rural regions*, which is easier for reporting purposes (there are 1,348 such regions in the EU-28) (Fig. 2.1). However, it should be borne in mind that the other types of region (intermediate, and predominantly urban) will contain some rural area. In some respects, their proximity to areas of high population density may give them both special employment problems and offer special solutions, such as the greater feasibility of commuting (in both directions); Eurostat [2017b] points out that where people work is not necessarily where they live.

Eurostat's statistics on rural regions typically base their reports on NUTS three-level units. Overall, in recent years (2014–2016) rural regions have covered 44% of the EU-28 territory, contained 19% of its population, 17% of total employment, and generated 13% of its gross value added (GVA) [European Commission, 2017] (Table 2.1). However, there are large differences between countries in these shares. For example, while in Ireland rural regions accounted for 90% of the territory and 60% of employment, in the Netherlands the respective figures were 2.1% and 0.6%. Such large differences are just one manifestation of the heterogeneity that characterizes many aspects of development of rural areas that extends to the problems these areas face and, thus rationally, to the policies applied to counter them.

2.3 Employment Patterns in Rural Regions

Some of the patterns seen in employment statistics are of critical significance to the way in which EU policy has attempted to promote jobs and incomes in rural areas. A common feature of rural regions, and one important in the context of policies to enhance employment, is that agriculture,

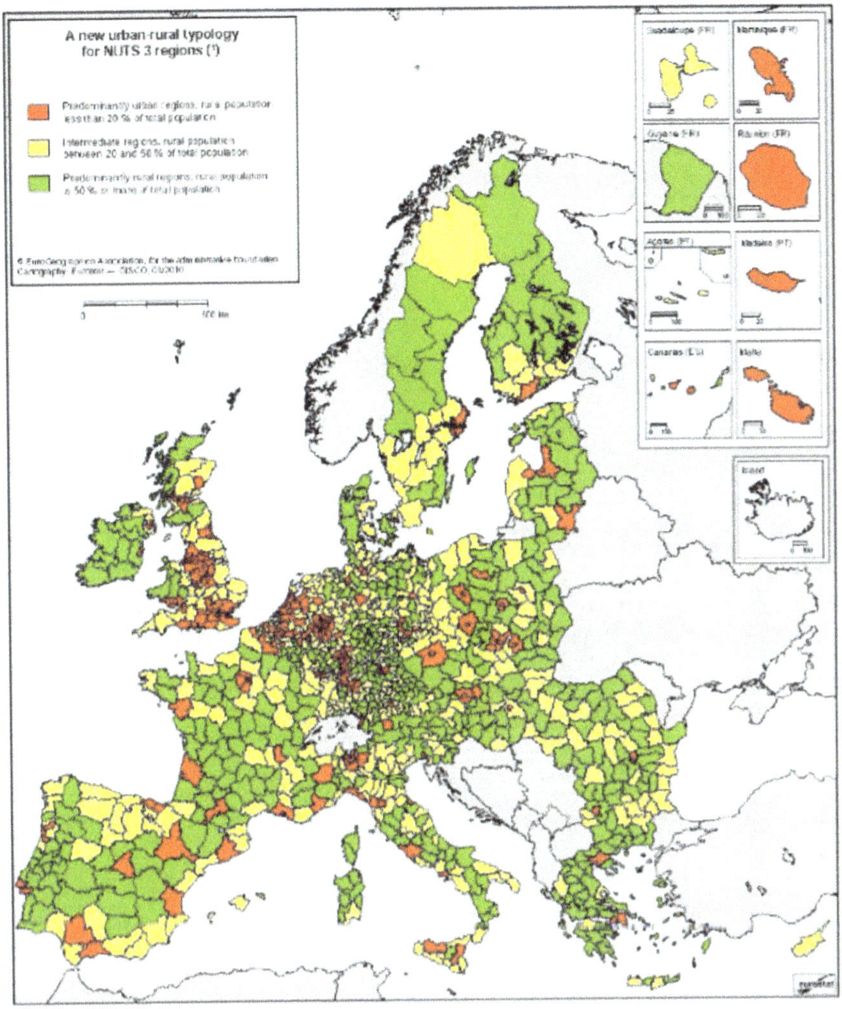

Fig. 2.1. Predominantly rural, intermediate, and predominantly urban regions in the EU.

Source: Eurostat.

forestry and fishing together represent only a small proportion of the economic activity in the rural regions of most MSs. as measured by GVA. For the EU-28 as a whole in 2014, this primary sector generated only 4.2% of GVA in rural regions; in contrast, the secondary sector (which includes industry and construction) formed 30.7%, and services — the

Table 2.1. Relative importance of rural regions in the EU and their employment structure.

	Share of national total in rural regions				Employment structure in rural regions (2014)		
EU MS	Territory (2015)	Employment	Population	GVA	Primary sector	Secondary sector	Tertiary sector
Belgium	32.6	6.6	8.5	5.3	3.3	19.2	77.5
Bulgaria	22.1	11.4	13.1	9.1	34.5	25.6	40
Czech Republic	36.7	20.7	21.2	18.3	5.9	43.2	53
Denmark	51.4	26.2	28.7	23.2	4.8	22	73.3
Germany	38.6	14.6	15.8	12.7	3.5	31.9	64.6
Estonia	81.6	40.1	45.0	29.9	8.1	31.8	60.1
Ireland	90.0	56.6	60.2	46.6	8.8	19.6	71.7
Greece	66.0	30.6	31.9	25.4	25.6	15.2	59.2
Spain	16.9	3.3	3.5	3.1	11.4	20.4	68.2
France	53.8	28.4	31.2	23.9	8	22.7	72.2
Croatia	62.9	36.1	43.1	34.0	7.4	33.4	59.2
Italy	24.0	9.2	9.6	8.8	7.2	24.8	68
Cyprus	—	—	—	—	—	—	—
Latvia	40.2	18.2	22.1	13.8	16.1	28.4	55.4
Lithuania	13.6	7.8	8.7	5.3	24.9	22.3	52.8
Luxembourg	—	—	—	—	—	—	—
Hungary	27.6	14.6	19.0	12.1	11.5	30.9	57.6
Malta	—	—	—	—	—	—	—
Netherlands	2.1	0.6	0.6	0.5	4.3	22.4	73.4
Austria	75.2	37.1	40.7	33.9	10.8	27.7	61.5
Poland	54.0	31.8	35.0	25.5	22.8	29.8	47.5
Portugal	79.0	32.1	31.4	27.8	22.5	21.7	55.7
Romania	67.8	52.4	53.8	36.6	39.7	27.3	33
Slovenia	72.8	53.1	58.6	49.3	12.2	35.3	52.5
Slovakia	46.0	32.1	37.5	29.1	4.3	33.4	62.4
Finland	82.4	37.8	40.1	34.5	7.8	25	67.2
Sweden	24.7	8.6	9.1	7.6	5.1	24.6	70.3
United Kingdom	29.5	3.5	3.6	2.6	6.3	21.8	71.9
EU-28	44.1	17.4	19.1	13.3	13.5	26.8	59.7
EU-15	42.7		15.4		7.6	24.9	67.6
EU-13	48.4		33.8		24.7	30.4	44.9

Source: Extracted from European Commission [2017].

major share — 65.1%. Only a few countries contained in their rural regions agricultural sectors that represented more than 10% of the GVA originating there (Bulgaria, Latvia and Romania), and in many of the older EU members, it was less than 3%. It follows that the economy in rural regions is likely to be principally affected by what is happening in non-agricultural sectors, and even large expansions in agriculture, forestry and fishing (combined) cannot greatly impact on overall GVA, simply because of the smallness of the primary sector.

As would be expected, within countries, agriculture, forestry and fishing are more important to employment in rural regions than in intermediate ones, and least important in urban ones. However, even in rural regions, agriculture is not the provider of the majority of jobs; Eurostat figures for 2016 show that in the rural regions of the EU, the primary sector accounted for only 13.5% of the total employment there (a larger figure than the share of GVA, suggesting relative lower factor rewards to labor). Again, differences were apparent between MSs, with the New Member States (NMSs) averaging 24.7% and the older Members 7.6%. In only a handful did the primary sector account for more than 20% of employment in rural areas (Bulgaria, Greece, Lithuania, Poland, Portugal and Romania). Thus, the often-assumed dominance of agricultural employment to rural jobs is simply not borne out by the data. It is the tertiary sector that provides more than half the total employment in rural regions, with the exception of Bulgaria, Poland and Romania. A study on rural regions and employment [Ecorys, 2010] for the European Commission pointed out that growth in services had been particularly strong in rural regions.

As suggested above, statistics on employment and economic activity are consistent with incomes being lower in rural regions. For the average of the years 2012–2014, the index of Gross Domestic Product (GDP) measured in Purchasing Power Standard (PPS) per capita was lowest in rural regions (index of 72.9, when EU-28 all regions = 100) and highest in urban regions (120.8). Incomes were lowest in the rural regions of EU-13 (48.0); furthermore, the gap between the rural and urban regions was more extreme among these countries that are recent entrants to the EU than among EU-15, though even there GDP per capita was about one quarter lower than in urban regions. This suggests that the quality of employment in rural regions may be a problem (low productivity leading to low earnings), particularly among the NMSs.

There are wide differences between rural regions in how their populations are changing. Eurostat [2013] pointed to a few EU-15 countries showing rises (including Belgium and the UK) as counter-urbanization overcomes the drift to urban centers, while many of the newer MSs showed falls, some quite sharp [European Commission, 2006]. Later data for 2011–2016 showed falls of more than 5% in Bulgaria, Latvia, Lithuania and Romania. Across the EU-28 there was a decline in the population of rural regions (−1.2%) whereas there were rises in intermediate and urban regions. Both older and NMSs saw lower population growth in their rural regions than elsewhere. The general European phenomenon of an aging population has been seen in a more extreme form in rural regions, with the share of the population aged over 65 being higher there than the national average in each EU-27 country, except Belgium and Poland [European Commission, 2013].[c]

Since 2008, the employment rate in rural regions has followed in broad terms the pattern seen in the general economy (Fig. 2.2). However, it is clear that the recessionary period from 2009 onwards has negatively affected rural areas more severely than intermediate and urban areas. Conversely, since the recovery started in 2013, the growth in employment in rural areas has at least matched that in other regions, though in absolute percentage terms, there is still a gap between rural regions and the others. By 2016, a situation had been reached in which the employment rate for persons aged 20–64 was the same across the types of region at EU-28 level, though this masked differences between the EU-15 and NMSs. In the older MSs, the rate of employment in rural regions was typically a little higher than in intermediate or urban regions (though there were occasional exceptions, such as Spain and Italy), whereas among the newer MSs, rural regions saw lower levels of employment than urban regions.

Statistics on the unemployment rate show, as would be expected, a falling trend in rural regions for the period 2013–2016. However, for the EU-28 as a whole, relatively high unemployment rates in rural regions is not a general feature; in only about a third of MSs was the unemployment

[c] Croatia joined the EU in 2013, and was not included in this publication.

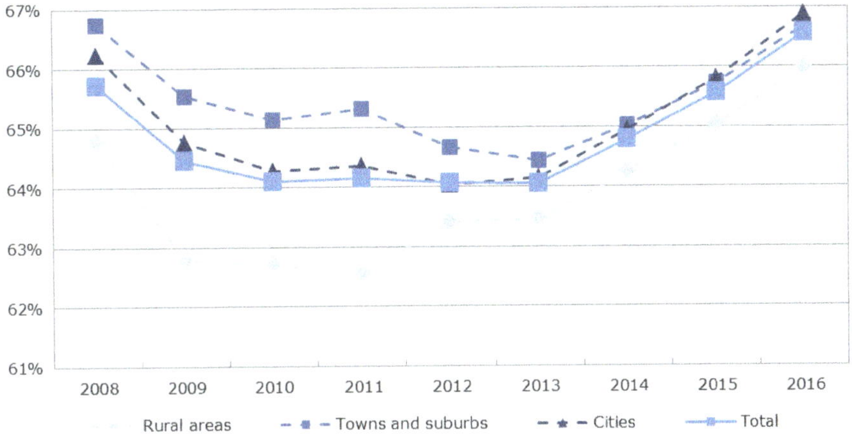

Fig. 2.2. Employment rate (15–64 years old) in the EU-28 and by type of area, 2008–2016.

Source: Eurostat.

rate in rural regions higher than the national average. Among the older MSs, high unemployment rates were more a characteristic of their urban regions, though among the NMSs, rates were highest in rural regions. Nevertheless, rural region unemployment rates were on average higher in the older MSs (8.6%) than in the new ones (7.4%). Based on somewhat earlier data, Ecorys [2010] concluded that unemployment is not predominantly a "rural" or an "urban" phenomenon but one of economic structures and favorable conditions for economic activity (e.g. accessibility, skilled work force). This appears to still apply.

An issue of obvious interest to this chapter is the extent to which EU policies have contributed to this pattern of rising employment and falling unemployment, in particular to the changes seen more recently.

2.4 EU Policies for Employment in Rural Areas

2.4.1 *Problems to be tackled*

Analysis of any area of policy has to start from the problems to be addressed. So, what are the problems related to employment that rural areas face, and how have these been changing? Among the factors that shape employment, which are capable of manipulation to increase the quantity and quality of employment opportunities? The analysis of rural area given above suggests that, though there is an employment gap between rural and other regions (a quantity issue), the bigger problem concerns the quality of employment as reflected in earnings.

Employment in rural regions, and the economic activity that generates jobs and incomes, faces some particular problems, though these will vary from one region to another.

- **Low population density:** By definition, EU rural regions are relatively sparsely populated, and this brings some drawbacks to economic activity and job creation. For example, local markets may be quite small, to the extent that heavy investment in capacity by business operators may simply not be justified by the returns that are to be earned. Both private sector retail service providers (e.g. supermarkets) and public sector health and education may find rural areas insufficiently populated to operate there.
- **Remoteness:** Many rural regions are remote from their main markets, so that costs of transport are higher than those faced by businesses located nearer their markets. In recognition of this, the EU regional typology has been developed to differentiate between rural regions that are close to a city and those that are remote.[d]
- **Poor infrastructure:** Road and rail infrastructure is often less well developed in rural areas, making the movement of goods and of people more expensive. Broadband and other digital connections often function less effectively [European Commission, 2018].
- **Relatively heavy dependence on the primary sector:** Though the economies of rural regions are not generally dominated by the primary sector, agriculture and forestry are more important there than in other regions. These industries are not among those that usually are growing quickly in terms of jobs and incomes.

[d] See http://ec.europa.eu/eurostat/statistics-explained/index.php/Regional_typologies_overview (accessed 17 May 2018).

- **Limited ability of labor to respond:** When the demand for labor in the primary sector is contracting, the ability of workers to adjust may be constrained by inappropriate skill sets; there is an educational shortfall in rural regions [European Commission, 2018]. The lack of local employment opportunities implies a probable need to move area (with related financial and social costs) or, at least, face long commuting journeys which carry costs both in terms of expenditure and in time spent. These impediments to adjustment will produce a gap between earnings in agriculture and those in other sectors and, at worst, unemployment.
- **Adverse demographics:** The aging population, coupled with relatively low proportions of young people that often reflects migration away of the more mobile and more able for better paid urban jobs, and sometimes falling populations, presents a range of problems to the creation of employment. Reducing access to services in rural areas make them less attractive as places to live and work.

But, it should be recognized that some of the characteristics that pose problems to the creation of employment (especially low population density and remoteness) are precisely the attributes that attract some new residents looking for pleasant places in which to reside or establish new businesses.

Also, it would be a mistake to see these problems of rural areas, and policies to address them, in isolation. Raising employment opportunities in rural regions may reduce migration to urban areas, and reduce unemployment and pressure on services there. And modern communications mean that people who are resident in rural areas can work in urban areas (and vice versa). Education, training and health services can be effectively delivered from urban sites if attention is given to overcoming access logistics.

2.4.2 *The rationale for intervention*

If problems exist, attention moves on to the rationale for intervention. What should be the role of government in such conditions? Attempts to negate the fundamental technical and economic forces at work that dictate low population densities and the changes seen over time in agriculture are doomed to failure — the public costs of manipulating them would be unsustainable. But there is a case for intervening to facilitate the adjustment process.

EU policies, including those on employment, are increasingly required by legislation to be based on a sound logic. The classic argument relies on three rationales.

(1) To counter market failure and promote efficiency, which includes actions that enable markets to function more effectively (such as by enhancing information flows on job opportunities and incomes), providing skills training where private choices do not generate socially optimal amounts (something that underlies the state provision of education generally) and enable externalities to be internalized (such as by incentivizing firms to cooperate where this generates positive benefits for the community as a whole).
(2) To achieve greater equity, such as by assisting farmers and other rural residents who are thrown into poverty because they are unable to adjust to the changing circumstance in which they find themselves.
(3) A political economy rationale, which implies that aid may be given less for its own sake but primarily to secure bigger changes elsewhere in the policy mix. As will be seen below, much of the support now labeled as "rural development" was initially seen as a way of making important reforms elsewhere in the CAP more acceptable to the farming community.

Of course, in addition to a sound rationale, technical fixes will need to be available in the form of schemes that use intervention instruments (such as investment grants, incentive payments and publicly provided advisory services and skills training) to achieve specified objectives related to the problems that have been identified. Also, there has to be evaluation to ensure that intervention brings anticipated net gains to society (expected benefits to society are at least as large as the anticipated costs). Such evaluations have to face the problem of establishing the counterfactual (what would have happened in the absence of the intervention) and thus of focusing on the additional impacts that result from implementing policy.

2.4.3 *Implementation of intervention*

Under EU policies, direct intervention in the employment levels and patterns seen in rural regions comes largely from actions under the Structural and Investment Funds, although, as has been pointed out earlier, these will be overlaid by a wide range of national policies and other EU policies that impact on employment indirectly. Among the latter, it is worth noting that what has become known as Pillar 1 of the CAP (direct income payments to farmers, production subsidies and market support) will affect employment in farm businesses, plus indirectly in the firms that supply their inputs and downstream operators such as food processors and elsewhere in the broader economy as farmers spend their supported income [Mattas and Loizou, 2017], though the economy-level impact will be diluted by the relatively small size of the farming sector in most MSs.

There are five EU Structural and Investment Funds that support the creation of more and better paid jobs in pursuit of the broad Europe 2020 strategy for smart, sustainable and inclusive growth, particularly the targets of raising employment levels and reducing poverty and social exclusion [European Commission, 2015a]. The activities under these funds are cofinanced by the EU budget and national budgets (in contrast with spending under Pillar 1, which is entirely financed by the EU budget). Allocation of resources is planned in periods of seven years under Multiannual Financial Frameworks (MFFs), the current one running from 2014 to 2020. These funds are as follows:

- **The European Regional Development Fund (ERDF):** This fund is focused primarily on regions that are lagging behind and is particularly concerned with large-scale infrastructure investments.
- **The European Social Fund (ESF):** This fund focuses on workers, young people and people seeking jobs by enhancing their skills and assisting their transition to employment.
- **The Cohesion Fund:** This fund is confined to countries that are lagging behind and thus not sharing in the growth in general prosperity; their Gross National Income (GNI) per capita has to be less than 90% of the EU-27 average. These comprise the NMSs plus Greece and Portugal.

- **The European Maritime and Fisheries Fund (EMFF):** This fund is mainly to do with the Common Fisheries Policy but may have implications for rural regions that happen to be coastal.
- **The European Agricultural Fund for Rural Development (EAFRD):** This fund forms Pillar 2 of the CAP and focuses on a mix of projects including structural change in agriculture, improvements in its economic performance, and agri-environmental programmes.

For the purposes of the ERDF, ESF and EAFRD regions are classed into three bands according to their GDP per capita compared to the EU average (less developed <75%, intermediate (also called transition) 75–90%, and more developed regions >90%). Though only one of these (the EAFRD) could be considered as being targeted at rural areas, the others impact on them because many of the less developed regions where average GDPs are lagging happen to be classed as rural.

Some idea of relative magnitudes is helpful. For the period 2014–2020, the total allocation from the EU budget to the Structural and Investment Funds was €351 billion, of which €182 billion went to the less developed regions from the ERDF, ESF and EAFRD. The Cohesion Fund was allocated €63 billion. The EAFRD allocation was €99 billion, though this was aimed at far more than employment creation; Matthews [2017] points out that only about 15% of Pillar 2 spending (already slim at a quarter of all spending on the CAP) is allocated to "social inclusion, poverty reduction and economic development", which would include job creation.

Though in the earlier phases of their operation, the Funds operated largely independently, since 2000 there has been an attempt to integrate them, thereby gaining synergy and raising efficiency by preventing duplication and avoiding gaps. A consequence is that, where in rural regions multiple funds are operating, it may be difficult to attribute changes in employment to individual projects.

2.4.4 *Rural development programs under the EAFRD*

From the early days of the EU, it was recognized that the CAP's ways of supporting agriculture (mainly through raising prices of farm commodities) contained inner contradictions and brought problems. While in the short term, the support might retain some employment in the primary sector, in the longer-term structural change (to fewer but larger commercial farms) and modernization (with less labor used) was inevitable. This carried implications for the future of rural society. It was clear that agriculture needed to be better integrated with the rest of the food chain and more strongly linked to sectors where there were increasing employment opportunities, such as tourism. At the same time, the developing farming systems were causing environmental damage. Several initiatives were developed to tackle the various issues, but not in a very holistic way [see Hill, 2012, Chapter 7].

The reorganization of EU agricultural policy under Agenda 2000 gave the opportunity to bring all these interventions together under the heading of the CAP's Pillar 2. The first Regulation (No. 1257/1999) covering the period 2000–2006 gave legality to the use of EU resources to part-finance actions listed in its Articles. Implementation was by MSs using Rural Development Programs (RDPs) proposed at national or sub-national levels[e] and needing approval by the European Commission. Though referred to as "rural development", these actions were not restricted to an economic interpretation. The heterogeneous collection that legislation stated could be supported by EU resources included assistance to farmer entry and exit, farm modernization, knowledge transfer and advisory services, farm business diversification, promotion of marketing and processing, afforestation and forest management, support to farming in less-favored areas (hills, uplands and other types) and, importantly, agri-environmental schemes (a feature that in the USA would be seen as part of environmental policy rather than rural development — see Blandford and Hill [2008]). It is perhaps understandable that, given the short time available for planning for the 2000–2006 RDPs, MSs tended to fit into it schemes that were already running rather than design afresh.

---

[e] Some MSs have a single RDP while other have multiple RDPs. For example, there are four separate RDPs in the UK where agriculture is a devolved responsibility, one each for England, Wales, Scotland and Northern Ireland. In total for the 2014–2020 period there were 115 RDPs across 28 EU MSs.

Subsequent Regulations have carried the process of Rural Development Plans at the national or regional level forward to the programming periods of 2007–2013 and 2014–2020. The eclectic mix of economic, social and environmental actions have been broadly maintained, with adjustments such as specifying minimum spends on certain areas. The number of jobs created (in supported projects) remains as a common indicator required by the European Commission, though there is some dispute about the accuracy with which this can be estimated. One notable change after the first programming period was to bring the Links between Actions for the Development of the Rural Economy (LEADER) approach into the mainstream of RDPs and to finance it from the EAFRD. Initially seen as a way of promoting and piloting innovation in rural development, this bottom-up approach builds on local initiatives and capacities to tackle local (mainly socio-economic) problems, including job creation. Local Action Groups (LAGs), made up of individuals, private and public sector organizations and often led by local government bodies, help in the design of interventions and are critical to operating the LEADER approach.

Job creation remains an aim. For the period 2014–2020 the EU-level target for RDPs was 124,000 non-agricultural jobs, of which 79,000 were in diversification and small and medium-sized enterprises, and 45,000 in activities associated with LEADER [European Commission, 2016b].

2.5 Does EU Policy Contribute to Rural Employment?

An important feature of the first Rural Development Regulation of 1999 was that it imposed a formal, systematic approach to assessing the performance of RDPs against the aims and objectives set for them, with *ex ante*, mid-term, and *ex post* evaluations to be carried out independently of MS administrations and submitted to the European Commission by specific dates [Bradley *et al.,* 2010]. The Common Monitoring and Evaluation Framework (CMEF) was set up for this purpose, with common evaluation questions across all the RDPs and the designation of indicators (inputs, outputs, results and impacts) that included the number of jobs created or protected, both at farm level and in related sectors (such as forestry contractors who planted trees). The Commission also took responsibility for having syntheses of the RDP reports made at EU level to give an indication of how the policy as a whole was performing. The commitment in legislation to evaluation of RDPs has endured with minor changes. Evaluation has also been expanded to embrace the CAP's Pillar 1.

Unfortunately, the publication of evaluation findings on the impacts of RDPs at the EU level is subject to substantial delay. The exercise to synthesize results from the *ex post* evaluations of RDPs operated in 2007–2013 has not yet been reported. The equivalent report on the impact of RDPs for the previous period (2000–2006) concluded, rather blandly, that rural development measures maintained and/or generated employment at local or regional level. Some measures supporting economic diversification (e.g. investments in farms, improving the processing and marketing of agricultural products, and diversifying agricultural activities and income sources) had an actual impact on both off-farm and on-farm employment, sometimes associated with improved equal opportunities. Two previously identified conclusions were underlined. First, measures addressing the wider rural economy appeared to have proportionately greater impacts on income and employment than purely agricultural measures. This is in line with the view of Matthews [2017] and others that a more efficient use of public funds comes from addressing problems of market failure, so that adjustment can take place and the broader economy can develop. Second, impacts were greater when measures were applied in combination or in synergy chains. This appears particularly true for the added impact of using training and advice in conjunction with investments on farms for purposes of diversification.

More recently, a study for the European Parliament [Schuh *et al.*, 2016], drawing on a wide range of evidence, concluded that the ability of CAP's Pillar 1 payments to farm operators to create jobs has been limited (that is, small at best) as there are contradictory effects on farm-level employment with, on the one hand, support tending to retain labor on farms that would otherwise not have survived while, on the other, encouraging the displacement of labor in the drive for productivity improvement (the decoupling of payments in the 2003 CAP reforms was thought to have such an effect). Pillar 2's approach using RDPs appears to have been more focused on creating off-farm jobs. However, funding support has been low, rather thinly spread, and not sustained in ways necessary to build on opportunities and deal with deeper structural problems.

Furthermore, concrete evidences of direct effects on rural employment are difficult to assess due to missing systematic reporting on job creation. This amounts to only a weak endorsement for the ability of agricultural support spending to impact on employment as a whole in rural areas.

Evaluation has also applied to the other EU Funds that have supported job creation, though until recently these tended to operate independently. In the period 2007–2014 the Regional and Cohesions Funds were estimated in *ex post* evaluations to have generated about 1.1 million new jobs (some nine times the target for RDPs in the subsequent period), though how many of these were in rural regions is not known [European Commission, 2016a]. In the latest programming period, evaluation of the European Structural and Investment Funds share a common base (the Common Provisions Regulation[f]) which, among other things, encourages the close working of evaluations of the ERDF, Cohesion Fund and the EAFRD where they share objectives, such as employment creation [Commission, 2015b]. This could be expected to result eventually in an integrated approach that should enable the impact of EU policies on rural employment to be properly assessed, though that is some way in the future.

In summary, while employment in rural regions suffered disproportionately in the economic depression from 2009, it has demonstrated substantial recovery, and from 2013 has shown growth that has at least matched that of other regions. EU policies intend to support employment creation, though it is far from certain that they, and in particular the CAP, have a material impact on recent changes in this important metric.

References

Blandford, D. and Hill, B. (2008). Guest Editorial: Directions in Rural Development Policy – Lessons from Both Sides of the Atlantic, *EuroChoices*, Special issue on *EU and US Rural Development Policies*, 7(1).

[f]Regulation (EU) No. 1303/2013 of the European Parliament and the Council of 17 December 2013 laying down common provisions on the ESI Funds, referred to as the CPR (Common Provisions Regulation).

Bradley, D., Dwyer, J. and Hill, B. (2010). The Evaluation of Rural Development in the EU, *EuroChoices*, Special Issue on *Evaluating Rural Development Policy*, 9(1), pp. 15–20.

Ecorys (2010). *Study on Employment, Growth and Innovation in Rural Areas* (*SEGIRA*). Rotterdam.

European Commission (2006). *Study on Employment in Rural Areas* (*SERA*). Commission, Brussels.

European Commission (2015a). *European Structural and Investment Funds 2014–2020: Official Texts and Commentaries.* Commission, Brussels.

European Commission (2015b). *Guidance Document on Evaluation Plans. Programming Period 2014–2020 Monitoring and Evaluation of European Cohesion Policy.* Commission, Brussels.

European Commission (2016a). *Ex Post Evaluation of the ERDF and Cohesion Fund 2007–2013.* Commission Staff Working Document, Commission, Brussels.

European Commission (2016b). *Facts and Figures: Rural Development in the European Union. Cork 2.0.* Commission, Brussels.

European Commission (2017). *CAP Context Indicators 2014–2020. Agriculture and Rural Development. 2017 Update.* Commission, Brussels.

European Commission (2018). *Rural Areas and the Primary Sector in the EU. DG Agriculture and Rural Development.* Unit Farm Economics, Commission, Brussels.

Eurostat (2010). *Regional Yearbook 2010.* ISSN 1830-9674. Section 15 'A Revised Urban-Rural Typology', Eurostat, Luxembourg.

Eurostat (2013). *Eurostat Pocketbooks: Agriculture, Forestry and Fishing Statistics*, 2013 edition. Eurostat, Luxembourg.

Eurostat (2017). *Regional Yearbook*, 2017 edition. Eurostat, Luxembourg.

Hill, B. (2012). Understanding the support of agriculture and rural development in the EU, Chapter 7 in *Understanding the Common Agricultural Policy.* Earthscan/Routledge.

Mattas, K. and Loizou, E. (2017). Point de vue — The CAP as a Job Stabilizer. Special Section on the CAP and Rural Jobs. *EuroChoices*, 16(3), pp. 23–26.

Matthews, A. (2017). Point de vue: How Can the CAP Promote Rural Jobs? Special Section on the CAP and Rural Jobs. *EuroChoices*, 16(3), pp. 18–21.

Schuh, B., Gorny, H., Kaucic, J., Kirchmayr-Novak, S., Vigani, M., Powell, J. and Hawketts, E. (2016). *The Role of the EU's Common Agricultural Policy in Creating Rural Jobs.* Study for the European Parliament, Brussels.

Chapter 3

US Policies and Rural Employment

David Blandford

Pennsylvania State University, State College, USA
dblandford@psu.edu

Following an analysis of the economic characteristics of rural areas in the United States and some of the social challenges that they face, trends in total employment and the structure of employment are described, followed by a description of policies at federal and state levels: primarily rural development policies at the federal level and economic development policies at the state level. In both cases, the emphasis is on infrastructural development as a means of improving the quality of life and increasing economic activity. Although some rural counties are experiencing population growth, the majority are losing residents. Rural counties tend to be less economically diversified than urban counties. They have a greater incidence of persistent unemployment and poverty, and lower educational levels in the workforce. Despite federal and state programs oriented toward improving rural infrastructure, there are significant deficiencies in key areas, such as transportation and telecommunications. A recent assessment indicates that a substantial increase in effort is required at all levels of government to improve the quality of life in rural areas and to strengthen the conditions for growth and employment creation.

3.1 Introduction

As in many other countries, defining what constitutes a "rural" area in the United States is challenging. More than two dozen definitions of rurality are currently used by federal agencies. The share of the total population identified as rural ranges from 17% to 49% depending on the definition used [Cromarty and Bucholtz, 2008]. Analysts of conditions in rural America most often use data on non-metropolitan (non-metro) areas, defined by the Office of Management and Budget (OMB) on the basis of counties or county-equivalent units (e.g. parishes and boroughs). Counties are the standard building block for assembling data and for monitoring and analyzing regional trends. Annual estimates of population, employment and income are available on a county or county-equivalent basis.

The federal agency primarily responsible for rural development programs is the US Department of Agriculture. The USDA's Economic Research Service (ERS) uses data for urban (metro) and rural (non-metro) areas to classify counties according to six mutually exclusive categories of economic dependence and six overlapping policy-relevant categories. These data provide insight into the economic and social characteristics of rural counties that are the focus of federal programs.

Metro (urban) counties contain one or more urbanized areas: high-density urban areas containing 50,000 people or more, and outlying counties that are economically tied to central counties, measured by the share of workers commuting on a daily basis to the central counties. Non-metro (rural) counties are outside the boundaries of metro areas and have no cities with 50,000 residents or more. There are currently 3,142 counties or their equivalents[a] in the United States, and the number varies widely among states. Excluding the federal capital (District of Columbia), the State of Delaware has the smallest number (3) and Texas the largest (254): the median number for the 50 states is 63.

[a]The term "county" is a unit of local government used in 48 of the 50 states: the equivalent units are "boroughs" in Alaska and "parishes" in Louisiana. Alaska also has 10 census areas that are treated as county-equivalent entities for statistical purposes. Cities that are administratively independent in Maryland, Missouri, Nevada and Virginia are also considered to be county-equivalents.

Almost 63% of U.S counties can be classified as rural; they tend to be large in area. The median size of rural counties (total of land and surface water) is 710 square miles, compared to 590 square miles for urban counties. However, the average size of rural counties in more remote parts of the country or those that were settled later tend to be larger. In Alaska, for example, the average size of the 29 counties (or equivalent administrative units) is over 13,000 square miles. The median size in Arizona, the last of the lower 48 states to be granted statehood in 1912, is over 4,600 square miles. As might be expected, the average population of rural counties (roughly 16,500 in 2017, based on Census Bureau estimates) is substantially smaller than for urban counties (roughly 98,000). Consequently, the average population density in urban counties is over six times greater than in rural counties (152 compared to 25 per square mile). The generally larger geographical area and lower population density of rural counties often create challenges for financing the provision and maintenance of local infrastructure (e.g. roads, water and sewage treatment facilities) and limit the size of local markets for goods and services.

3.2 Economic Characteristics of Rural Areas in the United States

The latest version of the ERS database (2015) classifies counties according to six types of economic dependence: farming, mining, manufacturing, federal/state government, recreation, and non-specialized economies (those in which none of these activities dominates). Counties are also classified according to policy-relevant social characteristics (low education, low employment, persistent poverty, persistent child poverty, population loss, and retirement destination). Table 3.1 summarizes the indicators relating to economic structure for rural and urban counties.

Several important differences between rural and urban areas are revealed in this table. First, the economies of urban areas tend to be more diversified, as revealed by the 56% or counties that have no dominant industry in terms of county earnings or employment. The economies of rural counties tend to be dominated by certain industries. Although it might be expected that farming is a major activity in many rural areas (22% of rural counties), it is also noteworthy that mining and

Table 3.1. Indicators of economic structure for rural and urban counties in the United States.

			Percentage for which the following are important					
	Number	(%)	Farm. (1)	Min. (2)	Man. (3)	Gov. (4)	Rec. (5)	Non. (6)
Rural	1,976	63	22	11	18	14	16	30
Urban	1,166	37	5	4	13	15	10	56
Total	3,142	100	16	8	16	15	14	39

Notes: Indicators, averages 2010–2012.
(1) Farming: 25% or more of earnings or 16% or more of employment.
(2) Mining: 13% or more of earnings or 8% or more of employment.
(3) Manufacturing: 23% or more of earnings or 16% or more of employment.
(4) Federal and state governments: 14% or more of earnings or 9% or more of employment.
(5) Recreation: identified by earnings and employment in related activities (see source for details).
(6) Not a farming, mining, manufacturing, government-dependent, or recreation county.
Source: USDA ERS, County typology codes update 2015, http://www.ers.usda.gov/data-products/county-typology-codes (accessed July 2018).

manufacturing are important in many cases. A larger percentage of rural counties have manufacturing as an important source of earnings and employment than urban counties. In many counties, both urban and rural, federal, state and local government employment is significant for the local economy.

As might be expected, recreational activity tends to be a more important source of economic activity in rural counties (16% of counties fall in the recreational category) due to the opportunities that rural areas can provide for outdoor recreational pursuits. However, the economic advantage conferred by natural amenities does not seem to be reflected strongly in the data on economic structure. Many urban areas also offer recreational attractions and these generate significant levels of earnings and employment.

The ERS database provides information on some policy-relevant social characteristics. Five of these are included in Table 3.2.

The data show that a higher proportion of rural counties have negative social characteristics compared to urban areas. Their populations tend to have lower educational levels and lower rates of employment. Rural areas are more likely to have declining populations and a greater incidence of

Table 3.2. Social indicators for rural and urban counties in the United States.

	Low education (1)	Low employment (2)	Population loss (3)	Retirement destination (4)	Persistent poverty (5)
Rural	19	36	24	10	15
Urban	9	16	5	21	4
Total	15	29	17	14	11

Notes:

(1) At least 20% or more of the residents aged 25–64 did not have a high-school diploma or equivalent (2008–2012).

(2) Less than 65% of residents aged 25–64 were employed in 2008–2012.

(3) The number of residents declined between the 1990 and 2000 censuses and between the 2000 and 2010 censuses.

(4) The number of residents aged 60 and older increased by 15% or more between 2000 and 2010.

(5) 20% or more of the residents were poor as measured by the 1980, 1990 and 2000 censuses and Census Bureau estimates for 2007–2011.

Source: Computed from USDA ERS, County typology codes update 2015, http://www.ers.usda.gov/data-products/county-typology-codes (accessed July 2018).

persistent poverty among remaining residents. A smaller proportion of rural counties appear to be retirement destinations, although rural counties located in particularly scenic areas (e.g. the Mountain West) have experienced modest population growth (roughly 1% between 2010 and 2016) [ERS, 2017]. As a further reflection of social disadvantage, the number of deaths from drug overdoses is increasing rapidly in rural areas; the ratio of deaths to population exceeded that in urban areas in 2015 for the first time [Mack *et al.*, 2017].

Taken together, the indicators in Tables 3.1 and 3.2 suggest that rural areas in the United States tend to be economically and socially disadvantaged compared to urban areas. The total population of rural counties declined by almost 200,000 between 2010 and 2016, with 1,351 counties (68% of the total number of rural counties) experiencing a combined loss in population of just under 790,000. Continuing a long-term trend, counties dependent on agriculture lost population, as did counties in manufacturing-dependent areas. Gains in population in rural counties in scenic areas or those affected by the recent expansion of the US oil and gas industry did not outweigh losses elsewhere.

An examination of the data in the ERS database reveals some interesting, statistically significant associations among some of the variables for rural counties. Perhaps, unsurprisingly, there is a highly significant correlation between low education levels and high unemployment, and between high unemployment and persistent poverty. But, it is also of interest that a significant negative correlation exists between high unemployment and the dominance of farming ($r = -0.21$, $t = 9.56$). This reflects the fact that the farming industry remains an important contributor to employment in many rural counties. The only other statistically significant correlation between employment and economic structure is a positive association between the importance of government activity and persistently high unemployment ($r = 0.19$, $t = 8.68$). State and local governments, and the Federal Government (particularly through the location and operation of military facilities) often attempt to compensate for a lack of employment opportunities in disadvantaged rural areas by creating government jobs.

3.3 Employment Trends in Rural Areas

Figure 3.1 shows trends in total employment (full-time and part-time) in rural and urban areas since 2001. The economic recession that followed the financial crisis of 2007–2008 resulted in a significant fall in US employment. The unemployment rate doubled from 5% at the beginning of 2008 to 10% by late 2009. Prior to the recession, the rate of job growth in urban areas had exceeded that in rural areas; and the rate of job creation was roughly twice as large as in rural areas. The recession resulted in the loss of a larger percentage of rural jobs (4.5%) than urban jobs (3.7%). With the subsequent economic recovery, employment growth in rural areas has continued to lag behind that in urban areas, as indicated by the growing divergence between the upper and lower lines in Fig. 3.1.

Table 3.3 shows that the number of jobs in urban areas increased by just over 13% between 2010 and 2016, compared to just over 4% in rural areas. The table also gives a breakdown of the change in employment by type of activity. The figures show that post-recession employment growth has been broad-based in urban areas. With the exception of government

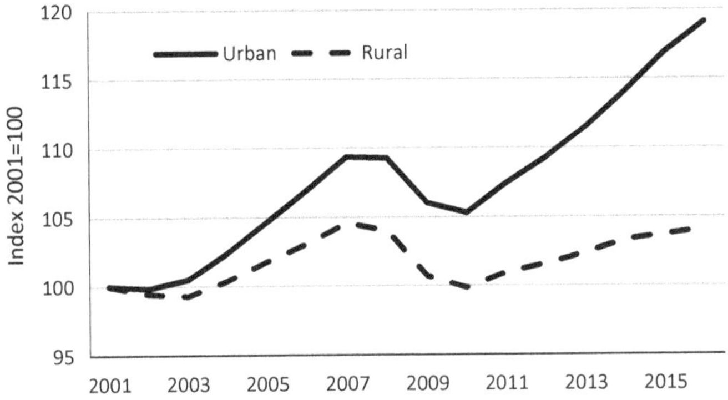

Fig. 3.1. Trends in employment in rural and urban areas in the US.

Source: Bureau of Economic Analysis, US Department of Commerce, http://www.bea.gov/Table/index-regional.cfm (accessed July 2018).

and government enterprises, employment in all categories increased. The median increase across all the categories listed was 15%. Increases in employment in areas that are important in urban economic structure (e.g. construction, retail trade, professional and technical services, and healthcare) have been particularly significant.

In contrast to urban areas, employment growth in rural areas has been far less robust (median increase of 5% for the categories listed), and there have been absolute declines in employment in several categories. The most significant, in terms of the contribution to total employment in 2016, were in government and government enterprises and farm employment.

Although the entries in Table 3.3 show that manufacturing employment increased in both urban and rural areas between 2010 and 2016, there has been a dramatic decline in total manufacturing employment since the turn of the century. US employment in manufacturing was 23% lower in 2016 than in 2001. Since manufacturing has typically constituted a larger share of total employment in rural areas (14% in 2001 compared to less than 10% in urban areas) the decline in employment in that sector has had a more pronounced effect in rural areas.

Estimates of the number of hired workers in agriculture in 2016 range from 820,000 (Department of Commerce) to 856,000 (Department of

Table 3.3. Changes in employment by category (2010–2016) and employment structure in urban and rural areas in the US (2016).

	Change in employment 2010–2016		Share of total employment in 2016	
Category of employment	Urban	Rural	Urban	Rural
Farm employment	1.2	–0.5	0.8	5.7
Forestry, fishing, and related activities	8.1	5.4	0.3	1.4
Mining, quarrying, oil and gas	15.0	5.6	0.6	2.0
Utilities	4.2	3.0	0.3	0.5
Construction	17.3	0.6	5.2	5.6
Manufacturing	8.1	9.0	6.2	10.7
Wholesale trade	15.5	11.9	3.7	2.8
Retail trade	11.2	4.6	9.9	11.0
Transportation and warehousing	33.7	12.6	3.7	3.4
Information	5.1	–8.7	1.9	0.8
Finance and insurance	8.1	–1.7	5.4	3.2
Real estate and rental and leasing	17.2	12.2	4.8	3.4
Professional, scientific, technical services	17.4	5.8	7.6	3.3
Management of companies	24.2	16.4	1.4	0.5
Administrative and support (1)	14.9	7.0	6.4	4.0
Educational services	15.6	12.0	2.6	1.5
Healthcare and social assistance	16.6	3.2	11.5	10.0
Arts, entertainment, and recreation	15.0	5.7	2.3	1.6
Accommodation and food services	21.6	11.2	7.5	7.1
Other services (except government)	17.7	8.6	5.9	6.0
Government and government enterprises	–1.0	–4.1	12.1	15.7
Federal civilian	–5.4	–12.0	1.5	1.1
Military	–8.1	–9.3	1.0	0.9
State and local	0.5	–2.9	9.6	13.6
State government	0.8	–3.7	2.7	3.3
Local government	0.4	–2.7	6.9	10.4
Total employment (number of jobs)	13.1	4.2		

Note: (1) includes waste management and remediation.

Source: Bureau of Economic Analysis, US Department of Commerce, http://www.bea.gov/Table/index-regional.cfm (accessed July 2018).

Labor). Many are part-time or seasonal workers and a significant number are immigrants. Survey data for fiscal years (FY) 2013–2014 indicate that 47% of farmworkers did not have a legal right to work in the United States [US Department of Labor, 2016].[b] The Pew Research Center estimates that the US civilian workforce included 8 million unauthorized immigrants in 2014 (5% of the workforce). However, the majority of these immigrants live in major metropolitan areas rather than in rural areas, and are most likely to have jobs in the service or construction industries [Pew Research Center, 2017].

3.4 Public Policies and Rural Employment

Rural areas are affected by a range of federal policies that influence economic activity and employment (e.g. taxation and public welfare policies). They are also influenced by policies at the state and local levels. Although the impact of policies may differ between urban and rural areas because of demographic differences, income levels and economic structure, most are not targeted specifically to either rural or urban areas. Consequently, the focus in the remainder of this chapter is on policies that are targeted to rural areas or have a significant impact on economic activity and employment in rural areas.

3.4.1 *Federal rural development programs*

Several rural development programs are operated at the federal level. They are authorized by the Farm Act — legislation approved every four or five years, and covering a range of activities conducted by the USDA [Johnson and Monke, 2018]. The Agricultural Act of 2014 covers five years (FY2014 to FY2018). The legislation authorizes programs in two expenditure categories: (1) mandatory programs for which expenditure estimates

[b]The Federal Government's FY extends from October to September. Hence FY19 extends from 1 October 2018 to 30 September 2019. The FY for two states (Alabama and Michigan) corresponds to the federal FY, in New York it ends in March and in Texas in August. For all the other states the FY runs from July to June. Unless otherwise indicated, data used in this chapter correspond to calendar years.

are prepared when the law is enacted, and (2) discretionary programs for which funds must be appropriated on an annual basis by the Congress. Mandatory programs dominate total expenditure, but most of the expenditure on rural development falls into the discretionary category. In FY2017, total discretionary outlays under the Agricultural Act accounted for roughly 19% of the $128 billion of total expenditure in that year [USDA, 2018].

Rural development programs are the responsibility of three agencies within USDA. The Rural Business-Cooperative Service (RBS) provides assistance for the development of business and industry, including small businesses, and renewable energy and energy improvement projects. The Rural Utilities Service (RUS) provides assistance for water and waste disposal, rural electric and telecommunications, including broadband access. The Rural Housing Service (RHS) provides assistance for home ownership, multi-family housing, and community facilities for health and public safety. The agencies provide financial and technical assistance to rural communities, residents, businesses, and private and public entities. Financial assistance includes direct and guaranteed loans, grants, and other payments. Several programs require or encourage recipients to contribute their own resources or to obtain third-party financing for projects, thereby leveraging Government support with private-sector finance. As noted earlier, only a small part of the expenditure on rural development falls into the mandatory category: this relates to the development of bioenergy and other forms of renewable energy (e.g. solar and wind) through the RBS.

Much of the funding provided through federal rural development programs is in the form of grants and loans and is directed toward infrastructure, particularly single family housing. Actual cash disbursements through the US Treasury in FY2017 to satisfy obligations (legally binding commitments) totaled $3,239 million (Fig. 3.2), equivalent to less than 3% of all USDA expenditure in that year. However, if the value of loan guarantees and other forms of assistance is included the number increases by more than 12-fold to $40,604 million, equivalent to almost 20% of the value of all USDA program activities in that year.

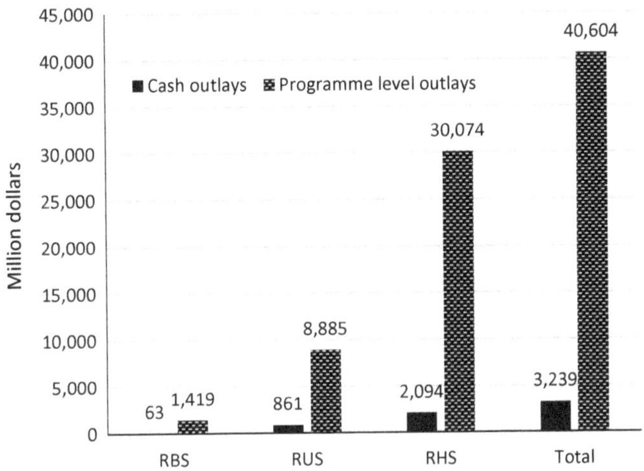

Fig. 3.2. US federal expenditure on rural development programs, FY2017.

Note: Totals include salaries and expenses.

Source: USDA FY2019 Budget Summary. www.usda.gov/our-agency/about-usda/budget (accessed July 2018).

3.4.2 *State and local rural development programs*

Many of the policies and programs that relate directly to economic development and employment are implemented at state and local levels. Available data suggest that the median expenditure per business establishment by the states on economic development activities in 2016 was equivalent to around 2% of state GDP per capita.[c]

While in many cases programs are targeted to economic development regardless of location, 10 states have taken legislative actions designed to promote development in rural areas [NCSL, 2018]. These range from the creation of councils or commissions to analyze rural issues, provide information on rural development and make recommendations to state

[c]Estimated from Council for Community and Economic Research database http://www.stateexpenditures.org. The figures refer to state budgeted/proposed expenditures for FY2016. Number of business establishments from the US Bureau of Labor Statistics. State GDP from the Bureau of Economic Analysis, US Department of Commerce.

legislatures on rural policy (e.g. Georgia, New Hampshire, New Mexico, New York, Pennsylvania and Wisconsin) to the provision of grants, tax credits or technical assistance to promote job creation in rural areas (Tennessee, Utah and Vermont). Maryland has a rural caucus of state legislators that promotes the interests of rural parts of the state.

There are substantial financial transfers from the Federal Government to the states for the implementation of programs in areas that affect economic activity, employment and quality of life. These transfers primarily involve health, public assistance and retirement pensions. However, the bulk of investment expenditures is funded at the state and local levels. In FY2015, 72% of spending on infrastructure came from state funds, including proceeds from the sale of bonds [CBPP, 2017].

In a recent assessment of the condition of America's infrastructure, the American Society of Civil Engineers [ASCE, 2017] awarded a D+ or "poor" rating. The estimated cost of bringing America's infrastructure to a state of good repair (a grade of B) by 2025 is $4.6 trillion, of which only about 55% has been committed by states, localities and the Federal Government.[d] Improving roads and bridges alone would require $1.1 trillion, more than has been allocated by all levels of government. A study of the impact of the projected underinvestment on economic activity estimates that it will result in 2.5 million fewer jobs by 2025 [ASCE, 2016]. In 2015, 15% of the nation's major rural roads (arterials and collectors) were rated in poor condition, 21% were rated in mediocre condition, 16% were rated in fair condition, and 48% were rated in good condition. In 2016, 10% of the nation's rural bridges were rated as structurally deficient [TRIP, 2017].

Another part of the economic infrastructure in which investment is lagging in rural areas is telecommunications. The Federal Communications Commission estimates that by the end of 2016 68.6% of Americans in rural areas had access to fixed high-speed broadband services (25 Mbps/3 Mbps), compared to 97.9% of Americans in urban areas; 98.1% of the

[d]The components included are: roads and bridges; rail, public transit and airports; dams, levees, inland waterways and ports; water, wastewater, waste and hazardous waste; schools; and public parks and recreation facilities.

country has access to either fixed terrestrial service or mobile LTE (4G mobile communications standard) but only 89.7% in rural areas [FCC, 2018]. A recent report by a USDA task force on agriculture and rural prosperity had as its first recommendation the expansion of reliable and affordable Internet connectivity in rural areas [USDA, 2017].

3.5 Does US Policy Contribute to Rural Employment?

Judging by recent economic performance and social indicators, current federal, state and local policies are having a limited impact on employment and well-being in rural areas in the United States. The Federal Interagency Taskforce established in 2017 to analyze rural prosperity made over 100 recommendations for legislative, regulatory and policy changes to promote growth and development in rural areas [USDA, 2017]. Many of these recommendations focus on improving infrastructure and quality of life to make rural areas more attractive to business and industry. While some rural areas are likely to prosper because of strong natural advantages, such as scenic beauty and other natural amenities, the majority appear to face the prospect of continued economic decline and population loss without a major intensification of rural development effort. Growing pressures on budgets at federal, state and local levels will make it extremely challenging to achieve this.

References

American Society of Civil Engineers (2016). *Failure to Act: Closing the Investment Gap for America's Economic Future.* ASCE. Washington, DC http://www.infrastructurereportcard.org/wp-content/uploads/2016/10/ASCE-Failure-to-Act-2016-FINAL.pdf (accessed July 2018).

American Society of Civil Engineers (2017). *2017 Infrastructure Report Card.* ASCE. Washington, DC http://www.infrastructurereportcard.org (accessed July 2018).

Center for Budget and Policy Priorities (2017). It's Time for States to Invest in Infrastructure. *Policy Futures Report.* CBPP. Washington, DC https://www.cbpp.org/research/state-budget-and-tax/its-time-for-states-to-invest-in-infrastructure (accessed July 2018).

Cromarty, J. and Bucholtz, S. (2008). Defining the "Rural" in Rural America. *Amber Waves* June 1. Economic Research Service, US Department of Agriculture, Washington DC http://www.ers.usda.gov/amber-waves/2008/june/defining-the-rural-in-rural-america (accessed July 2018).

Economic Research Service (2017). *Rural America at a Glance: 2017 Edition.* Economic Information Bulletin 182. Economic Research Service, US Department of Agriculture. Washington, DC http://www.ers.usda.gov/publications/pub-details/?pubid=85739 (accessed July 2018).

Federal Communications Commission (2018). *2018 Broadband Deployment Report.* FCC, Washington DC http://www.fcc.gov/reports-research/reports/broadband-progress-reports/2018-broadband-deployment-report (accessed July 2018).

Johnson, R. and Monke, J. (2018). *What is the Farm Bill?* Congressional Research Service, Washington DC April 26. http://www.hsdl.org/?view&did=810176 (accessed July 2018).

Mack, K. A., Jones, C. M. and Ballesteros, M. F. (2017). Illicit Drug Use, Illicit Drug Disorders, and Drug Overdose Deaths in Metropolitan and Nonmetropolitan Areas — United States. Centers for Disease Control and Prevention. *Morbidity and Mortality Weekly Report Surveillance Summaries* 66 (No. SS 19): 1–22. www.cdc.gov/mmwr/volumes/66/ss/ss6619a1.htm (accessed July 2018).

National Council of State Legislatures (2018). *State Legislative Rural Development Councils.* NCSL. Washington, DC http://www.ncsl.org/research/agriculture-and-rural-development/state-legislative-rural-development-efforts.aspx (accessed July 2018).

Pew Research Center (2017). Key Facts about U.S Immigrants. *Fact-tank: News on the Numbers.* May 3. Washington, DC http://www.pewresearch.org/fact-tank/2017/05/03/key-findings-about-u-s-immigrants (accessed July 2018).

TRIP (2017). *Rural Connections: Challenges and Opportunities in America's Heartland.* June. TRIP National Transportation Research Group. Washington, DC http://www.tripnet.org/docs/Rural_Roads_TRIP_Report_2017.pdf (accessed July 2018).

United States Department of Agriculture (2017). *Report to the President of the United States from the Task Force on Agriculture and Rural Prosperity.* USDA. Washington, DC http://www.usda.gov/sites/default/files/documents/rural-prosperity-report.pdf (accessed July 2018).

United States Department of Agriculture (2018). *FY 2019 Budget Summary.* http://www.usda.gov/our-agency/about-usda/budget (accessed July 2018).

United States Department of Labor (2016). *A Demographic and Employment Profile of United States Farmworkers. Findings from the National Agricultural Workers Survey (NAWS) 2013–2014*. Washington, DC http://www.doleta.gov/agworker/pdf/NAWS_Research_Report_12_Final_508_Compliant.pdf (accessed July 2018).

Part B
Trends in Rural Employment

Chapter 4

Rural Employment Trends in the EU

David Harvey

University of Newcastle upon Tyne, UK
david.harvey@ncl.ac.uk

The EU's rural areas reflect the history, geography and politics of the Member States (MSs), as well as general patterns of socio-economic development. As a consequence, they display very considerable diversity and heterogeneity. Rural areas and their employment levels are generally more politically important in the EU than in the US, as reflected by the prominence of agricultural and rural policies in the EU. However, the patterns of rural development and employment do not suggest that the agri-food sector can be relied on as a major engine of rural development and employment in the EU. An evolutionary perspective of economic development strongly suggests that endogenous, locally induced and potentially self-sustaining growth is possible and capable of cultivation by appropriate policies and strategies.

4.1 Introduction

A major difference between Europe and the United States is that the average population density is more than three times higher in the EU, at 112 per square kilometer, *vs.* 34 per square kilometer in the US. EU population densities range from fewer than 50 per square kilometer in the Scandinavian and Baltic countries (similar to Washington State and Texas) to more than 200 per square kilometer in Germany, the UK, Belgium and the Netherlands (similar to Connecticut and Massachusetts). In both the US and the EU, rural areas have become distinct from cities and towns as a complex consequence of history, geography and politics, in conjunction with general socio-economic patterns of human development.

Economic development, and hence employment, tends to focus on urban areas, attracting people and wealth (capital) and leading to further development — encouraged by economies of scale in the provision of both public and private services. Typically, urban centers develop at natural transportation nodes, in the lowlands, close to rivers or the coast, and often on Grade 1 farmland, as illustrated in both the *Eurostat Regional Yearbook* [European Commission, 2017b, Map 2, p. 12] and the Eurostat Geostat population grid [European Commission, 2017c].

As Chapter 2 has already indicated, EU rural areas are both difficult to define sensibly and also widely heterogeneous. In particular, they are not predominantly agricultural. Nevertheless, there is a general trajectory for rural employment and development discernable from the historical development of modern economies. It has long been recognized [e.g. Johnston and Mellor, 1961] that economic growth implies a relative decline in agriculture as a generator of both incomes and employment. With increasing incomes, we spend a smaller fraction of our incomes on food production, if not also processing and preparation. It follows that fewer people are able to earn a full-time living from farming and find something else to do as economies grow and societies develop. As a consequence, and other things (e.g. trade patterns) being equal, rural economies (as predominantly agricultural economies) will decline, unless they also develop and grow other activities and livelihoods. Myrdal [1957; see also, Fujita, 2007] argued that market forces would reinforce regional disparities by exploiting agglomeration economies of scale, while new economic geography theories [Krugman, 1991] extend the concepts of divergence between core and peripheral economies, based on imperfect markets, transportation, communication and transaction costs. Copus *et al.* [2006], using data for 2001, identify a long-established process of urbanization in the EU, consistent with these divergence predictions and drawing both population and economic activity out of rural areas, especially those which are more remote.

However, these authors also note a counter-urbanization process in the EU, where both employment and economic activity flow from more concentrated urban areas into the more accessible rural regions. In addition, these authors also note rather clear North–South and East–West patterns, reflecting both different stages in economic development as well as differences in natural and cultural environments, and different political histories. Between 1995 and 2000, Copus *et al.* [2006] find that 40% of rural regions in the EU suffered a decline in population, with one in five experiencing declines resulting from both natural net birth rates and out migration. On the other hand, 40% of rural regions enjoyed an increase in their populations, with 20% experiencing increases in population from both net births and inward migration. These authors also discuss the difficulties associated with classifying rurality solely on the basis of population densities. Among the options they discuss is one which (a) restricts the urban classification to areas (communes) with populations >10,000 and (b) includes an index of peripherality.

> The member states most affected (by the exclusion of small communes) are France and Czech Republic, where a considerable share of the national territory moves from significantly to predominantly rural. In France this is the consequence of the numerous very small communes (low number of inhabitants, small in size, but high population density). In the original OECD classification, the relevant NUTS 3 regions are considered as urban since population density exceeds 150 inhabitants and the sum accounts for more than 15% of the region's population. In the modified version, these communes are considered as rural, since they have less than 10,000 inhabitants [Copus *et al.*, 2006, p. 168].
>
> The index of peripherality shows a core-periphery pattern for EU27's NUTS3 regions, with the core regions situated in Eastern and Southern England, Benelux, the North of France, Northern and Western Germany and parts of Denmark. Also some regions in Northern Italy show above-average values. The more peripheral parts of Europe are constituted by Southern France, the central Spanish, Mid and South Italy as well as Austria, Hungary, Slovakia and Czech Republic. The Scandinavian as well as the Baltic countries show above-average accessibility only in the more populated coastal regions while other parts of these countries (especially in Scandinavia) tend to be highly peripheral.

Table 4.1. Modified classification of EU regions.

	Pop share (%)	Area share (%)	Pop density (inhab per square kilometer)
Predominantly urban	27.7	3.4	1390.9
Significantly rural — accessible	17.8	9.3	270.2
Significantly rural — peripheral	14.7	12.7	152.9
Predominantly rural — accessible	13.9	14.5	130.5
Predominantly rural — peripheral	26.0	60.1	74.1

Source: Copus *et al.* [2006, p. 171].

> The New Member States (including Romania, Bulgaria) and Greece are almost exclusively characterized by high peripherality [Copus *et al.*, 2006, p. 155].

The reclassification of Nomenclature for Territorial Units for Statistics (NUTS) Level 3 (NUTS3) regions (excluding the UK, for which sufficient data were not available) results in the distributions of population and total areas, as shown in Table 4.1.

This introduction indicates that there are two major issues to be addressed in a discussion of rural employment trends in the EU. First, what are the existing patterns and trends of rural employment and development in Europe? Second, how might we explain existing patterns and, if possible, speculate on the likely reasons for changes and trends in these patterns? The following two sections explore these two major issues.

4.2 Rural Areas in the EU

Apart from marked differences in national treatments of property rights associated with land, general patterns of rural economic development have taken place in much of Europe against a background of two major additional factors, in comparison with the United States. First, much of Europe has been rather densely populated for much longer than the US. In essence, European rural areas have developed from peasant, self-sufficient farming communities, with substantial histories and cultural ties (still evident, especially in Romania and Bulgaria). Second, and more importantly, Europe has experienced very substantial political contest and associated change. The accession of the New Member States (NMSs) to the EU, following the collapse of the Berlin Wall and the former USSR, has been the most obvious and recent example. In the NMSs, the patterns of rural development have often been rather different from those in Western Europe, notwithstanding their lagged economic development. The disintegration of the collective, state and commune farms (and associated activities and services) has redistributed property rights over land and associated physical capital to former owners, with consequent effects on both farm and rural economic structures: see, e.g. Hartvigsen [2013], who concludes:

> Land reforms have resulted in different outcomes, including quite different farm structures. Before 1989, the farm structures in the study countries (with the exception of Poland and Yugoslavia) were dominated by large-scale cooperatives and state farms. The land reforms after 1989 have resulted in a complete breakup of these farm structures in some of the countries, while in other countries the farm structures remain dominated by large-scale corporate farms (often being the successors of the cooperatives and state farms) that now operate on lease agreements with the private owners of the land. The differences in the farm structures that emerged from the land reform process can, at least to a large degree, be explained by the chosen land reform approaches in each country [Hartvigsen, 2013, p. 49].

In addition, the effects of the great recession following the credit crunch in 2008 have been differentiated in Europe by the consequences of the associated Euro crisis. In particular, Greece, and to a lesser extent Spain, Portugal, Ireland and Italy, have seen substantial reductions of growth rates and rises in unemployment to a much greater extent than elsewhere in Europe. However, as noted by Hill in this book, recent trends in rural employment in the EU have echoed those in the rest of the economy, following the global credit crunch in 2008, and subsequent prolonged recession and gradual recovery. European rural areas in general did not suffer higher unemployment rates than the suburbs or cities, while employment rates in rural areas are now converging on those in the towns and cities across Europe [European Commission, 2018]. However,

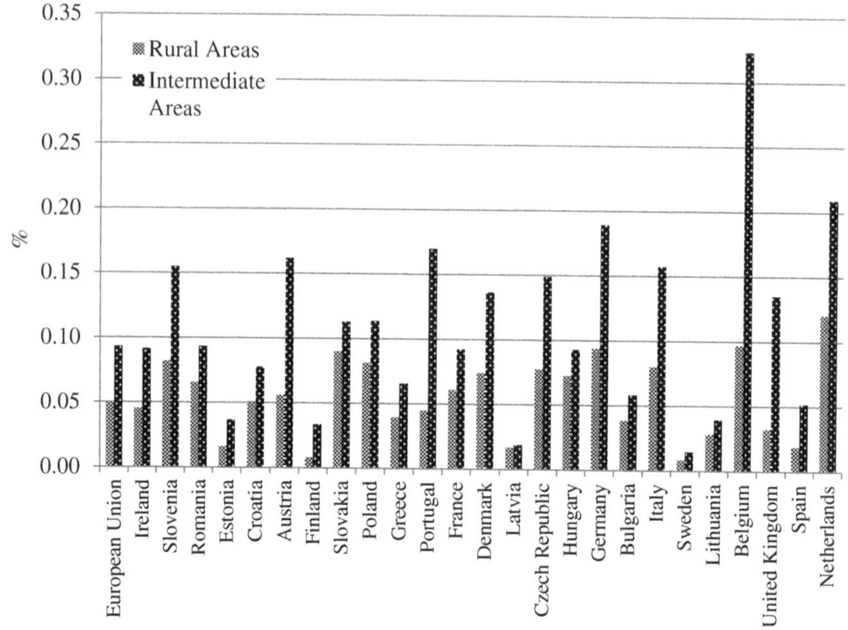

Fig. 4.1. European Union population densities (000 per square kilometer), 2015.
Source: European Commission [2017a, Table CCI 04].

average rates of employment and unemployment over time conceal much heterogeneity and do not provide much information about the particular conditions or likely future prospects in European rural areas.

The European Commission defines rurality in terms of population densities, based on a population grid of 1 square kilometer in combination with a minimum population threshold.[a] However, as Fig. 4.1 shows, the classification conceals a great deal of variation across the EU. In Fig. 4.1, the Member States (MSs) of the EU are ordered by the proportion of the total population living in rural areas, which almost linearly declines from

[a] *Cities* (alternative name: *densely-populated areas*): at least 50% of the population lives in an urban center. *Towns and suburbs* (alternative name: *intermediate density areas*): less than 50% lives in an urban center but more than 50% lives in an urban cluster. *Rural areas* (alternative name: *thinly populated areas*): more than 50% of the population lives in rural grid cells [European Commission, 2015].

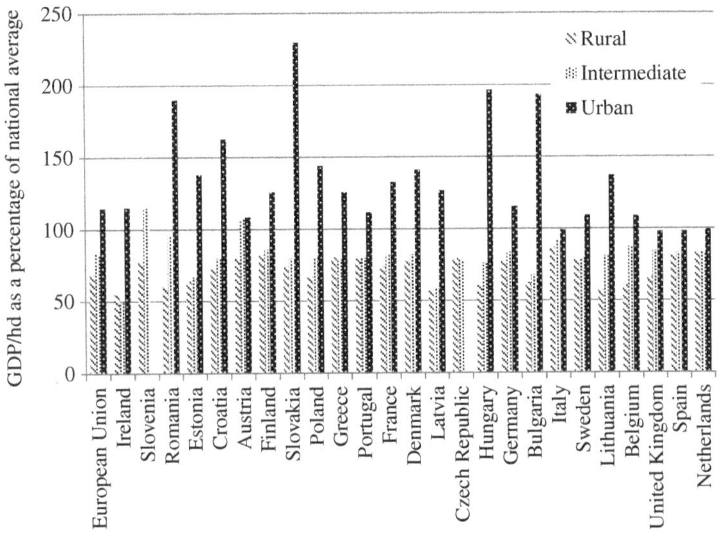

Fig. 4.2. GDP per head by rurality, 2014, as a proportion of the national average in the EU MSs.

Note: Urban data are not available for the Czech Republic or Slovenia.

Source: European Commission [2017a, Table CCI 08].

60% in Ireland and 58% in Slovenia, to 3.5% in the UK and Spain and 0.6% in the Netherlands.[b] As can be seen, the density of population in rural and intermediate areas varies substantially. Rural areas in, for example, Spain and the United Kingdom are substantially less densely populated than those in the Netherlands, Belgium, Italy or Germany. Of course, there is also very substantial variation within these countries, which is concealed by these national averages.

It is not easy to estimate average incomes within the different regions of a country, since people live and work in different locations [European Commission, 2017b, 2018]. However, Fig. 4.2 illustrates the estimated

[b]The statistics provided by the European Commission [2017a] show the population distribution by type of region (rural, intermediate, urban), where Ireland is clearly the most rural, and Lithuania being recorded as having only 8.7% living in rural regions although 63.5% live in intermediate regions. Figure 4.1 is drawn from the CAP context indicators; see also European Commission [2018, p. 10].

differences in GDP per head between the different rural, intermediate and urban areas in the EU MSs, compared with their respective national averages, with countries ordered as Fig. 4.1. Rural areas are universally poorer than the national averages, and generally poorer than their intermediate peers, while urban areas are almost universally richer, though in Italy, Spain, the UK and the Netherlands there is no apparent distinction at this level of aggregation. The apparent income gaps between the rural and urban areas are generally larger in the NMSs, encouraging a continued migration from rural to urban areas in these countries, especially in Slovakia and Romania [European Commission, 2018]. The rural/urban differentials are generally smaller in the EU-15, reflecting their more advanced economic development, and typically associated with either relatively stable population distributions between the areas or, as in the UK, with reverse migration from urban to intermediate and rural areas.

Although rural areas might be expected to rely heavily on agriculture and related industries (the primary sector, including mining and fishing), this is not the case. As Fig. 4.3 shows, the primary sector accounts for a small proportion of total economic activity across the whole of the EU. Only in Romania and Bulgaria does this proportion reach 20%. For most countries, the proportion is well below 10%. Again, while most primary sector activity might be expected to occur in the predominantly rural areas, it only contributes 4% of gross value added (GVA) in rural areas on average across the whole EU, though it is twice as important (at 8%) in the NMSs than in the EU-15 [European Commission, 2018]. It is noticeable that, even in Ireland, as the most rural country in Europe, the primary sector only accounted for 5.5% of total activity in 2016.

As the European Commission [2018] notes:

> In Bulgaria, Lithuania, Latvia and Romania the primary sector still represents around 10% or more of total GVA in rural areas, followed by Estonia, Spain, Croatia, Greece and Hungary (between 8 and 10%). By contrast, in Belgium, Germany and Ireland the primary sector accounts for less than 3% of the total GVA in rural areas.

Chapter 14 of the *Eurostat Regional Yearbook* [European Commission, 2017b] focuses on rural areas. This reports that the risk of poverty or

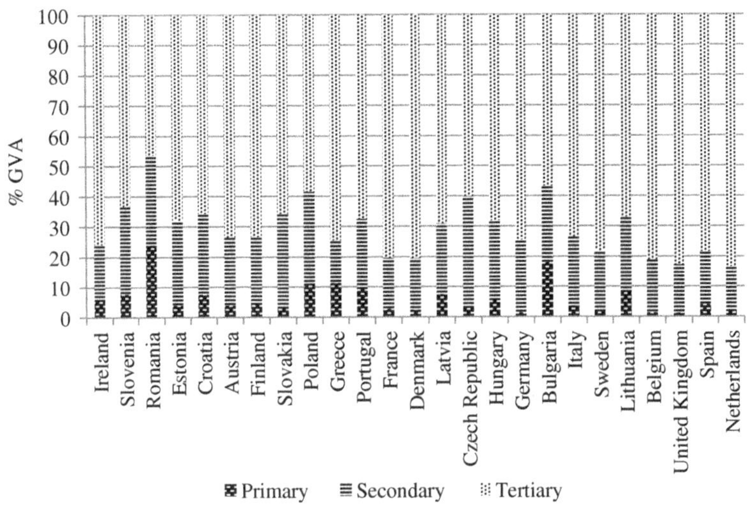

Fig. 4.3. Distribution of gross value added by type of region in the EU MSs 2016.
Source: European Commission [2017a, Table CCI 10].

social exclusion tends to be higher for rural populations in Eastern, Baltic and Southern MSs, in contrast to the Western and Northern MSs, where it is often higher for people living in cities [European Commission, 2017b, p. 255]. Similarly, the share of people between 18 and 24 neither in employment, nor education, nor training (NEET) tends to be higher in rural areas in most of the Eastern and Southern EU MSs, in contrast to the western States, where NEET rates are often higher in cities [European Commission, 2017b, p. 262]. Likewise, unemployment rates tend to be lower in the rural areas of the northern and western MSs than in the urban areas, while the opposite is the case in the Eastern States [European Commission, 2017b, p. 263].

Ecorys [2010] provides the most recent and comprehensive analysis of trends in rural employment and economic growth in rural areas in the EU, on the basis of NUTS3 data (the most disaggregated level in areal terms) over the period 1995–2007. This trend analysis echoes that found by Copus *et al.* [2006] with the primary sector (agriculture, forestry, fishing and mining) generally declining and the tertiary (service) sector increasing in both income (GVA) and employment terms. This study emphasizes [e.g. European Commission, 2017b, p. 21] that the manufacturing and service sectors are the main drivers of economic growth in the rural areas. Although population densities appear to remain relatively stable in all areas, rural area populations are aging, with many accessible rural areas showing signs of counter-urbanization [European Commission, 2017b, p. 22]. On the other hand, the remote and mountainous parts of central and northern Europe, as well as much of southern Europe, are experiencing continued population decline.

Ecorys [2010] used these data, characterizing the current state and recent history of each of the NUTS3 regions in the EU, to group the regions into similar types. This analysis identified specific clusters or types of NUTS3 regions, based on 24 variables reflecting their demography, land cover, and socio-economic character and recent trends, including employment and GVA. The identified clusters are mainly driven by: employment in the primary sector; population density and change in density; land cover (artificial or natural), reflecting the territorial definition of the regions [Ecorys, 2010, p. 173], which is reassuringly similar to intuitive perceptions of rurality. However, the report notes that removing these main clustering drivers did not result in any substantial change in the cluster types, suggesting that the socio-economic conditions reflect and complement the natural, physical and demographic characters of the regional clusters.

Apart from the four types of city regions, the remaining 11 clusters are essentially different sorts of rural and intermediate regional types[c]:

- **Lowland "intensive" farming:** This includes largely lowland parts of the Benelux countries and Great Britain, and a limited number of regions in France, Greece and Bulgaria, characterized by their predominantly urban/intermediate character (in terms of population density) with comparably high economic performance, and experiencing increased population and consequent pressure on land use — at the expense of agricultural land. This tendency is also underlined by the

[c] For the purposes of this chapter, the clusters were edited and renamed by the author.

above-average increase of the tertiary sector in these regions. This cluster is more heterogeneous than most and is the second largest.[d]

- **"Traditional" European rural areas:** These include predominantly rural areas (low population density and low artificial surface) in France and Northern Italy (the economically better performing Italian regions), as well as Spain and Portugal, Central Europe (parts of Austria, Hungary and the Czech Republic, as well as Slovakia), showing average economic performance with a stable economic structure, but experiencing significant economic decline, especially in the secondary sector — in terms of performance, though not employment — with the other economic sectors staying stable. The tourism sector performs better than the EU average in this cluster.
- **Less developed "less favored" areas:** These include rural Southern and Northern EU periphery, i.e. parts of Spain, Southern Italy (Mezzogiorno), parts of Greece, Scotland, Sweden and Finland as well as the Austrian Alps, with climatic and topographic specifics (Northern periphery and Alps) or climatic specifics of extreme South and North, and Alpine Climate, showing low population density with below average economic performance but relatively stable sectoral balance. Unemployment rates decreased significantly compared to the EU average, with highly developed tourism. Relatively low-skilled farmers can be found.
- **Developed coasts and mountains:** These include coastal regions in Spain, France, Italy, Bulgaria and Great Britain as well as parts of the Alpine arc, and the Pyrenees, with common topographic conditions either by the sea or in mountain areas. One significant common characteristic is tourism, with outstanding and increasing tourism infrastructure, with significant urban areas, and a strong tertiary sector. Significantly increasing population density generates pressure on land.
- **Eastern European borderland:** This includes very remote rural areas at the Eastern border of the European Union in Poland, Romania and some parts of Bulgaria, characterized by very low economic

[d] Unfortunately, Ecorys [2010] does not report the detailed statistics of the clusters, but instead maps and describes them.

performance though with relatively high growth rates, dependent on farmers, albeit with limited formal skills, experiencing rapid shifts from primary to other sectors — especially the tertiary sector or out-migration (the highest share in the EU). Tourism is underdeveloped.

- **Agriculture in transition:** This includes large parts of the Baltic countries, parts of Eastern Poland and parts of Slovenia, with low economic performance but comparably strong growth rates. One can note agriculture declining from a high level and the secondary sector growing. The tertiary sector, including tourism, is not yet significant. CAP Pillar 2 funding is three times higher than the EU average.
- **Intermediate manufacturing:** This includes intermediate regions (rather than predominantly rural) in Western Germany (except the cities), Southern Sweden and parts of Slovenia with average economic performance, with relatively low shares of agriculture in employment and economic performance, but with highly skilled agricultural managers. Strong secondary and tertiary sectors are found with relatively high growth rates, though not at the expense of agriculture. However, increasing pressure on land may result from a shift in economic activity. Farmers respond to these trends by diversifying their income (above-average share of other gainful activities by farmers).
- **Shrinking manufacturing:** This includes intermediate regions in Germany with the bulk located in Eastern Germany and the Northern part of Denmark, showing below-average economic performance, and marking the German East-West divide with relatively slow but steady development, mostly accounted for by industry and services, but suffering a relatively high unemployment rates and shrinking populations, and associated aging. Agriculture is a relatively small employer, though with a good proportion of well-trained farmers and a relatively high share of on-farm diversification. Tourism is underdeveloped.
- **Recovering manufacturing:** This includes intermediate industrial areas in West Poland, Czech Republic, Slovakia and Bulgaria. Strong economic growth and a large decrease in unemployment rates can be noted compared to the EU average — though from a comparably high level. Agriculture is still relatively important but shedding labor to the secondary sector. Tourism is undeveloped and population is shrinking.

- **Rural development "winners":** This includes a heterogeneous cluster of rural regions, ranging from Eastern Portugal, Central Spain and Central France, Ireland, parts of Scotland and large parts of Finland, and including areas in Austria and Greece. Average economic performance (GDP per capita and employment), with a modest shift from agriculture to other sectors, though farming/forestry still important, with farm managers comparably well trained. This cluster clearly reflects the inclusion of CAP funding as a cluster dimension: Pillar 1 support is about three times the EU average, and significantly higher Pillar 2 (rural development spending) (€63.6/€5.3 per capita compared with €14.2/€2.7 EU averages).
- **"Less favored area" small-scale farming:** This includes rural, agriculturally dominated peripheral regions in the South and North of Europe (Spain, Portugal, Greece, Danube-Bulgaria, Bulgarian mountains, and some Baltic regions). One can note a very stable agricultural sector (small change in primary sector employment), but the primary sector GVA (2000–2006) is very weak (–6.7% *vs.* 1.3% on EU average), with very low economic performance and relatively high unemployment rates. The secondary and tertiary sectors are undeveloped. Significantly lower levels (8.7%) of managers are found with basic or full agricultural training compared to the EU average (42.4%).

There is clearly some overlap between this peripheral farming cluster and the "Rural Development Winners" cluster, though Ecorys reports that the latter cluster also includes some regions from the Traditional Rural Areas, and from the Lowland Intensive and Intermediate Manufacturing clusters. As the report also notes, the fact that the inclusion of CAP spending does not alter the clustering of EU regions very much might imply that the spending is reasonably targeted, or that the spending has not made much difference to the patterns and extent of rural development.

4.3 What Determines Rural Development and Employment?

The mosaic pattern of rural regions in the EU raises the critical question of how these different clusters emerge and evolve. The economic principles governing development can be outlined in terms of the efficient and effective use of scarce resources, otherwise known as capitals: natural (environmental); human; social (and cultural); physical; spatial [Ellis, 2000]. This Sustainable Livelihoods framework does not typically identify spatial capital as a separate dimension of the overall resource base. Instead, it refers to financial capital. However, finance is the major means of converting both income streams and different resource bases into each other, rather than constituting a logically separate sort of capital.[e]

Terluin [2003] reviews the development of various theories about how global and local forces interact in the context of different regional conditions to make the most effective and efficient use of these capitals (i.e. to develop). She also tests the various hypotheses advanced in the literature against the patterns of rural development evidenced in 18 case study regions in the EU, nine of which are described as "leading" and are paired to and compared with nine lagging regions in similar geographical areas. Terluin finds strong supporting evidence for theories which are as follows:

(1) ascribe an active role to local actors and leaders through both internal and external networks to stimulate employment and growth (the mixed exogenous/endogenous development model);
(2) attribute growth and development to well-developed self-help capacities (community led development);
(3) assign central importance to the exploitation of rural amenities, social and cultural capitals (the effective mobilization and use of local immobile resources [Bryden, 1998]).

Given sufficient stocks of the five main capitals, rural employment depends on the character and capacities of local communities and on their internal and external socio-economic networks and communications. The stronger these are, the stronger rural development is expected to be.

---

[e] Finance is a transformation system, while the remaining capitals are structures. Positional (spatial) capital, on the other hand, includes a critical feature of much of the rural resource base — where it is in relation to other people and other capitals, including its temporal relationships, and where things and people are in relation to their histories.

However, Terluin's approach to the examination of these theories runs the risk of confusing the direction of causality. It may be that successful, leading communities develop and exhibit these capacities and networks, rather than that these networks and capacities determine development. Petrick [2013] notes that economists have not paid much attention to the social coordination and communication processes emphasized by the neo-endogenous theories [Ray, 2006]. He develops an evolutionary (game theory) model to link typical economic perspectives on the development process with those from other social sciences [p. 709]:

> Based on the idea that coordination costs among agents are higher in rural than in urban areas plus the behavioural assumption of evolutionary learning without perfect foresight, a number of surprising insights are generated (from the neo-classical economic perspective). In an environment of decentralized interaction, there may be self-reinforcing processes of either growth or decline that are contingent on the regional history. Depending on these processes, there may emerge a global mosaic of coexisting prosperous and deserted rural regions, and Pareto-inferior outcomes may persist for a long time.... The evolutionary game depicts the simultaneous outmigration and investment inactivity observed in many rural regions.

This evolutionary model refocuses the conventional economic approach from effective resource allocation to the organization and interaction of the agents (people). The model is minimal and highly stylized, simply distinguishing between mobile and immobile people (echoing Bryden's conception above) and representing investment in the local community as either active or inactive. There are gains to be made if people stay and invest, but also individual gains from moving (migrating from the area), while investment is obviously costly in the short term. Since investment requires some confidence that the investment will pay-off, the model includes a primitive learning process, whereby the pay-offs depend on the behaviors (moving and investment) of the agents in previous rounds of the evolutionary game. As Petrick says [p. 721]:

> Note how the evolutionary process gives meaning to the idea of endogenous development. Ray (2006) stressed the bottom-up trajectory of this process, which characterises the decentralised, self organised interaction

> of local stake holders independent of external steering or planning. In the evolutionary model, this is interpreted as a process of 'spontaneous order' that is determined by countless interactions of individuals. Adaptive agents carrying simple behavioural rules reach, by trial and error, an outcome whose aggregate properties are not known to them beforehand and are thus not pursued intentionally.

Petrick concludes [p. 733]:

> Evaluated against the background of neo-classical growth theory, the model emphasises that the combination of factors to generate economic activity in rural areas is not automatic. In addition, it requires more than a change in production technology to stimulate growth. The present model rather highlights the need for coordination among different rural stake holders – the young and mobile who bring new ideas but may easily leave to urban centres, and the older immobile who have better access to tacit knowledge and financial capital but depend on the presence of the mobile. As the agglomeration benefits typical to urban centres are missing (in this simple model), bringing both groups together in a rural setting is not trivial and implies that gains could be had from the involvement of an externally supported governance mechanism. Such a mechanism — broadly representing activities funded by LEADER-type measures (see Hill, Chapter 2) — potentially helps rural people to stem the tide of rural decline and opens their eyes towards the alternative options of rural income generation they have. However, this happens only if a sufficient number of rural actors can be convinced that non-best play is beneficial to them in the longer run.

This model is clearly a highly simplified representation of the motives and interacting forces operating in rural areas. However, it also clearly illustrates that endogenous local behaviors can either generate spontaneous endogenous growth as agents choose to stay and invest, or lead to progressive decline as agents decide to leave and not to invest. Without some change in peoples' motivations and actions, progressive decline generates path dependence often seen in lagging rural areas. Lack of investment (in any of the basic capitals) tends to be self-reinforcing unless there is either a stimulus for growth from the rest of the economy (exogenous growth), or some local impetus for self-help capacity-building and development of local competitive advantages and mobilization of resources (endogenous growth).

4.4 Conclusions

This chapter has sketched the general patterns and trends in rural employment in the EU. The primary message is that, while there is very substantial heterogeneity in these patterns across Europe, they are generally consistent with a broad picture of the relative economic development of rural areas as national and regional economies develop. In these broad terms, rural areas are likely to experience relative decline in the earlier stages of economic development, but generally recover as economic development progresses. Although rural areas are typically conceived as being largely agricultural (or forestry or wilderness), their economic and employment structures tend to echo and reflect those of their more urban neighbors. As such, the future prospects for employment and incomes in rural areas will be heavily dependent on national and regional economic growth and development, including the development of transport and communication links. However, an evolutionary perspective (illustrated by Petrick [2013]) strongly suggests that declining and lagging rural communities can be "cultivated" and stimulated to become more engaged and prosperous under the right conditions. This perspective clearly suggests that there is a role for purposive public (collective) intervention to stimulate local endogenous growth, which in turn can become self-sustaining and progressive.

References

Bryden, J. M. (1998). Development Strategies for Remote Rural Regions: What do we Know so Far? Paper presented at the *OECD International Conference on Remote Rural Areas — Developing through Natural and Cultural Assets*, Albarracin, Spain, 5–6 November.

Copus, A., Hall, C., Barnes, A., Dalton, G., Cook, P., Weingarten, P., Baum, S., Stange, H., Lindner, C., Hill, A., Eiden, G., McQuaid, R., Grieg, M. and Johansson, M. (2006). *Study on Employment in Rural Areas* (for European

Commission Directorate General for Agriculture), Scottish Agricultural College, Aberdeen, UK. https://www.napier.ac.uk/~/media/worktribe/output-246104/serareport1ruraleu272006pdf.pdf (accessed 7 November 2018).

Ecorys (2010). *Study on Employment, Growth and Innovation in Rural Areas (SEGIRA)*. Ecorys, Rotterdam. https://ec.europa.eu/agriculture/sites/agriculture/files/external-studies/2010/employment/full-text_en.pdf (accessed 7 November 2018).

Ellis, F. (2000). *Rural Livelihoods and Diversity in Developing Countries.* Oxford University Press, Oxford.

European Commission (2015). *Statistics Explained: Glossary.* https://ec.europa.eu/eurostat/statistics-explained/index.php?title=Glossary:Degree_of_urbanisation (accessed 7 November 2018).

European Commission (2017a). *CAP Context Indicators.* https://ec.europa.eu/agriculture/cap-indicators/context/2017_en (accessed 7 November 2018).

European Commission (2017b). *Eurostat Regional Yearbook*, Brussels, Belgium. https://ec.europa.eu/eurostat/web/products-statistical-books/-/KS-HA-17-001 (accessed 7 November 2018).

European Commission (2017c). *Population Maps.* http://ec.europa.eu/eurostat/statistical-atlas/gis/viewer (accessed 7 November 2018).

European Commission (2018). *Rural Areas and the Primary Sector in the EU*, DG Agriculture and Rural Development, Unit Farm Economics, Brussels, Belgium. https://ec.europa.eu/agriculture/sites/agriculture/files/statistics/facts-figures/eu-rural-areas-primary-sector.pdf (accessed 7 November 2018).

Fujita, N. (2007). Myrdal's theory of cumulative causation. *Evolutionary and Institutional Economics Review*, 3(2), pp. 275–283.

Hartvigsen, M. (2013). *Land Reform in Central and Eastern Europe After 1989 and its Outcome in the Form of Farm Structures and Land Fragmentation*, Land Tenure Working Paper 24, FAO, Rome.

Johnston, B. F. and Mellor, J. W. (1961). The role of agriculture in economic development. *American Economic Review*, 51(4), pp. 566–593.

Krugman, P. R. (1991). Increasing returns and economic geography. *Journal of Political Economy*, 99, pp. 483–499.

Myrdal, G. (1957). *Economic Theory and Underdeveloped Regions*. Gerald Duckworth & Co., London.

Petrick, M. (2013). Reversing the rural race to the bottom: An evolutionary model of neo-endogenous rural development. *European Review of Agricultural Economics*, 40(4), pp. 707–735, https://doi.org/10.1093/erae/jbt019 (accessed 7 October 2018).

Ray, C. (2006). Neo-endogenous rural development in the EU. In P. J. Cloke, T. Marsden and P. H. Mooney (eds.), *Handbook of Rural Studies*. London: SAGE Publications, pp. 278–291.

Terluin, I. J. (2003). Differences in economic development in rural regions of advanced countries: An overview and critical analysis of theories. *Journal of Rural Studies*, 19, pp. 327–344.

Chapter 5

Special Study: The Productivity of Family and Hired Labor in EU Arable Farming

Mathias Kloss*,‡ and Martin Petrick†

**University Hospital Halle, Saale, Germany*
†Leibniz Institute of Agricultural Development in Transition Economies (IAMO), Halle, Saale, Germany
‡mkloss@posteo.de

This chapter investigates the impact of labor force composition on agricultural output in EU arable farming. We determine the relative productivity of family and hired labor in five EU member states using FADN data for the years 2001–2008. The results reject the notion that hired labor is generally less productive than family workers. In fact, farms with a higher share of hired workers are more productive than pure family farms in countries traditionally characterized by family labor, namely France and West Germany. Here, an increase in reliance on hired labor or the shift of family labor to more productive tasks could raise productivity. This finding calls into question a main pillar of the received family farm theory. In two of the three countries, we find no statistically different effects of either type of labor. For the United Kingdom, we find the classical case with family farms being more productive than those relying on hired labor.

5.1 Introduction

According to a widely accepted view, large-scale farming operations involving many workers under a centralized management authority are economically inferior to smaller family-run businesses, at least in the temperate zones. The two maintained hypotheses of the underlying "family farm theory" are as follows: (1) technological-scale economies are typically exhausted before farm size exceeds the labor capacity of a family; and (2) growth of the labor force beyond family members is inhibited by rising supervision costs. These hypotheses used to be supported by a large body of empirical literature from developed and developing countries [Brewster, 1950; Schmitt, 1991; Hayami and Otsuka, 1993; Allen and Lueck, 1998; Eastwood *et al.*, 2010]. For many decades after World War II, the economic and social superiority of family farms over agriculture based on hired labor was a widely held notion among researchers, governments and international organizations.

However, even in agricultural regions traditionally dominated by small to medium-sized family farm operations, such as Western Europe or the US, farm sizes have been growing and, more importantly, the share of hired workers in total labor force has been slowly but steadily increasing [Blanc *et al.*, 2008; Darpeix *et al.*, 2014]. According to figures by Eurostat [2016], regularly employed non-family members on average contributed 15.4% of the total agricultural workload in the EU-28 in 2013, whereas irregularly employed non-family members contributed another 8.1%. This share has been on the rise for years, especially with regard to regularly employed hired labor. These workers replace family members on a year-round basis rather than complementing them during harvest time — a fact that calls into question the validity of hypothesis (2) outlined above (Fig. 5.1).

The typical argument for different productivities of hired and family labor is based on the idea of diverging incentives. Hired labor is usually not a residual income claimant, and its effort cannot commonly be observed because of the special nature of agricultural production (e.g. seasonality, weather effects). Therefore, hired laborers have incentives to "shirk", resulting in effort levels that are only a fraction of those achieved by family labor. As a result, both kinds of labor are not easily substituted.

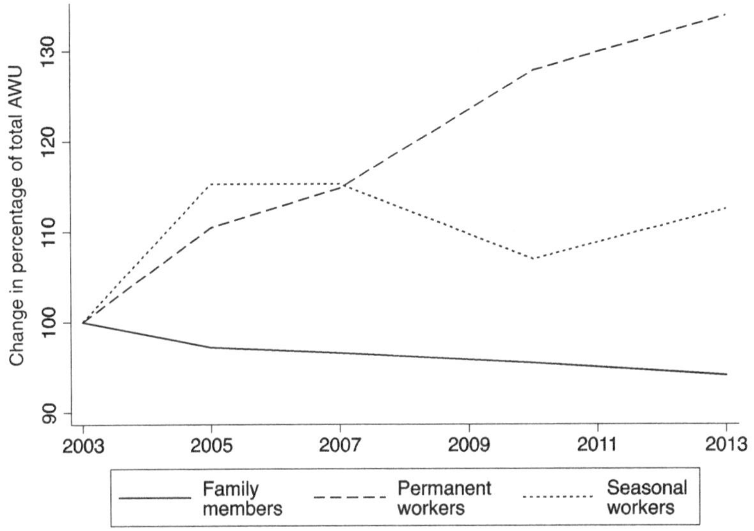

Fig. 5.1. Change in the composition of the agricultural labor force in EU-28.

Notes: 2003 = 100. AWU, Annual Working Units. Family consists of permanent family labor including holders and members of the sole holder's family. Permanent workers consist of regularly employed non-family members. Seasonal workers comprise irregularly employed non-family members.

Source: Authors' compilation based on European Commission [2012, 2013] and Eurostat [2016].

This perceived problem can be mitigated by hired labor supervision. Hence, transaction costs in the form of supervision costs arise, making farm production based on hired labor more expensive.

On the other hand, farms with a large stock of workers may allow specialization and the division of labor into distinct tasks [Allen and Lueck, 1998; Kimhi, 2009]. For example, family members might concentrate on management and/or supervision tasks, while hired laborers specialize in non-managerial tasks. To the extent that modern farming technologies allow such specialization benefits, the productivity of hired labor may well exceed that of a family member who is a "jack of all trades but the master of none".[a]

[a]Productivity differences may also be due to family members and workers possessing different levels of education and technical expertise. While the positive effects of farmers' human capital on production decisions have been analyzed, we know relatively little about the effects of workers' education.

5.2 Empirical Approach and Data

Given these conflicting views, it is useful to examine the relative productivity of family compared to hired labor by confronting accepted wisdom with new empirical evidence. We did this by extending the methodological approach of Bardhan [1973], Deolalikar and Vijverberg [1983, 1987] and Frisvold [1994] who investigated this question in the developing country context of India, using an estimation procedure introduced by Wooldridge [2009], hereafter Wooldridge/Levinsohn/Petrin (WLP).[b]

In order to assess the effective labor effort, a production function was estimated for each country using two methods: (1) standard Ordinary Least Squares (OLS) as a baseline, and (2) our preferred estimator suggested by WLP. The primary interest was in an estimate of what we call the "effective labor effort parameter" which measures how a farm's labor force composition affects total farm productivity. If this parameter exceeds the value 0, a higher share of family labor increases total farm productivity; if lower than 0, total farm productivity decreases with a higher share of family labor [see Kloss and Petrick, 2018 for details].

The database was a panel originating from the Farm Accountancy Data Network (FADN) of five EU member states: Denmark, France, Germany (West), Italy and the United Kingdom (UK) — countries that rely more or less heavily on family labor. Data was available for the years 2001–2008. The sample included full-time arable farms and reflected diverse farm structures in EU arable farming, including traditional family-type farming (e.g. France and Italy) as well as relatively high shares of hired labor (e.g. the UK).

The EU's FADN provides a stratified farm-level data set that holds accountancy data for 25 of the 27 EU Member States.[c] The stratification criteria are region, economic size and type of farming — full-time field crop farms (TF1) in the present analysis. This means that the farm's operation is the core activity for the farmer with at least 40 operating hours per

[b]The WLP estimator is especially useful in an agricultural context [Petrick and Kloss, 2018]. For detailed results per estimator and country, as well as plausibility and robustness checks, we refer to Kloss and Petrick [2018].

[c]During the analyzed period, the EU had 27 Member States since Croatia joined the Union in 2013.

week [European Commission, 2014; FADN data]. Output was measured as total farm output in euros (€), and land input as total utilized agricultural area (UAA), including owned and rented land, and land in sharecropping, in hectares (ha). Material or working capital input was measured by total intermediate consumption (in €), consisting of total specific costs (for seeds and seedlings, crop protection and other inputs) and overheads (comprising "supply costs linked to production activity", e.g. costs for energy such as fuel and electricity) arising from production in the accounting year; the latter are usually the single largest position in the materials input [European Commission, 2011]. The costs of fertilizer in materials input were not included, since land and fertilizer are highly correlated, suggesting that farmers utilize land and fertilizer inputs in an (almost) fixed ratio. Fixed capital was approximated by using the opening valuation of machinery and buildings. In order to estimate effective labor use, information on hired and family labor working time separately was needed, in addition to total labor hours which is readily available in the FADN data.[d] Monetary values were deflated to real values in 2005 prices using appropriate price indices.

Table 5.1 summarizes the number of farms for each country in our sample, the labor force composition (average percentage of family labor), and the other variable means. The sample covered a total of 3,314 farms.

Table 5.1. Sample size and variable means.

Country	Farms	Family labor in percentage of total labor	Total labor	Output	Land	Materials	Capital
Denmark	208	84.52	2.8	180.4	122.7	98.0	840.0
France	1,030	84.11	3.2	155.8	143.5	85.1	160.1
Germany (West)	566	84.70	4.2	150.9	92.3	84.7	153.9
Italy	1,322	88.55	3.6	60.6	44.7	23.8	125.2
United Kingdom	188	64.76	6.3	278.1	248.7	157.2	239.3

Notes: Total labor in 1,000 hours. Output, materials and capital in €1,000. Land in ha.

Source: Authors' calculations, based on FADN data.

[d]More information on these variables, including their FADN codes, is available from Kloss and Petrick [2018].

The numbers on output reflect the different forms of agricultural organization outlined before. Further confirming the picture conveyed in Fig. 5.1, the dominant type of labor in EU arable farming is family labor. For a full set of descriptive statistics, see Kloss and Petrick [2018].

5.3 Results

Table 5.2 presents the sample sizes, and the point estimates with their standard errors of the effective labor effort parameter, for each country and the two estimation methods.

Compared to the WLP estimates, the OLS estimator detects labor force heterogeneity in one more case — Denmark. The reason for this result is probably an upward-biased OLS estimate of the parameter. Such a result is commonly observed for the OLS estimator in presence of endogeneity.

Regarding the preferred estimates, the following picture unfolds. In Denmark and Italy, the parameter is not significantly different from zero, meaning that the null hypothesis of perfect substitution between hired and family labor cannot be rejected. The small- and medium-scale agricultural structures of West Germany and France exhibit negative parameter values

Table 5.2. Effective labor effort parameter estimates.

	OLS			WLP		
Country	*N*	Parameter	SE	*N*	Parameter	SE
Denmark	605	0.290***	0.108	605	0.117	0.090
France	4,289	−0.554**	0.217	4,289	−0.481**	0.214
Germany (West)	2,408	−1.641**	0.698	2,408	−1.517**	0.615
Italy	3,545	−0.274	0.221	3,545	−0.165	0.198
United Kingdom	612	0.190**	0.090	612	0.215**	0.095

Notes: OLS = Ordinary Least Squares estimation. WLP = Wooldridge/Levinsohn/Petrin estimation. *N* = sample size (no. of farms). SE = standard error of parameter. Year dummy variables included in both OLS and WLP models. *** (**, *) significant at the 1% (5%, 10%) level, based on SEs robust to clustering in groups.

Source: Authors' calculations.

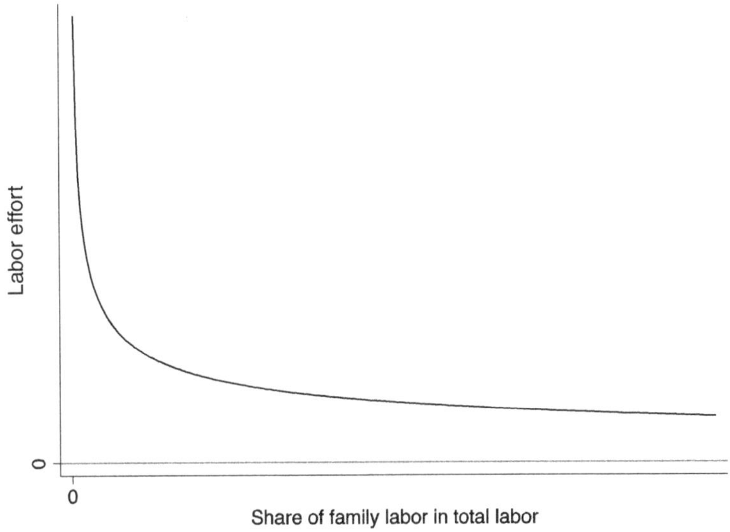

Fig. 5.2. Effective labor as a function of family labor share in total labor if parameter value negative.

Note: Graphical representation for hired labor being more productive than family labor and constant total labor input.

Source: Authors' elaboration.

that are significantly different from zero. This result implies that effective labor effort is a monotonically decreasing function of the share of family labor (Fig. 5.2).

Hence, farms relying on hired labor are more productive than family farms, and farms relying almost completely on hired labor are particularly productive. Moreover, the productivity loss created by a higher share of family labor declines as the ratio of family to total labor expressed in the effective labor effort function increases [cf. Bardhan, 1973, p. 1381]. It is probably in these instances where hired labor specializes in high-productivity tasks and/or family labor focuses on low-productivity tasks. In contrast, the classical case of family members being more productive than hired labor (a positive parameter value) is only observed for the United Kingdom — the extent being moderate. In this case, there is an argument for labor supervision that might increase the productivity of hired workers. The largest productivity differential between family and hired labor is exhibited by West Germany, where, for example, an increase in the share of hired labor time in total labor time from 20% to 30% amounts to an average increase in labor productivity by €0.56/hour or about 2.4% — up to €23.50/hour.[e]

5.4 Conclusions

Contrary to received wisdom, we found that farms with a higher share of hired labor are more productive than family farms in the small- and medium-scale agrarian structures of France and West Germany. According to our estimates, hired labor performs the high-productivity tasks in these countries. In such a situation, an increase in reliance on hired labor or a shift of family labor to more productive tasks raises productivity. Hence, labor market reforms should aim at providing incentives to hire specialized labor. For instance, programs to train and hire skilled labor could improve their inflow into agricultural labor markets. In Denmark and Italy, we found no evidence for labor force heterogeneity. We regard it an interesting question for future research to find out why hired labor in arable farming is so productive in France and West Germany, two countries traditionally characterized by family farms. One possible explanation is that farm technology, e.g. modern tractors and other field machinery using precision-farming methods, has reached such levels of sophistication that benefits from labor specialization can be reaped. On the other hand, farming in the UK traditionally displays high levels of hired labor, which may to a larger extent consist of lower-qualified personnel subject to the classical incentive problems. Our data did not allow us to explicitly address the effects of skills and technical expertise of family *vs.* hired workers, and we regard this as an important area for future research.

Our results call into question the general validity of one of the received family farm theory's main pillars, i.e. the dominant effect of supervision costs on hired labor productivity. Countries regarded as traditional strongholds of the family farm have apparently crossed a

[e] Calculation based on the sample means of the different inputs and the WLP production function estimates.

technological threshold where specialization of hired labor overcompensates for the negative effects of workers' moral hazard, i.e. that their work is not easily verifiable and enforceable. Factors such as, the increasing importance of non-traditional and non-agricultural sources of farm household income are likely reinforcing this trend.

References

Allen, D. W. and Lueck, D. (1998). The nature of the farm. *Journal of Law and Economics*, 41(2), pp. 343–386.

Bardhan, P. K. (1973). Size, productivity, and returns to scale: An analysis of farm-level data in Indian agriculture. *Journal of Political Economy*, 81(6), pp. 1370–1386.

Blanc, M., Cahuzac, E., Elyakime, B. and Tahar, G. (2008). Demand for on-farm permanent hired labour on family holdings. *European Review of Agricultural Economics*, 35(4), pp. 493–518.

Brewster, J. M. (1950). The machine process in agriculture and industry. *Journal of Farm Economics*, 32, pp. 69–81.

Darpeix, A., Bignebat, C. and Perrier-Cornet, P. (2014). Demand for seasonal wage labour in agriculture: What does family farming hide? *Journal of Agricultural Economics*, 65(1), pp. 257–272.

Deolalikar, A. B. and Vijverberg, W. P. M. (1983). The heterogeneity of family and hired labor in agricultural production: A test using district level data from India. *Journal of Development Economics*, 8(2), pp. 45–69.

Deolalikar, A. B. and Vijverberg, W. P. M. (1987). Test of heterogeneity of family and hired labour in Asian agriculture. *Oxford Bulletin of Economics and Statistics*, 49(3), 291–305.

Eastwood, R., Lipton, M. and Newell, A. (2010). Farm size. In P. L. Pingali and R. E. Evenson (eds.), *Handbook of Agricultural Economics*, Vol. 4, Elsevier, Amsterdam, pp. 3323–3397.

European Commission (2011). *Definitions of Variables used in FADN Standard Results*. Brussels.

European Commission (2012). *Agriculture in the European Union*. Statistical and Economic Information. Report 2012. Luxembourg.

European Commission (2013). *Agriculture in the European Union*. Statistical and Economic Information. Report 2013. Luxembourg.

European Commission (2014). *FADN: Field of Survey*. http://ec.europa.eu/agriculture/rica/methodology1_en.cfm#tuof (accessed 7 October 2018).

Eurostat (2016). *Eurostat Statistical Books: Agriculture, Forestry and Fishery Statistics*. Luxembourg.

Frisvold, G. B. (1994). Does supervision matter? Some hypothesis tests using Indian farm-level data. *Journal of Development Economics*, 43(2), pp. 217–238.

Hayami, Y. and Otsuka, K. (1993). *The Economics of Contract Choice: An Agrarian Perspective*. Clarendon Press, Oxford.

Kimhi, A. (2009). Demand for on-farm permanent hired labour on family holdings: A comment. *European Review of Agricultural Economics*, 36(3), pp. 447–452.

Kloss, M. and Petrick, M. (2018). *The Productivity of Family and Hired Labour in EU Arable Farming*. IAMO Discussion Paper No. 174, Halle (Saale). https://www.iamo.de/fileadmin/documents/dp174.pdf (accessed 7 October 2018).

Levinsohn, J. and Petrin, A. (2003). Estimating Production Functions Using Inputs to Control for Unobservables. *Review of Economic Studies*, 70(2), pp. 317–341.

Petrick, M. and Kloss, M. (2018). Identifying agricultural factor productivity from micro-data: A review of approaches with an application to EU countries. *German Journal of Agricultural Economics*, 67(2), pp. 67–79.

Schmitt, G. (1991). Why is the agriculture of advanced Western economies still organized by family farms? Will this continue to be so in the future? *European Review of Agricultural Economics*, 18(3–4), pp. 443–458.

Wooldridge, J. M. (2009). On estimating firm-level production functions using proxy variables to control for unobservables. *Economics Letters*, 104(3), pp. 112–114.

Chapter 6

Entrepreneurship in Rural Employment in the US

Tessa Conroy*, Steven Deller and Matthew Kures

University of Wisconsin–Madison, Madison, WI, USA
**tessa.conroy@wisc.edu*

Since the Great Recession (2007–2009), the job recovery in non-metropolitan counties has been less robust than in metropolitan counties. Part of that may be due to the industrial composition of rural areas, which have larger manufacturing and agricultural sectors than metropolitan areas. These two sectors, which have been growing in productivity and output, are doing so with less labor and therefore generate a smaller share of employment than they once did. Non-metropolitan counties have also lost employer businesses, meaning that there are fewer businesses to create job opportunities. Although these factors may make job growth more challenging, there may be untapped potential in non-metropolitan areas. The number of non-employer businesses in these areas has been growing and the rate of proprietorship is high compared to metropolitan areas. These entrepreneurial characteristics suggest that non-metropolitan areas have a foundation to support job growth. Historically, entrepreneurship has proven to be an important source of job creation, with new and young businesses generating close to half of all new jobs. Thus, non-metropolitan communities may find it strategic to access their most entrepreneurial populations and support new businesses to foster long-term job growth.

6.1 Introduction

The rural–urban divide in the USA has become a common point of discussion since the recent presidential election in 2016. These conversations have pointed to stark differences between large cities and the relatively sparsely populated surrounding areas. Often, urban areas are characterized as more politically progressive, wealthier and better educated, but also unaware of how communities across the vast and rural part of the country live. Rural residents often are characterized as being relatively conservative and hard-working, but faced with challenges such as lower levels of education, low employment growth, and higher rates of poverty, to name a few.

City residents tend to view all rural residents as a homogeneous pool, and *vice versa*, rural residents tend to pool all urban-dwellers together, but the rural–urban divide has a local character that varies by state and region. In Colorado, the Interstate 25 corridor extending north and south from Denver along the Front Range, which largely captures the more urban and mountainous part of the state, is distinct from the more rural, flat and agricultural eastern part of the state. Similarly, in Washington and Oregon, the Interstate 5 corridor stretching from Seattle through Portland between the Pacific Coast and the Cascade Mountains is far more urban than the eastern sides of each state. In Wisconsin, Madison and Milwaukee in the southeast often are pitted against the interests of the rest of state and seen as getting a disproportionate share of resources and political attention [Cramer, 2016].

Although the rural–urban divide varies across regions, there are real and important trends that can be observed broadly. In particular, the economies of rural communities have not performed as well as the economies of metro areas coming out of the Great Recession. Perhaps, this is because industries that tend to have a larger presence in rural communities have struggled in recent years. At the same time, rural communities do seem to be quite entrepreneurial when compared to urban areas. As shown by Haltiwanger *et al.* [2013], the health of the economy is largely driven by business start-ups or entrepreneurship. This rich tradition of rural entrepreneurialism could be an overlooked factor when trying to understand differences in employment outcomes across the rural–urban divide.

In this chapter, we focus attention on the role of self-employment and entrepreneurialism in helping to better understand that divide.

6.2 General Employment Trends

During the Great Recession, job loss was more severe in rural counties than in urban counties. Rural areas also had a slower rate of job recovery and subsequent growth (Fig. 6.1).[a] This means that urban areas did not suffer to the same extent as rural areas in terms of relative jobs lost and urban areas recovered more quickly from their losses than rural communities did. By 2012, urban counties regained all the jobs that were eliminated during the Recession, but, as of 2016, rural areas had still not fully recouped their losses.

The differences in employment growth rates across metro and non-metro areas may also partially influence an increase in the number of long-distance commuters among non-metro residents (Fig. 6.2). For instance, an analysis of a nine-state area in the upper Midwest suggests that the share of non-metro commuters traveling 50 miles or more each way grew noticeably between 2006 and 2014 [Kures *et al.*, 2018]. Indeed, many of these long-distance commuters reside in outlying rural regions around employment centers in large metro areas. Although these commuters likely weigh many factors, such as housing costs and quality-of-life differences, when deciding to travel long distances, the levels of employment opportunities in non-metro areas may be considered as well.

A key factor in the tepid job growth in rural areas during the recovery may be the industrial composition of rural areas. If we look at the sources of income by industry, rural America is far more reliant on agriculture, manufacturing and the public sector (Fig. 6.3) than metro areas are. The public sector — schools, post offices, and road departments, as examples — in rural areas has been especially vulnerable to changes in public fiscal policies. Because of significant declines in tax revenues at all levels of government during the Great Recession, many rural areas faced disproportionate reductions in government spending. There was, however,

[a] Rural counties are synonymous with non-metropolitan counties. Urban counties are metropolitan counties.

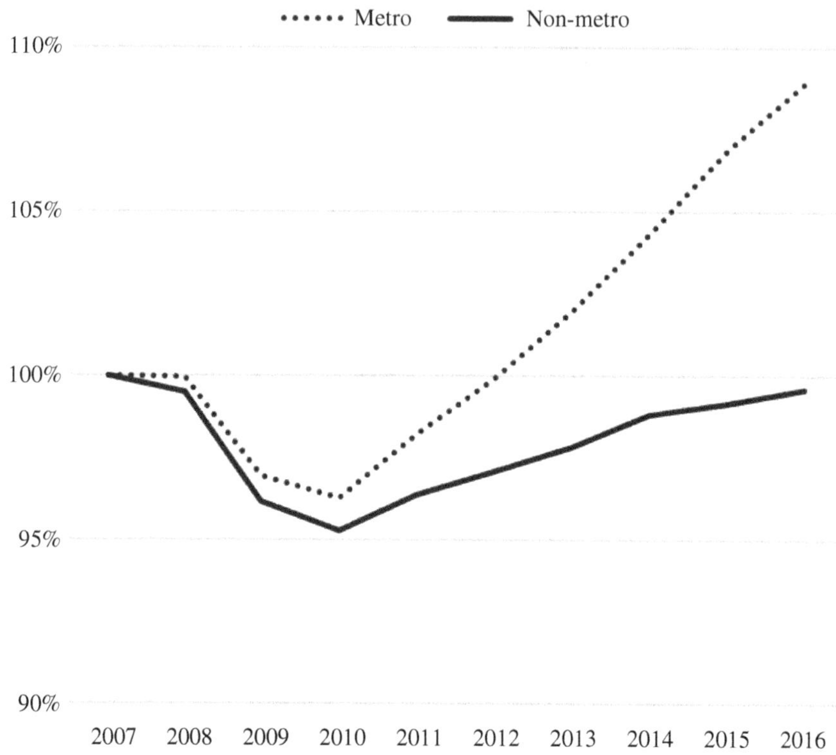

Fig. 6.1. Non-farm employment growth.

Source: Authors' analysis of data from the Bureau of Economic Analysis.

significant variation in how states, and as a result many local governments, responded to the loss of revenues. Some states, such as Wisconsin under Governor Scott Walker and Kansas under Governor Sam Brownback, addressed revenue shortfalls by drastically reducing expenditures, which translated into fewer jobs. Rickman and Wang [2018] found that the "fiscal austerity" states tended to perform more poorly than states that took a more balanced approach to revenue shortfalls using a mix of expenditure reductions and tax increases. Because so many more rural states pursued policies of fiscal austerity, they may have been more exposed to job reductions.

Manufacturing and agriculture, often viewed as central to many rural economies, are success stories in terms of output and productivity growth but are employing a smaller and smaller share of the workforce. Increases

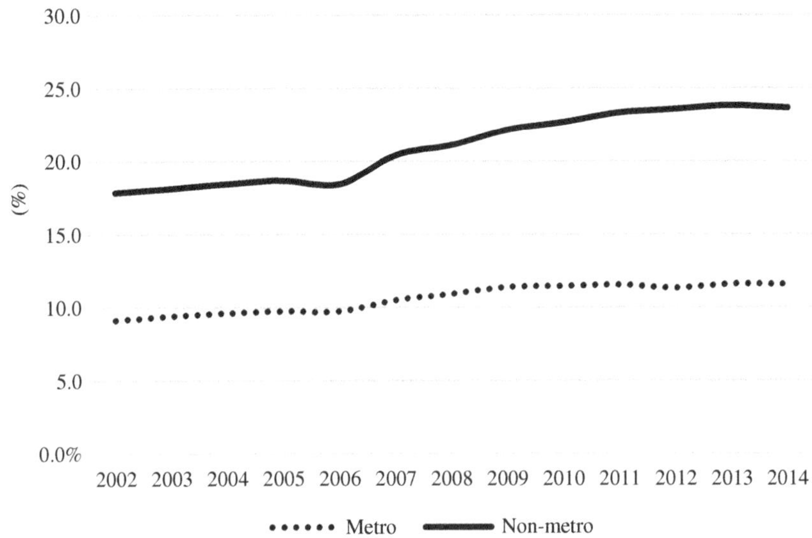

Fig. 6.2. Share of workers commuting 50 miles or more each way.

Source: Authors' analysis of the Longitudinal Employer-Household Dynamics (LEHD) Origin-Destination Employment Statistics.

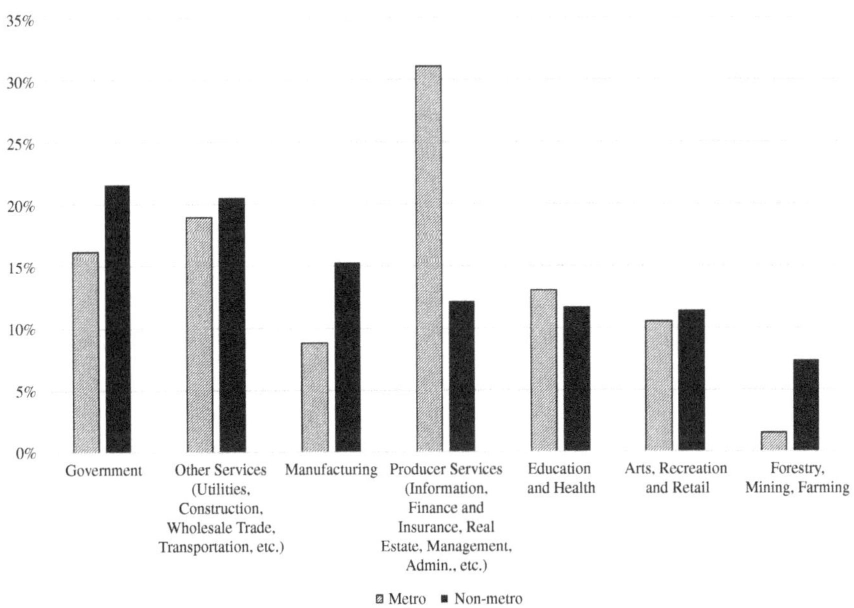

Fig. 6.3. Source of income by sector, 2016.

Source: Authors' analysis of data from the Bureau of Economic Analysis.

in productivity and automation have allowed manufacturers to "do more with less". Manufacturing, in particular, has struggled in the face of globalization. Labor-intensive routine manufacturers that focused on producing commodities found that competition from overseas altered market structures. These domestic manufacturers were forced to either enter bankruptcy or relocate overseas to drive down the costs of operations.

Undoubtedly, rural areas disproportionately felt the massive loss of jobs in manufacturing, particularly routine manufacturing, from the late 1990s to the early 2000s. Autor *et al.* [2018] show that, during the period from 1990 to 2014, trade shocks stemming from international manufacturing competition reduced men's relative earnings, marriage rates, and fertility rates. Shocks to earnings also increased male idleness and premature mortality and, perhaps not surprisingly, increased the share of unwed mothers and the share of children living in poverty-stricken, single-headed households. To the extent that manufacturing job losses were more severe in rural areas, we also might expect the social ills that come with these labor demand shocks to be more severe in rural areas.

Given the historically large presence of manufacturing in rural areas, it is not surprising that many communities focus on manufacturing with recruitment and attraction efforts. Many communities have tried to incentivize a large firm, often a manufacturer, to move to their community in hopes of the new firm offering large numbers of jobs. Although there are examples of communities successfully recruiting a large manufacturer, these are generally rare. In general, manufacturers seldom move, and those that do are quite small and move only short distances [Conroy *et al.*, 2016]. The firms that can do precise cost analysis and consider distant new locations are few, as are the communities that can afford the expense of a lucrative incentive package. Further, the rural economy is diverse, and focusing on just one sector may result in missed opportunities.

Farming remains important for many rural areas, but not for as many areas as widely believed. Using the US Department of Agriculture (USDA) Economic Research Service's (ERS) definition of farm-dependent counties, only 391 of the 1,976 non-metropolitan counties in the United States, or fewer than one in five, depend on farming as a primary source of economic activity. Most of these counties are clustered in the Great Plains and many states, such as New York and Alabama, have no farm-dependent counties. However, farming was a source of stability throughout the Great Recession and the recovery years that immediately followed. High commodity prices and favorable growing conditions made farming a source of strong economic activity for many rural areas. Unfortunately, over the past few years, commodity prices have declined, resulting in a weaker farm economy.

6.3 The Rise of Non-Employer Businesses

Although the industrial structure of a region plays an important role in determining its employment trajectory, the type of firms in the region can be equally important. The size, or employment power, of a firm is especially important. Just as large manufacturers are becoming fewer and fewer, a much nimbler form of businesses has been rising in its place, namely, non-employer businesses. These businesses without any employees consist largely of individual contractors and have become synonymous with companies like Uber. More and more companies are choosing to contract services rather than hire employees to perform these services in-house. Consequently, we see more people working for themselves and fewer new businesses with employees.

This trend toward non-employer establishments can be seen in Fig. 6.4. First and importantly, the number of employer businesses in non-metropolitan counties has declined since 2001. So, there are fewer businesses in rural areas hiring employees — not to mention paying good wages and offering benefits — today than in 2001. Given this decline in the number of businesses that have workers, it is not surprising that job growth has been lacking in rural areas. Meanwhile, in urban areas, the number of employer establishments has grown, as has the number of jobs.

The trend in non-employer firms is perhaps even more interesting. In rural America, the number of non-employers has grown, suggesting that more and more people are working for themselves, perhaps partly due to weak employment prospects in traditional wage-and-salary jobs. The growth in non-employer businesses in urban areas is even more striking. By far and away, non-employer businesses in metro economies make up the fastest-growing segment, easily outpacing that in rural counties. Although the gig economy has long been in place with many lawyers,

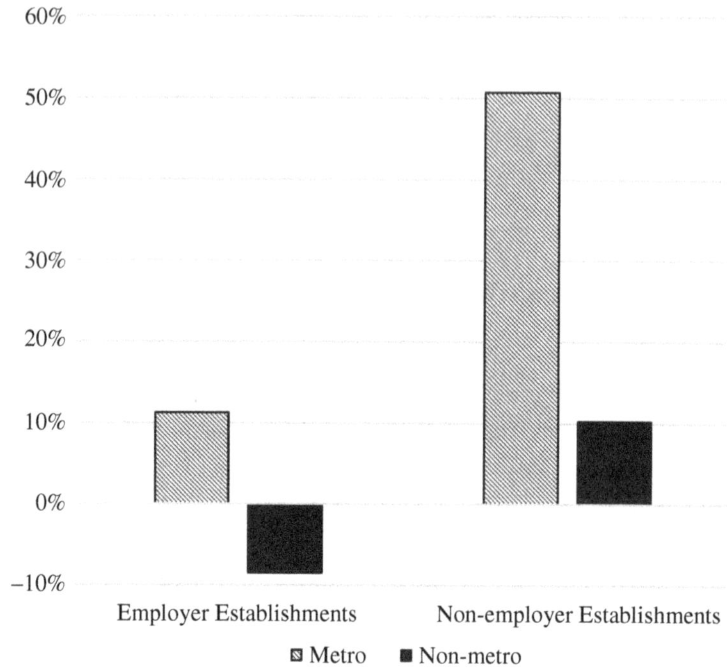

Fig. 6.4. Growth in employer and non-employer establishments, 2001–2015.
Source: Authors' analysis of data from the County Business Patterns and Non-Employer Statistics.

hairstylists and accountants working for themselves, it does seem to have accelerated in recent years, especially in urban areas. Thus, while the Great Recession may have accelerated this trend, the downturn did not initiate the rise of non-employers.

6.4 Proprietorship

The rise of non-employers in urban areas compared to rural areas could indicate that urban areas are home to small, thriving, entrepreneurial businesses. However, the number of proprietorships per 1,000 residents[b] indicates that, in fact, this increase in entrepreneurial non-employer businesses may not be a case of urban counties outperforming rural areas (Fig. 6.5).

[b]A proprietorship is a tax status that is indicative of at least one self-employed person.

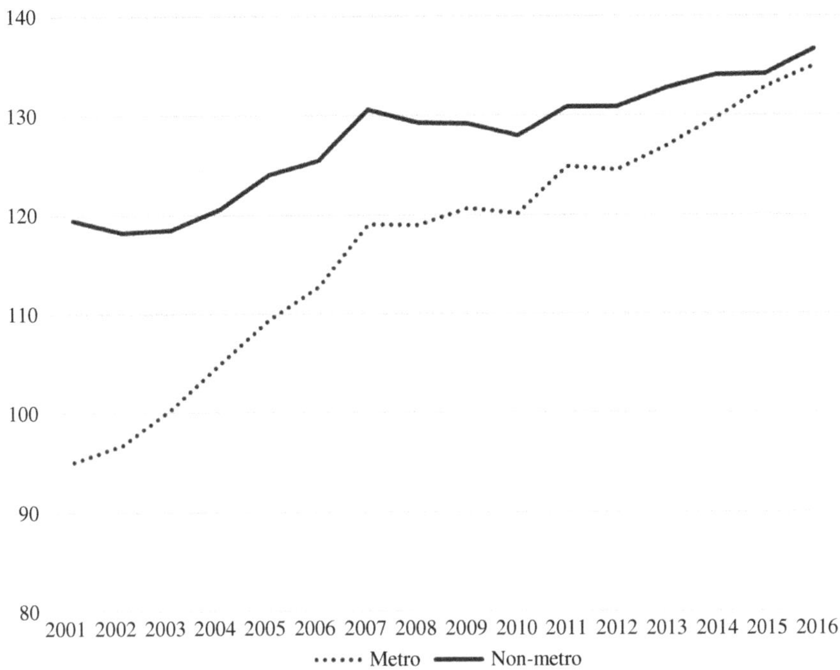

Fig. 6.5. Proprietorships per 1,000 residents.

Source: Authors' analysis of data from the Bureau of Economic Analysis.

Proprietorship activity is an area in which urban areas are catching up to more rural counties, which have long had more proprietorships than urban areas, a signal of rural entrepreneurialism. This entrepreneurial tendency is perhaps to be expected, given that farm proprietorships are included in the total number of proprietorships and farming is a largely rural and, arguably, a quite entrepreneurial occupation. In recent years, urban counties have been catching up. So, although analysis provided in Fig. 6.4 might make it seem that urban areas are leading in this kind of entrepreneurial activity, in which people are striking out on their own, this is not necessarily the case. Placed in context, as in Fig. 6.5, we can see that rural counties seem to have had some comparative advantage in proprietorship.

Often, proprietorship is underemphasized in policy discussions because those discussions typically focus on wage-and-salary positions. Yet, these conventional wage jobs are seemingly becoming scarcer. The type of job that is typically not discussed, let alone counted in some employment statistics, is the type that a person creates for himself or herself. Consequently, policies can lean toward supporting employer firms in lieu of supporting entrepreneurial ventures. This bias of support can be compounded by political interests as well. Given the length of an election cycle and visibility of these initiatives, a political official may reasonably prefer the short-term payoff of recruiting a firm with 50 employees over supporting 20 sole proprietors who may go on to hire another one to two workers over the next year, even though entrepreneurs are much less likely to move for a better incentive package, and are more likely to invest in their local community compared to large footloose firms that are motivated by incentive packages.

6.5 Young Firms and Job Creation

The entrepreneurial foundations shown in the high rates of proprietorship in rural areas are promising for rural job growth. Entrepreneurship has proven critical to economic performance, including income growth, poverty alleviation and job creation [Shrestha *et al.*, 2007, Goetz *et al.*, 2012; Bunten *et al.*, 2015]. Further, Haltiwanger *et al.* [2013] show that new and young firms are a critical source of new jobs. Historically, new firms alone have generated one-third of gross job growth annually. Though weaker in recent years, new and young firms still produce the largest component of gross job growth.

Figure 6.6 shows the share of job creation by establishment age in total (across both rural and urban areas). In 2001, new and young firms (those under 5-years old) created just over half of gross jobs. New firms alone, defined as those less than 1 year old, generated 30% of gross jobs. For comparison, the age category covering the 5-year increment from age five to nine generated just 14% of all jobs. That is to say, new businesses generated more than twice as many jobs as all firms from age five to nine. Last, mature establishments more than 10 years old produced just slightly more jobs than new establishments, at 34%.

More recent data, however, do suggest a shift. In 2017, the share of job creation from establishments under age five fell to 41% from 52% in 2001.

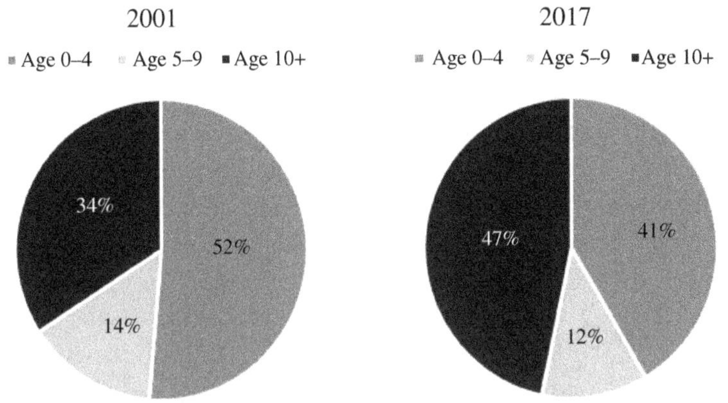

Fig. 6.6. Share of job creation by firm age, 2001 and 2017.

Source: Authors' analysis of data from the Bureau of Economic Analysis.

The share from new establishments alone declined from 30% to 24%. In place of new firms, the share of job creation from the most mature firms has risen substantially, now generating 47% of gross jobs, up from 34%.

The shift toward relying on more mature firms is potentially problematic for several reasons. First, productivity of new businesses drops rapidly with age [Alon *et al.*, 2017]. Not only does this matter for regional output but also for workers' wages, as compensation is tied to productivity. The more workers we have in the most productive firms, the more upward pressure there is on wage growth. To the extent that workers are shifting into less productive firms, we might expect less wage growth. Indeed, long-run declines in start-up activity may be tied to decades of stagnant wages. Thus, start-up activity is important not just for job quantity but also job quality.

Second, although these figures focus on gross job creation, net job creation — the difference between those created and destroyed — is equally, if not more, important. New firms, by definition, do not destroy any jobs and thus have positive net job creation. Mature firms of every other age category do destroy jobs if they contract or close entirely. On average, after age zero, businesses destroy more jobs than they create, resulting in negative net job creation [EIG, 2017]. Thus, it is essential to have the positive net job creation from new firms to offset these losses.

For rural economies with their strong entrepreneurial roots, the job potential of young firms is promising. It does seem that additional support for new and young firms in rural areas could be an effective way to boost job creation. Helping them transition into the stages where they are hiring their first employees seems especially important because, in aggregate, this would increase the number of employers, and with it the number of jobs, not to mention the potential benefits in terms of productivity and wage growth.

6.6 Business Survival

The promise of entrepreneurship for job growth is based not only on the high rate of proprietorship in rural counties. Businesses in rural communities also are more likely to survive up to 5 years than those in metro areas. In Fig. 6.7, we show the survival rate of new businesses with the share of each cohort that reached age five between 1995 and 2012.[c] There is almost a survival gradient, with establishments in the most rural counties having the highest five-year survival rate to establishments in the most urban counties having the lowest survival rate.

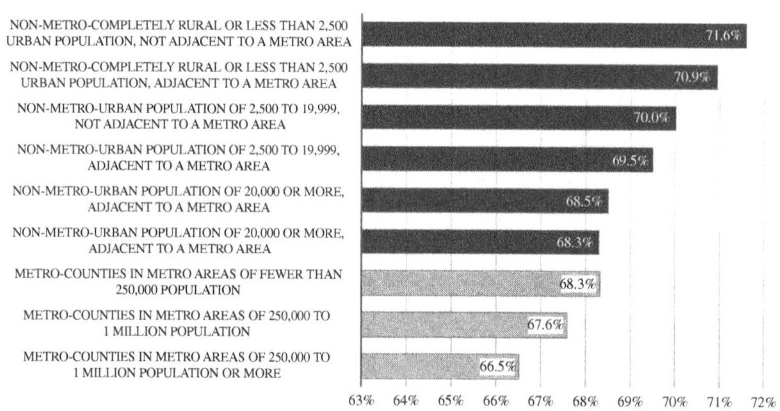

Fig. 6.7. Five-year business survival rates, county average by rural–urban continuum code (age five between 1995 and 2012).

Source: Reproduced from Deller and Conroy [2016].

[c]For a more detailed discussion of business survival rates across the urban–rural divide, see Deller and Conroy [2016, 2017].

Arguably, this is because there is less competitive pressure in a rural area: fewer new businesses enter the market, making it easier for marginal businesses that would not last in a more competitive environment to stay open. It also may be a testament to the resourcefulness of rural areas. With limited job opportunities, people who are unable to move because of the expense, for example, or who simply prefer to stay may resort to working for themselves. Similarly, because of few other options, they may have to find a way to sustain their business as their primary job, leading to higher survival rates.

6.7 Entrepreneurial Populations

Given that rural communities may want to pursue entrepreneurial strategies for job growth, they need to determine who in their communities has the most potential as entrepreneurs. Sometimes in rural communities, it is tempting to look at the large outflows of young populations and focus on how to retain or attract people. But when it comes to start-up activity, there are several other demographics that can be targeted for entrepreneurial development.

The US population is aging, especially in some rural areas. Often, this older demographic is overlooked when it comes to economic development, but recent retirees may be valuable for their economic potential. People who are retired or about to retire have had the opportunity to accumulate some financial wealth and work experience. Further, many retirees are ready to step away from their full-time careers but would still like to be productive. This desire to work in a new capacity, combined with their human and financial capital, makes recent retirees and soon-to-be retired people a pool of potential entrepreneurs. There is evidence of this in that rural areas that have seen an influx of in-migration of an older generation also have better entrepreneurial outcomes than areas without such an influx [Deller *et al.*, 2018].

Second, immigrant or foreign-born populations tend to be especially inclined toward entrepreneurship. Immigrants are nearly twice as likely as native-born residents to start a business [Jackson, 2015]. This appears to be a largely urban phenomenon; however, data are limited for thoroughly studying this relationship in rural settings. The data also may be skewed by southern border and coastal states that have very large cities and large immigrant populations, such as California. Comparatively, the Midwest, for example, has fewer major metro areas and is less diverse.

Still, the entrepreneurialism of immigrants in cities is noteworthy. Perhaps it has less to do with the urban setting and more to do with having a large enough immigrant population to create both strong social capital and unique market opportunities. The social capital in some communities provides a network that can support business owners on the supply side as they procure inputs and establish their businesses, and that network can also be sufficiently large to provide a strong consumer base. This community-based social capital can establish itself among a group of immigrants in large urban settings. However, in rural settings, there may not be a sufficiently large immigrant population to create its own network that can support a business owner. Instead, a rural community may have to be especially intentional in integrating its diverse set of business owners into the primary business network in order to support them — particularly racial and ethnic minorities that are likely less networked, putting them at a disadvantage.

Last, the relatively overeducated in rural areas also may be a promising entrepreneurial population. Rural areas can be very desirable places to live because they are relatively affordable, less congested, and high in natural amenities. To the extent that highly educated workers have several options of where to seek work, they may choose such desirable rural communities. However, in some communities, the job offerings of local employers are not well-matched to the residents' skills. In many rural communities, the residents' skills exceed the skills that employers require. Consequently, residents may be considered relatively overeducated, having education and skills beyond what is needed for their jobs. Thus, there is a skills surplus in some rural counties [Moore, 2005]. These underemployed residents may find the alternative of working for themselves especially attractive. In becoming an entrepreneur, these educated workers could create positions for themselves and choose to live in their preferred location. Indeed, there is evidence that high-amenity, overeducated regions are more entrepreneurial than regions with fewer amenities and a skills shortage [Conroy and Watson, 2018].

6.8 Implications for Economic Development

The high rates of proprietorship and business survival point to a strategy for job growth in rural communities. As a critical source of job creation, entrepreneurs and their new businesses are a vital component of long-term economic growth. Entrepreneurship enhances economic growth by influencing all sectors, rather than focusing purely on agriculture or manufacturing. This enhances the diversity of a community, which can lend to stability during a downturn [Deller and Watson, 2016; Deller *et al.*, 2017]. Many communities already have talented populations with entrepreneurial potential: these include immigrants, retirees and the soon-to-be retired, as well as the overeducated and underemployed. Taken together, these factors point to the local asset-based development of entrepreneurial potential as a way to increase economic growth.

References

Alon, T., Berger, D., Dent, R. and Pugsley, B. (2017). *Older and Slower: The Startup Deficit's Lasting Effects on Aggregate Productivity Growth*. Working Paper No. 23875. National Bureau of Economic Research.

Autor, D., Dorn, D. and Hanson, G. (2018). *When Work Disappears: Manufacturing Decline and Falling Marriage-Market Value of Young Men*. Working Paper No. 23173. National Bureau of Economic Research.

Bunten, D., Weiler, S., Thompson, E. C. and Zahran, S. (2015). Entrepreneurship, information, and growth, *Journal of Regulatory Science*, 55(4), pp. 560–584.

Conroy, T. and Watson, P. (2018). *Betting the Over/Under: Education and Entrepreneurship*. Working Paper. Available from chapter author.

Conroy, T., Deller, S. and Tsvetkova, A. (2016). Regional business climate and interstate manufacturing relocation decisions. *Regional Science and Urban Economics*, 60, pp. 155–168.

Cramer, K. J. (2016). *The Politics of Resentment: Rural Consciousness in Wisconsin and the Rise of Scott Walker*. University of Chicago Press, Chicago.

Deller, S. C. and Conroy, T. (2016). Survival rates of rural businesses: What the evidence tells us. *Choices*, 31(4), pp. 1–5.

Deller, S. C. and Conroy, T. (2017). Business survival rates across the urban–rural divide. *Community Development*, 48(1), pp. 67–85.

Deller, S. C., Conroy, T. and Watson, P. (2017). Women business owners: A source of stability during the great recession? *Applied Economics*, 49(56), pp. 5686–5697.

Deller, S., and Watson, P. (2016). Did regional economic diversity influence the effects of the great recession? *Economic Enquiry*, 54(4), pp. 1824–1838.

Deller, S., Kures, M. and Conroy, T. (2019). Rural entrepreneurship and migration. *Journal of Rural Studies*, 66, pp. 30–42.

Economic Innovation Group (EIG) (2017). *Dynamism in Retreat: Consequences for Regions, Markets, and Workers*. https://eig.org/dynamism (accessed July 2018).

Goetz, S. J., Fleming, D. A. and Rupasingha, A. (2012). The economic impacts of self-employment. *Journal of Agricultural Economics*, 3 (August), pp. 315–321.

Haltiwanger, J., Jarmin, R. S. and Miranda, J. (2013). Who creates jobs? Small versus large versus young. *Review of Economics and Statistics*, XCV(2), pp. 347–361.

Jackson, C. (2015). *Lessons from the Kauffman Index: Immigrants are Infused with Entrepreneurial Energy*. Kauffman Currents. https://www.kauffman.org/blogs/currents/2015/06/lessons-from-the-kauffman-index-immigrants (accessed July 2018).

Kures, M., Deller, S. and Conroy, T. (2018). *Patterns and Determinants of Stretch Commuting Across the Rural-Urban Continuum*. Working Paper. Available from chapter authors.

Moore, S. (2005). *Regional Asset Indicators: Tapping the Skills Surplus*, Center for the Study of Rural America, Federal Reserve Bank of Kansas City.

Rickman, D. S. and Wang, H. (2018). Two tales of two US states: Regional fiscal austerity and economic performance. *Regional Science and Urban Economics*, 68, pp. 46–55.

Shrestha, S. S., Goetz, S. J. and Rupasingha, A. (2007). Proprietorship formations and US job growth. *Review of Regional Studies*, 37(2), pp. 146–168.

Part C
Farm Policies and Rural Jobs

Chapter 7

CAP and Rural Jobs: Analysis of Studies

Mauro Vigani*, John Powell and Janet Dwyer

Countryside and Community Research Institute, University of Gloucestershire, UK
**mvigani@glos.ac.uk*

This chapter summarizes understanding of the impact of the European Union's Common Agricultural Policy (CAP) upon rural and agricultural jobs by reviewing the published literature on this topic over the past 30 years. It considers policy modifications over the period in which these studies were conducted and how these changes are likely to have affected the overall pattern and balance of CAP impacts upon rural jobs, within and beyond the farm sector. This chapter starts by summarizing the intervention logic of CAP instruments in order to anticipate the kinds of impact that such policies might generate and to consider how they would vary in time and space. After describing the methodological approach for the literature review, some patterns that emerged in the literature are discussed in order to illustrate the link between predicted theoretical outcomes and actual employment outcomes.

7.1 The Intervention Logic of the CAP and its Implications for Employment Impacts

The likely impact of the Common Agricultural Policy (CAP) upon rural employment can be considered from a number of different perspectives. First, economic theory can be explored for suggestions concerning the implications of policy intervention in the agricultural sector at a strategic level. Second, at a more detailed level, the employment impacts of the mix and overall balance of different types of policy lever applied under the CAP can be examined. Third, the recorded or demonstrated changes in employment that appear to be connected to the CAP and its changes over time, within specific geographical and socio-economic contexts around Europe, can be explored. It is only when the findings of all three of these kinds of analysis are combined that it is possible to draw reasoned, detailed and relatively robust conclusions concerning the impact of the policy upon agricultural and rural employment.

The economic theory of competitive markets suggests that, when policymakers decide to intervene in markets to provide additional resources, or to improve the economic conditions within a particular sector of the economy, they are likely to create a situation in which that sector attracts and retains more resources than it might have done without the policy intervention. It might therefore be anticipated that a policy such as the CAP, with objectives to stabilize prices and/or to support farm incomes, *inter alia*, would encourage the retention of capital, labor and land in farming which might otherwise have left the sector as it develops over time. However, the relative strength of this effect will be influenced by market conditions, and by policies targeting other sectors of the economy. If other sectors are more attractive economically than agriculture, even when it has additional government support, then labor and other resources will flow out of agriculture, subject to conditions such as elasticities of substitution and labor mobility. Thus, although the impact of the CAP relative to the counterfactual might be to retain jobs in farming, the overall trend may still be a movement of employment from agriculture to other areas.

The CAP consists of a wide variety of policy instruments; some act as general support to the sector in a relatively untargeted way, while others have specific goals and targets for which they are carefully designed and implemented. The relatively untargeted measures in the current CAP, for example, include decoupled support under Pillar 1, which pays a standard payment per hectare to keep land in good agricultural condition and to provide an element of income support and stability to farming businesses. When it comes to targeted support, there are at least three main types:

1. those which encourage investment in the agricultural sector to improve its productivity and profitability;
2. those which support disadvantaged territories where without aid agricultural land might be abandoned; and,
3. those which focus upon investment in the wider rural economy beyond agriculture (e.g. support for tourism or craft activities, renewable energy generation, and business diversification).

The anticipated impact upon rural employment would be different for each kind of targeted support. Aid designed to stimulate improved productivity would be likely to lead to declining use of labor in existing farm businesses. On the other hand, aid which targets support to areas facing constraints would tend to encourage the retention of labor within farming, and this might also be done in such a way as to stimulate other rural economic activities, particularly in areas that are relatively spatially remote from other types of economic influence. Thus, in theory it might be possible to understand the impact of the CAP upon rural employment by considering the balance of funding between these different kinds of targeted and untargeted policy instrument, whereas in practice it is very difficult. The wide range of expected impacts must be tempered by a consideration of local context, and the dynamic interplay of agricultural and rural economic drivers with trends occurring in the wider economy. Furthermore, impact will depend upon policy performance and evaluation over many years has revealed plentiful examples where policies fail to deliver, for a variety of reasons. There are thus, limitations to what can be predicted from theory and *a priori* expectations concerning the impact of the CAP on rural employment across the varied territory of the European Union.

7.2 Methods and Results

7.2.1 *Methodological approach*

Over the past 30 years, a variety of studies have researched the impact of the CAP on agricultural and rural employment. In order to compile an exhaustive collection of these studies, a systematic literature review was conducted, covering literature pertaining to all Member States (MSs) of the EU and their regions for the period from the 1992 CAP reform up to March 2018.

The literature search utilized several different sources: the library databases of the University of Gloucestershire (DISCOVERY), the University of Bath (PRIMO search) and the University of East Anglia (UEA Library Search). In addition, the resources of international institutions, such as the European Commission repository, the Joint Research Centre repository and the OECD library, were incorporated, along with online resources identified using Google Scholar, Agra-Europe and AgEcon Search. A snowball approach was applied by screening the reference lists in each identified source and working backwards from these to find further relevant articles.

Different keywords and search terms were applied. Keywords were related to jobs (employment, labor, job, job creation, migration, work) and to the CAP (agriculture, rural, development, CAP, pillar, decoupling, reform, European Union, European Commission, European Parliament, EU). Different combinations of these keywords were applied to the databases with appropriate Boolean operators in two different time periods, between 28 January and 3 February 2016 [Schuh *et al.*, 2016], and then updated between 12 and 14 March 2018.

The initial searches identified more than 1,500 records, which were then narrowed down to relevant studies using a screening strategy based on a set of exclusion and inclusion criteria. First, the literature was screened to eliminate duplicates and newspaper articles to avoid potential strong ideological bias. Second, the following inclusion and exclusion criteria were applied to titles and abstracts:

- **Inclusion criteria:** Countries and regions in EU MSs; all measures and instruments of Pillars 1 and 2 of the CAP and its reforms since

1992; the impact of the CAP on agricultural and rural employment, structural change (entry/exit), migration of workers across sectors, farmers' time allocation decisions between on- and off-farm work; *ex ante* and *ex post* analyses; quantitative and qualitative analyses.
- **Exclusion criteria:** Countries that are not EU MSs; policies or regulations different from the CAP and its Pillars and reforms; studies for which the full text is not available/accessible; studies published in a language different from English and/or before 1999.

For all those studies for which both abstract and title met the criteria, the full text was obtained and the inclusion/exclusion criteria were reapplied to the full text. At the end of this systematic process, a total of 58 studies were retained for the literature review (academic articles, conference proceedings/working papers, government documents and reports, books).

7.2.2 *Results of the literature review*

The results of the systematic literature review were organized with reference to the main periods of reform of the CAP and also by differences between Pillar 1 and Pillar 2. Initial analysis of the studies revealed a wide focus of attention in terms of time, policy area, methodology applied, and whether the study was *ex ante* (i.e. forecasting impacts) or *ex post* (evaluating what had happened). Table 7.1 provides an overview of the breakdown of studies across policy reform periods, focus of analysis and net effect reports (i.e. positive or negative).

Overall, some authors highlighted that the progressive liberalization promoted by the CAP reforms over time had led to a reduction of the number of agricultural and rural jobs [e.g. Baum *et al.*, 2006; Helming *et al.*, 2008; Elek *et al.*, 2010; Vereijken and Hermans, 2010; Manos *et al.*, 2013]. However, because of the heterogeneity across MSs and regions in terms of farming systems and market structures, it is difficult to make simple generalizations concerning the effect of the CAP on agricultural and rural employment. The policy supports for farm income, investment and training appear to have helped maintain agricultural jobs and create temporary employment opportunities in some rural areas [e.g. EC, 2006;

Table 7.1. Results of systematic literature review.

No. of studies	Reform	Method	*Ex ante*/*Ex post*	Net effect
5	1992	Quantitative	*Ex post*	Positive
5	Agenda 2000	Quantitative	*Ex post* and *ex ante*	Positive and negative
27	2003	Quantitative	*Ex post* and *ex ante*	Positive and negative
5	"Health Check"	Mixed	*Ex post*	Positive and negative
3	2013	Mixed	*Ex ante*	Positive and negative
3	Toward 2020	Quantitative	*Ex ante*	Positive and negative
16	Not specified	Mixed	*Ex post* and *ex ante*	Positive and negative

Notes: The total sum of studies in column one exceeds 58, which is the number of articles/papers/books collected with the systematic literature review, because some of the authors have analyzed more reforms in a single publication. "Not specified" means that the studies are assessing the CAP employment impact without focusing on specific reforms.

Breustedt and Glauben, 2007; Křístková and Ratinger, 2012; Kaditi, 2013; Olper *et al.*, 2014], but not all studies supported this. Therefore, it is probably correct to say that the effect of CAP subsidies on employment can be either positive or negative, depending on the type of policy instrument and the way that the CAP is implemented at national or regional level [e.g. Petrick and Zier, 2012; European Court of Auditors, 2013; Dupraz and Latruffe, 2015]. At a strategic level, however, the CAP may have promoted a more intensive and mechanized agriculture, which would suggest a net negative impact upon farm employment [e.g. Alexiadis *et al.*, 2013].

Expectations and outcomes: A comparison

Table 7.2 compares the theoretically informed expected outcomes of the CAP focus in relation to jobs (in both the agricultural sector and rural areas more widely), with predicted and actual outcomes from the 1960s to the present. It summarizes the main policy changes over the period enabling an overview of how key changes in direction have altered the relationship between CAP support and employment.

Table 7.2 suggests that in the early period (1960s and 1970s) the price support focus of the CAP would maintain labor in the agricultural sector,

Table 7.2. Comparison of expected employment impacts arising from CAP changes with study outcomes.

Time period	Policy focus	Expected employment impacts	Outcomes of studies
1960–1970	Guaranteed prices to producers of some of the main European agricultural commodities including: • dairy products • beef and sheep meat • wheat, barley, other arable crops • selected permanent crops, fruits and vegetables.	Promote overall retention of resources in the farm sector and restructuring, which would substitute labor by capital, particularly in MSs where land tenure and inheritance laws facilitated structural change. Less Favored Area (LFA) support likely to promote labor retention in areas where support was at a significant scale and targeted to active farmers. In some MSs, LFA payments made to absentee landowners and/or offered at low levels, thus employment impacts would be negligible.	No studies identified
1980–1990	Policy shift away from production support toward partial decoupling. More use of aid to target specific non-production outcomes. Aids for environmental management and set-aside more important. Broader rural development support under the EC Structural Fund programs.	Partially decoupled direct payments (largest element in CAP spending) might maintain production, but not necessarily support labor use. Continuing structural investment aids would stimulate the replacement of labor by capital in many situations. Growth of decoupled and environmental aid might weaken links between public funding and the retention of labor, particularly where agri-environment measures promoted extensification, and aid required only minimal retention of land in "good agricultural and environmental condition".	Rural development support (Greece): decreased rural–urban job migration; maintained agricultural jobs. Support reduced impacts of structural change in agriculture more generally. Crop subsidies decreased on-farm labor. Agri-environmental support increased on-farm labor.

(Continued)

Table 7.2. (*Continued*)

Time period	Policy focus	Expected employment impacts	Outcomes of studies
2000–2010	"Agenda 2000" package, created the two-Pillar CAP. EU enlargement in 2004 to embrace 10 NMSs. Overall balance of spending in the policy shifted more toward rural development.	Anticipated creation of new jobs in rural areas, both on-and off-farm. Relatively more significant in the NMSs, where Pillar 2 spending for the first four years after accession was commonly more significant than Pillar 1 aid.	Slightly negative or no impact on agricultural and rural employment. Decoupling removed incentives to maintain production; labor could be diverted to other activities; reduced rate of farmers leaving the sector. Varied response by sector and MS. Pillar 1 cross-compliance conditions could decrease on-farm employment in regions of the EU-15 where extensification of production takes place, with wider impacts on supply chains. Decrease in recorded farm employment.
2010 onwards	More mixed and more spatially disparate focus. NMSs increasingly received more decoupled Pillar 1 aid. Balance of Pillar 1 and Pillar 2 spent across the MSs varies considerably.	Anticipated to induce the shedding of labor from farms in cases where structural change develops relatively easily, but patterns of impact upon employment will vary across MS. Pillar 2 variability will induce local variation in employment effects as there is a wide range of choices for Managing Authorities regarding balance and targeting of resources (e.g. agri-environmental management, farm modernization, support for economic diversification).	Wide variation in balance between Pillar 1 and Pillar 2 funding across MSs, affects employment outcomes. NMSs received more decoupled Pillar 1 aid. *Ex ante* study suggests an agricultural labor subsidy could marginally increase labor.

although restructuring, and capital investment would be likely to decrease labor requirements in some MSs. During that period the European Community was small (only six countries, increasing to nine after the first enlargement in 1973), and agricultural policy was driven by notions of the need for a high level of self-sufficiency following the Second World War rationing, which had continued into the 1950s in some countries.

Starting in the 1990s, there was a move toward reducing the link between production and subsidy, with the realization that this would be likely to involve a reduction in agricultural labor. The key change was the 1992 CAP reform, which involved a move away from production support (i.e. a limited level of decoupling), wider use of targeted aid to deliver non-production outcomes, and the beginnings of broader rural development support under Structural Fund programs. The literature survey identified five studies that analyzed the impact of the reformed CAP from 1992, using data for the years 1990–1999. Specific studies found that rural development funds in some areas (such as Greece) reduced the rate of job migration from rural to urban areas and retained people in agriculture [Psaltopoulos *et al.*, 2006], or reduced the impact of structural change in agriculture [Breustedt and Glauben, 2007]. In addition, one study [Dupraz and Latruffe, 2015] noted that CAP crop subsidies had a negative impact upon on-farm labor in the 1990s, while agri-environmental measures had a positive impact. The limited focus of the five studies supports the anticipated policy outcomes, with various elements of the CAP starting to pull in different directions. Broader rural development funding tended to slow the rate of rural to urban migration, and while agri-environmental agreements enhanced the demand for on-farm labor. The far larger proportion of funding going to subsidize production worked in the opposite direction as capital investment and restructuring increased.

The decade after 2000 saw the formation of the two-Pillar CAP and EU enlargement through the addition of 10 New Member States (NMSs) in 2004. The period was dominated by the 2003 CAP reform, which decoupled farm payments from production. With an increase in rural development (Pillar 2) funding, additional jobs could be expected, especially in the NMSs, where Pillar 2 spending for the first four years after accession was commonly more significant than Pillar 1 aid.

Table 7.1 illustrates the significance of this major change in policy in that almost half of the studies from the literature survey focus on the 2003 reform period and a further five studies examined the "Agenda 2000" reform. This was the most studied period of policy change in the research literature as it introduced many changes to Pillar 1 (especially through the decoupling of direct payments, compulsory cross-compliance and optional modulation[a]), and significantly increased support for wider rural development.

Among the 27 studies (including both *ex ante* and *ex post* analyses) focusing on the 2003 CAP reform, there are some differences of opinion among the authors. The majority concluded that overall the 2003 reform had either a negative impact on agricultural and rural employment [Gohin and Latruffe, 2006; Elek *et al.* 2011; Genius, 2013], or had no significant impact [Corsi and Salvioni, 2012; Douarin, 2008] in rural employment terms. The main channel of impact was through the effects of decoupling of subsidies from agricultural production. Whereas previously subsidized production had acted as a support for rural employment, once the link was broken there was no incentive to maintain production, and labor could be freed to undertake other forms of activities (diversification). Several authors suggested that coupled payments, by being linked to production, provided an incentive to increase the time spent working on the farm, especially on family farms. In contrast, decoupled payments, by guaranteeing sufficient farm income without requiring more work, provided farmers with more time either for leisure or for off-farm work. The outcomes suggest a decrease in recorded farm employment [Agrosynergie 2011; Viaggi *et al.*, 2011; Hennessy and Rehman, 2008; Balamou *et al.*, 2008; Tranter *et al.*, 2007].

However, the picture is a complex one, varying by both agricultural sector and MS, and complicated by the addition of 10 new EU MSs in 2004 with very different socio-economic conditions. In the livestock sector (beef and dairy), for example, some authors undertaking *ex ante*

---

[a]Modulation is the reduction of direct payment awards and the transfer of the money thus "saved" from Pillar 1. Subsequent CAP reforms have involved "degressivity" (reductions in higher awards), "capping" (upper limits to such awards), and direct budget transfers between Pillar 1 and Pillar 2.

studies [Hennessy and Rehman, 2006] suggested that off-farm work and structural change would be accelerated after decoupling, while in the tobacco sector Manos *et al.* [2009] indicated that decoupling would lead to an increase in unemployment. An alternative explanation [Breustedt and Glauben, 2007] recognized that the overall effect of decoupling is ambiguous, as it enables farmers to cut back or cease commercial production while continuing to receive CAP support, resulting in a reduction in farmers leaving the agricultural sector. However, more recent studies that could rely on long farm-level panel data for all MSs found that, on average, at EU level both coupled and decoupled payments contributed to reduce the rate of out-migration of labor from the agricultural sector [Olper *et al.*, 2014]. This finding is consistent with predictions from theory [Barkley, 1990] concerning the impact of support reducing the incentives to exit the sector and providing returns to the farmer, although in the form of welfare transferred from other groups of the society.

There are suggestions from some authors that the cross-compliance conditions introduced into Pillar 1 by the 2003 CAP reform might also have a negative employment impact [Baum *et al.*, 2006], particularly in regions of the EU-15 where an expected extensification of production (i.e. lower inputs and increased set-aside) would be likely to decrease employment. Reductions in agricultural sector employment arising from extensification would also be likely to have both upstream and downstream impacts on supply chains, as demand for goods and services declined.

In terms of rural development (Pillar 2), the studies also indicate a more complex response than that anticipated. The expected outcome of policy change was an increase in employment both on-farm and in the wider rural areas. The assumption underlying the reform was that decoupling would free farmers to invest in production and also to diversify, while Pillar 2 support would provide a wider array of jobs in the local economy, making rural areas more attractive and retaining both services and a working age population. In practice, the outcomes vary across MSs depending on eligibility for Pillar 1 support, the selection of Pillar 2 measures and the effectiveness with which they were implemented.

Only three studies were identified in the literature survey for the period 2010 leading up to 2020, and they suggest both positive and negative outcomes for employment. The current period exhibits a more complex and spatially differentiated situation making the impact of policies difficult to predict. The NMSs have increasingly received more decoupled Pillar 1 aid, and the balance of Pillars 1 and 2 spending across the EU has varied considerably. One *ex ante* evaluation using partial and general equilibrium models [Helming and Tabeau, 2017] has indicated that by reallocating Pillar 1 budgets to a coupled agricultural labor subsidy, the average employment in agriculture in the EU could increase by 0.6–1.6% in the current programming period up to 2020.

7.3 Quantification of Policy Impacts on Employment

A limited number of studies attempted to quantify the impacts of the 2003 reform (see Table 7.3) in terms of its impacts on employment numbers. A study focusing on Austria [Neuwirth *et al.*, 2010] estimated that, if the money used for CAP subsidies were used in other economic sectors, an estimated net total of 33,000 agricultural jobs would have been lost. Overall, however, the literature shows that decoupling could have provoked an overall loss of agricultural jobs. One Scottish study [Topp and Mitchell, 2003] forecasts that the 2003 CAP Reform would reduce employment between 4,900 and 7,800 in a single Scottish region, while a wider perspective undertaken some years later [Gohin and Latruffe, 2006] estimated that decoupling may have lost 85,000 to 134,000 full-time on-farm workers across the entire EU-15 (i.e. an average of 5,000–9,000 jobs per MS). An *ex ante* evaluation using CGE models compared impacts in Greece and Scotland [Balamou *et al.*, 2008], noting that a 30% decrease in coupled support resulted in a 2.65% decrease in employment in Greek rural areas and a 0.21% decrease in Scottish rural areas. In contrast, an *ex post* evaluation with econometric analysis [Olper *et al.*, 2014] estimated that CAP payments over the period 1990–2009 prevented the exit of 27,000 workers from the farming sector, equivalent to approximately 1,420 per year. These findings are supported by an additional *ex post* evaluation [Neuwirth *et al.*, 2010] which determined that direct payments had maintained 40,000–50,000 agricultural jobs.

In terms of Pillar 2 impacts, a small-scale study focused on the forestry sector in Scotland estimated that the 2000–2006 Scottish Rural Development Program (RDP) generated about 2,780 full time equivalent

Table 7.3. Estimated effects of different measures and reforms of the CAP.

Source	Year	Policy proposal	Method	Impact
Topp and Mitchell	2003	Agenda 2000	*Ex ante* evaluation with mathematical programming	5,000–8,000 agricultural jobs lost
European Commission	2006	The LEADER II initiative	*Ex post* evaluation with statistical data analysis	100,000 agricultural jobs created
SAC	2006	Scottish RDP 2000–2006: Forestry scheme	*Ex ante* evaluation with expert interviews	2,780 jobs created in nurseries, contracting and in-house staff
Bournaris and Manos	2012	Pillar 2: Alternative crops and Agri-environment schemes	*Ex ante* evaluation with a scenario analysis	(i) −2.7% of total labor with only Single Farm Payment (SFP) (ii) +2% of total labor with adoption of alternative crops under SFP
European Commission	2015	Pillar 2: 2014–2020 RDP programs	*Ex post* evaluation with statistical data analysis	(i) 60,000 non-agricultural start-ups across all MSs (ii) LEADER approach will cover 51% of EU rural population (iii) 3.9 million training places to improve rural labor skills
Gohin and Latruffe	2006	Decoupling	*Ex ante* evaluation with equilibrium models	(i) 85,000–134,000 farm jobs lost (ii) 3,000 jobs created in food industry

(Continued)

Table 7.3. (*Continued*)

Source	Year	Policy proposal	Method	Impact
Balamou *et al.*	2008	Decoupling: 30% decrease in coupled support	*Ex ante* evaluation with CGE models	(i) 2.65% decrease in employment in Greek rural areas (ii) 0.21% decrease in employment in Scottish rural areas
Neuwirth *et al.*	2010	Direct payments	*Ex post* evaluation with statistical data analysis	40,000–50,000 agricultural jobs maintained
CAP-IRE	2011	Complete removal of the CAP	*Ex ante* evaluation with multiple methods	30% of farmers exiting the agricultural sector
Latruffe *et al.*	2013	Complete removal of the CAP	*Ex ante* evaluation with econometric analysis	21% of farmers exiting the agricultural sector
Olper *et al.*	2014	Total CAP payments	*Ex post* evaluation with econometric analysis	27,000 agricultural jobs maintained
Helming and Tabeau	2017	Pillar 1 budgets reallocated to a farm labor subsidy	*Ex ante* evaluation with equilibrium models	Average employment in EU agriculture could increase by 0.6–1.6%

jobs [SAC, 2006], while the European Commission [2006] stated that rural diversification measures of the LEADER II initiative helped to both secure agricultural jobs and create temporary jobs through environmental and village renewal activities. The number of jobs maintained and/or created were estimated to be in the region of 100,000, half of which were available to women. An *ex ante* evaluation of Pillar 2 based on a scenario analysis [Bournaris and Manos, 2012] exploring the effects of alternative crops and agri-environment schemes suggested that under current conditions the SFP would decrease labor by 2.7%, while a scenario that enabled adoption of alternative crops under SFP would lead to a 2% increase in total labor. However, in none of the examples is it possible to determine the duration of the jobs beyond the reporting period, nor the nature of the work itself (e.g. skilled *vs.* unskilled; temporary, seasonal, or casual).

7.4 Conclusions

In general, the quantitative studies examined in the literature survey find that the influence of the CAP on agricultural and rural jobs increases with the amount of support received, and this is linked to higher farm income, capital, investments and productivity induced by the policy. Indeed, up until recently, the CAP has supported intensive and highly mechanized farming. However, the overall effect of Pillar 1 support has been one of slowing the decline in or maintaining the actual number of jobs in agriculture rather than creating new jobs: direct subsidies can augment farms' financial access to investments which tend to increase the agricultural productivity per unit of labor rather than creating a demand for new labor. The impact of Pillar 2 on employment is more difficult to estimate as it varies widely depending on MS goals, selection of measures and the effectiveness of program delivery. Regarding Pillar 2, there is little indication of the permanence of jobs beyond the funding period.

Did the evidence from empirical analysis confirm theoretical expectations? The answer cannot be as unequivocal as one would desire. Complexity arises not only because of the differences across the labor markets and agricultural systems of EU MSs, but because the way that policies are implemented at national/regional level plays a major role in the accessibility of and returns from funding. This latter point is an issue largely ignored in the literature, with a few noticeable exceptions [e.g. Angioloni *et al.*, 2017].

Changing impacts of the CAP upon rural and agricultural employment could be anticipated over the current programming period (to 2020), and ones that are increasingly geographically differentiated over time. Patterns will increasingly be influenced by national and regional choices concerning CAP spending priorities, as well as by the underlying structural, legal and fiscal frameworks that shape the processes of structural change in the sector and in the wider rural economy of each MS.

References

Agrosynergie (2011). Evaluation of Income Effects of Direct Support. Framework Contract No. 30-CE-0223110/00-78. *Evaluation of CAP Measures Concerning Sectors Subject to Past or Present Direct Support — Lot 1: Horizontal Issues*. Final Report.

Alexiadis, S., Ladias, C. and Hasanagas, N. (2013). A regional perspective of the common agricultural policy. *Land Use Policy*, 30(1), pp. 665–669.

Angioloni, S., Sherry, E. and Wu, Z. (2017). Evaluating the Effectiveness of Axis 3-LEADER Grants on Job Creation. Paper for presentation at the 91th AES Conference, Dublin, Ireland, April.

Balamou, E., Pouliakas, K., Roberts, D. and Psaltopoulos, D. (2008). Modelling the Rural-urban Effects of Changes in Agricultural Policies. Paper for presentation at the 107th EAAE Seminar *Modelling of Agricultural and Rural Development Policies*. Sevilla, Spain, January–February.

Barkley, A. P. (1990). The determinants of the migration of labor out of agriculture in the United States, 1940–85(3). *American Journal of Agricultural Economics*, 72, pp. 567–573.

Baum, S., Cook, P., Stange, H. and Weingarten, P. (2006). Agricultural Employment Trends in an Enlarged European Union: Does the CAP Reform/introduction Matter? Poster paper prepared for presentation at the *International Association of Agricultural Economists Conference*, Gold Coast, Australia, August.

Bournaris, T. and Manos, B. (2012). European Union agricultural policy scenarios' impacts on social sustainability of agricultural holdings. *International Journal of Sustainable Development & World Ecology*, 19(5), pp. 426–432.

Breustedt, G. and Glauben, T. (2007). Driving forces behind exiting from farming in Western Europe. *Journal of Agricultural Economics*, 58(1), pp. 115–127.

CAP-IRE (2011). *Assessing the Multiple Impacts of the Common Agricultural Policies (CAP) on Rural Economies.* Project Final Report. https://cordis.europa.eu/project/rcn/88424_en.html (accessed 7 October 2018).

Corsi, A. and Salvioni, C. (2012). Did the CAP Reform Affect Off-farm Labor Participation in Italian Farms? Paper for presentation at the 1st AIEAA Conference *Towards a Sustainable Bio-economy: Economic Issues and Policy Challenges*, June, Trento, Italy.

Douarin, E. (2008). Do Decoupled Payments Really Encourage Farmers to Work More Off Farm? A Microlevel Analysis of Incentives and Preferences. Paper prepared for the 12th EAAE Congress. https://ageconsearch.umn.edu/bitstream/44024/2/352.pdf (accessed 7 November 2018).

Dupraz, P. and Latruffe, L. (2015). Trends in family labor, hired labor and contract work on French field crop farms: The role of the Common Agricultural Policy. *Food Policy*, 51, pp. 104–118.

Elek, S., Fertő, I. and Forgács, C. (2010). The possible effects of the CAP Reform on farm employment in Hungary. *Agricultural Economic Review,* 11(2). Available at: http://www.eng.auth.gr/mattas/11.2.3.pdf (accessed 7 October 2018).

European Commission (2006). *Employment in Rural Areas: Closing the Jobs Gap.* COM(2006) 857 final. Brussels, 21.12.2006.

European Commission (2015). *Food & Farming: Focus on Jobs and Growth.* Publication prepared for the EU Agricultural Outlook Conference, Brussels. December.

European Court of Auditors (2013). *Have the Member States and the Commission Achieved Value for Money with the Measures for Diversifying the Rural Economy?* Special Report No. 6/2013. Luxembourg: Publications Office of the European Union.

Genius, M. (2013). Production and off-farm employment decisions of Greek and Hungarian farmers in the light of the last CAP reform. *Agricultural Economic Review*, 14(2), 1–16.

Gohin, A. and Latruffe, L. (2006). The Luxembourg common agricultural policy reform and the European food industries: What's at stake? *Canadian Journal of Agricultural Economics*, 54, pp. 175–194.

Helming J. and Tabeau A. (2018) The economic, environmental and agricultural land use effects in the European Union of agricultural labour subsidies under the Common Agricultural Policy. *Regional Environmental Change*, 18(23), pp. 763–773.

Helming, J. F. M., Verhoog, D., Meijl van H. and Nowicki, P. (2008). Effects of CAP Reform on Regional Employment in the EU. Paper prepared for presentation at the 12th EAAE Congress People, *Food and Environments: Global Trends and European Strategies*, Gent, Belgium, August.

Hennessy, T. C. and Rehman, T. (2006). Modelling the Impact of Decoupling on Structural Change in Farming: Integrating Econometric Estimation and Optimisation. Paper prepared for presentation at the IAAE Conference, Gold Coast, Australia, August.

Hennessy, T. C. and Rehman, T. (2008). Assessing the impact of the 'decoupling' reform of the common agricultural policy on Irish farmers' off-farm labor market participation decisions. *Journal of Agricultural Economics*, 59(1), pp. 41–56.

Kaditi, E. A. (2013). The Impact of CAP Reforms on Farm Labor Structure, Working Paper No. 63, Factor Markets Project, August.

Křístková, Z. and Ratinger, T. (2012). Impact of the CAP´s Second Pillar Budget Reform on the Czech Economy. Agris on-line Papers in *Economics and Informatics*, 4, pp. 49–59.

Latruffe, L., Dupuy, A. and Desjeux, Y. (2013). What would farmers' strategies be in a no-CAP situation? An illustration from two regions in France. *Journal of Rural Studies*, 32, pp. 10–25.

Manos, B., Bournaris, Th. and Chatzinikolaou, P. (2011). Impact assessment of CAP policies on social sustainability in rural areas: An application in Northern Greece. *Operations Research*, 11(1), pp. 77–92.

Manos, B., Bournaris, Th., Chatzinikolaou, P. and Papathanasiou, J. (2009). Evaluation of tobacco cultivation alternatives under the EU common agricultural policy (CAP). *Journal of Policy Modelling*, 31(2), pp. 225–238.

Manos, B., Bournaris, Th., Chatzinikolaou, P., Berbel, J., Nikolov, D. (2013). Effects of CAP policy on farm household behaviour and social sustainability. *Land Use Policy*, 31, pp. 166–181.

Neuwirth, J., Ortner, K. and Wagner, K. (2010). Economic Effects of the Common Agricultural Policy on Employment in Austria, Presentation to 7th ERDN Conference, 29–30 October 2009, Debrecen, Hungary. https://www.agraroekonomik.at/fileadmin/download/ERDN_2009_Ortner.pdf (accessed 8 July 2018).

Olper, A., Raimondi, V., Cavicchioli, D. and Vigani, M. (2014). Do CAP payments reduce farm labor migration? A panel data analysis across EU regions. *European Review of Agricultural Economics*, 41(5), pp. 843–873.

Petrick, M. and Zier, P. (2012). Common agricultural policy effects on dynamic labor use in agriculture. *Food Policy*, 37(6), pp. 671–678.

Psaltopoulos, D., Balamou, E. and Thomson, K. J. (2006). Rural–urban impacts of CAP measures in Greece: An inter-regional SAM approach. *Journal of Agricultural Economics*, 57(3), pp. 441–458.

SAC (2006). Ex-Post Evaluation of the Scottish Rural Development Programme (2000–2006). Report prepared for the Scottish Government.

Schuh, B., Gorny, H., Kaucic, J., Kirchmayr-Novak, S., Vigani, M., Powell, J. and Hawketts, E. (2016). The Role of the EU's Common Agricultural Policy in Creating Rural Jobs. Research for AGRI Committee of the European Parliament. IP/B/AGRI/IC/2015_158.

Topp, C. F. E. and Mitchell, M. (2003). Forecasting the environmental and socio-economic consequences of changes in the common agricultural policy. *Agricultural Systems*, 76(1), pp. 227–252.

Tranter, R. B., Swinbank, A., Wooldridge, M. J., Costa, L., Knapp, T., Little, G. P. J. and Sottomayor, M. L. (2007). Implications for food production, land use and rural development of the European Union's Single Farm Payment: Indications from a survey of farmers' intentions in Germany, Portugal and the UK. *Food Policy*, 32(5–6), pp. 656–671.

Vereijken, P. H. and Hermans, C. M. L. (2010). A quick scan tool to assess the relative prospects of European regions for sustainable agriculture in a liberal market. *Land Use Policy*, 27(2), pp. 440–448.

Viaggi, D., Raggi, M. and Gomez y Paloma, S. (2011). Understanding the determinants of investment reactions to decoupling of the common agricultural policy. *Land Use Policy*, 28(3), pp. 495–505.

Chapter 8

Special Study: The Importance of Territorial Diversity: Employment Effects of the CAP's Pillars 1 and 2 in Rural Areas in Italy

Francesco Mantino

Council for Agricultural Research and Analysis of Agricultural Economics-Policies and Bio-Economy, Rome, Italy
francesco.mantino@crea.gov.it

Several recent studies have dealt with the Common Agricultural Policy's (CAP's) impacts on employment in agriculture. Most show that generally the effects of Pillar 1 are negative for both family and hired labor. Employment effects of Pillar 2 Rural Development Plan (RDP) measures seem more controversial. In this chapter, the CAP's impact on agricultural employment in three types of area (Urban, Intermediate and Peripheral) is evaluated in terms of the following: (a) farm structure and socio-economic context (land area and productivity, incomes and immigration); (b) various types of CAP expenditures. The results suggest that structural and context variables contribute to changes in farm employment more than policy measures. Amongst the latter, Pillar 1 income payments to farmers appear to have affected farm employment negatively in most areas, perhaps due to the introduction of activities requiring lower labor input, or to risk-averse behavior by farmers. The Pillar 2 RDP measures all showed positive effects, but not always statistically significant. These RDP effects differ according to measure type: farm and agro-industrial investment support generates higher employment effects than other types of support. In some cases, investment in rural diversification also contributes to farm employment.

8.1 Introduction

Agricultural employment is not only a national issue, but is also increasingly becoming a territorial issue and an indicator of strong territorial disparities within the EU. There is continuous outmigration from European rural areas, but this is particularly strong in the most peripheral rural areas. This trend threatens to hamper development opportunities in these areas, and also their future economic and social resilience. Consequently, new and increasing disparities are being created between intensive and high-productivity rural areas, and marginal ones.

What role did the Common Agricultural Policy (CAP) play in creating agricultural employment opportunities in recent times? This question has been at the center of the political and academic debate for different reasons: (a) agricultural employment is still relevant in predominantly rural areas of EU-27 developed economies (5% of the total value added and 16% of total employment) [EC, 2011]; and (b) according the EU's Lisbon Strategy for 2007–2013 and its EUROPE 2020 strategy for 2014–2020, agriculture should contribute to creating employment opportunities like any other sector.

This chapter aims to identify the determinants of CAP impact on agricultural employment in Italian agriculture in the 2007–2014 period and to analyze the diversity of this policy impact in different territorial settings, in particular, diversities between the most Peripheral Areas on one side, and Urban, Peri-urban and Intermediate Areas on the other.

8.2 Theoretical Background and Recent Trends in the Italian Agricultural Labor Market

8.2.1 *Theoretical background*

Several recent econometric studies have dealt with the CAP's impacts on employment in agriculture: most show that the effects of the CAP's Pillar

1 are generally negative (with some exceptions, e.g. [Nordin, 2014]), for both family and hired labor. This conclusion is statistically robust, and supported by homogeneous results in different regional settings and different econometric methods [Kaditi, 2013]. Negative impacts can arise for two reasons [Dupraz and Latruffe, 2015; Petrick and Zier, 2011]: (a) decoupling payments from production makes it possible to reduce farm employment without reducing the subsidy, which becomes an income subsidy; (b) over time, there is a change toward labor-saving types of farming. Petrick and Zier [2011] also support a third reason: in some cases, direct payments provide financial resources for labor-saving investments. Coupled payments generate negative effects as well: this is true in the Greek case [Kaditi, 2013] and in three German Länder examined by Petrick and Zier [2011]. Nevertheless, Dupraz and Latruffe [2015] conclude that crop payments have negative effects on family employment, which would be substituted by hired and contract labor. Livestock payments, instead, would have positive effects on family and contract employment, while negative on hired work.

Employment effects of rural development measures seem more controversial. In the studies examined here, the farm investment support has no statistically significant effects, although in most cases the observed effect is positive. Petrick and Zier [2011] conclude that support for processing and marketing investment had a negative effect in Germany, in both the short and medium terms, probably due to the adoption of labor-saving technologies. Less Favored Area (LFA) payments show positive effects only in France, with negative effects elsewhere. Agro-environmental payments generate positive effects in two cases, i.e. conservation practices (e.g. winter crops in France) and organic production techniques (e.g. in Germany), which generally need more labor. In general, these studies scarcely explore support measures for rural diversification and quality of life; the small RDP budget in some cases and the indirect effects on farm labor make the econometric estimates more difficult and less significant. In Germany, Petrick and Zier [2011] explain the negative effects of these measures on farm employment through the improved opportunities of off-farm work.

A common drawback of these studies is that little attention has been paid to the territorial (infra-regional) diversity of these effects. Two reasons for this are the lack of appropriate and comparable data at the territorial level, and the implicit assumption that structural and institutional differences among countries (the macro-level) are more important than territorial diversity in explaining the CAP's employment impact. Our central hypothesis is that territorial diversity strongly affects farm labor use at regional and sub-regional levels. This implies that the analysis of policy impacts should be carried out below Eurostat's Nomenclature of Territorial Units for Statistics (NUTS) level 2. The Lisbon Treaty states that all policies should contribute to territorial and social cohesion, and strengthens the need to include territorial diversity when looking at how the CAP has affected territorial cohesion.

8.2.2 *Trends in Italian agricultural labor markets: Territorial diversity*

Patterns and trends in agricultural employment differ greatly according to the type of socio-economic system. To identify these differences, we use a territorial typology which has been adopted in Italy to deliver the National Strategy for Inner Areas (NSIA). This is a special national program, co-funded by European Structural and Investment Funds (ESIFs) over the period 2014–2020, that aims to enhance public services and local development opportunities in the most remote rural areas [Ministry of Economic Development, 2014; Lucatelli, 2013]. It includes four types of areas, with population shares in parentheses:

(1) **Urban Poles**, identified by the metropolitan areas and principal cities in each region (40%);
(2) **Areas with Broad Economic Development ("Belt Areas")**, including the most industrialized and intensive agriculture and agri-food sectors (37%);
(3) **Intermediate Areas**, characterized by more extensive and diversified agriculture, and medium-low access to public services (15%);
(4) **Peripheral (and Ultra-peripheral) Areas**, characterized by problematic access to services, due partly to low economic development and partly to shrinking public resources (8%).

In the three decades, 1982–2010, both Urban Poles and Peripheral Areas lost population, though for different reasons. Increasing urbanization costs affected the cities, while the Peripheral Areas suffered from worsening service standards and lack of employment opportunities. Between 2001 and 2011, the number of immigrants (from other EU countries, and refugees) tripled in all areas, but more so in the Belt Areas where demand for labor was higher.

Over 60% of national agricultural production comes from the Belt and Intermediate Areas (with 45% of total farmed area), while the Peripheral Areas produce only 13% from over a quarter of the total area (Table 8.1). The quality of natural resources and the availability of services and infrastructure explain this disparity: Belt Areas have land productivity values three times those in Peripheral Areas. The difference in the Gross Agricultural Product (GAP) per full-time employee in agriculture, measured in Annual Work Units (AWUs) and per farm, contributes to explaining why the farm labor force has tended to decline in the last 30 years most in Peripheral Areas.

Agricultural labor markets are characterized by three main structural trends: (a) steady decline in the agricultural labor force (Fig. 8.1), at least until 2008, when the trend becomes a slight increase due to the return of labor to agriculture during the economic crisis; (b) decline in agricultural labor much more evident in Peripheral Areas (–52%) than in other areas over 1981–2011, and in most recent period (2001–2011), the trend has been less positive in Peripheral Areas than elsewhere (Fig. 8.2); (c) family labor as the main contributor to the agricultural labor force decline, while hired labor had a quite opposite trend (Fig. 8.3). These divergent trends are more evident in Urban Poles and Belt Areas, where off-farm labor opportunities are more relevant for farm family members, and consequently the share of hired labor in the farm activities has become more relevant than family share. These structural trends reveal that agricultural labor markets work in different ways at territorial level, and that these differences should be taken into account in the evaluation of policy effects on employment.

In contrast to area shares (in terms of Utilized Agricultural Area, UAA) and GAP, about 60% of total CAP Pillars 1 and 2 payments in 2010 went to Belt and Intermediate Areas, while 23% went to Peripheral Areas, where the share of total CAP expenditures represents more than one-third of the value of agricultural production.

Table 8.1. Main agricultural diversities between territorial socio-economic systems in Italy.

	Utilized agricultural area 2010 (hectares)			Gross agricultural production 2010				Change in agricultural employment 1981–2011	CAP subsidies/ GAP 2010
Type of area	Area ('000 ha)	(%)	Change (%) 1982–2010	Million (€)	(%)	Per UAA (€)	Per farm unit (€)	(%)	(%)
Urban Poles	1,823	14.2	−16.8	7,936	16.0	4,353	34,256	−28.4	2.71
Belt Areas	3,999	31.1	−15.8	21,591	43.7	5,400	39,194	−43.3	2.01
Intermediate	3,537	27.5	−20.7	13,291	26.9	3,757	27,305	−46.3	2.87
Peripheral	3,497	27.2	−21.1	6,641	13.4	1,899	18,890	−52.4	4.82
Total	12,856	100	−18.8	49,459	100	3,847	30,514	−43	2.73

Source: Author's elaboration from Agricultural Census (2010), FADN, and Population Census (2010).

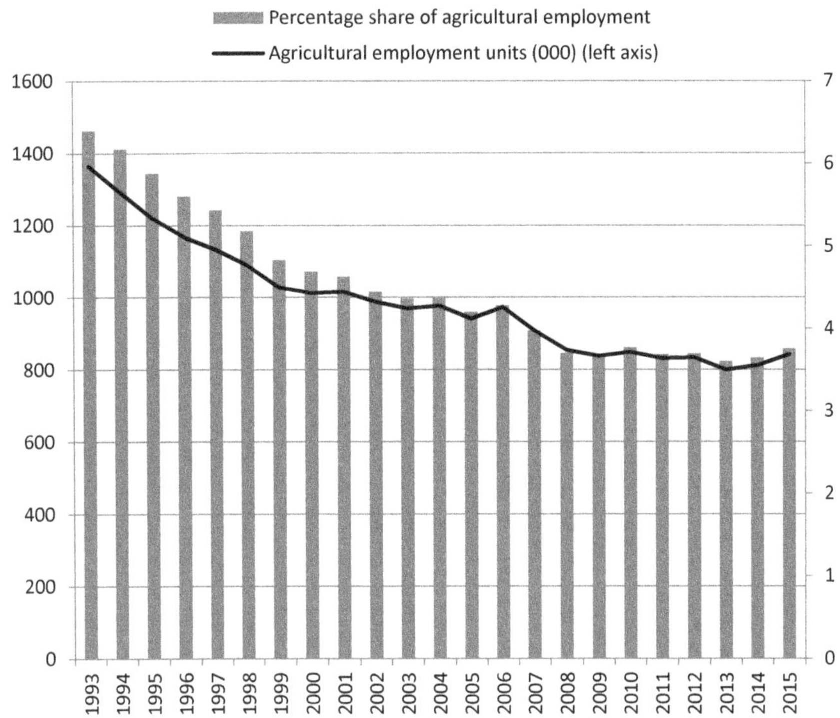

Fig. 8.1. Trends in level and relative share of agricultural employment in Italy, 1993–2015.
Source: Author's elaboration from ISTAT (National Institute of Statistics).

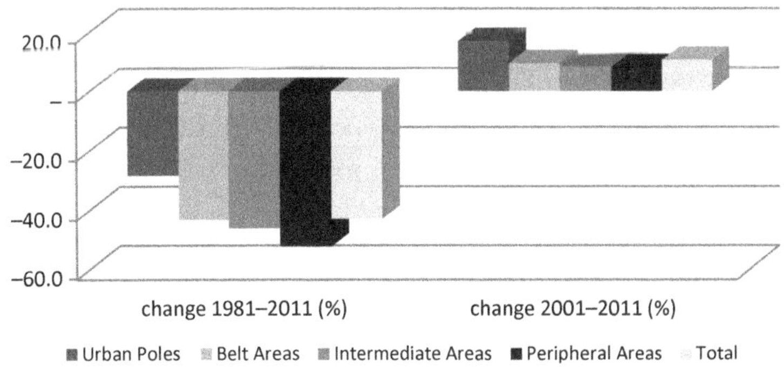

Fig. 8.2. Diversity of trends in agricultural employment by type of area in Italy.
Source: Author's elaboration from Agricultural Census Data (1981, 2001, 2011).

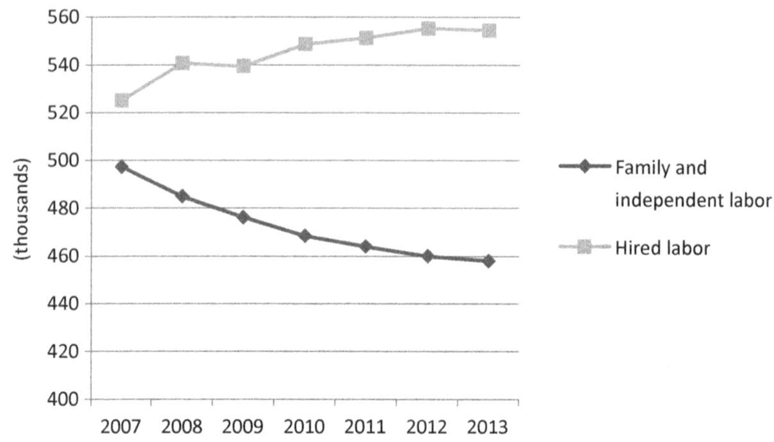

Fig. 8.3. Trends in family and hired agricultural employment in Italy, 2007–2013.
Source: Author's elaboration from ISTAT (National Institute of Statistics)

Each type of area displays a different profile of CAP expenditures (Fig. 8.4). In Urban Pole agriculture, expenditures for rural development measures play an important role, notably Agro-Environmental Measures (AEMs) and farm and agro-industrial investments. In Belt Areas, the Single-Farm Payment (SFP) is the key measure, while farm investment supports play a relatively minor role. In Intermediate and Peripheral Areas, CAP support is almost equally distributed between SFPs and rural development measures. Two critical issues emerge from the expenditure profile in the Peripheral Areas. First, most of the rural development support comes from AEMs and compensatory allowances in LFAs, while farm investment support is lower than in other areas. Second, support for rural diversification, which according to rural development programs is expected to be important, does not differ from the national average (Fig. 8.4).

8.3 The Econometric Model and its Results

The CAP's impact on agricultural employment was evaluated through an econometric model which tries to explain farm labor use in the year 2014 as dependent on two groups of variables: (a) farm structure and socio-economic context (UAA, land productivity, per capita income and immigration); (b) types of CAP expenditures (SFPs, coupled payments, LFA

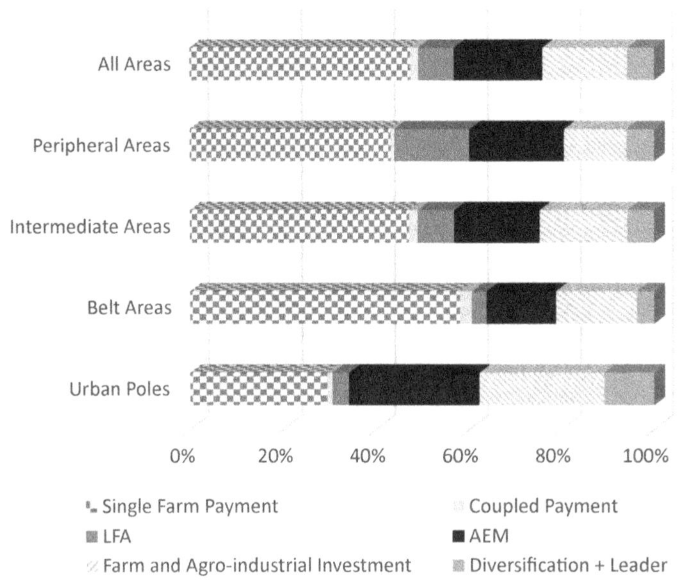

Fig. 8.4. Percentage distribution of the CAP support by each type of socio-economic areas in Italy, 2007–2013.

Source: Author's elaboration from data of the National Payment Agency (AGEA).

and other natural handicaps payments, agro-environmental and Natura 2000 payments, farm and agro-industry investments,[a] and farm diversification and quality of life in rural areas investments[b]).[c] Data used in the model were collected at the Local Administrative Unit (LAU2) level (the municipality) for the period 2007–2013.

Tables 8.2 and 8.3 show the results of the model estimated at national level and in each type of area and also the average elasticity coefficients.[d]

---

[a] Investments in farms and agro-industries include not only investments in physical assets, but also setting up of young farmers, training and advisory services, processing and marketing, rural infrastructures (rural roads, water, electricity, broad band provision, etc.), and non-productive investments (e.g. stone walls, land reclamation, etc.).

[b] Diversification and quality of life include non-agricultural activities, small-scale infrastructures and services for rural populations, rural tourism, small- and medium-sized enterprises in craft and manufacturing sector, and all investments within the LEADER approach.

[c] Similar work has been undertaken by the World Bank [2018].

[d] Elasticity coefficients measure the % change in farm labor in response to a 1% of change in each independent variable.

Table 8.2. Results from the regression model.

Dependent variable: Total annual work units, 2014	Regression coefficients			
	Typology of areas			
Independent variables	All areas	Urban poles and belt areas	Intermediate areas	Peripheral and ultra-peripheral areas
Constant	2.707**	–9.226	1.768	2.724
Structural and context variables:				
Utilized agricultural area (2010)	0.616***	0.724***	0.542***	0.473***
Farm land production/ha (2010)	0.598***	0.728***	0.573***	0.470***
Per capita available income (2009)	–0.815***	0.058	–0.586**	–0.693**
Immigrants (average 2001–2010)	0.167***	0.176***	0.083***	0.083*
Policy variables/ha, (2007–2013):				
Coupled payments (Art. 68)	–0.077*	–0.307***	–0.341***	–0.478***
Direct payments	–0.110***	0.206**	–0.215***	–0.069
Agro-environmental payments	–0.037	–0.045	0.040	0.235**
Less-favored area payments	0.058***	0.303***	–0.081**	–0.092
Investment in agriculture	0.067**	0.109*	0.217***	0.245*
Investment in rural diversification	0.072***	–0.075	0.088**	0.039
No. of observations	8057	3888	4158	1812
Goodness of fit (adjusted *R*-squared)	0.792	0.660	0.580	0.550
F-test	3066***	741.6***	577.7***	220.4***

Note: ***, **, *values statistically significant at the 1%, 5% and 10% levels, respectively.

Source: Author's calculations.

Table 8.3. Selected elasticity coefficients from the regression model.

Type of CAP instrument (2007–2013)	All areas	Urban poles and belt areas	Intermediate areas	Peripheral and ultra-peripheral areas
Coupled payments/ha	−0.02	−0.05	−0.07	−0.10
Single-farm payments/ha	−0.77	1.25	−1.67	
Agro-environmental payments/ha				0.30
LFAs payments/ha	0.04	0.09	−0.09	
Investment in agriculture/ha	0.18	0.29	0.62	0.67
Investment in rural diversification/ha	0.07		0.13	

Source: Author's calculations.

In general, the statistical results are quite good: most of the coefficients are statistically significant, and the overall explanatory power is high (about 80% of the total variance).

The results suggest that structural and context variables contribute to changes in farm employment more than policy measures. Immigration appeared to provide opportunities for using less expensive labor and/or replacing family labor that could be allocated to more profitable non-farm employment in the local area or elsewhere. Better-paid off-farm jobs also reduced the labor force available for farming.

Focusing on policy measures, Pillar 1 measures (SFPs and payments coupled to farm production) appear to affect farm employment negatively in most areas, perhaps due to the introduction of activities requiring lower labor input, or to risk-averse behavior by farmers who benefit from SFPs, thus tending to limit farm development. This result is consistent with other studies [EP, 2016a; Dupraz and Latruffe, 2015; Kaditi, 2013]. The only exception to this can be found in Urban Poles and Belt Areas, where the average elasticity of SFP is quite high (Table 8.3), probably due to the high productivity of the agricultural resources of these areas and their closeness to rich urban markets, both factors keeping the intensity of use of labor at high levels.

The Pillar 2 measures of the RDP all show positive effects, but not always statistically significant ones. These RDP effects differ according

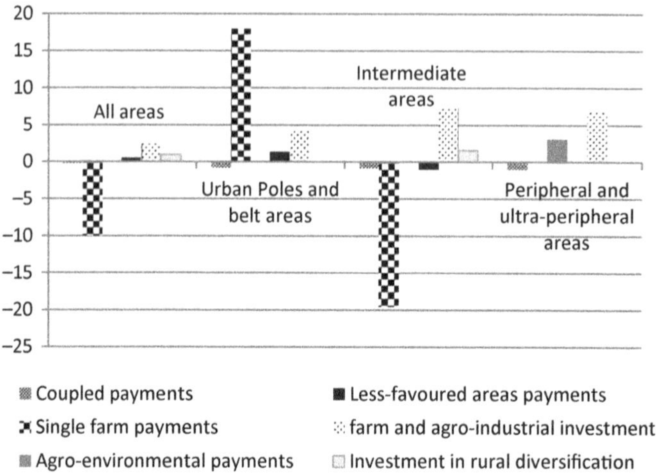

Fig. 8.5. Employment net effects in each type of areas (no. of working units per municipality).
Source: Author's calculations.

to the type of measure: farm and agro-industrial investment support generates higher employment effects than AEM and LFA. In some cases, investment in rural diversification also contributes to farm employment. Farm and agro-industrial investment improve farm competitiveness and labor growth, instead of facilitating labor substitution through technological development, as some studies seem to suggest happens in other countries.

Figure 8.5 shows specific effects of single CAP measures in the diverse territorial settings. The employment effects of farm investment support increase from Belt Areas to Intermediate and Peripheral Areas, while for rural diversification the employment effects are generally low, and visible only in Intermediate Areas. The diversity of policy impact at territorial level can be explained by three main factors: (a) in several RDP, approval of funding is conditional on proof of achieving an employment target; (b) the presence of idle/underutilized human resources in agriculture is higher in the less developed areas (Intermediate and Peripheral); (c) the intensity of public expenditure per hectare is usually higher in some areas than elsewhere. The first and second factors may explain the highest employment effects of farm and agro-industrial investment in Intermediate and Peripheral Areas, while the third factor explains why employment effects of rural diversification are higher in Intermediate Areas than elsewhere. It is worth noticing that AEM payments generate employment effects only in Peripheral Areas, where more sustainable agricultural practices are more in line with the usual practices already in place in these areas. The results concerning LFA payments are unexpected; they provide positive, but very low, effects in Urban Poles and Belt Areas, and negative (but not statistically significant) effects in Intermediate and Peripheral Areas. In other words, LFA payments provide negative effects just where they are expected to influence positively the stay in agriculture of farm holders and/or family members.

8.4 Conclusions: Policy Implications

The above findings provide fresh insights into the role of the two CAP Pillars and the political impetus for changes in the EU framework of rules for these two Pillars. This is timely in the light of the recent CAP reform post-2020 Regulations published by the European Commission (DG AGRI) following its Communication on "Modernizing and Simplifying the CAP". The main policy tools of Pillar 1 appear — in this study — to have unwelcome effects on agricultural employment in most areas. Such measures were not specifically designed to create jobs, but to ensure the production of food and socio-environmentally sustainable land management practices. It must be pointed out that there is a stream of literature emphasizing the role of Pillar 1 [Mattas and Loizou, 2018] in maintaining several farm activities that otherwise would be reduced or even cease, with devastating consequences on the farm employment.

On the other hand, Pillar 2 rural development measures display positive employment effects. However, the intensity of these effects is strongly related to the type of area: farm and agro-industrial investment support has higher impact in areas where there is still a great amount of idle/underutilized human resources (the less developed areas). The net effects of the LFA payments are negligible or even negative. Thus, given the objective of creating jobs in more Peripheral Areas, where job opportunities are lower than elsewhere, policymakers should increase the role of those measures supporting investment in farm-based and rural diversification. This confirms the "new rural paradigm" concept [OECD, 2006] which emphasizes that interventions should be investment-based rather than subsidy-based. Moreover, more targeted job-creation tools are likely to produce new jobs at lower cost than current Pillar 1 measures [EP, 2016b]. Interventions should help farmers and local communities to overcome specific barriers and constraints to improve their productivity [Matthews, 2017], prioritizing "smart" support measures such as innovation and knowledge transfer, better organization within the supply chain [Mantino and Forcina, 2018], improved infrastructures including high-quality broadband provision, new facilities in renewable energy, etc. These kinds of policy support will be possible in the period after 2020, but they will be strongly dependent on the amount of financial resources available in the Strategic CAP Plans[e] once the funds are allocated to Pillar 1 measures.

The implications are not limited to the composition of policy instruments, but also concern the approach of policy intervention. This requires a more territorially targeted and differentiated approach and, consequently, the possibility to design at sub-regional level the appropriate CAP mix. In Peripheral Areas, for example, Pillar 1 and LFA payments currently altogether account for more than 60% of total CAP payments, while these areas need instead a high proportion of diversification support. In sum, a more flexibly applied CAP is needed, capable of addressing diverse territorial needs, and strengthened by rules of policy design and implementation more oriented toward the pursuit of territorial cohesion.

References

Dupraz, P. and Latruffe, L. (2015). Trends in family labour, hired labour and contract work on French field crop farms: The role of the common agricultural policy. *Food Policy*, 51, pp. 104–118.

European Commission, DG AGRI (2010). Europeans, Agriculture and the Common Agricultural Policy, Special Eurobarometer 336. http://ec.europa.eu/public_opinion/archives/ebs/ebs_294_en.pdf (accessed 8 October 2018).

[e]These plans are to be drawn up by Member States (and approved by the European Commission) in order to show how they will apply the CAP after 2020.

European Parliament (EP), Committee on Agriculture and Rural Development (2010). On the Future of the Common Agricultural Policy After 2013, document EP 439.972. http://www.europarl.europa.eu/sides/getDoc.do?type=REPORT&reference=A7-2010-0204&language=EN (accessed 8 October 2018).

European Parliament, Directorate-General for Internal Policies, Policy Department B-Structural and Cohesion Policies (2016a). The Role of the EU's Common Agricultural Policy in Creating Rural Jobs, European Union. http://www.europarl.europa.eu/RegData/etudes/STUD/2016/573418/IPOL_STU(2016)573418_EN.pdf (accessed 8 October 2018).

European Parliament, Directorate-General for Internal Policies, Policy Department B-Structural and Cohesion Policies (2016b). CAP Reform Post 2020 — Challenges in Agriculture, Workshop Documentation, European Union. http://www.europarl.europa.eu/RegData/etudes/STUD/2016/585898/IPOL_STU(2016)585898_EN.pdf (accessed 8 October 2018).

Kaditi, E. A. (2013). The Impact of CAP Reforms on Farm Labour Structure, Factor Markets Project Working Paper No. 63, 245123-FP7-KBBE-2009-3. https://www.ceps.eu/system/files/FM%20WP%20No%2063%20Impact%20of%20CAP%20Reforms_Edited.pdf (accessed 8 October 2018).

Lucatelli, S. (2013). *A Strategy for 'Inner Areas' in Italy*, presentation at OECD Conference, Bologna, 23 October. http://www.oecd.org/cfe/regional-policy/1.2%20Promoting%20Growth.pdf (accessed 8 October 2018).

Mantino, F. (2017). Employment effects of the CAP in Italian agriculture: Territorial diversity and policy effectiveness, *EuroChoices* 16(3), pp. 12–16.

Mantino, F. and Forcina, B. (2018). Market, Policies and local governance as drivers of environmental public benefits: The case of the localised processed tomato in Northern Italy. *Agriculture*, 8, p. 34.

Mattas, K. and Loizou, E. (2017). The CAP as a job stabiliser. *EuroChoices* 16(3), pp. 23–26.

Matthews, A. (2017). How can the CAP promote rural jobs? *EuroChoices* 16(3), pp. 18–21.

Ministry of Economic Development (2014). A Strategy for Inner Areas in Italy: Definition, Objectives, Tools and Governance, Materiali UVAL. http://www.agenziacoesione.gov.it/opencms/export/sites/dps/it/documentazione/servizi/materiali_uval/Documenti/MUVAL_31_Aree_interne_ENG.pdf (accessed 8 October 2018).

Nordin, M. (2014). Does the decoupling reform affect agricultural employment in Sweden? Evidence from an exogenous change. *Journal of Agricultural Economics*, 65(3), pp. 616–636.

OECD (2006). *The New Rural Paradigm: Policies and Governance*, OECD Publishing, Paris.

Petrick, M. and Zier, P. (2012a). Common Agricultural Policy Effects on Dynamic Labour Use in Agriculture, SiAg-Working Paper 12. http://edoc.hu-berlin.de/series/siag-working-paper/2012-12/PDF/12.pdf (accessed 8 October 2018).

Petrick, M. and Zier, P. (2012b). Common agricultural policy effects on dynamic labour use in agriculture, *Food Policy*, 37, pp. 671–678.

Schuh, B., Gorny H., Kaucic, J., Kirchmayr-Novak, S., Vigani, M., Powell, J. and Hawketts, E. (2016). Research for Agri Committee — The Role of the EU's Common Agricultural Policy in Creating Rural Jobs, IP/B/AGRI/IC/2015_158, Brussels: European Parliament, Directorate General for Internal Policies.

World Bank (2018). Thinking CAP. Supporting Agricultural Jobs and Incomes in the EU, EU Regular Economic Report 4, World Bank Report on the European Union, Washington DC.

Chapter 9

Employment Effects of CAP Payments in the UK Non-Farm Economy

Marian Rizov*, Sophia M. Davidova† and Alastair Bailey†

*University of Lincoln, Brayford Pool, Lincoln, UK
† School of Economics, University of Kent, Canterbury, UK
*mrizov@lincoln.ac.uk

The effects of the Common Agricultural Policy (CAP) payments on indirectly generated non-farm jobs in small- and medium-sized enterprises (SMEs) are central to job creation. This chapter examines whether there are differences in these effects according to business location (rural or urban), the agricultural supply chain, and according to CAP pillars, using both static and dynamic models of employment. The results suggest positive net spillovers of CAP payments to non-farm employment. Although their magnitudes are small, they are economically significant. In general, Pillar 1 has a stronger positive employment effect than Pillar 2, but Pillar 2 payments have a stronger positive effect per Euro spent in rural areas and within the agricultural supply chain.

9.1 Introduction

This chapter investigates the contribution of the EU's Common Agricultural Policy (CAP) payments to non-farm sector employment in both rural and urban areas in the United Kingdom (UK) through its direct and indirect effects on agriculture's upstream and downstream industries, and the economic diversification of rural areas. In recent years, given the difficult recovery from the 2008 financial crisis, the provision of employment is of primary interest to policymakers and to millions of UK citizens. Additionally, whatever the UK Brexit package[a] may be, it is almost certain that the ways in which agriculture is supported will change.

For decades, CAP payments have implicitly maintained the level of agricultural employment, or at least slowed down its decline under the pressures of technical and structural change. In the face of these forces, the CAP could hardly have further substantial impact in the direction of job creation or even job maintenance in primary agriculture, although the need to increase the CAP's contribution to employment has been emphasized on many occasions by the European Commission and European Parliament, and was included as one of the three objectives of rural development support for 2014–2020 [Art. 4, Regulation (EU) No. 1305/2013]. However, in reality, the CAP contributions to employment may have been more important than they appear at first glance due to possible inter-industry spillovers on non-farm employment which are often not accounted for.

Against this backdrop, the objective of this chapter is to estimate the effect of CAP payments on indirectly generated non-farm jobs. In particular, the study focuses on three key questions: (i) whether CAP payments are positively associated with non-farm employment; (ii) whether there are differences in the effect according to business location (rural or urban) and within agricultural supply chain; and (iii) whether Pillar 1 direct payments and Pillar 2 rural development payments have different employment effects.

A report [EP, 2016] for the European Parliament Committee on Agriculture and Rural Development (COMAGRI) reviewed 53 studies concerning the role of CAP in the creation of rural jobs. The structured literature review is discussed in detail in Chapter 7. Of these studies, 16 reported a negative effect on employment in agriculture, nine a positive one, eight a mixed effect, depending on farm structure and rural economy,

---

[a] At time of writing, Brexit is the short portmanteau term for British exit from the European Union, as voted for in a UK referendum in June 2016, and due to take place on 29 March 2019.

and six found no effect. However, all these studies either focused on agriculture and rural jobs, or on labor migration out of agriculture. More recently, Blomquist and Nordin [2017] examined the CAP's impact on regional employment beyond agriculture in Sweden and estimated the cost per job as equal to $26,000. Earlier, Petrick and Zier [2012] found higher costs (€50,000 per job) in East Germany.

9.2 The Evolution of CAP Subsidies and the Implications for Employment

The CAP Health Check of 2008 did not change the fundamental decisions taken in the 2003 reforms, i.e. the introduction of a decoupled (from production) Single-Farm Payment (SFP) to farmers, conditional on environmental and other cross-compliance requirements, and keeping the land in Good Agricultural and Environmental Conditions (GAEC), as the main feature of Pillar 1, but it decreased the remaining coupled payments, increased modulation of funds from Pillar 1 to Pillar 2, and removed arable land set aside. It also provided the EU Member States (MSs) with flexible possibilities (the so-called Article 68 measures) to assist subsectors of agriculture with special problems.

SFPs may affect non-agricultural employment through two main channels, both of which would lead to expansion in the demand faced by non-farm sector firms: its "coupled" effect on farm investments and output levels and its "decoupled" effect on household consumption. In the first, SFPs may be invested in farm production and thus, increase or maintain employment in agriculture and in up- and downstream industries. They may also have wealth and insurance effects that may increase the input use and output levels, and affect investment decisions as farmers save and invest more, as well as increase the liquidity of credit-constrained households. Decoupled income support to farmers can also affect income-leisure and labor allocation decisions, as well as the consumption of the farm household. Farm household income/expenditure effects are generated mainly in rural areas but may or may not correlate with increased employment in those areas, taking into account purchases at a distance and services provided from urban areas. Moreover, direct payments are well known to "leak" out in higher land rents (the price of the land input), paid to landowners who may not live in the locality. A consequence of the appropriation of a high share of payments by landowners means that the local multiplier effect of CAP Pillar 1 payments is likely to be lower in those areas where there is a high proportion of rented land, as higher rents go to landowners who do not always live in the same locality. However, while the presence of leakages is an important consideration, which generally applies to farmers' purchasing power and expenditure, the analytical framework used in this chapter is built on the idea of economywide spillovers and the data employed capture economywide effects.

Rural development measures in Pillar 2 can affect non-farm employment through a wide range of channels. Rizov [2004, 2005] studied the CAP's effect on the organization and performance of rural communities since the introduction of Pillar 2 in 1999, e.g. through diversification of economic activities. However, such measures may create employment both within the local rural community and beyond, in the urban areas, thus emphasizing the general interdependency of rural and urban areas. Similar to Pillar 1, first-order effects are due to the flow of funds into some rural households which increases their purchasing power. Additionally, measures for investments in physical assets — farm modernization, infrastructure, energy-saving technologies — may influence employment in research and development, construction, technical services, etc. Business start-up aid for young farmers and for non-farm enterprises, as well as village renewal support, can have a direct effect on employment in rural and surrounding urban areas. Support to enhance biodiversity and the provision of higher-value ecosystem services may help to create non-farm jobs in rural tourism and associated services. Policy developments within the food system, e.g. short food chains, organic box trade and traceability, can produce employment growth along the entire agri-food supply chain.

However, the form and the level of CAP payments vary across the UK. Table 9.1 presents some indicators that exemplify the striking differences in agricultural sectors across its four constituent countries (England, Northern Ireland, Scotland and Wales).

Table 9.2 presents the CAP payments by Pillar in the UK and the constituent countries since 2010 — the first year available which falls within the period of analysis in this paper. The constituent countries

Table 9.1. Indicators of UK farming by constituent country, 2013.

Indicators	England	Northern Ireland	Scotland	Wales
Total agricultural area (million ha)	9.5	1.0	6.2	1.7
Number of farms ('000)	101	24.5	52.7	42.3
Average farm size (ha)	90	41	106	37
Crops/grass/rough grazing (percentage of total agric. area)	40	5	10	5
Grass (percentage of total agric. area)	44	78	24	68
Rough grazing (percentage of total agric. area)	10	17	66	27
Designated less favored area (%)	17	70	85	81
Gross output/farm (£'000)	189.3	78.4	59.6	26.1
Gross output/ha (£)	2016	1925	507	879
Net farm income (£'000)	34	13	21	17

Source: Allen *et al.* [2014].

implemented SFPs differently: Scotland and Wales introduced the SFP on a historical basis, England opted for a dynamic hybrid version, and Northern Ireland for a static hybrid one.

9.3 Theoretical Framework: A Firm Employment Function

The theoretical framework employed in the analysis includes the following:

- Smolny's [1998] monopolistic competition model with delays in adjustment in output price, employment, and capacity.
- As regards the timing of effects, only output is considered endogenous in the short run, while employment and prices adjust in the medium run, due to delays arising from contractual conditions and various types of uncertainty. Production capacities and technologies react only in the long run.

Table 9.2. CAP payments by funding stream and constituent country, € million.*

	2010	2011	2012	2013	2014
UK Total	*4337*	*4327*	*4433*	*4417*	*4299*
Pillar 1	3424	3309	3348	3326	3234
of which: DP	3325	3304	3290	3285	3195
CMO	99	5	58	41	39
Pillar 2**	913	1018	1085	1091	1065
of which EAFRD	512	653	742	752	798
England Total	*2761*	*2696*	*2777*	*2792*	*2714*
Pillar 1	2199	2099	2146	2126	2048
of which: DP	2100	2094	2088	2085	2009
CMO	99	5	58	41	39
Pillar 2**	562	597	631	666	666
of which EAFRD	348	448	470	532	563
Wales Total	*413*	*417*	*426*	*406*	*413*
Pillar 1 DP	316	312	309	309	301
Pillar 2**	97	105	117	97	112
of which EAFRD	38	45	54	48	54
Scotland Total	*779*	*826*	*840*	*819*	*757*
Pillar 1 DP	589	583	584	583	566
Pillar 2**	190	243	256	236	191
of which EAFRD	92	123	167	113	119
Northern Ireland Total	*384*	*388*	*390*	*400*	*415*
Pillar 1 DP	320	315	309	308	319
Pillar 2**	64	73	81	92	96
of which EAFRD	34	37	51	59	62

Notes: DP — Direct Payments (aka SFP); CMO — Common Market Organization; EAFRD — European Agricultural Fund for Rural Development. *Annual data is for the EU financial year 16 October–15 October. **The difference between the total Pillar 2 and the amount received from EAFRD indicates the national cofinancing.
Source: DEFRA [2015].

- Demand for the firm's product is assumed dependent on prices and on other factors such as aggregate industry demand and its shifters induced by market factors or policies, as well as CAP expenditures (which may affect volatility as well as level).
- Short-run firm supply is determined by capital and labor as inputs, with output determined as the minimum of supply and demand.
- In the medium term, employment may be determined by capacity constraints, with price rather than employment adjusting. However, in the more likely case, employment and price are jointly determined.

Demand shifts due to the spillovers and diversification effect of CAP payments lead to growth in employment. Uncertainty reduces optimal employment and increases the price through the costs of underutilization of employment. However, as argued earlier, if CAP payments reduce uncertainty, then there will be less underutilization of labor, and employment would rise in relative terms.

9.4 Data and Estimation Strategy

Firm (company) data for over 2 million firms over the period 2008–2014 was extracted from the Financial Analysis Made Easy (FAME) dataset of Bureau van Dijk and combined with detailed subsidy data extracted from the CAP Payments database of the UK Department of Environment, Food, and Rural Affairs (DEFRA). Firm data coverage compared with national statistics is very good as regards sales (89%) and employment (90%). The analysis focuses on the effect on employment in small- and medium-sized enterprises (SMEs), defined as businesses with fewer than 250 employees, and typical of most rural businesses. In 2013, SMEs represented over 99% of all private-sector businesses in the UK and accounted for 59.3% of private-sector employment and for 48.1% of private-sector turnover [Department for Business Innovation and Skills, 2013]. The period covered ranges from 2008, the year of the European Commission's CAP Health Check, to 2014, the first transitional year of the "new" CAP for the period 2014–2020.

The CAP payment information covers four years — 2008, 2010, 2012 and 2014 — and comprises the amount of total payments and its three components: Common Market Organization (CMO) and Direct Payments (DPs) made under CAP's Pillar 1, and rural development payments made under Pillar 2.

The industry sectors in the FAME dataset are identified on the basis of the 2007 UK Standard Industrial Classification (SIC) at the two- or four-digit level. All nominal monetary variables were deflated to real values using appropriate indices. The input–output (I–O) shares of the agriculture, forestry and fishing sector in all other sectors were obtained from symmetric OECD I–O tables, averaged over the 2005–2010 period, and weights were used to represent inclusion or otherwise in the agricultural supply chain, including the manufacturing of inputs to agriculture (e.g. fertilizers, pesticides and other agrochemical products; machinery for agriculture, forestry and for food processing; renting or leasing of agricultural machinery and equipment) and industries downstream encompassing food processing and wholesale of agricultural raw materials and live animals.

Definition of variables and descriptive statistics calculated from the estimated sample of SMEs are reported in Table 9.3, and average SME characteristics by rural and urban locations in Table 9.4. Generally, there are no important differences in summary statistics between rural and urban firms, but rural SMEs are slightly larger as measured by employment and smaller in assets, and they face smaller local market demand. The cost of employees (and their wages) also is lower in rural SMEs. In rural areas, more CAP payments are received than in the urban areas as exemplified by the total subsidy and the higher share of direct payments. The location-based (postal district) CAP payments measure confounds the amount of payments received by individual farms with the size of the farm sector at the location considered; nevertheless, such measure of intensity of the CAP payments suffices for our analytical purposes.

9.5 Results

The estimation results from the SME sample, for the static and dynamic models, are presented in Tables 9.5 and 9.6. CAP payments have a statistically significant effect in both models. While the magnitudes of the coefficients appear small, they are of economic significance. The elasticity of

Table 9.3. Definition of variables and summary statistics.

Variable	Definition	Mean (S.D.)
Employment	Number of full-time equivalent firm workers, log	3.07 (1.50)
Market demand	Annual 2-digit SIC by TTWA aggregated demand in £'000, log	13.83 (3.41)
Demand variance	Firm revenue deviation from 2-digit SIC geometric mean	0.99 (2.11)
Cost per employee	Annual firm wage bill per FTE worker in £'000, log	2.99 (1.24)
Firm size	Value of firm total assets in £'000, log	7.18 (2.60)
Firm age	Firm age in years	17.98 (17.93)
Total subsidy	Value of total CAP subsidies (Pillars 1 and 2) at 4-digit postcode district in £'000, log	8.78 (1.79)
CMO share	Share of common market organization (CMO) subsidy, Pillar 1	0.04 (0.11)
DP share	Share of direct payments (DP) aka SFP, Pillar 1	0.67 (0.41)
Pillar 1 share	Share of Pillar 1 (CMO + DP)	0.71 (0.39)
Pillar 2 share	Share of rural development payments (RD)	0.29 (0.39)
Manufacturing	Dummy for aggregate manufacturing industries	0.12 (0.33)
Construction	Dummy for construction and utilities industries	0.09 (0.28)
Services	Dummy for aggregate service industries	0.79 (0.41)
Rural area	Dummy for rural areas according to the DEFRA (wider) definition of rurality	0.17 (0.38)
Ag. supply chain	Dummy for 4-digit SIC industries comprising the agricultural supply chain	0.02 (0.12)

Notes: Total number of observations: 190,348 for 2008, 2010, 2012 and 2014.
Source: Authors' calculations.

employment with respect to total CAP payments is 0.014 (Table 9.5, column (1)), which means that completely removing the CAP payments in the UK would result in a 1.4% drop in employment in non-farm SMEs from the current level, *ceteris paribus*, equivalent to about 220,000 jobs.

In Table 9.5, column (2), total CAP payments are decomposed into Pillar 1 and Pillar 2, which show different effect magnitudes. The contribution

Table 9.4. Summary statistics for rural and urban samples of SMEs.

Variable	Rural mean (S.D.)	Urban mean (S.D.)
Employment	3.09 (1.55)	3.06 (1.49)
Employment growth	0.01 (0.20)	0.01 (0.23)
Market demand	11.84 (3.40)	14.24 (3.26)
Demand variance	0.81 (2.06)	1.03 (2.12)
Cost per employee	2.82 (1.21)	3.03 (1.24)
Firm size	7.12 (2.61)	7.19 (2.59)
Firm age	18.65 (17.97)	17.85 (17.92)
Total subsidy	9.08 (1.79)	8.71 (1.78)
CMO share	0.02 (0.09)	0.04 (0.12)
DP share	0.76 (0.34)	0.66 (0.42)
Pillar 1 share	0.78 (0.33)	0.70 (0.40)
RD share	0.22 (0.33)	0.30 (0.40)
Manufacturing	0.16 (0.36)	0.12 (0.32)
Construction	0.10 (0.30)	0.08 (0.28)
Services	0.74 (0.44)	0.80 (0.40)
Ag. supply chain	0.03 (0.17)	0.01 (0.11)
Number of observations	32,788	157,560

Source: Authors' calculations.

of Pillar 1 to non-farm employment is 1.0% or 150,000 jobs, and Pillar 2 contributes 0.5% or around 70,000 non-farm jobs. In column (3), where the CAP payments are treated as endogenous and instrumented with the share of arable land, the results remain similar to the ones discussed previously.

In the dynamic models (Table 9.6), short-run and long-run effects could be distinguished. The total short-run effect of CAP payments is 0.9%, while the long-run effect is about 1.4%, similar to the static model estimate. The effects of Pillars 1 and 2 are estimated as 0.6% and 0.3%, respectively, generally preserving the relative importance of the two pillars from the static model analysis. Importantly, the static and dynamic analyses seem to produce comparable and consistent results. The finding that Pillar 1 has a stronger impact on employment than Pillar 2 suggests

Table 9.5. Regression results for the full SME sample, static specifications.

Dependent variable	Log of employment, ln(empl)		
Explanatory variables	(1)	(2)	(3)
Total subsidy	0.014** (0.002)	—	—
Total subsidy (instrumented)	—	—	0.018** (0.004)
Pillar 1 share	0.023** (0.006)	—	0.024** (0.006)
Pillar 1 subsidy	—	0.010** (0.001)	—
Pillar 2 subsidy	—	0.005** (0.001)	—
Market demand	0.105** (0.007)	0.105** (0.007)	0.105** (0.007)
Demand variance	−0.183** (0.032)	−0.183** (0.033)	−0.184** (0.033)
Cost per employee	−0.226** (0.085)	−0.228** (0.088)	−0.221** (0.090)
Firm size	0.088** (0.014)	0.087** (0.014)	0.087** (0.015)
Firm age	0.017** (0.002)	0.017** (0.002)	0.017** (0.002)
Rural area	0.114** (0.014)	0.111** (0.013)	0.110** (0.014)
Ag. supply chain	0.248** (0.067)	0.248** (0.067)	0.248** (0.067)
2010	−0.111** (0.007)	−0.110** (0.008)	−0.110** (0.007)
2012	−0.151** (0.010)	−0.154** (0.009)	−0.164** (0.009)
2014	−0.171** (0.012)	−0.170** (0.012)	−0.169** (0.012)
Number of observations	190,348	190,348	190,348
Number of instruments	45	45	45
AR(1), p-value	0.01	0.01	0.02
AR(2), p-value	0.63	0.52	0.43
Hansen J, p-value	0.36	0.30	0.28

Notes: Robust standard errors are reported in parentheses; level of significance **1%, *5%. A set of 1-digit SIC industry dummies with reference category food processing is included in all regressions.
Source: Authors' calculations.

Table 9.6. Regression results for the full SME sample, dynamic specifications.

Dependent variable	Log of employment, ln(empl)		
Explanatory variables	(1)	(2)	(3)
Lagged ln(empl)	0.350**	0.351**	0.350**
	(0.013)	(0.013)	(0.013)
Total subsidy	0.009**	—	—
	(0.001)		
Total subsidy (instrumented)	—	—	0.012**
			(0.002)
Pillar 1 share	0.020**	—	0.022**
	(0.003)		(0.003)
Pillar 1 subsidy	—	0.006**	—
		(0.000)	
Pillar 2 subsidy	—	0.003**	—
		(0.000)	
Market demand	0.084**	0.085**	0.085**
	(0.006)	(0.007)	(0.006)
Demand variance	−0.277**	−0.281**	−0.289**
	(0.017)	(0.018)	(0.017)
Cost per employee	−0.180**	−0.180**	−0.179**
	(0.051)	(0.050)	(0.050)
Firm size	0.216**	0.215**	0.217**
	(0.026)	(0.027)	(0.027)
Firm age	0.019**	0.019**	0.018**
	(0.005)	(0.005)	(0.005)
Rural area	0.051**	0.050**	0.048**
	(0.011)	(0.012)	(0.012)
Ag. supply chain	0.031	0.029	0.028
	(0.017)	(0.017)	(0.016)
2010	−0.069**	−0.068**	−0.068**
	(0.006)	(0.006)	(0.006)
2012	−0.068**	−0.074**	−0.076**
	(0.012)	(0.011)	(0.012)
2014	−0.076**	−0.074**	−0.074**
	(0.013)	(0.013)	(0.013)
Number of observations	174,731	174,731	174,731
Number of instruments	48	48	48
AR(1), *p*-value	0.00	0.00	0.00
AR(2), *p*-value	0.15	0.14	0.13
Hansen J, *p*-value	0.45	0.46	0.45

Notes: Robust standard errors are reported in parentheses; level of significance **1%, *5%. A set of 1-digit SIC industry dummies with reference category food processing is included in all regressions.
Source: Authors' calculations.

that, although in theory decoupled from farm output, Pillar 1 payments do in fact affect the supply and demand linkages between farms and firms. Furthermore, the Pillar 1 and Pillar 2 payments appear to have heterogeneous effects on non-farm employment; these deserve further investigation.

Estimation of interaction terms suggests that the long-run impact of CAP payments on employment is relatively concentrated in the rural SMEs and within the agricultural supply chain, with the CAP payments bringing extra employment mostly in rural areas relative to urban areas. Regarding the agricultural supply chain employment, the interaction term suggests that again CAP payments play a very important role for job creation in the industries up- and downstream of agriculture, with the effect of Pillar 1 remaining larger than Pillar 2.

Considering that rural SMEs employed over 2 million people in 2015 [ONS, 2015], completely removing the CAP payments *ceteris paribus* would lead to losing around 45,000 rural jobs as the negative impact on the rural labor market would be economically (and socially) significant. Interestingly, the contribution of Pillar 2 to rural employment is higher (1.2%) than that of Pillar 1 (1.0%). Considering that the Pillar 2 payments are just under a half of the Pillar 1 payments, the difference is even more pronounced per Euro spent.

The contribution to employment in the agricultural supply chain of Pillar 1 is about 17% and of Pillar 2 about 14%. Clearly, per Euro spent, the contribution of Pillar 2 is again higher than Pillar 1. The fact that CAP payments show higher overall employment maintenance in the agricultural supply chain compared to the rest of the economy suggests that farmers' spending on production and consumption activities, along the farm supply chain, generates spillovers that are important for non-farm employment.

9.6 Conclusions

The market-distorting effects of the CAP have been subject to many criticisms by economists. However, this study has found net positive effects of CAP payments on non-farm UK employment, with relatively stronger effects per Euro spent of Pillar 2 rural development payments than Pillar 1 direct payments, especially in rural areas and within the agricultural supply chain. The magnitude of the overall estimated effect (elasticity) is

1.4%, which is relatively small but of economic significance. The UK has one of the more flexible and efficient labor markets in Europe, and one characterized by relatively low unemployment during the period of analysis. Thus, these results could be considered as toward the lower bound of CAP employment effects in the EU non-farm economy.

Under an extreme policy scenario in which the CAP payments were completely removed without compensating/countervailing measures (and neutral tax policy), the impact on UK employment would amount to about 220,000 jobs lost. Furthermore, the impact in rural areas would be more than two times stronger, in percentage terms, which equates to about 45,000 jobs lost. In the industries comprising the agricultural supply chain, the effect is also substantial, at about a 32% total reduction in employment.

The results suggest that the removal of CAP payments could have rural development implications beyond employment lost, e.g. higher rural unemployment and a possible outflow of population from rural areas. Furthermore, if the extra jobs at firm level supported by the CAP were removed, some firms might become unviable and exit in the long run.

These results should not be interpreted as an attempt to justify the role of CAP subsidies as a job creation policy across the EU because there might be other non-agricultural, labor market policies which could be more efficient in increasing or sustaining employment opportunities in non-farm enterprises. Nevertheless, a broad approach is necessary in analyzing the implications of the CAP, as its impact is felt well beyond agriculture.

References

Allen, M., Downing, E., Edwards, T., Seaton, N. and Semple, M. (2014). CAP Reform 2014–20: EU Agreement and Implementation in the UK and Ireland, RP14/56, 30 October 2014, House of Commons library, http://researchbriefings.parliament.uk/ResearchBriefing/Summary/RP14-56 (accessed 8 October 2018).

Blomquist, J. and Nordin, M. (2017). Do the CAP subsidies increase employment in Sweden? Estimating the effects of government transfers using an exogenous change in the CAP. *Regional Science and Urban Economics*, 63(C), pp. 13–24.

Department for Business Innovation and Skills (2013). *SMEs: The Key Enablers of Business Success and the Economic Rationale for Government Intervention*, BIS Analysis Paper No. 2 (December).

Department for Environment, Food & Rural Affairs (DEFRA) (2015). Agriculture in the United Kingdom 2014. https://www.gov.uk/government/statistics/agriculture-in-the-united-kingdom-2014 (accessed 7 November 2018).

European Parliament (EP) (2016). The Role of the EU's Common Agricultural Policy in Creating Rural Jobs, Agriculture and Rural Development, Research paper for AGRI Committee. http://www.europarl.europa.eu/RegData/etudes/STUD/2016/573418/IPOL_STU(2016)573418_EN.pdf (accessed 8 October 2018).

Office for National Statistics (ONS) (2015). Inter Departmental Business Register (IDBR), 2014/15, http://www.ons.gov.uk/ons/about-ons/products-and-services/idbr/index.html (accessed 8 October 2018).

Petrick, M. and Zier, P. (2012). Common agricultural policy effects on dynamic labour use in agriculture. *Food Policy*, 37(6), pp. 671–678.

Rizov, M. (2004). Rural development and welfare implications of CAP reforms. *Journal of Policy Modeling*, 26(2), pp. 209–222.

Rizov, M. (2005). Rural development under the European CAP: The role of diversity. *Social Science Journal*, 42(4), pp. 621–628.

Smolny, W. (1998). Monopolistic price setting and supply rigidities in a disequilibrium framework. *Economic Theory*, 11, pp. 157–169.

Chapter 10

US Farm Bill Policies: Impacts on Rural Economic Development

Mary Ahearn

2413 Mumford Dr., Silver Spring, MD, USA
mahearn54@aol.com

The US Farm Bill is organized as a collection of titles that cover policies on a common topic, including rural development, and has been renewed approximately every five years since 1933. The rural development portion of the bill provides for the US Department of Agriculture's rural development programs: Rural Utilities, Rural Housing and Rural Business-Cooperative services. Most programs administered by USDA's Rural Development mission area are funded through annual, discretionary appropriations, and the Farm Bill and other acts provide the authority for these appropriations. Rural development generally takes place at the local, usually county, level, where leaders access the programs offered through the Farm Bill and other federal, state, and private sources. The Farm Bill also provides for agricultural support: agricultural support issues garner most of the political attention during development of the bill as the current challenges facing agricultural competitiveness and farm returns are considered in detail. It is common to equate rural policy with agricultural policy, but most rural communities and rural households are not dependent on or engaged with agricultural production. Other national policies — such as health, education, and tax policies — and market and non-market forces affect rural development outcomes, in addition to Farm Bill policies.

10.1 Introduction

In the minds of many policymakers and the broad public, rural economic development is synonymous with agricultural sector development. This view is rooted in the history of the United States at a time when most rural residents were farmers or employed in other economic sectors dependent on the vast natural resources in rural America. That history also explains why the so-called "Farm Bill" includes a rural development portion and why the US Department of Agriculture was named the lead federal agency for coordinating rural policy in the Rural Development Act of 1972.

Although the US Department of Agriculture (USDA) has the responsibility for coordinating rural policy for the federal government, it is by no means responsible for most policies affecting rural America. As an example of the dispersion of rural policies across the federal government, when the current Secretary of Agriculture assembled a task force on the topic, he drew in representatives from more than 21 federal agencies, offices, and departments [USDA, 2017]. Moreover, as noted elsewhere in this volume, many other national policies, such as health, education, and tax policies, and market and non-market forces, affect rural development outcomes, besides Farm Bill policies. Although federal policies affecting rural development goals and outcomes are dispersed, the US Farm Bill is arguably the single most important piece of dedicated rural legislation. Therefore, the purpose of this chapter is to describe the policies of the Farm Bills directed at rural development, in contrast to the policies in the bill strictly addressing agricultural production issues.

10.2 Rural Development Portion of the Farm Bill in a Broader Rural Policy Context

Rural development policy as presented at the national level is often a statement of goals for a more prosperous rural America. Generally, each new administration offers a statement of the current economic conditions and trends in rural America along with a set of general goals that are consistent with the administration's overall political philosophy. The latest statement was released in October 2017 as the *Report to the President of the United States from the Taskforce on Agriculture and Rural Prosperity*

[USDA, 2017]. The general goals were organized around five key indicators: e-connectivity, quality of life, rural workforce, technological innovation, and economic development. The report also called for the establishment of a commission to oversee the recommendations and an advisory council to the commission. The strategies to address each of the general goal areas encouraged removal of regulations, further assessments of the problem, private–public partnerships, and greater high-level coordination across government agencies. Absent was a strong sense of a call for increased federal spending on current or new rural development programs.

By necessity, the practice of rural development policies is place-based and reflects the uniqueness of any one rural area. Since development takes place at the local level, in the United States this is generally the county level of government. There are 3,007 counties in the United States, and nearly two-thirds of them are classified as non-metropolitan, i.e. rural.[a]

---

[a]This is based on the Office of Management and Budget (OMB) classification, which defines non-metropolitan areas as counties that are not metropolitan counties, where metropolitan counties are defined as central counties which contain a core urban area of 50,000 or more population and outlying counties that are economically tied to the core counties. However, it should be noted that there are two major ways in which official statistics are reported, based on the definition of the US Census Bureau or the definition of the OMB [Ratcliffe, 2012]. The US Census Bureau defines rural areas as areas that are not urban, where urban is either an urbanized area of 50,000 or more people or an urban cluster of at least 2,500 (with at least 1,500 outside of institutions), but less than 50,000 people. The Census Bureau's urban areas are used as one of the building blocks in OMB's designation. Since the designation is based on county units, this means that metropolitan counties can, and often do, have parts that are as designated as rural according to the US Census Bureau. Data users who are interested in time trends should keep in mind that population and development change continuously over time and space, as population centers grow or decline. However, the designations as urban/rural or metropolitan/non-metropolitan are not updated frequently to match this continuous development. Both official designations are based primarily on the decennial Census of Population. The latest census was for 2010 and designations were announced in 2012; these designations will continue until sometime after the 2020 Census of Population. Therefore, this means that if a rural area develops and increases in population — often the rural areas with the fastest-growing economies — at some point it may be classified as urban. It is not uncommon, regardless of definition, to refer to both OMB's non-metropolitan areas and the Census's rural areas as rural areas, as is done in this chapter.

State-level and national-level programs, as well as some private programs, provide selective, piecemeal resources to counties and other local jurisdictions under a variety of access points and requirements.

Although rural development activities take place at the local level, they also take place in the context of a rural region. A variety of efforts have recognized the advantages of coordinating development activities across contiguous rural areas and across government and private program opportunities for individual communities. For example, there are regional coordination activities in largely rural and/or economically depressed areas, such as the *Appalachian Regional Commission,* which was established in 1953 and is largely federally funded. More recently, since 2009, the USDA's Rural Development mission area has financially supported the *Stronger Economies Together* program to help counties work with other jurisdictions in their region in engaging in rural development strategies and activities. At least 94 rural regions in 32 states have been engaged with this program. Another recent example of the coordination across program resources was the *Strikeforce* of the previous USDA administration, which helped more than 500 persistent-poverty areas coordinate across programs to attain local area goals. These types of collaboration achieve economies in planning and are better able to capitalize on opportunities that do not necessarily follow traditional political boundaries, and they are critical in serving the needs of low-income communities that lack effective community leadership and planning resources.

Social scientists and public administration experts often lament the fact that the United States does not have a strong, directed rural development policy. Frankly, however, the process of rural development is extremely complex and varied. What works for one community will not necessarily work for another with a differing set of capital endowments. What works at one point in time may not work at another, due to the dynamic economic environment. Moreover, there is not always a consensus on shared goals or outcomes of rural development programs. The complexity of the rural development process, with a multitude of factors at play affecting any one development outcome, also means that evaluation of rural development programs is a challenge. Rural development agencies regularly ask program participants to report their outcomes, but due to the complexities of factors affecting outcomes, such as employment impacts, there is no ideal and rigorous manner in which these evaluations are conducted.

A rich social science literature exists in the fields of domestic rural development and regional economics. This includes well-developed theories about the development process and empirical tests of those theories. It is beyond the scope of this chapter to review that literature; in addition, its lessons do not drive US rural policy development. However, the review of Isserman *et al.* [2009] (Isserman, Feser and Warren, IFW) is worth mentioning because it was specifically commissioned by the mission area whose programs are funded by the Farm Bill, that is UDSA Rural Development. IFW provide a review of the literature and an empirical analysis of a composite indicator of rural "prosperity." Their outcome indicator of prosperity was based on low poverty rates, low unemployment rates, higher educational attainment, and good housing conditions. Other theories focus on single-variable outcome indicators, such as poverty rates or unemployment, and still others focus on competitiveness or growth of a region. More recently, as inequality has increased in the country, there has been a focus on reduced income inequality as a rural development goal [Chetty *et al.*, 2014]. A major challenge exists in empirical testing of various theories of development because of the multitude of factors and the sorting of causation in the rural development process.

10.3 What is the US Farm Bill?

Each new Farm Bill has a unique, formal name and number, but the current version of the legislation at any one point in time is informally referred to as the Farm Bill. The Bill is organized as a collection of titles that cover policies on a common topic, such as dairy policy or conservation policy. The number and name of titles varies with each Farm Bill. In recent decades, the Bill has been renewed approximately every five years. The first Farm Bill became law in 1933. It was part of the sweeping legislative agenda of what is known as the New Deal, under President Franklin D. Roosevelt, to help the United States recover from the Great Depression. The first Farm Bill was a critical part of the New Deal legislative complement because fully 25% of the US population then lived on farms, compared to less than 2% today. Formally, the current legislation is the 2014 Agricultural Act, signed into law on 7 February 2014, by President Barack Obama, with an expiration date of 30 September 2018. Before any one Farm Bill expires, it is either extended or a new piece of legislation is designed. The US House of Representatives and the US Senate must both pass separate versions of a Farm Bill before agreement on a single bill is voted on and sent to the President for his or her signature.

Local economic development, other than sector-based agricultural policies, was not a focus of federal policy until the 1950s [Rasmussen, 1986; Deller and Goetz, 2009] and gained some momentum in the 1970s, including in the Farm Bill of the time. For example, an earlier 1970 Agricultural Act states that: "The highest priority must be given to the revitalization and development of rural areas." Rural development did not even merit its own portion of a Farm Bill until the Food, Agriculture, Conservation, and Trade Act of 1990. It is fair to say that rural development, aside from agriculture policy, is still not a high priority — let alone the highest priority — as measured by attention in the policy development process or by budget outlays. The highest priorities are the agricultural commodity and the nutrition portions of the Bill. In the 2014 Farm Bill, for example, the rural development portion represents only 22 out of the 356 pages [Smith, 2015].

10.4 The Role of Agriculture in Rural Development

At the time of the New Deal — when the basic structure of US current farm policies was established — rural areas were dominated by farming, and agricultural policies provided the needed support and a safety net for much of rural America. Furthermore, it was widely acknowledged that the farm population was economically disadvantaged. Empirical analysis in the 1980s offered an updated and more accurate view of this perception of rural America and the role for place-based, rather than sector-based, policies. First, an Economic Research Service (ERS) report [Bender *et al.*, 1985] capitalized on newly accessible computing power and county-level datasets to offer a typology of counties that dispelled the notion that all, or even the majority of, local rural economies were dominated by agriculture. This report provided the basis of what is currently known as the ERS county typology codes and demonstrated the diversity across rural America. (The current set of typologies includes six economic dependence codes, such as farm-dependent, as well as seven policy relevant types, such as persistent-poverty counties [USDA, ERS, 2015a]). Bender *et al.* [1985] reported that 29% of counties were classified as farming-dependent — where 20% or more of the labor and proprietor income came from farming — using 1975–1979 data and largely concentrated in the North Central and Great Plains regions. Only 13% of the non-metro population resided in farm-dependent counties at that time, and in the intervening (more than three) decades the share of counties and the non-metro population they represent has significantly declined. Figure 10.1 shows the trend in the share of counties with 20% or more of labor and proprietor income from farming.

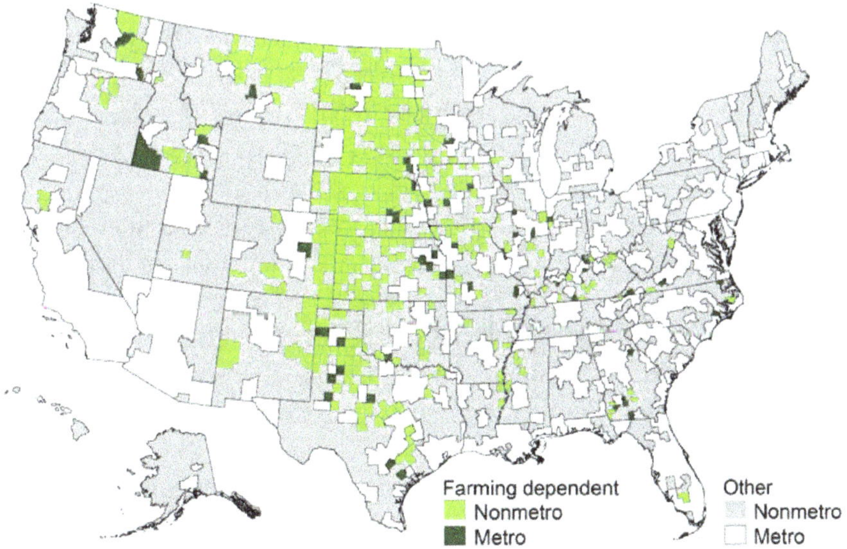

Fig. 10.1. Farming-dependent counties in the US, 2015 revision.

Notes: County boundaries are drawn for the farming-dependent counties only. Such counties are those where 25% or more of the county's average annual labor income and proprietors' earnings is derived from farming, or 16% or more of the jobs were in farming, as measured by 2010–2012 Bureau of Economic Analysis, Local Area Personal Income and Employment data.

Source: USDA, Economic Research Service, using data from the Bureau of Economic Analysis.

The second data-dependent contribution to the policy discussion was to dispel the notion that farm households were economically disadvantaged relative to other US households. In the wake of the farm financial crisis of the 1980s, USDA invested in the Farm Costs and Returns Survey, the precursor to the Agricultural Resource Management Survey, designed to statistically represent the income and wealth of households associated with the principal farm operators. Prior to that time, farm household income statistics did not rely on statistically representative data (instead, these were constructed based on assumptions about related data) and portrayed the farm operator population with significantly lower household income; farm household wealth data did not exist. The analysis provided in Ahearn *et al.* [1988] and a congressional publication at the time [Ahearn, 1986], along with the annual ERS statistical release of farm financial indicators, established that farm households were not economically disadvantaged, a fact that has become widely acknowledged in most policy circles. Indeed, farm households were shown to have incomes at least as high as US households (see Chapter 13) and more than four times the household wealth.

Aside from these straightforward descriptive statistics, a large social science literature rigorously considers the role of agriculture as a source of rural growth. Again, providing a review of that literature is beyond the scope of this chapter, but an important example of that literature is Kilkenny and Partridge [2009]. They considered agriculture in the context of the export-base hypothesis of rural growth and reviewed the empirical literature based on that hypothesis. They also reported on their own empirical analysis of agriculture employment as a source of rural growth and found that agricultural employment is not the only, or best, driver of rural growth.

The acknowledgment of the diminished role of agriculture in nonmetro areas and the strong financial position of farm families does not mean that agriculture, or agricultural policy, is economically unimportant to rural development goals. Interestingly, a changing food environment, with consumers' preferences for local and regional food sources, is one of the drivers of these changes. This has meant that the 2014 Act includes several programs related to regional food systems and these programs are of interest to many rural communities. For example, the Farmers' Market and Local Food Promotion Program (administered by the Agricultural Marketing Service of USDA) in the horticulture portion of the Farm Bill, while available to both rural and urban areas, has garnered a great deal of interest in the rural development practitioner community and spawned a growth in farmers' markets nationwide from fewer than 2,000 in 1994 to more than 8,000 in 2014. To date, the social science literature has not shown significant returns to local food farming [Ahearn *et al.*, 2018; Detre *et al.*, 2011] nor development impacts from the growth in regional food systems, except in select regions [Brown *et al.*, 2014; Hughes and Boys, 2015], but it is still an emerging literature as local and regional food systems take hold.

Not unrelated to rural development programs are programs in the 2014 Act associated with sustainable agriculture and support of beginning farmers. As with the local foods movement, interest has been growing among some farm groups for greater support of these programs. Often, advocates for these relatively new initiatives indicate that there is anecdotal evidence that support for farmers who adopt sustainable agricultural practices and for beginning farmers has positive rural development outcomes. This is something difficult to evaluate at this emergent level. The addition of programs that focus on the characteristics of people, such as beginning farmers, socially disadvantaged farmers, or managers of farmer markets, allows for better targeting of agricultural programs to people and communities rather than to commodities or land.

10.5 The Rural Development Portion of the 2014 Farm Bill

The 2014 Farm Bill represents about 2% of the federal budget, and rural development programs in the Bill are less than 0.03% of that amount. Based on budget outlays alone, it is clear that rural development policies are a low priority relative to the nutrition programs and the programs directed toward agricultural producers. The bulk of rural development programs in the Bill are in Title VI, Rural Development, and many of these programs were an extension from prior legislation, although in some cases with new authorization levels [US Congressional Research Service, 2014]. However, there are also programs of interest to rural communities in other portions of the 2014 Bill, such as the Rural Energy for America program in Title IX on energy, and the Farmers' Market and Local Food Promotion Program in Title X on horticulture.

Besides authorizations from the Consolidated Farm and Rural Development Act of 1972, rural development programs administered by the USDA also are authorized under the 1990 Act, the Rural Electrification Act of 1936, and the Housing Act of 1949 (a complete history is provided in Cowan [2014]). Most programs administered by USDA Rural Development are funded through annual, discretionary appropriations, while the Farm Bill and the other Acts provide the authority for these appropriations. Relative to the 2008 Farm Bill levels, the rural development portion received a small budget increase in the 2014 Farm Bill, in contrast to the major portions garnering most of the Bill funding for farm commodity subsidies, nutrition and conservation which provided small budgetary savings. (For a detailed comparison of the Sections of the rural development portion in 2014 in a side-by-side analysis including the 2008 and the Senate and House bills, see US Congressional Research Service [2014].)

USDA Rural Development programs are grouped within three agencies: Rural Utilities, Rural Housing and Rural Business-Cooperative services. Table 10.1 reports the expenditures (i.e. enacted amounts) in each major program area from 2008 to 2015. In previous years, Rural Utilities received the largest share of the rural development budget, but the 2010 increase in Rural Housing represented a 65% increase over 2009 and was followed by a 2011 increase of 78% over 2010. Most of this increase was due to the increase in single-family housing unsubsidized guaranteed loans (Sec. 502) in response to the 2008 economy-wide recession. In light of the increasing interest in providing rural areas with improved internet access and the relative lack of private investment,[b] there is a growing demand for additional funding in the rural utilities program area.

The various programs in each agency include direct and guaranteed loans, grants, technical assistance and other payments. Some programs

[b] Inadequacy of high-speed broadband coverage in rural areas relative to sub-urban and urban areas is well documented — the so-called "digital divide" [Horrigan and Duggan, 2015].

Table 10.1. Rural development loan and grant programs in the US, fiscal year budget authority (in $ millions).

	2008	2009	2010	2011	2012	2013	2014	2015	2016	2017	2018
Rural utilities	775	4,464	694	635	587	555	685	537	602	695	690
Rural housing	1,332	2,074	1,893	1,893	1,521	1,414	1,694	1,714	2,036	2,068	2,055
Rural business & cooperative	178	516	554	292	201	118	379	200	209	167	166
Total loan and grant programs	2,285	7,054	3,141	2,820	2,309	2,087	2,758	2,451	2,847	2,962	2,911

Source: Office of Budget Planning and Analysis, USDA.

assist intermediaries that then provide services to the intended beneficiaries, and some programs require recipients to leverage USDA support with private-sector financing. The majority of financial assistance in USDA's rural development loan programs operate at a low subsidy rate — the actual amount of subsidy depends on default rates, interest rates, and whether there are fees. Access to capital can be very fragmented for a rural community, and the programs of USDA Rural Development are an important option. This also makes local leadership and planning necessary inputs into the development process. Rural areas face challenges in independently financing infrastructure improvements. For example, unlike urban communities, they cannot issue their own public bonds to pay for infrastructure improvements. Rural businesses face challenges in securing financing, in part due to bank consolidation. This is in spite of the fact that rural businesses may be good investments — Scruggs [2009] reported that investments in rural areas of California performed on par with those in Silicon Valley.

10.6 Rural Development in the Making of the 2018 Farm Bill

The writing of any Farm Bill takes place in the context of the larger economic and political environment of the time. The rural development portion of the 2014 Act, for example, was written in the context of economic disadvantage for the non-metro population, the diversity of rural economies, and a recognition, and renewed reminder, of the wealth that non-metro areas provide the nation as a whole.

More broadly, a major political disagreement emerged during the writing of the 2014 Farm Bill and has lingered with conservatives who are interested in curtailing all farm subsidies and welfare programs to low-income households, including the food assistance programs of the Farm Bill, known as the Supplemental Nutritional Assistance Program (SNAP). Because the various interests reflected in the Farm Bill — farm, conservation, nutrition and rural development — have benefited from negotiating among elected officials to produce a multiple-purpose bill, conservative officials attempted during the debates leading up to the 2014 Bill to separate various portions. In particular, there was an interest on the part of conservatives in separating the portion addressing nutrition from the rest of the Farm Bill [Wilde, 2016]. However, farm and nutrition interest groups successfully resisted this approach, in recognition that they would be unlikely to garner the necessary votes for their constituents without the traditional alliance.

The political and economic context of the writing of the 2018 Farm Bill includes the lingering interest and increased clout of many conservative Republicans to curtail the spending of the next Farm Bill. However, the political environment also has shifted due to the increased gridlock resulting from the election of Donald Trump. Rural populations voted overwhelmingly for him due to his ability to harness their dissatisfaction with their current economic and social environment [Catte, 2018]. About 46 million people, or 14% of the US population, live in areas classified as non-metropolitan or rural areas. In the constitutional system of the electoral college, every state begins with two electoral votes regardless of its population size, and the number of remaining electoral college votes are allocated based on the population size of the state (with each state being guaranteed a minimum of one more, for a total of three). The winner of the state election takes all the electoral votes (except in Maine and Nebraska). Therefore, because of the guaranteed minimum number of electoral votes, regardless of population size, rural states continue to have significant influence — or as one commentator phrased it, as a result of the electoral college, rural America "retains vastly disproportionate electoral strength" [Badger, 2016]. Many in rural and agricultural policy circles are pointing to the election outcome as one that will — or could, or should, or might — mean a greater policy focus on enhanced opportunities in rural America. To date, there has been no evidence that the current administration is responsive to the special needs of the majority of nonfarm rural residents, as evidenced by the President's budget released in February 2018, slashing most rural-specific programs.

In anticipation of the expiration date of the 2014 Farm Bill, the US House of Representatives passed its version of the next Farm Bill on 21 June 2018, following the Senate's passage of its version on 13 June 2018. There are always issues to be resolved between the two chambers through a conference process, but the 2018 conference promises to be especially challenging, because the version passed in the House of Representatives was not done in a bipartisan fashion. Republicans control the House by a wide margin and sought only to bring agreement among fellow Republicans, and, as a sign of the gridlock in US politics during this period, even the Republican-only agreement was difficult to accomplish.

One positive outcome for rural America in both the House and Senate 2018 Bills is increased resources for expanding broadband internet coverage to more rural areas. The intense political battles expected with finding agreement on the next Farm Bill have nothing to do with the Bill's rural development programs. The most notable conflict in conference will come from the lack of agreement about the addition of work requirements allowing a subset of SNAP recipients to receive support. Another difference to be addressed in conference is agricultural subsidy limitations, with the House seeking to expand eligibility and limits from current law, and the Senate seeking to reduce both eligibility and payment limits. The rural development programs of Farm Bills are generally not controversial, and some might say they are even ignored in debate. An exception to this in 2018 involves the Secretary of Agriculture's interest in abolishing the position of Under Secretary for Rural Development within USDA. Some lawmakers have argued that this will reduce the ability of Congress to provide oversight to the executive branch's management of rural development programs and otherwise lower the priority of rural issues within the USDA. In times of extreme conflict, being largely ignored has its advantages. However, continued funding of rural development programs may be held hostage to the major sources of disagreement relating to the Under Secretary position, agricultural subsidies, and especially nutrition programs for low-income households.

10.7 Concluding Comments

Special-interest farm groups and many elected officials from farming areas have continued to use misleading rhetoric that providing subsidies to farmers is the equivalent of supporting rural America. This is in spite of the social science literature on the limited role played by agriculture in enhanced rural development outcomes and the simple descriptive statistics on the dependence of communities and farm households on farm production activities. Given farm households' dependence on off-farm sources of income, a vibrant and diversified rural economy is critical to the sustainability of their farm businesses.

Regional science is far from an exact science, but design of rural development policies has the benefit of several lessons that have emerged in the previous decades. This includes a recognition that one size does not fit all. Hence, the Farm Bill approach of funding an assortment of programs providing support of basic inputs into development has some advantages for communities with leaders able to access and integrate the programs to accomplish the development objectives of any particular community. These programs include programs outside USDA and traditional Farm Bill-funded programs.

Major shifts in rural development policy, as is true for urban development policy, have especially been driven by differing visions for the appropriate role of government in a market economy in the development process. There is a shared view of the important role of government in investing in people, e.g. education, health care, worker training, household safety net, and in providing local infrastructure investment, e.g. roads, bridges, waterways, and especially broadband infrastructure. But beyond that general vision, there is little agreement on the total levels of funding, the responsibility for funding among levels of government, and the direction of public funds for investments in people or infrastructure.

References

Ahearn, M. (1986). An Income Comparison of Farm and Nonfarm People, in *New Dimensions in Rural Policy: Building Upon Our Heritage*, Joint Economic Committee of the US Congress, 99th Congress, 2nd Session, S. Prt. 99–153, June 5, Washington, DC.

Ahearn, M. C., Liang, K. and Goetz, S. (2018). Farm business financial performance in local foods value chains, *Agricultural Finance Review*, 78(4), pp. 470–488.

Badger, E. (2016). As American as apple pie? The rural vote's disproportionate slice of power, *New York Times*, November 20. http://www.nytimes.com/2016/11/21/upshot/as-american-as-apple-pie-the-rural-votes-disproportionate-slice-of-power.html?_r=0 (accessed 8 October 2018).

Bender, L., Green, B., Hady, T., Kuehn, J., Nelson, M., Perkinson, L. and Ross, P. (1985). *The Diverse Social and Economic Structure of Nonmetropolitan America,* ERS, USDA, RDRR No. 49, Washington, DC.

Brown, J., Goetz, S., Ahearn, M. and Liang, K. (2014). Linkages between community focused agriculture, farm sales, and regional growth, *Economic Development Quarterly*, February, 28: pp. 5–16.

Catte, E. (2018). *What You Are Getting Wrong about Appalachia.* Belt Publishing, Cleveland, OH.

Chetty, R., Hendren, N., Kline, P. and Saez, E. (2014). *Where is the Land of Opportunity? The Geography of Intergenerational Mobility in the United States.* NBER Working Paper No. 19843.

Cowan, T. (2014). *An Overview of the USDA Rural Development Programs,* US Congressional Research Service, RL31837, Feb. 18, GPO, Washington, DC. https://www.hsdl.org/?home (accessed 8 October 2018).

Deller, S. and Goetz, S. (2009). Historical description of economic development policy. In Goetz, S., S. Deller, and T. Harris (eds.), *Targeting Regional Economic Development,* Chapter 2. Routledge, New York, pp. 17–34.

Detre, J., Mark, T., Mishra, A. and Adhikari, A. (2011). Linkage between direct marketing and farm income: A double-hurdle approach, *Agribusiness*, 27(1), pp. 19–33.

Horrigan, J. and Duggan, M. (2015). *Home Broadband 2015*, http://www.pewinternet.org/2015/12/21/home-broadband-2015/ (accessed 7 November 2018).

Hughes, D. and Boys, K. (2015). What we know and don't know about the economic development benefits of local food systems, *Choices*, Q1, http://www.choicesmagazine.org/UserFiles/file/cmsarticle_413.pdf (accessed 8 October 2018).

Isserman, A., Feser, E. and Warren, D. (2009). Why some rural places prosper and others do not, *International Regional Science Review*, 32(3), pp. 300–342.

Kilkenny, M. and Partridge, M. (2009). Export sectors and rural development, *American Journal of Agricultural Economics*, 91(4) (November), pp. 910–929.

Rasmussen, W. (1986). Agricultural and rural policy: A historical note, in New *Dimensions in Rural Policy: Building Upon Our Heritage*, Studies prepared for the use of the Subcommittee on Agriculture and Transportation, Joint Economic Committee of the Congress of the United States, US GPO, Washington, DC, pp. 32–38.

Ratcliffe, M. (2012). *A Century of Delineating a Changing Landscape: the Census Bureau's Urban and Rural Classification, 1910 to 2010.* US Bureau Geography Division, http://www2.census.gov/geo/pdfs/reference/ua/Century_of_Defining_Urban.pdf (accessed 8 October 2018).

Scruggs, P. (2009). *The Role of Equity Capital in Rural Communities*, unpublished paper, http://community-wealth.org/content/role-equity-capital-rural-communities (accessed 8 October 2018).

Smith, V. (2015). *The Economic and Welfare and Trade Implications of the 2014 Farm Bill,* Emerald, UK.

US Congressional Research Service (2014). *The 2014 Farm Bill (P.L. 113–79): Summary and Side-by-Side* (Ralph M. Chite, Coordinator), Report 7-5700, Washington, DC, http://nationalaglawcenter.org/wp-content/uploads/2014/02/R43076.pdf (accessed 7 November 2018).

US Department of Agriculture and Rural Prosperity Taskforce (2017). *Report to the President of the United States from the Taskforce on Agriculture and Rural Prosperity* (Secretary Sonny Perdue, Chair), October 21, Washington, DC, https://www.usda.gov/sites/default/files/documents/rural-prosperity-report.pdf (accessed 7 November 2018).

US Department of Agriculture, Office of Budget and Program Analysis (2018). *FY 2019 Budget Summary*, Revised February 16. Washington, DC, https://www.obpa.usda.gov/budsum/fy19budsum.pdf (accessed 7 November 2018).

Wilde, P. (2016). The nutrition title's long, sometimes strained, but not yet broken, marriage with the Farm Bill, *Choices*, Q4. http://www.choicesmagazine.org/choices-magazine/theme-articles/looking-ahead-to-the-next-farm-bill/the-nutrition-titles-long-sometimes-strained-but-not-yet-broken-marriage-with-the-farm-bill (accessed 7 November 2018).

Chapter 11

Special Study: Public Policy, Lending and Social Equity Issues for Rural America

Charles Dodson

USDA Farm Service Agency, Economic Policy Analysis Staff, Washington, DC, USA
charles.dodson@wdc.usda.gov

The United States has been involved in farm credit markets for more than 100 years. When federal credit programs were originally enacted, small family farms played a dominant role in the rural economy. Consequently, improving farm incomes had more of an impact on bolstering the rural economy. But with farm consolidation, declining rural populations and declining federal budget resources, policy objectives have evolved to reflect the changing structure. Rather than enhancing overall farm income, programs have become tailored to address specific market failures or achieve specific social objectives. The Farm Credit System (FCS) addresses broad-based credit availability issues related to informational asymmetries and non-competitive markets. Credit programs administered by USDA's Farm Service Agency (FSA) are designed specifically to serve creditworthy farm businesses that are of higher risk. FSA's direct loan programs, which are costlier to administer, have become directed toward groups and purposes where the net social benefit is greater. This includes encouraging new entrants into farming, especially members of socially disadvantaged groups, and, more recently, promoting organic and farm-to-table types of agriculture. FSA-guaranteed lending has evolved as a cost-efficient method to serve mid- and large-size family farms suffering temporary financial hardships.

11.1 Introduction

Public credit programs play a pivotal role in economic policy throughout the world. More than 2,000 credit programs are administered by governments in more than 100 countries [Green, 2003]. Policymakers use these programs to enhance economic growth, increase employment, and achieve objectives related to social equity. Mechanisms used may include loans either made directly or guaranteed through a government agency, interest subsidies and sponsorship of private enterprises whose role is to ensure a reliable supply of credit. This study discusses federal farm credit policy as it pertains to the United States. The country has a long history of involvement in farm credit markets and has developed a multifaceted approach that utilizes multiple mechanisms to cope with various actual and potential market failures. Specifically, the justification for credit intervention and economic impacts are discussed. Also discussed, are roles played by Federal institutions in improving the performance of farm credit markets.

11.2 Justification for Credit Market Intervention

A government's involvement in credit markets typically is based on the perception of market failure where a less-than-optimal amount of credit is extended, resulting in some feasible investment projects not being undertaken. A credit market failure may be the result of an information failure, discrimination, lack of competition, and/or incomplete markets. Stiglitz and Weiss [1981], in their seminal paper, demonstrated how informational asymmetries may distort credit markets. As defined by them, credit rationing is the inability of a firm or individual to obtain credit despite being creditworthy. In the case of credit rationing, informational asymmetries, or imperfect information, can make it difficult for a lender to verify a borrower's repayment ability, resulting in denials of feasible loan applications, which thereby create inefficiencies [Mankiw, 1986]. Stiglitz and

Weiss argue that concerns about adverse selection would deter lenders from increasing interest rates in response to imperfect information, resulting in lenders restricting, or rationing, the supply of credit. In this case, adverse selection implies that a higher interest rate would encourage borrowers to engage in riskier enterprises, further increasing the uncertainty of repayment. However, adverse selection may not be a big concern among farm lenders because of the availability of non-price mechanisms and the use of risk-based pricing [Barry *et al.*, 2000]. Lenders may utilize restrictive loan covenants, collateral pledging, default penalties and insurance requirements to respond to imperfect information. Since most lenders utilize a risk-adjusted pricing scheme, which bases rates on credit classification, uncertainty could result in borrowers being misclassified into higher-risk categories and likely paying higher interest rates. Thus, imperfect information can have wide-ranging adverse consequences for borrowers through unwarranted loan denials, risk misclassifications, or restrictive non-price mechanisms that constrain asset flexibility and investment choices.

Farm businesses have characteristics that make them more susceptible to the adverse consequences of imperfect information. Credit evaluation of agricultural enterprises may require specialized knowledge and technical expertise. Weather-related risk and cyclical production increase the variability of returns, making loan repayments more uncertain. Industrialization and farm consolidation have increased the complexity of farm business organizational structure and working capital needs. Farming tends to be in less populated areas, away from cities or towns where most lenders are located. Furthermore, smaller community banks that historically have been an important source of agricultural credit may be less able to withstand these risks. Each of these factors increase a lender's costs of evaluation and monitoring, which can, in turn, constrain credit availability. These conditions are exacerbated for young and beginning farmers, who are likely to lack sufficient credit history to evaluate their credit potential [Hartarska and Nadolnyak, 2012].

Credit market intervention also may be undertaken to achieve social objectives such as facilitation of wealth creation among racial and ethnic groups that may have suffered past discrimination. Black, Hispanic, American Indian and women farmers have all made claims of past inequitable treatment by USDA farm lending programs. Claims of blacks and American Indians were recognized as a class and reached settlement agreements [Cowen and Feder, 2013b]. USDA voluntarily established an administrative claims process in 2011 in response to ongoing claims of discrimination of women and Hispanics [Cowen and Feder, 2013a]. Even though recent studies have shown no evidence of continuing discrimination [Escalante *et al.*, 2006; Dodson, 2013], providing credit to socially disadvantaged groups, including women and minorities, remains a key focus of US farm credit policy. About 20% of all farm loans USDA makes annually are to socially disadvantaged farmers [USDA, 2017a, 2017b]. Besides alleviating impacts of past discrimination, credit also may be used to encourage new entrants as an effort to increase overall diversity. In 2012, women represented 14.5% of primary farm operators and racial minorities represented only 7.7% [USDA, 2014].

Federal credit programs may be used to exploit externalities by addressing incomplete markets. Examples include providing credit enhancements that encourage the production of healthier foods or promote conservation practices. More than 40% of the rural population has been characterized as living in food deserts, which are characterized by a shortage of grocery stores, farmers' markets and healthy food providers [Dutko *et al.*, 2012]. USDA's microloan program is an example of a credit enhancement designed to encourage adoption of organic practices by smaller-scale farms that supply retail outlets, such as farmers' markets [USDA, 2016]. USDA's conservation loan program was created to facilitate conversion to organic farming and enable farmers to install conservation practices [USDA, 2017a, 2017b].

11.3 Impacts of Credit Market Interventions

Interventions that reduce credit constraints would be expected to increase output and employment. This can occur through additional risk reduction, and the removal of non-price risk management mechanisms. Additional is the incremental investment that would not have been undertaken in the absence of a credit market intervention. By reducing the unsystematic risk associated with lending to a specialized enterprise or a geographic region, federal credit programs increase lender liquidity and, consequently, credit availability. Likewise, the risk reduction resulting from a credit market intervention can lessen the need for lenders to require additional loan security or to implement restrictive covenants that would constrain a borrower's investment decisions and limit growth potential.

Empirical studies have quantified some of the adverse effects associated with a credit market failure. A credit constraint lowers the agricultural value of production [Briggeman *et al.*, 2009] and limits a farmer's ability to accumulate capital [Barry *et al.*, 2000]. As would be expected given asset fixity and cyclical production, US farm credit markets have been found to be characterized by disequilibrium, which was particularly pronounced during the 1980s farm financial crisis [Hubbs and Keuthe, 2017]. Numerous non-agricultural studies have shown a positive impact on aggregate output and employment from public credit programs. Guaranteed credit programs increase employment, especially in low-income markets [Craig *et al.*, 2007]. Also, the receipt of guaranteed loan increases a firm's performance, job creation and exports [Cowling and Siepel, 2013]. The availability of credit programs enables incremental investment and is greater during credit crunches [Honohan, 2010].

Although interventions in credit markets can have positive consequences, there are also criticisms. Despite benefits to borrowers, public credit programs can place private lenders at a competitive disadvantage, resulting in public entities crowding out private lenders [Robbins, 2009; Lins and Barry, 1984]. Crowding out reduces the net social benefit of subsidized credit programs [Jensen, 2000]. It has also been argued that, by lowering the effective loan rate for borrowers, federal credit programs can lead to overinvestment or can induce borrowers to substitute debt for equity or capital for labor [Bosworth *et al.*, 1987].

11.4 Federal Farm Credit Programs in the United States

Credit has been a component of US farm policy for more than 100 years. Over this time, US farm credit policy has evolved to improve market efficiency by increasing competition, lowering transaction costs, and reducing problems of asymmetric information [Lee and Irwin, 1996; Barry, 1995]. Passage of the Federal Farm Loan Act catalyzed the formation of the Farm Credit System (FCS) as it operates today to provide credit to farmers and rural communities on a cooperative basis. The USDA has been involved in providing credit to farmers since the Great Depression. Initially providing only direct loans, USDA implemented a loan guarantee program in the 1980s. Today, each of these FCS mechanisms serves a unique role in agricultural credit markets defined along the lines of farm typology and financial risk.

FCS primarily addresses broad-based credit availability issues affecting farmers and rural America. In 2018, FCS included 69 retail lending associations that made and serviced loans made directly to farmers, agribusiness and rural homeowners. It also included Farmer Mac, which provided a secondary market for agricultural real estate and rural housing mortgage loans. Combined, Farmer Mac and FCS associations provided 42% of all farm lending in 2016 (Fig. 11.1).

As a specialized agricultural lender, FCS possesses the unique expertise that may be necessary to evaluate the creditworthiness of farm business. Since it serves the entire US, it can address potential non-competitive markets in areas with few farm lenders. As a Government-Sponsored Enterprise (GSE), FCS benefits from the implicit guarantee of the US Treasury. Consequently, FCS has excellent access to bond markets, providing a reliable supply of capital necessary to fund loans. This mechanism addresses issues resulting from the disequilibrium of loan demand

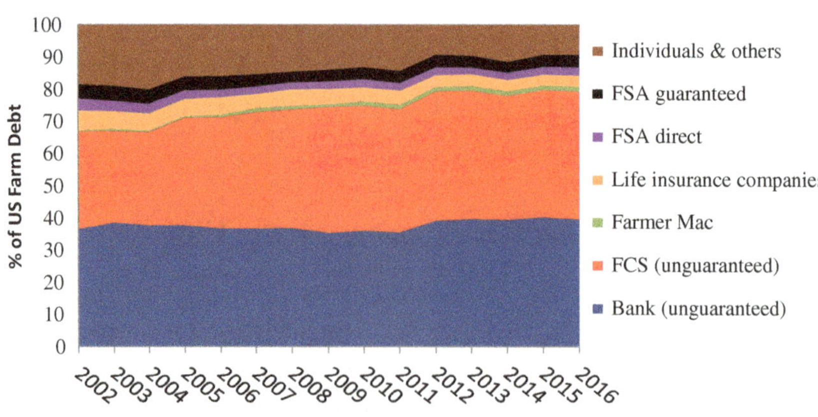

Fig. 11.1. Market share of total farm debt held by lender group.
Source: USDA Economic Research Service Farm Income & Wealth Statistics.

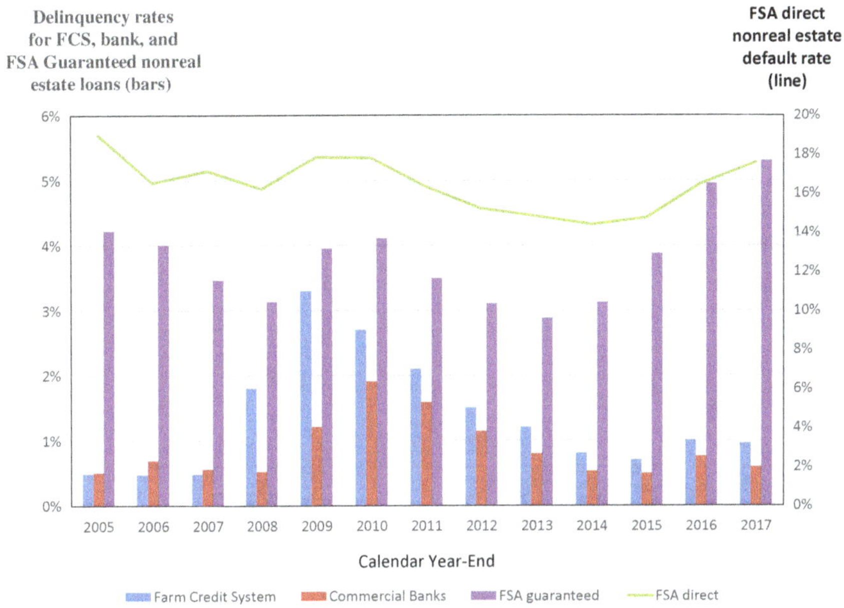

Fig. 11.2. Default rates on farm real estate loans by lender group at calendar year-end.

Source: Annual financial reports of the farm credit system funding corporation; Kansas City Federal Reserve Bank Agricultural Finance Databook; USDA FSA R540 and GROG databases.

and credit availability that may be caused by the cyclicality of agricultural production. As a GSE, FCS imposes no direct cost on the US Treasury. Also, its financial strength and overall portfolio quality imply low risk. FCS institutions are financially sound with an average capital/assets ratio of 16.9% in 2018 [Farm Credit Funding Corporation, 2018]. Non-accrual farm loans at FCS institutions were 1.1% of total farm loans in 2018 and have been less than those of banks over the past 10 years (Fig. 11.2).

Although FCS lenders effectively serve to reduce any broad-based market failures affecting farm borrowers, they have not been as effective at serving the needs of smaller family farms. During 2014–2016, 29.4% of indebted small family farms where farming is the primary occupation indicated having an FCS loan, compared to 40.6% for large family farms (see Table 11.1).[a] Likewise, 27.2% of all part-time farmers had an FCS

[a] Small family farms are defined to include farming operations with less than $350,000 in gross cash farm income. This definition is based on the typology developed by USDA's Economic Research Service [Hoppe and MacDonald, 2013].

Table 11.1. Average shares of indebted farms with term debt owed to major lender groups, by USDA ERS farm typology, 2014–2016.

			Farm Service Agency		
	FCS (%)	Banks (%)	Direct (%)	Guaranteed (%)	Direct and/or Guaranteed (%)
Small family farms					
Farming occupation	29.4	65.5	6.3	2.3	9.9
Part-time	27.2	67.2	4.9	1.5	6.8
Mid-size family farm	39.3	61.0	4.8	6.0	14.0
Large family farm	40.6	62.1	2.8	7.85.1	12.9
All indebted farms	31.2	65.4	4.1	6.3	9.2

Note: Categories based on ERS farm typology [Hoppe and MacDonald, 2013].
Source: USDA ARMS and FSA farm loan data.

loan over the three-year period. But since part-time farmers primarily rely on non-farm income, they are less likely to meet FCS eligibility criteria, which stipulate that qualified loan applicants be *bonafide* farmers.

Credit programs administered by USDA's Farm Service Agency (FSA) are specifically designed to serve creditworthy farm businesses that are of higher risk. This includes farmers suffering a financial hardship, farmers with limited capital to offer as loan collateral, or beginning farmers with limited credit history. FSA makes and services direct loans through staff located in local offices. Qualified commercial, cooperative, or non-profit lenders originate and service guaranteed loans. Qualified lenders make applications for loan guarantees to local FSA offices. Under a loan guarantee, FSA guarantees repayment of up to 95% of the principal balance. All loan guarantees are loss-sharing, which means that FSA will reimburse the lender for losses incurred if the loan goes into default, including loss of loan principal, some accrued interest and certain liquidation costs.

Not only do FSA's direct and guaranteed loan programs have different delivery mechanisms, they have different roles. Direct loans serve a much riskier clientele, as indicated by higher default rates for non-real estate loans, which are four times that of guarantees (Fig. 11.2) Also, direct lending requires a larger investment in staff and overhead, resulting in greater administrative costs [USDA, 2006]. The higher costs in combination with federal budget constraints have resulted in most USDA farm lending occurring through guarantees. Because direct programs require more public resources, loans are mostly targeted to groups for whom the net social benefit is expected to be greater. Although direct loans comprise only 2.5% of the total farm debt in 2016, the program is highly targeted, with 75% of loan funds reserved for use by beginning farmers, veterans and socially disadvantaged groups.

While the overall market share for guaranteed loans in 2016 was only 2.9%, the share of mid- and large-size farms using these programs was larger. Among the large-size farm operations, 7.8% of those with debt had an FSA guaranteed loan (Table 11.1). With more than $1 million in annual sales, these operations have large working capital needs, and are more likely to include complex business structures such as limited partnerships, family corporations and embedded entities. As such, issues of asymmetric information are accentuated, especially among those of higher risk. This is especially important for community banks that may be less able to withstand the risk associated with lending to larger farm businesses. Community banks, defined as those with less than $1 billion in total assets, supply 60% of total bank credit to farms [Dodson, 2014]. Guarantees are especially important to small community banks that have less than $250 million in assets. This group of banks made up more than 60% of FSA loan guarantees to banks.

The market segmentation between direct and guaranteed programs is achieved through differences in loan size limits, targeting and a nuance in eligibility requirements. Besides operating a family farm, qualified guaranteed applicants must have an acceptable credit history, yet be unable to obtain a loan at reasonable rates and terms from a private lender "without a guarantee". Qualified direct applicants must meet the same criteria except for the clause "without a guarantee". These stipulations limit FSA guarantees to a narrow niche in the creditworthiness spectrum between unguaranteed commercial loans and direct FSA loans. Direct loan size limits of $300,000 for farm real estate and non-real estate loans limit the ability to serve larger farms. In comparison, guaranteed loan limits were $1.39 million in 2018 and are adjusted annually based on changes in prices paid by farmers. Also, the beginning and socially disadvantaged groups targeted by direct loans are more likely to operate smaller farms than non-targeted groups.

As previously discussed, there are noteworthy risks of credit market intervention. Specifically, if not carefully administered, intervention can create distortions and inefficiencies. With respect to US farm credit markets, several institutional provisions exist to curtail any adverse impacts. Both FCS and FSA lending programs are governed by extensive federal regulations. The Farm Credit Act of 1971 established criteria for borrower eligibility and loan purposes. It also provided enforcement authority to the Farm Credit Administration to assure that FCS lending institutions are run in a prudent manner and that regulations are followed. Likewise, the Consolidated Farm and Rural Development Act of 1972 set forth the regulations that govern delivery of USDA farm credit programs. The Secretary of Agriculture is responsible for overseeing and implementing these provisions. The Federal Credit Reform Act of 1990 required a more accurate budgetary accounting of all federal credit programs [United States Government Accountability Office, 2016]. Consequently, the scarcity of federal budget resources imposes a constraint on the amount of direct and guaranteed loan funds available each fiscal year. Finally, if existing laws and regulations fail to curtail market distortions, Congress can intervene by replacing or changing current legislation.

11.5 Summary

Access to a reliable and affordable source of credit has been shown to have positive impacts on a firm's production, performance and growth potential. Improving access to credit for farm businesses has been a longstanding goal of federal credit policy. Cyclical production, non-competitive market, and vulnerability to weather increase a lender's uncertainty of loan repayment. Because of this informational asymmetry, farm borrowers are more likely to experience an unwarranted loan denial, risk misclassification, or restrictive non-price mechanisms that constrains asset flexibility and investment choices. Over 100 years, US federal farm credit policy has evolved to address credit market vulnerability using a multifaceted approach that includes a GSE (FCS), a federal loan guarantee program and a direct lending program which are administered through USDA. Each of these mechanisms serves a unique role in facilitating the flow of credit to agriculture. A key objective of the FCS is to assure a consistent and reliable source of credit to the farm sector by addressing broad-based issues more likely to affect a large share of total farms. This can include the overall availability of credit to the farm sector, non-competitive markets, or informational asymmetries affecting farmers as a group. As a GSE, the FCS imposes little direct cost on the government. Direct and guaranteed credit programs, which do impose costs on the government, are targeted to address specific idiosyncratic factors, such as providing credit to targeted groups or those suffering a temporary financial setback. In establishing federal farm credit policy, policymakers implemented an extensive set of regulations as a protection against market distortions.

References

Barry, P. J. (1995). *The Effects of Credit Policies on US Agriculture*. AEI Press, Washington, DC.

Barry, P. J. and Robison, L. J. (2001). Agricultural finance: Credit, credit constraints, and consequences. In B. L. Gardner and G. C. Rausser (eds.), *Handbook of Agricultural Economics*. Elsevier, Amsterdam, NY, pp. 513–571.

Barry, P., Bierlen, R. and Sotomayor, N. (2000). Financial structure of farm businesses under imperfect capital markets. *American Journal of Agricultural Economics*, 82, pp. 920 933.

Bosworth, B., Carron, A. and Rhyne, E. (1987). *The Economics of Federal Credit Programs*, Brookings Institution, Washington, DC.

Briggeman, B. C., Towe, C. A. and Morehart, M. J. (2009). Credit constraints: Their existence, determinants, and implications for US farm and nonfarm sole proprietorships. *American Journal of Agricultural Economics*, 91(1), pp. 275–289.

Cowan, T. and Feder, J. (2013a). *Garcia v. Vilsack: A Policy and Legal Analysis of a USDA Discrimination Case*, CRS Report to Congress 7-5700. Congressional Research Service. February. http://nationalaglawcenter.org/wp-content/uploads/assets/crs/R40988.pdf (accessed 8 October 2018).

Cowan, T. and Feder, J. (2013b). *The Pigford Cases: USDA Settlement of Discrimination Suits by Black Farmers*. CRS Report to Congress 7-5700. Congressional Research Service. March 2013. http://nationalaglawcenter.org/wp-content/uploads/assets/crs/RS20430.pdf (accessed 8 October 2018).

Cowling, M. and Siepel, J. (2013). Public intervention in UK small firm credit markets: Value-for-money or waste of scarce resources? *Technovation*, 33, pp. 265–275.

Craig, B. R., Jackson, W. E III, and Thomson, J. B. (2007). *On Government Intervention in the Small-Firm Credit Market and its Effect on Economic Performance*. Federal Reserve Bank of Cleveland, Working Paper 07-02.

Dodson, C. B. (2013). *Racial/ethnic Discrimination in USDA's Direct Farm Lending Programs*, Paper for presentation at the AAE/ CAES Joint Annual Meeting, Washington, DC, August 4–6. http://ageconsearch.umn.edu/bitstream/150492/2/Dodson_AAEA_WDC_2013_revised.pdf (accessed 8 October 2018).

Dodson, C. B. (2014). Bank size, lending paradigms, and usage of farm service agency's guaranteed loan programs. *Agricultural Finance Review*, 74(1), 133–152.

Dutko, P., Ver Ploeg, M. and Farrigan, T. (2012). *Characteristics and Influential Factors of Food Deserts*, ERR-140, US Department of Agriculture, Economic Research Service, August.

Farm Credit Funding Corporation (2018). First Quarter 2018. *Quarterly Information Statement of the Farm Credit System*, Jersey City, NJ, May 18.

Green, A. (2003). *Credit Guarantee Schemes for Small Enterprises: an Effective Instrument to Promote Private Sector-Led Growth?* SME Technical Working Paper No. 10. UNIDO, Vienna. https://www.unido.org/sites/default/files/2007-11/18223_PSDseries10_0.pdf (accessed 8 October 2018).

Hartarska, V. and Nadolnyak, D. (2012). Financing constraints and access to credit in a postcrisis environment: Evidence from new farmers in Alabama. *Journal of Agricultural and Applied Economics*, 44(4), pp. 607–621.

Honohan, P. (2010). Partial credit guarantees: Principles and practice. *Journal of Financial Stability*, 6, pp. 1–9.

Hoppe, R. A. and MacDonald, J. M. (2013). *Updating the ERS Farm Typology*. Economic Research Service Economic Information Bulletin No. 110, April. www.ers.usda.gov/webdocs/publications/43742/36482_eib110.pdf?v=41368 (accessed 8 October 2018).

Hubbs, T. and Kuethe, T. (2017). A disequilibrium evaluation of public intervention in agricultural credit markets. *Agricultural Finance Review*, 77(1), pp. 37–49.

Jensen, F. E. (2000). The farm credit system as a government sponsored enterprise. *Review of Agricultural Economics*, 22(2), pp. 326–335.

Lee, W. and Irwin, G. (1996). Restructuring the farm credit system: A progress report. *Agricultural Finance Review*, 56, pp. 1–21.

Lins, D. A. and Barry, P. J. (1984). Agency status for the farm credit system. *American Journal of Agricultural Economics*, 66(5), pp. 601–606.

Mankiw, N. G. (1986). The allocation of credit and financial collapse. *Quarterly Journal of Economics*, 101 (Aug), pp. 455–470.

Robbins, E. (2009). Lending competition of community banks and the farm credit system, *Financial Industry Perspectives*, Federal Reserve Bank of Kansas City, Kansas City, MO, pp. 1–16. https://www.kansascityfed.org/publicat/fip/LendingCompetition08-09.pdf (accessed 8 October 2018).

Stiglitz, J. and Weiss, A. (1981). Credit rationing in markets with imperfect information. *American Economic Review*, 71(3), pp. 393–410.

United States Department of Agriculture (2006). *Evaluating the Relative Cost Effectiveness of the Farm Service Agency's Farm Loan Programs*. Report to Congress, August. https://www.fsa.usda.gov/Assets/USDA-FSA-Public/usdafiles/EPAS/PDF/farm_loan_study_august_06.pdf (accessed 8 October 2018).

United States Department of Agriculture (2014). *2012 Census of Agriculture, Summary and State Data*, Vol. 1, Geographic Area Series. Part 51. AC-12-A-51. National Agricultural Statistics Service. Washington, DC.

United States Department of Agriculture (2016). *Fact Sheet: Microloans*, Farm Service Agency, February. https://www.fsa.usda.gov/Assets/USDA-FSA-Public/usdafiles/FactSheets/2016/FACT%20SHEET%20-%20Microloans%20(Revised%2002-29-16).pdf (accessed 8 October 2018).

United States Department of Agriculture (2017a). *Fact Sheet: Conservation Loan Program*, Farm Service Agency, March. https://www.fsa.usda.gov/Assets/USDA-FSA-Public/usdafiles/FactSheets/2017/conservation_loan_program_march2017.pdf (accessed 8 October 2018).

United States Department of Agriculture (2017b). *Fact Sheet: Loans for Socially-Disadvantaged Farmers and Ranchers*, Farm Service Agency, March. https://www.fsa.usda.gov/Assets/USDA-FSA-Public/usdafiles/FactSheets/2017/loans_for_socially_disadvantaged_farmers_and_ranchers_march2017.pdf (accessed 8 October 2018).

United States Government Accountability Office (2016). *Credit Reform: Current Method to Estimate Credit Subsidy Costs is More Appropriate for Budget Estimates Than a Fair Value Approach*, GAO-16-41, Washington, DC. https://www.gao.gov/assets/680/674905.pdf (accessed 8 October 2018).

Part D
Entry, Exit of Farmers and Migration

Chapter 12

Entry and Exit of Farmers Across the EU

Davide Viaggi

Department of Agricultural and Food Sciences,
University of Bologna, Italy
davide.viaggi@unibo.it

The objective of this chapter is to investigate the dynamics of entry and exit from the farming sector across the EU, based on a review of the literature and recent policy and statistical documents. First, it summarizes the main data available on this topic. Second, it illustrates the determinants of entry and exit, including policy, as well as the relationships between entry and exit. Finally, the chapter highlights the current policy setting in the EU concerning measures directly addressing exit/entry issues. The concluding section outlines future policy design issues and needs.

12.1 Introduction

The entry and exit of operators from the farming sector is a key issue, closely connected with several topics relevant to the sector. First, the number of farmers is related to farm size, with implications for competitiveness. Second, new entrants and age structures are related to entrepreneurship, innovation and investment. Third, entry/exit dynamics are at the core of the interplay between farming, the rural economy and rural social structures. The objective of this chapter is to investigate the dynamics of farmer entry and exit across the EU, based on a review of the literature, including recent policy and statistical documents.

In the past, farm entry and exit were largely connected with the retirement of old farmers and their replacement by more youthful ones, mostly, if not exclusively, from the same family. This "succession" story is now changing significantly for several reasons, including the entrance of entrepreneurs/employees without a farming household background, and of new legal entities not represented by a single human being. Current trends are also linked to migration issues and to new urban–rural relationships.

Historically, policy has had an important influence on early retirement as well as on the entrance of younger farmers, and this remains a strong focus of attention in current and probably future policy settings.

12.2 Trends in Entry and Exit in the EU

In recent decades, EU agriculture has been dominated by high rates of farmer exit, accompanied by low entry rates. Employment in agriculture has constantly decreased, with a notable reduction by 26% between 2005 and 2014. This trend can be associated with both demographic aspects of agricultural employment and structural change affecting farm numbers.

Concerning age structure, in 2013, about one-third of all farmers in the EU were older than 65, while only about 6% of farmers were younger than 35 years. The ratio between farmers younger than 35 and older than 55 varies notably among regions and countries, with peaks below 0.05 and in a much lower number of areas over 0.50 (Fig. 12.1) [European Commission, 2018a]. Younger farmers are usually managing larger farms, while holdings managed by older farmers are on average smaller. The number of farms itself has been dropping over time in Europe.

The imbalance between entry and exit is partly due to obstacles faced by young farmers in setting up new farm businesses. These include access to land and capital, as well as the reluctance of some older farmers to retire. Causes of imbalance can also be connected to national issues, such as taxation, and land and inheritance legislation, which are typically very different across countries [European Commission, 2018b].

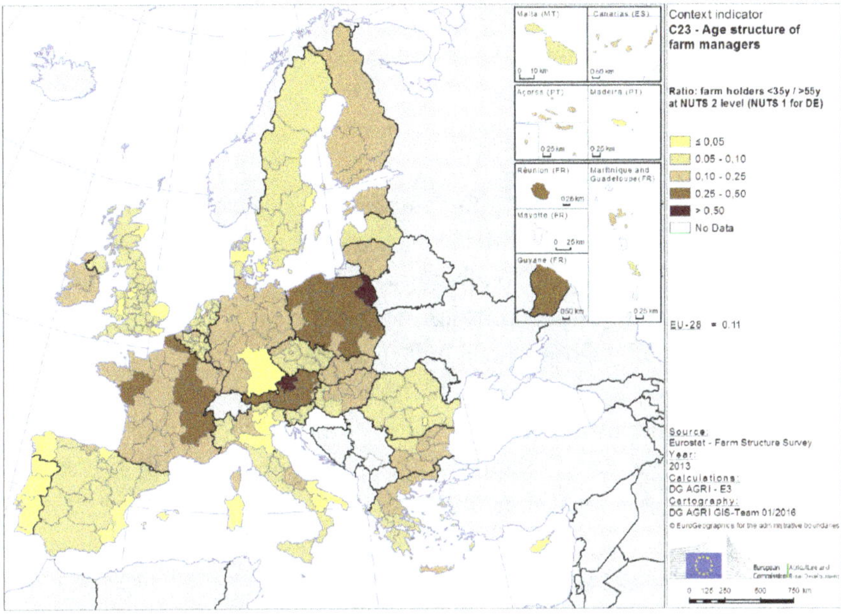

Fig. 12.1. Age structure of farm managers.

Source: European Commission [2017].

12.3 Determinants of Entry and Exit and the Role of Policy

Entry and exit are complex dynamic processes, and many papers [Barnes *et al.*, 2015; Bertoni and Cavicchioli, 2016] emphasize path dependency, i.e. the historical links between decisions taken or developments occurring in one period and then in another. First, it should be noted that entry and exit are connected to each other due to the fact that a new farmer can take up a farm only when a previous one leaves. On the other hand, individual exit may be easier when there is the opportunity of entry by a young successor. There are also different forms of collaboration between entrant and leaving farmers. For example, a retiring farmer can leave actual farm management to other, more active farmers, e.g. renting tenants or contractors. There is also a gray area concerning the role of retired farmers still living on farms or that of potential successors in farm management before they take up the business formally. Finally, while much of the literature sees the exit/entry decision as part of a succession process within the same household, the process is made more flexible and less "mechanical" by the increasing role of different legal forms of farm businesses, such as partnerships.

Exit is largely connected with demographic aspects, in particular the aging of farmers. However, other factors, such as profitability, play an important role, and this can be often traced to observable farm characteristics, such as size and specialization, with the regular message from the literature that smaller farmers can exit more easily, and thus are the first to exit. Further determinants may be technology (e.g. organic farming), the amount of labor available per hectare, or the number of full-time farm workers or their gender [Ferjani *et al.*, 2015; Raggi *et al.*, 2013; Latruffe *et al.*, 2013]. Exogenous factors linked to location are also important, such as land productivity, the availability of services or alternative opportunities for employment. For example, population density of the area has been found to have a significant effect on exit in Tuscany (Landi *et al.*, 2016).

In some areas, other, more local, factors may be important; for example Viira *et al.* [2013] observe that farms from land obtained through restitution at the beginning of the transition process in the former centrally planned economies of Central and Eastern Europe (CEE) tend to have different dynamics, due to the fact that the farmers are emotionally inclined to maintain the farms of their forefathers. The role and level of connectivity with the social environment are also important. For example, Flaten [2017] reports that sheep farmers in Norway with a positive view of the local farming community are less likely to exit.

Entry is largely connected to the opportunities for income and quality of life envisaged in the farming sector. In this respect, relative income levels compared to other sectors are important, and depend on general economic trends. The economic and financial crisis of the late 2000s increased expectations of opportunities and stability in agriculture compared with other sectors. Entry is also connected to education and training choices, so that aspects related to culture and vision of the farming sector, especially amongst the more youthful, may be relevant.

Altogether, three main types of new entrants can be identified [Davidova, 2014; i Rico and Fuller, 2016; Hassink *et al.*, 2016]:

(1) successors from existing farm households;
(2) newcomers from different sectors;
(3) employees from other sectors and with former links with farming households, coming back due to economic needs.

These three entry groups display rather different characteristics. In particular, the newcomers bring often rather different approaches and visions, and can be seen as promoting new forms of rurality [i Rico and Fuller, 2016]. On the other hand, they often face more difficulties in entering the sector.

Barriers to entry, especially the high initial investment required for farming activity and access to land, are at the core of the understanding of the mechanism of entry. In this area, alternative forms of farm acquisition, such as renting or partnership, are a key area of investigation [Leonard *et al.*, 2017].

The issue of entry is often associated with the contrast between young new entrants and older farmers in terms of effects on farm performance and policy responses. Recent analyses also focus on the fact that young farmers may be rather heterogeneous in terms of performance related to different aspects of farm management [McKillop *et al.*, 2018], especially in relation to continuity and discontinuity of practices. However, recent literature highlights that this is not straightforward, as both family and non-family transfers entail elements of both continuity and discontinuity in farming practices [Joosse and Grubbström, 2017].

Differences between new entrants in terms of entrepreneurship are also relevant. In particular, new farmers with high confidence in their entrepreneurial competencies tend to identify more new business opportunities, while new part-time farmers, who see farming rather as their second job, are less likely to identify such opportunities [Pindado *et al.*, 2018].

These differences are still poorly explored by the literature, but have relevant policy implications, in order to ensure that incentives provided to young farmers better reflect and pursue policy objectives. Several studies emphasize the role of policy in affecting the exit/continuation decision, including the succession process. The withdrawal of CAP payments is discussed in Latruffe *et al.* [2013] and Raggi *et al.* [2013], who found that the number of exiting farmers could increase by 20–40%, depending on the areas.

Barnes *et al.* [2015] considered different scenarios including increased stable and decreased CAP payments. Faced with the first two scenarios, most farmers stated a desire to stay in farming and maintain their current trajectory. Under the lower payments scenario, the share of farmers stating they would exit the industry more than doubled, from 4% to 9%. Decoupling of CAP payments from production levels has been found to accelerate the disinvestment process and farm exit [Kazukauskas *et al.*, 2013]. The reform of the milk quota system has also been investigated, and found to stimulate decisions to exit the dairy sector (and farming) in less competitive areas [Dervillé *et al.*, 2017; O'Donnell *et al.*, 2011; Pieralli *et al.*, 2017]. The transitional CAP measure available in the New Member States to support semi-subsistence farms undergoing restructuring was found to affect negatively exit rates in Estonia [Viira *et al.*, 2013].

In general, it is agreed that policies supporting early retirement have little effect, while policies encouraging uptake of farms by new entrants are more effective [Davis *et al.*, 2013]. However, different instruments can have rather different impacts. For example, Davis *et al.* [2013] investigated the possible impacts of New Entrant Schemes Ireland and found that an interest rate subsidy on farm development loans had a more positive potential impact than other options, such as a working capital installation grant.

Most of these analyses are based on stated intentions, which may be more or less realistic proxies of actual behavior. Thus, they may fail to provide good estimates, especially when considering major choices linked to complex dynamic process typical of the exit process [Viira *et al.*, 2014].

Also, in many cases, the net role of policy may be questioned, as many of the entry/exit changes that are claimed to be due to policy might have happened anyway. However, even in this case, policy may affect timing and modalities of entry/exit, or influence the decisions expected from new entry, e.g. investment and innovation.

12.4 Current Policy Setting and its Evolution

Based on the above discussion, any policy measure affecting the profitability of farming may also affect the dynamics of entry and exit. Besides this "trivial" consideration, there are basically three types of policy measures related to exit/entry [European Parliament, 2017]:

(1) Measures directly providing incentives to retirement or first settlement of young farmers, such as CAP Pillar 2 start-up grants.
(2) Measures oriented at guaranteeing higher income to young farmers, such as the young farmer top-up schemes in Pillar 1.
(3) Age-differentiated support (e.g. higher share of cofinancing) or selection procedures ensuring higher score and hence easier access to funding for young farmers, for example in the investment measures in Pillar 2.

There is also evidence that the rural development instrument LEADER has had a role in encouraging activity by young farmers.

The role of policy components in affecting entry–exit dynamics depends on both contextual conditions and on policy implementation, especially in Pillar 2. General income support through the Young Farmers Payment scheme, especially since the payment is decoupled, is reported to reduce the incentives of farmers to retire [Bika, 2007].

So far, the documented role of young farmer payments (see item 2 above) is minor, as the first year of implementation of the 2014–2020 CAP only included about 4.1% of basic payment applications and about 0.6% of the actual payments [European Commission, 2018a]. The role of young farmer measures in Pillar 2 is also controversial, and in general has attracted low attention in Rural Development Programs [European Commission, 2018b]. However, it should be noted that the role of Pillar 2 measures and prescriptions greatly depends on details of the implementation process, so that real effort and practical effects are difficult to disentangle. Young farmers remain an issue in CAP proposals for the period 2021–2027 [European Commission, 2018b], e.g. Member States should allocate at least 2% of their direct payments to help young farmers get set up, complemented by support for measures facilitating access to land, and exchange schemes for young rural people.

12.5 Conclusions and Perspectives

Entry and exit from the farming sector remain a major issue for the competitiveness of the sector and a key topic for policy. Its role has evolved from a simple issue of aging to a topic of dynamism and competence flow that can allow a vibrant development of the sector in light of the current focus on innovation and interplay with global value chains. This evolution of topics is also visible in policies, where attention to age is more and more spread across measures, especially those concerning investment and innovation.

References

Barnes, A., Sutherland, L.-A., Toma, L., Matthews, K. and Thomson, S. G. (2015). The effect of the common agricultural policy reforms on intentions towards food production: Evidence from livestock farmers. *Land Use Policy*, 50, pp. 548–558.

Bertoni, D. and Cavicchioli, D. (2016). Process description, qualitative analysis and causal relationships in farm succession. *CAB Reviews: Perspectives in Agriculture, Veterinary Science, Nutrition and Natural Resources*, 11(43), pp. 1–11.

Bika, Z. (2007). The territorial impact of the farmers' early retirement scheme. *Sociologia Ruralis*, 47, pp. 246–272.

Davidova, S. (2014). Small and semi-subsistence farms in the EU: Significance and development paths. *EuroChoices*, 13(1), pp. 5–9.

Davis, J., Caskie, P. and Wallace, M. (2013). Promoting structural adjustment in agriculture: The economics of New Entrant Schemes for farmers. *Food Policy*, 40, pp. 90–96.

Dervillé, M., Allaire, G., Maigné, E. and Cahuzac, E. (2017). Internal and contextual drivers of dairy restructuring: Evidence from French mountainous areas and post-quota prospects. *Agricultural Economics*, 48(1), pp. 91–103.

European Commission (2017). *CAP Context Indicators 2014–2020* (2017 update), Bruxelles. https://ec.europa.eu/agriculture/cap-indicators/context/2017_en (accessed 29 March 2019).

European Commission (2018a). *Modernising and Simplifying the CAP: Economic Challenges Facing EU Agriculture*. Background Document, Bruxelles.

European Commission (2018b). *Modernising and Simplifying the CAP: Socio-Economic Challenges Facing EU Agriculture and Rural Areas.* Background Document, Bruxelles.

European Parliament (2017). Young Farmers — Policy Implementation After the 2013 CAP Reform, study report for Policy Department for Structural and Cohesion Policies, Directorate-General for Internal Policies, Brussels.

Ferjani, A., Zimmermann, A. and Roesch, A. (2015). Determining factors of farm exit in agriculture in Switzerland. *Agricultural Economic Review*, 16(1), pp. 59–72.

Flaten, O. (2017). Factors affecting exit intentions in Norwegian sheep farms. *Small Ruminant Research*, 150, pp. 1–7.

Hassink, J., Hulsink, W. and Grin, J. (2016). Entrepreneurship in agriculture and healthcare: Different entry strategies of care farmers. *Journal of Rural Studies*, 43, pp. 27–39.

i Rico, N. M. and Fuller, A. M. (2016). Newcomers to farming: Towards a new rurality in Europe. *Documents d'Analisi Geografica*, 62(3), pp. 531–551.

Joosse, S. and Grubbström, A. (2017). Continuity in farming — Not just family business. *Journal of Rural Studies*, 50, pp. 198–208.

Kazukauskas, A., Newman, C., Clancy, D. and Sauer, J. (2013). Disinvestment, farm size, and gradual farm exit: The impact of subsidy decoupling in a European context. *American Journal of Agricultural Economics*, 95(5), pp. 1068–1087.

Landi, C., Stefani, G., Rocchi, B., Lombardi, G. V. and Giampaolo, S. (2016). Regional differentiation and farm exit: A hierarchical model for Tuscany. *Journal of Agricultural Economics*, 67(1), pp. 208–230.

Latruffe, L., Dupuy, A. and Desjeux, Y. (2013). What would farmers' strategies be in a no-CAP situation? An illustration from two regions in France. *Journal of Rural Studies*, 32, pp. 10–25.

Leonard, B., Mahon, M., Kinsella, A., Donoghue, C., Farrell, M., Curran, T. and Hennessy, T. (2017). The potential of farm partnerships to facilitate farm succession and inheritance. *International Journal of Agricultural Management*, 6(1), pp. 4–19.

McKillop, J., Heanue, K. and Kinsella, J. (2018). Are all young farmers the same? An exploratory analysis of on-farm innovation on dairy and drystock farms in the Republic of Ireland. *Journal of Agricultural Education and Extension*, 24(2), pp. 137–151.

O'Donnell, S., Horan, B., Butler, A. M. and Shalloo, L. (2011). A survey of the factors affecting the future intentions of Irish dairy farmers. *Journal of Agricultural Science,* 149, pp. 647–654.

Pieralli, S., Hüttel, S. and Odening, M. (2017). Abandonment of milk production under uncertainty and inefficiency: The case of western German Farms. *European Review of Agricultural Economics*, 44(3), pp. 425–454.

Pindado, E., Sánchez, M., Verstegen, J. A. A. M. and Lans, T. (2018). Searching for the entrepreneurs among new entrants in European Agriculture: The role of human and social capital. *Land Use Policy*, 77, pp. 19–30.

Raggi, M., Sardonini, L. and Viaggi, D. (2013). The effects of the Common Agricultural Policy on exit strategies and land re-allocation. *Land Use Policy*, 31, pp. 114–125.

Viira, A.-H., Põder, A. and Värnik, R. (2013). The determinants of farm growth, Decline and exit in Estonia. *German Journal of Agricultural Economy*, 62(1), pp. 52–64.

Viira, A.-H., Põder, A. and Värnik, R. (2014). Discrepancies between the intentions and behaviour of farm operators in the contexts of farm growth, decline, continuation and exit: Evidence from Estonia. *German Journal of Agricultural Economy*, 63(1), pp. 46–62.

Chapter 13

US Trends in Farm and Off-Farm Rural Employment

J. Michael Harris* and Ashok K. Mishra†

**USDA Economic Research Service, Resource and Rural Economics Division, Washington, DC, USA*

†Morrison School of Agribusiness, W. P. Carey School of Business, Arizona State University, USA

†Ashok.K.Mishra@asu.edu

Agriculture is one of the most productive sectors in the US economy. The amount of labor used in farming has declined since the early years of farming. The long-term trend of less-farm labor and more of the other farm inputs has allowed farm operators and other family members to allocate more time to off-farm jobs. Most farmers receive income from off-farm work, but small-scale operations rely on off-farm income to sustain their operations. More than half of US farm operations are small-scale and have annual sales of less than $10,000.

13.1 Introduction

To date, the US farm economy has contracted from a peak in 2012 when commodity prices hit record highs. Because of these economic conditions, farms have employed belt-tightening measures such as reducing production costs and living expenses. Many also are seeking off-farm income opportunities, and farm households have been boosting income streams for several decades. Today, off-farm employment is the primary source of income for many farm households. Both farm and non-farm activities compete for scarce management time, and economic decisions often are shaped by time allocation within a farm household. According to the 2012 agricultural census, 77% of principal operators lived on their farm, and about 70% report that less than 25% of their household income comes from farming. About 61% worked some days off the farm, and about 52% had a primary occupation other than farming.

To better understand how US farm operators, spouses and family members allocate labor between farm and off-farm, this chapter uses the USDA Agricultural Resource Management Survey to summarize current trends in farm labor allocation and the impact on farm income and wealth.

Definition of farm household

Primary operator farm households can be organized as individual operations, partnerships, and family corporations. These farms are closely held (legally controlled) by their operator and the operator's household. Farm operator households exclude households associated with farms organized as non-family corporations or cooperatives, as well as households in which the operator is a hired manager. Household members include all individuals who depend on the household for financial support, whether they live in the household or not. Students away at school, for example, are counted as household members if they are dependents.

13.2 Theoretical Drivers of Off-Farm Employment

Decisions by farm households to allocate labor between the farm and off-farm opportunities reflect the implicit rewards of labor allocation. Decision-making follows the theory of time allocation [Becker, 1981], in which households maximize their utility function. The allocation of farm labor can be modeled using a household production model that combines agricultural production, consumption and labor supply decisions in a single framework to maximize the utility function [O'Brien and Hennessy, 2006].

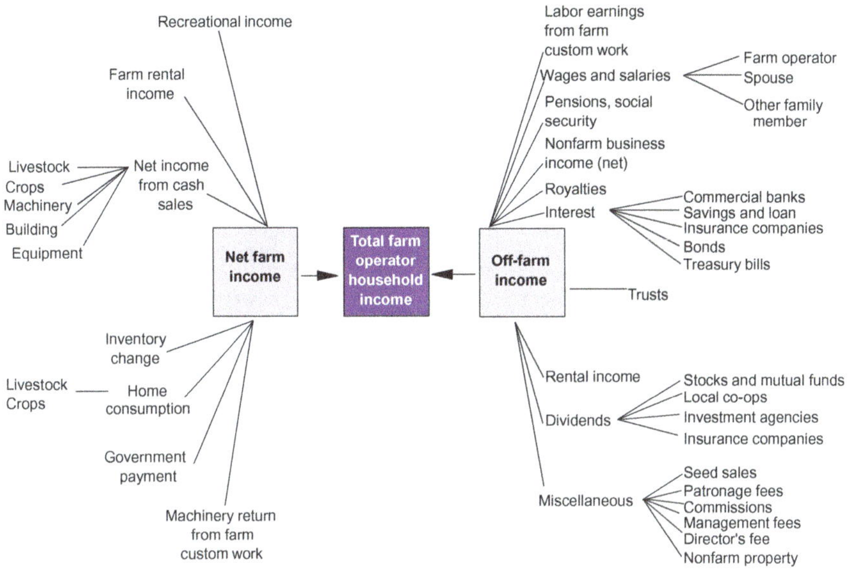

Fig. 13.1. Sources of farm household income.

Source: Mishra *et al.* [2002].

Theoretically, family characteristics (especially size) are an important driver of the economic well-being of households, coupled with resources, production and employment levels, and the ability of income to meet consumption, savings, and other household needs (Fig. 13.1).

Some important other drivers include the presence of young children and other family members. Mishra and Goodwin [1998] found that the presence of children under 13 years old significantly reduces off-farm labor supply, and Woldehanna *et al.* [2000] found that households with large family sizes are more likely to work off-farm. Other drivers are also important: wealthier households may be less risk-averse, which may decrease their incentive to work off-farm; human capital factors influence the labor allocation decision, specifically age; and older farm operators are less likely than younger farm operators to work off-farm [Mishra and Goodwin, 1998]. Farm characteristics must also be considered when looking at drivers of labor allocation. For example, Mishra and Goodwin [1997] found that the larger the farm, the lower the probability that

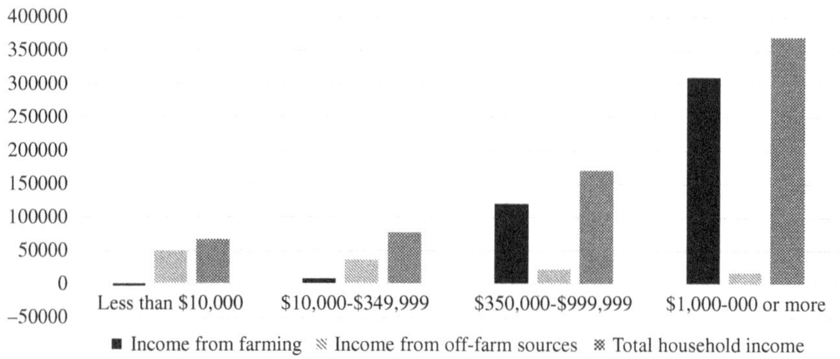

Fig. 13.2. Small-scale farms depend more on off-farm income compared to large farms, 2016.

Note: Sales equal cash income before expenses.
Source: USDA Agricultural Resource Management Survey, ERS and NASS, 2006.

farmers work off-farm, and in 2002, the same authors also found that dual careers (where both operators and spouses have off-farm work) are pursued by households operating large farms.

The importance of farm business size is demonstrated in Fig. 13.2. Farms that have gross sales of less than $10,000 account for about 50% of US farms, but for only about 1% of production. Typically, these farms depend on off-farm sources for the majority of household income. As the size of farm increases, income from farming increases. The largest farms earn the most from farming, and most of their income comes from farming. In fact, most farmers receive income from off-farm work, but small-scale operations rely on off-farm income to sustain their operations. More than half of US farm operations are small-scale and have annual sales of less than $10,000. Both median household and farming income increase with size. Among the largest commercial farm households, earnings reached $365,069 in 2016. Most of these earnings came from farming.

13.3 Off-Farm Work and Income in US Farm Households

US agriculture is one of the most productive sectors in the US economy. Mishra *et al.* [2002] examined the well-being of US farm households using traditional measures such as total household income, but also farm household wealth and expenditures. They found that, although farm business income varies considerably, farm household income is relatively stable. Using cross-sectional data from the Agricultural Resource Management Survey (ARMS), they found that off-farm income played a larger role in total household income in 1999 than in 1993, a trend that has continued into the 21st century. Consequently, the farm business played a smaller role as a source of income and in determining household well-being.

In a farm household, many factors influence the allocation of labor, including the amount of labor needed for the farming operation, the skill set of household members, and off-farm labor opportunities. The amount of labor used in farming has declined since the early years of farming. The long-term trend of less farm labor and more of the other farm inputs has allowed farm operators and other family members to allocate more time to off-farm jobs. ARMS data can be used to examine trends in off-farm employment (Fig. 13.3). In 2016, 59% of principal operators worked off the farm, and 45% of spouses also worked off the farm. The general pattern is somewhat stable, with increases for both principal operators and their spouses. There is a noticeable drop for spouses from 2012 to 2014, a period of good financial conditions for the farm sector. Off-farm employment is sensitive to several economic factors including macroeconomic conditions and profitability in the farm sector.

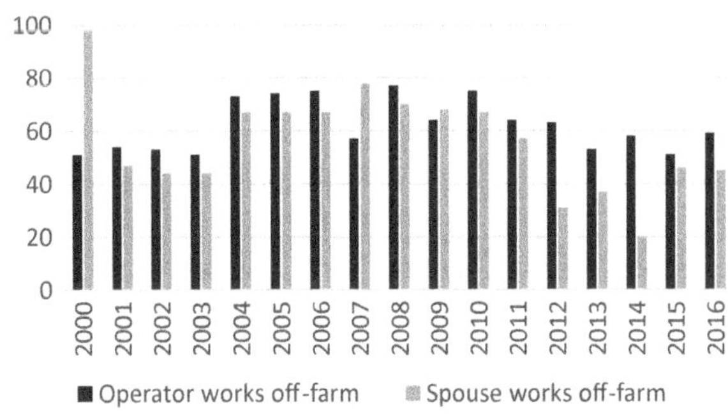

Fig. 13.3. Percentage of principal operators and spouses who work off-farm, 2000–2016.

Source: USDA ARMS, ERS and NASS, 2000–2016.

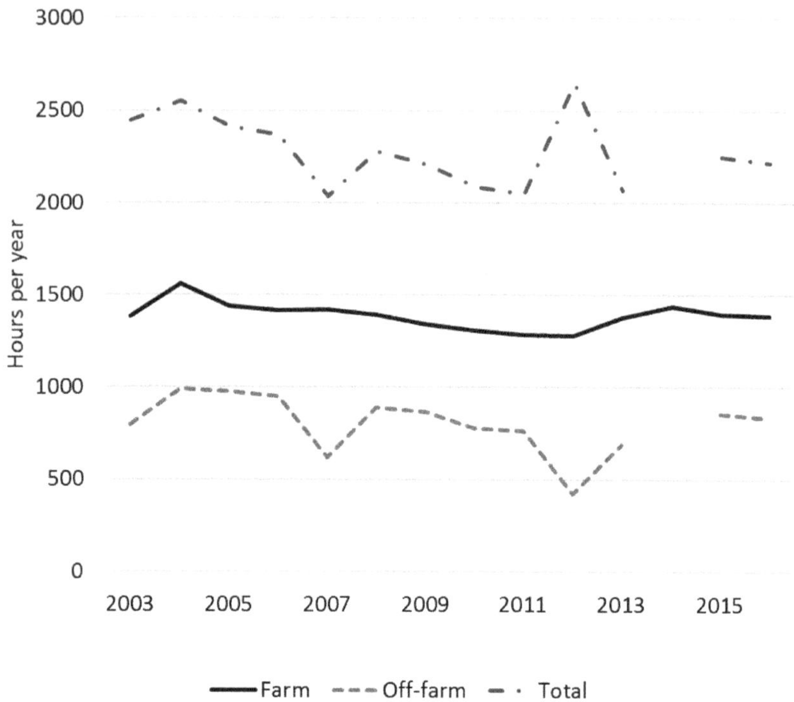

Fig. 13.4. Time allocation in farm, off-farm activities per year, by farm operators, 2003–2016.

Source: USDA ARMS, ERS and NASS, 2003–2016.

Data from the USDA's Economic Research Service (ERS) reveal that over the 2003–2016 period, farm operators spent on average 2,278 hours per year on both farming and off-farm activities. The farm operators spent the majority of the hours (1,387 hours per year) in farm-related activities and about 801 hours per year on off-farm work (Fig. 13.4). It should be noted that the number of farm and off-farm hours differs by farm size and farm specialization. Specifically, consistent with other studies [Mishra *et al.*, 2002; Prager and Burns, 2018], operators of intermediate, commercial, and dairy farms spent significantly more hours on the farm and very few hours in off-farm work. Finally, ERS data show that spouses reported significantly lower total number of hours worked, about 1,027 hours per year, on farm and off-farm activities (Fig. 13.5). Note that spouses also tend to spend time in home production (taking care of household chores,

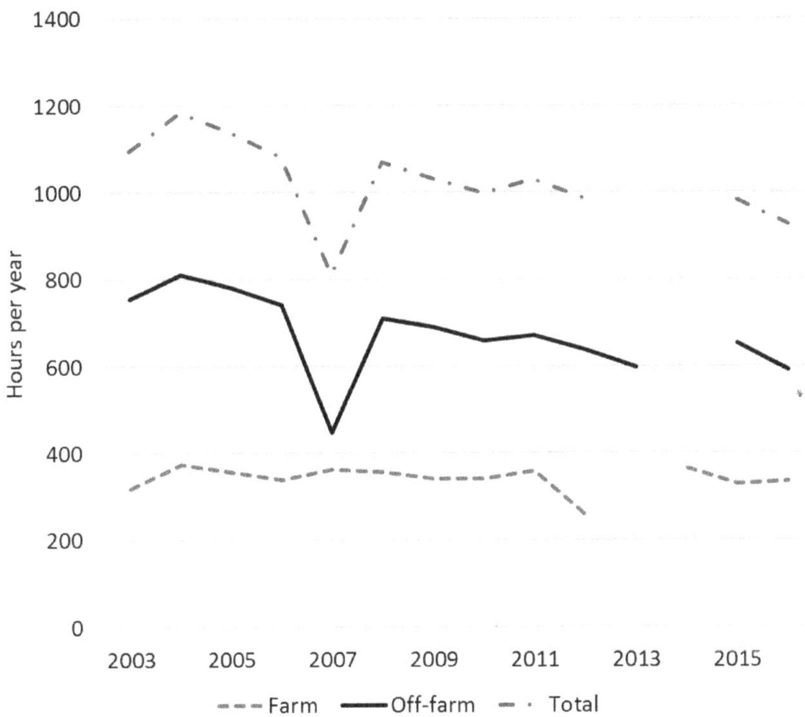

Fig. 13.5. Time allocation in farm, off-farm activities per year, by spouses 2003–2016.

Source: USDA ARMS, ERS and NASS, 2003–2016.

children, and food preparation, etc.), which is not counted in the total hours of work. Additionally, spouses, on average, spend twice as many hours in off-farm work (672 hours per year) than in farm work (341 hours per year). During the 2003–2016 period, significant variability occurs in the number of hours of farm and off-farm work for both operators and spouses (Figs. 13.4. and 13.5). Additionally, the total work (farm and off-farm), farm and off-farm work hours per year show a downward trend (data in the missing years were not collected by ERS). This could be attributed to better measurement, reporting, accounting, and farm mechanization.

Figure 13.6 reports the percentage of operators and spouses who work 35 or more hours off the farm. Note that data for hours of farm and

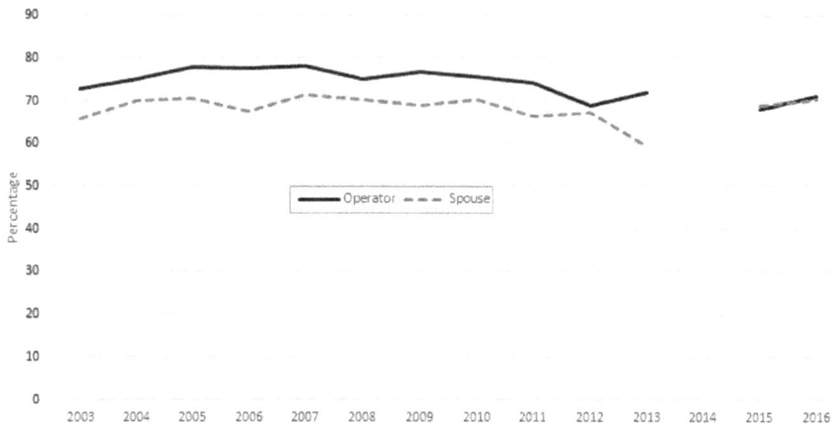

Fig. 13.6. Percentage of operators and spouses working more than 35 hours per week in off-farm jobs, 2003–2016.

Source: USDA ARMS, ERS and NASS, 2003–2016.

off-farm work for 2014 were not collected by the ERS. On average over the 2003–2016 period, of the operators reporting off-farm work, more than 75% reported working 35 or more hours per week — nearly full-time work. Similarly, of the spouses reporting off-farm work, more than 68% reported working 35 or more hours per week, again full-time off-farm work.

In 2016, median farm operator household income exceeded median US household income by 29% ($76,250 compared to $59,039, see Table 13.1). ERS classifies farm households into three types based on the farm or ranch they operate (the "collapsed typology" [Hoppe and MacDonald, 2013]): residence farms, in which the principal operator is primarily employed off-farm or is retired from farming; intermediate farms, in which the primary occupation of the principal operator is farming, but the farm operation earns less than $350,000 in gross cash farm income; and commercial farms, those operations earning $350,000 or more in gross cash farm income. Farm households identified with residence farms — those either retired from farming or with an off-farm occupation — earned the highest amount of off-farm income; however, off-farm income was important to both intermediate and commercial farms as well. Households associated with intermediate farms earned positive average income ($8,201) from farming, but median household

Table 13.1. Principal US farm operator household finances, 2013–2016.

Item	2013	2014	2015	2016
Number of family farms	2,045,352	2,053,008	2,032,300	2,027,269
	Income, median dollars per household			
Farm income	−644	−118	−765	−940
Off-farm income	62,500	70,000	67,500	66,468
Earned income	40,737	42,257	38,270	40,000
Unearned income	20,742	27,439	25,013	24,962
Total household income	73,219	81,637	76,735	76,250
US household income*	53,585	53,657	56,516	59,039
	Income, average dollars per household			
Farm income	30,639	31,025	24,740	24,731
Off-farm income	90,481	103,140	95,140	93,187
Earned income	66,053	71,754	65,814	65,680
Unearned income	24,428	31,386	29,326	27,506
Total household income	121,120	134,164	119,880	117,918
US household income*	75,195	75,738	79,263	83,143
	Balance sheet, median dollars per household			
Total household assets	917,534	1,043,700	966,000	1,014,218
Farm assets	437,375	440,326	438,775	480,500
Non-farm assets	322,234	399,545	297,000	331,250
Total household debt	65,519	85,376	90,562	76,377
Farm debt	800	900	938	950
Non-farm debt	30,000	45,000	37,917	39,000
Household net worth	804,500	872,251	827,307	896,811
	Balance sheet, average dollars per household			
Total household assets	1,466,569	1,674,467	1,590,217	1,751,763
Farm assets	948,116	998,082	1,003,551	1,131,480
Non-farm assets	518,453	676,385	586,666	620,283
Total household debt	153,593	205,024	190,885	185,679
Farm debt	80,655	100,288	101,430	99,664
Non-farm debt	72,938	104,736	89,454	86,014
Household net worth	1,312,976	1,469,443	1,399,332	1,566,084

Note: *Estimates of US household income are produced by the US Census Bureau, Current Population Reports, P60-259, Income and Poverty in the United States: 2016 (and earlier editions).
Source: USDA ARMS, ERS and NASS, 2013–2016.

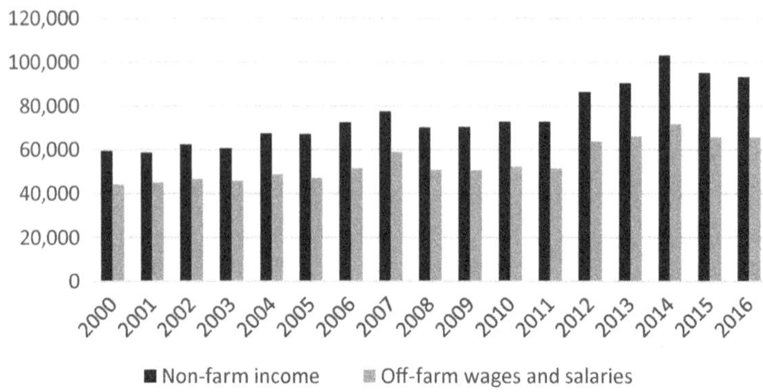

Fig. 13.7. Income earned from off-farm wages and net farm income of US farms 2000–2016.

Source: USDA ARMS, ERS and NASS, years 2000–2016.

income from farming has remained very small ($428). Intermediate farm households have been reliant on off-farm income, earning $55,000 from all off-farm sources in 2016. It is the commercial farm households — those operating farms with at least $350,000 in farm household — who derive a majority of their income from farming.

In fact, in 2016, only 37% of residence farm households earned positive farm income, yet these households earned only 7% of their total household income from farming. Just over half (53%) of intermediate farm households earned positive farm income, which totaled 27% of these households' total income. Conversely, 86% of commercial farm households had a positive flow of income from their farming operation, which accounted for 77% of their (much larger) household income. Though they received more on-farm income than residence farm owners and more off-farm income than those operating commercial farms, intermediate farm households earned the lowest overall income, $57,594, in 2016. The median commercial farm household earned $143,968 in on-farm income, about four times the $39,000 earned from off-farm sources. As with residential farms, the total income of intermediate and commercial farm households over the last 20 years has increased substantially [USDA-ERS, 2016].

Figure 13.7 shows that the majority of off-farm income earned by farm operator households was about 58% in 2016 [USDA-ERS, 2016].

This earned income comes from wages and salaries earned by members of the household. The remainder of non-farm income comes from transfers (18%) and from non-farm businesses (12%).

13.4 Farm Households Working More Off-Farm and Accumulating Wealth

Over the past 20 years, farm business households have seen an increase in their median incomes after adjusting for inflation. In 1996, the median annual income of farm business households was $35,166, compared to $76,483 for self-employed households. By 2016, the median income of farm business households had increased to $64,929, compared to $84,459 for self-employed households. Figure 13.7 shows the contribution of off-farm employment to total household income from 2000 to 2016. Farm households typically receive income from both farm and off-farm sources. The total median income of US farm households increased steadily over 2010–2014, reaching an estimated $81,637 in 2014 in nominal terms (USDA-ERS, 2016). Median household income fell 6% in 2015 and remained flat in 2016. Median farm income earned by farm households is estimated at −$940 in 2016. In recent years, slightly more than half of farm households have had negative farm income each year. Most of these households earn positive off-farm income.

Two major trends have shaped the increase in farm household wealth over the past two decades: an increase in the income of farm households, and the large-scale rise in farmland value over that period. A large portion of the total value of farm and non-farm assets of farm households is captured in real estate holdings. The primary dwelling of roughly half of all residence households and two-thirds of all intermediate and commercial households is owned by the farm operation. About 80% of total farm assets and almost one-third of non-farm assets are in real estate (including both land and structures). Since 1970, the value of farmland real estate — the major source of wealth for farm households — has grown significantly.

In 2016, the median wealth of US households was about $97,300 while the average farm household had a median wealth of $897,000,

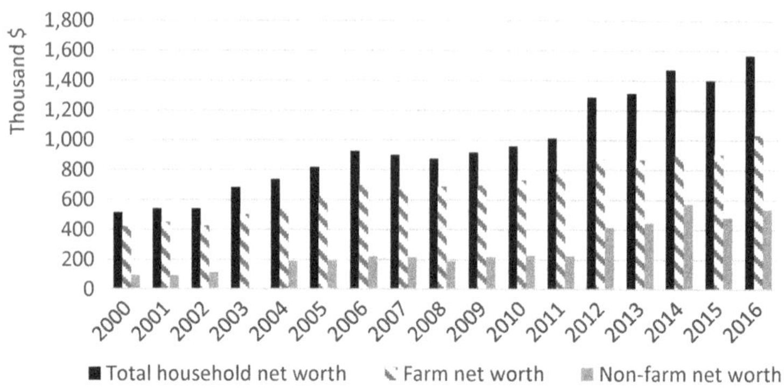

Fig. 13.8. Average farm household net worth, 2016.
Source: USDA ARMS, ERS and NASS, 2000–2016.

about nine times that amount. Households operating commercial farms had \$2.8 million in total wealth at the median. Most large farm operations hold farmland or other real estate, and even smaller farms own much of their equipment. As with farm income, the wealth of farm households varies depending on the type of farm. Because they produce less, the median residence farm households own fewer farm assets (\$359,500) and a similar amount in non-farm assets (\$352,500). Intermediate farms own about twice as much in farm assets (\$656,096) than in non-farm assets (\$264,800), and much more than residence farm households [USDA-ERS, 2016]. On the other hand, commercial farm households, with more than \$350,000 in annual gross cash farm income, hold more than four-fifths of their assets in their farm operation (\$2.7 million), with the rest in non-farm assets (\$433,750). Household wealth is shown in Fig. 13.8. This considerable wealth has accumulated steadily over the last two decades. Concomitant with the increase in farmland real estate, average household net worth increased by more than 50% since 2004. Across all farm households, total household net worth — farm and non-farm assets less farm and non-farm debt — totaled nearly \$900,000 in 2004. It has grown steadily, at an average rate of 5% per year, to \$2.8 million in 2016. Increases in the later years are due to increasing farm and non-farm assets. Note the increases in non-farm assets in the household portfolio.

13.5 Summary

Farm households are faced with decisions about how to allocate their limited resources among farm and non-farm activities. In the US, off-farm work is no longer viewed as a transitional position between the agricultural and the industrial economy, but as a lifestyle choice, with farming as a second job. Off-farm employment often is done for the sake of securing retirement and health benefits. In addition, farm households are no different from other households in pursuing two careers and diversifying earnings. More than half of all US farm operators work off-farm, and nearly half of all spouses also are employed off the farm.

The farm business as a source of income has played an increasingly smaller role in determining the well-being of US farm households. About 79% of total farm household income in 2016 originated from off-farm sources. The contribution of earned income (off-farm wages and salaries) alone amounted to 53% of total farm household income. Farm household income is relatively stable, but changes in farm output, commodity prices, and business cycles, along with macro-economic policies, all contribute to its variability. Since these factors are beyond any farmer's control, many farm households have relied successfully on off-farm income to stabilize their total household income.

The age and status of the farm operator (life cycle) mostly determine the level and sources of household income, and wealth, farm type and size, operator education, farm tenure, and family size are also factors. Among the contributing factors, size of the farming operation is a major factor, but location of the farm operation also affects farms in rural areas (especially those near urban areas), and off-farm income can be the dominant source of household earnings.

References

Becker, G. S. (1981). *A Treatise on the Family*. Harvard University Press, Cambridge, MA.

Hoppe, R. A. and MacDonald, J. M. (2013). *Updating the ERS Farm Typology*. US Department of Agriculture, Economic Research Service.

Mishra, A. K. and Goodwin, B. K. (1997). Farm income variability and the supply of off-farm labor. *American Journal of Agricultural Economics*, 79(3), pp. 880–887.

Mishra, A. K. and Goodwin, B. K. (1998). Income risk and allocation of labour time: An Empirical investigation. *Applied Economics*, (30), pp. 1549–1555.

Mishra, A. K., Morehart, M., El-Osta, H., Johnson, J. and Hopkins, J. (2002). *Income, Wealth, and Well-being of Farm Operator Households*. Agricultural Economics Report # 812, US Department of Agriculture, Economic Research Service, Washington, DC.

O'Brien, M. and Hennessy, T. (2006). *An Examination of the Contribution of Off-farm to the Viability and Sustainability of Farm Households and the Productivity of Farm Businesses*, Rural Economy Research Centre, Galway, Ireland.

Prager, D. and Burns, C. (2018). The effects of US agricultural policies on farm household income and labor. In Mishra, Viaggi and Gomez y Paloma (eds.), *Public Policy in Agriculture: Impact on Labor Supply and Household Income*. Routledge, Oxon, UK.

USDA Economic Research Service (ERS) (2016). *Farm Household Income and Characteristics*, https://www.ers.usda.gov/data-products/farm-household-income-and-characteristics (accessed 22 March 2019).

Woldehanna, T., Lansink, A. O. and Peerlings, J. (2000). Off-farm work decisions on dutch cash crop farms and the 1992 and agenda 2000 CAP Reforms. *Applied Economics*, 22(2), pp. 163–171.

Chapter 14

Wage, Employment and Demographic Trends for Hired Farmworkers in the US*

Thomas Hertz

Economic Research Service, USDA, Washington, DC, USA
thertz@ers.usda.gov

Real hourly wages, annual hours of work and annual earnings of US farmworkers are rising both in absolute terms and in relation to workers in the non-farm economy. This is likely driven by a combination of the reduced rate of net immigration from Mexico, rising minimum wages and rising labor demand. In fiscal years 2013–2014, just 2% of the crop farm workforce were recent immigrants, compared to 23% in fiscal years 1999–2000. These recent immigrants tend to be young, so that in their absence the farm workforce is aging and less geographically mobile than in past years. Growers have responded by adopting new technologies to raise labor productivity, switching to less labor-intensive crops and increasing their use of the H-2A visa program, which brings foreign-born workers to the US on a temporary basis. Thus far, these adjustments appear to have succeeded in restraining the growth in labor costs as a share of total cash expenses or gross cash income.

*The findings and conclusions in this chapter have not been formally disseminated by the US Department of Agriculture and should not be construed to represent any agency determination or policy. This research was supported by the intramural research program of the US Department of Agriculture, Economic Research Service.

14.1 Introduction

This chapter focuses on the US hired farm workforce, a relatively small slice of the rural workforce but one whose economic status is important to monitor for at least three reasons. First, hired farmworkers are typically poorly educated and have relatively low annual earnings, high unemployment rates and high rates of family poverty. Tracking their progress can thus tell us something about how well rural economies are providing for one of their more disadvantaged constituencies. Second, in the US, as in many industrialized nations, most wage and salary workers in agriculture are foreign born, and many lack legal immigration status. The recent shift on both sides of the Atlantic toward nativist political regimes has turned up the heat on the debate over illegal immigration, exposing the conflict between those who rely on unauthorized foreign labor, including many farmers, and those who would reduce the numbers of immigrant workers, whether in hopes of raising wages and creating employment opportunities for the native-born or in furtherance of other, non-economic objectives. Research on farmworker wage, employment and demographic trends is an input into this important and contentious debate. Third, hired labor accounts for a significant share of operating expenses for many farmers, particularly in fruits, vegetables and horticulture, and in the hog and dairy industries. Trends in labor costs and availability influence farmers' crop selection and production practices, and rising costs may accelerate the long-run trend toward larger and more mechanized farm operations, which in turn has ramifications for income and wealth inequality in rural areas [MacDonald *et al.*, 2018].

This chapter addresses aspects of each of these issues, beginning with an overview of economic and demographic trends among farmworkers and their families. This analysis is not restricted to rural areas. As it happens, only about 40% of hired farmworkers in the US live in counties that are deemed non-metropolitan, which is the most commonly used definition of rurality. This primarily reflects the fact that most of the main farming areas in California, Arizona and other Western states lie in geographically large counties that include major cities and are hence defined as metropolitan.

The data for this chapter come from a variety of sources. The longest-running survey of farmworkers is the Department of Labor's National

Agricultural Workers Survey (NAWS), which has been collecting detailed economic, demographic and health-related data since 1989. However, it covers non-supervisory laborers in crop agriculture only; other occupations are excluded, as are all livestock workers and the foreign-born seasonal workers who are temporarily admitted to the US via the H-2A visa program. The USDA's Farm Labor Survey (FLS) includes these missing categories, and is the source for the industry-wide hourly wage data reported below. The Census Bureau's American Community Survey (ACS) is used for industry-wide demographic data. It should be noted that the ACS uses a household-based as opposed to a farm-based sampling strategy, which generally finds lower shares of immigrant workers than does the NAWS. It is also unclear how well the ACS is able to represent the growing number of H-2A workers. Finally, the USDA's Agricultural Resources Management Survey (ARMS) provides data on labor cost shares.

14.2 Farmworkers' Real Wages and Annual Earnings Continue to Rise

Real hourly wage rates have been trending upward for the past 30 years for farmworkers, both in absolute terms and as a percentage of average wages in the non-farm economy. Figure 14.1 reports real wages from 1989 to 2017 for non-supervisory crop and livestock laborers and the average for all farm occupations. Real farm wages have risen at just under 1% per year, but have increased faster since 2011. In 1989, the average non-supervisory farm laborer earned $9.61 per hour (at 2017 prices), which was 51% of the average for production and non-supervisory workers in the non-farm economy.[a] By 2017, the non-supervisory farm wage had risen to $12.47, which was 57% of the non-farm average. Farm workers are thus making gradual progress in closing the farm/non-farm wage gap that is found in virtually every country.

[a]The non-farm wage is taken from the Bureau of Labor Statistics' Current Employment Statistics; the definition of the production and non-supervisory category may be found at: https://www.bls.gov/web/empsit/cesfaq.htm (accessed 6 November 2018).

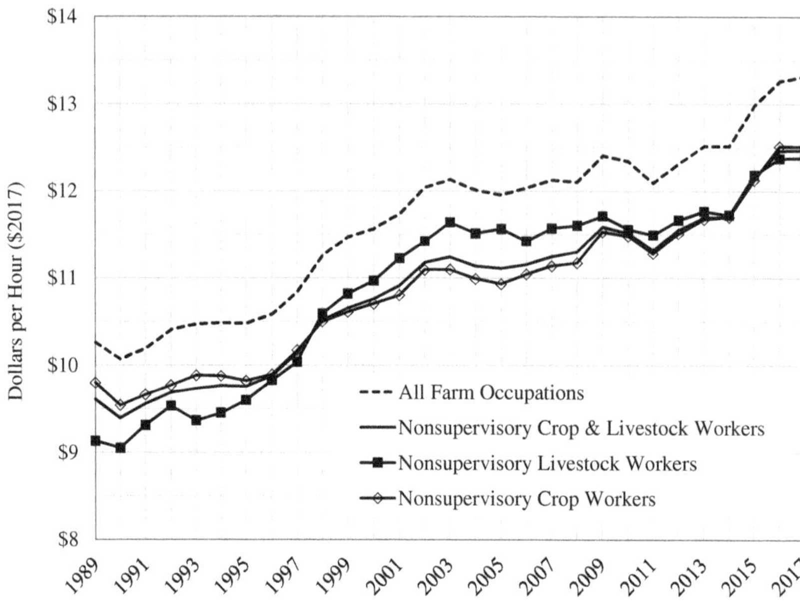

Fig. 14.1. Average real hourly wages in agriculture.

Note: Adjusted for inflation using the Bureau of Labor Statistics' CPI-U-RS.

Source: Author's analysis using data from USDA, FLS.

Wage growth since 2011 has been driven by a number of factors. In recent years, increases in state minimum wages have played an important role, and scheduled increases will raise farm wages further [Ifft and Grout, 2017]. California, which is home to roughly one-quarter of the nation's farmworkers and produces 55% of US fruits and vegetables, raised the state minimum wage from $8 to $9 per hour in July 2014 and to $10 per hour in January 2016. As of January 2018, the minimum was $10.50 per hour for establishments with 25 employees or fewer and $11 per hour for larger employers. By January 2023, the state minimum will be $15 for all employers, with time-and-a-half wages required for hours in excess of eight per day or 40 per week.[b] Arizona, New York, Oregon and Washington

[b]Overtime provisions will be implemented in stages, starting in January 2019. Smaller employers will be fully included by January 2025. The full text of the relevant legislation is available at: https://leginfo.legislature.ca.gov/faces/billTextClient.xhtml?bill_id=201520160AB1066 (accessed 29 June 2018).

also had minimum wages above $10 per hour in 2018, with further increases scheduled. Together with California, these states produced 72% of US fruits and vegetables in 2015.

A second important driver of wage growth has been the slowdown in immigration to the US. Net migration from Mexico to the US turned negative in the wake of the Great Recession, and has remained depressed due to demographic and economic changes in Mexico [Charlton and Taylor, 2016], and increased enforcement of immigration restrictions in the U.S [Alden, 2017]. This has reduced the estimated size of the Mexican-born population in the US from 12.75 million in 2007 to 12.03 million in 2015, a decline of 6% [Cohn *et al.*, 2017], and reduced the number of unauthorized immigrants from Mexico from 6.9 million to 5.6 million, a decline of 19% [Passel and Cohn, 2017]. Because roughly two-thirds of the crop farm workforce is Mexican-born, and two-thirds of this group are unauthorized,[c] these population declines have likely reduced the supply of labor to US agriculture.

Wages also are being driven upward by a recent rise in labor demand. For the past century, both the absolute numbers of farmers and hired farmworkers, and their share of the US population, have followed a long-run downward trend, as is true in all industrialized nations. But lately, farm wage and salary employment has been rising. According to estimates from the Bureau of Economic Analysis, wage and salary employment on farms and in agricultural support services reached its nadir in 2008, at 1.175 million, but by 2016 had rebounded to 1.344 million, an increase of 14%.[d]

---

[c]The NAWS is unique among farm labor data sources in that it queries workers about their legal immigration status. In recent years, roughly half of the overall crop farm workforce has been unauthorized. While many argue that this can only be an underestimate, it is worth noting that, over the years, fully 98% of immigrants who have been in the US for at most one year have reported being unauthorized, suggesting that the NAWS is successful in eliciting this information in face-to-face interviews. However, because the NAWS interviews workers only with permission of their employer, it remains possible that biases in employer non-participation may result in an undercount of the unauthorized.

[d]This is an estimate of the annual average number of people employed for wages in either full or part-time farm-related jobs, with no attempt to standardize for hours worked per week. It is not a count of the number of separate individuals who work on farms at some time during the year; that figure is generally roughly twice as high as average annual

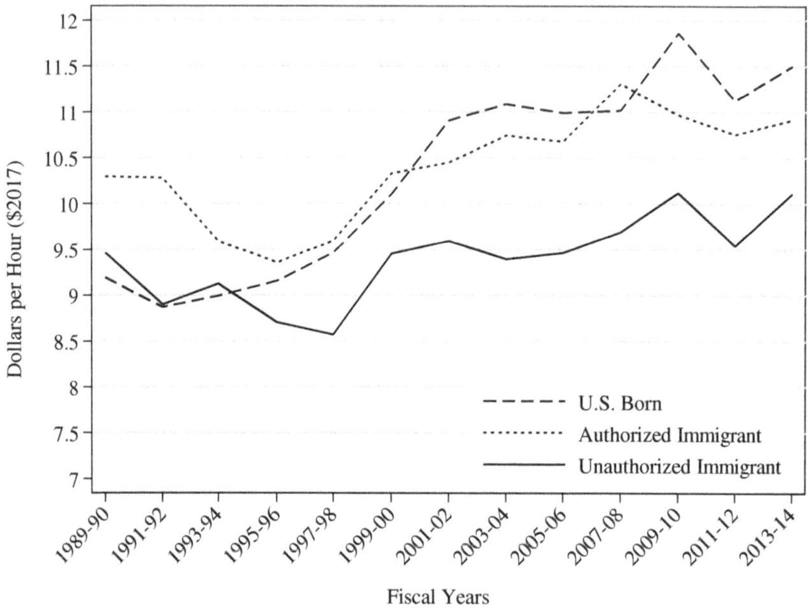

Fig. 14.2. Average real hourly wages of crop farmworkers.

Note: Adjusted for inflation using the Bureau of Labor Statistics' CPI-U-RS. "Authorized immigrants" include naturalized citizens and lawful permanent residents.

Source: Author's analysis of data from Department of Labor, National Agricultural Workers Survey.

This growth reflects increases in both directly hired workers (up 12%, to 820,000) and in agricultural support services (up 18%, to 524,000), the bulk of which consists of farm labor contract workers.

Figure 14.2 illustrates trends in average real hourly wages for unauthorized immigrants, authorized immigrants (including naturalized citizens and legal permanent residents, or green-card holders), and US-born non-supervisory crop farmworkers. Note that these data end in fiscal years (FY) 2013–2014, and so do not capture the most recent increases.[e]

employment, reflecting the fact that many farmworkers do not work a full 52 weeks per year in agriculture.

[e]These wage rates are somewhat lower than the averages reported in Fig. 14.1, from the Farm Labor Survey. This may reflect differences in the composition of the samples of farmworkers covered by the two surveys.

Average hourly wages for unauthorized immigrant workers in FY2013–2014 were about 80 cents per hour less (about 7% less) than for their authorized immigrant counterparts. This gap is reduced by about half when we take account of differences in age, work experience, and education, using regression-based methods (results not shown in figure).

Figure 14.3 demonstrates that annual hours of farm work also have risen, particularly for unauthorized immigrants. For much of the past 30 years, unauthorized workers worked 300–400 fewer hours per year than authorized immigrants. In FY2013–2014, however, unauthorized workers averaged 1,684 annual hours, compared to 1,613 for authorized immigrants.

In Figure 14.4, we see the combined effect of rising hourly wages and rising hours of work for crop farmworkers, which has been to double average annual real earnings from farm work in 20 years for unauthorized

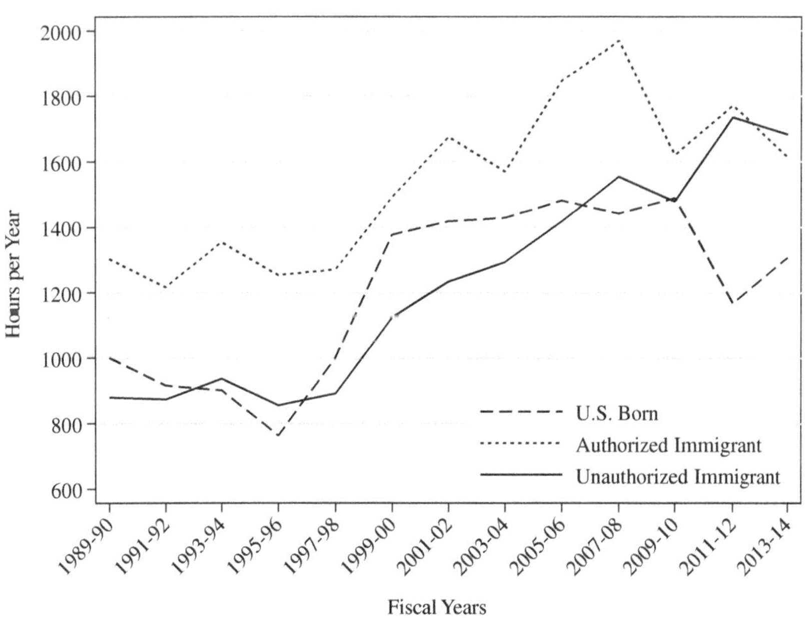

Fig. 14.3. Average annual hours of farm work for crop farmworkers.

Note: "Authorized immigrants" include naturalized citizens and lawful permanent residents.

Source: Author's analysis of data from Department of Labor, National Agricultural Workers Survey.

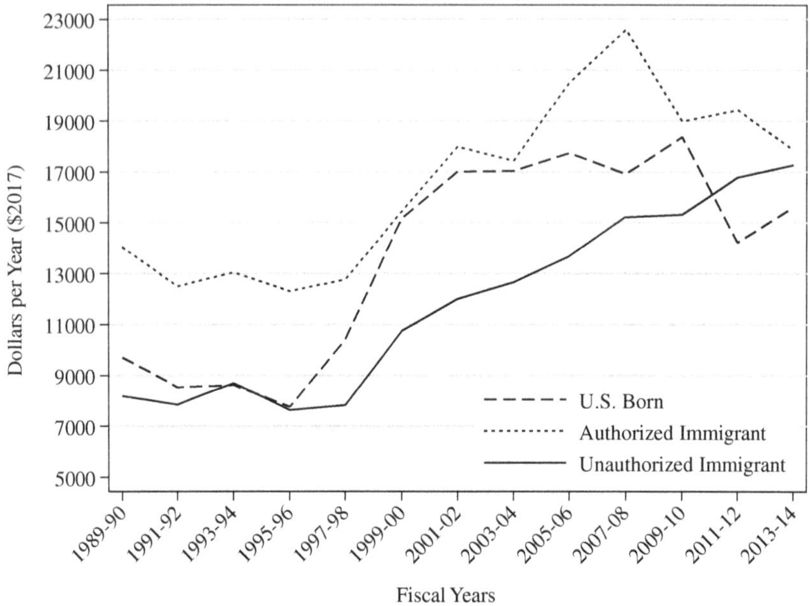

Fig. 14.4. Average real annual farm earnings for crop farmworkers.

Note: Adjusted for inflation using the Bureau of Labor Statistics' CPI-U-RS. "Authorized immigrants" include naturalized citizens and lawful permanent residents.

Source: Author's analysis of data from Department of Labor, National Agricultural Workers Survey.

workers (to $17,300 in 2017 dollars) and to increase them by about 37% for authorized immigrants (to $17,900), while US-born crop farmworkers saw their annual earnings from farm work rise by about 81% (to $15,600). This convergence in the earnings of the various legal status categories is clearer when earnings from non-farm employment are included: US-born, authorized immigrant and unauthorized immigrant crop farmworkers had total earnings of $20,400, $19,600 and $19,000, respectively, in FY2013–2014 (numbers not shown in figure).

14.3 Immigrant Farmworkers are More Settled, and Their Average Age is Rising

The increase in annual hours of work described above has been facilitated by an increase in the proportion of the year that unauthorized farm workers spend in the US (i.e., a reduction in time spent abroad), as shown in Fig. 14.5. This chart excludes recent immigrants, in order to provide a more accurate picture of the time allocation of those who could potentially have spent a full year in the US. Between FY1991 and FY1998, unauthorized immigrant crop farmworkers typically spent 8–11 weeks out of the country; from FY1999 to FY2008, that figure ranged between three and seven weeks; and from FY2009 forward it has averaged just one week.

This decline reflects a combination of factors, including changing demographics in Mexico, changing economic conditions in both Mexico and the US, and the fact that stricter enforcement of immigration restrictions, particularly since 2011, has increased both the risk of apprehension associated with crossing the border and the negative consequences for those apprehended [Alden, 2017]. Thus, some of the decline in labor supply brought about by the decline in net migration to the US from Mexico has been offset by the fact that prior years' immigrants are staying in the country for a great proportion of the year.

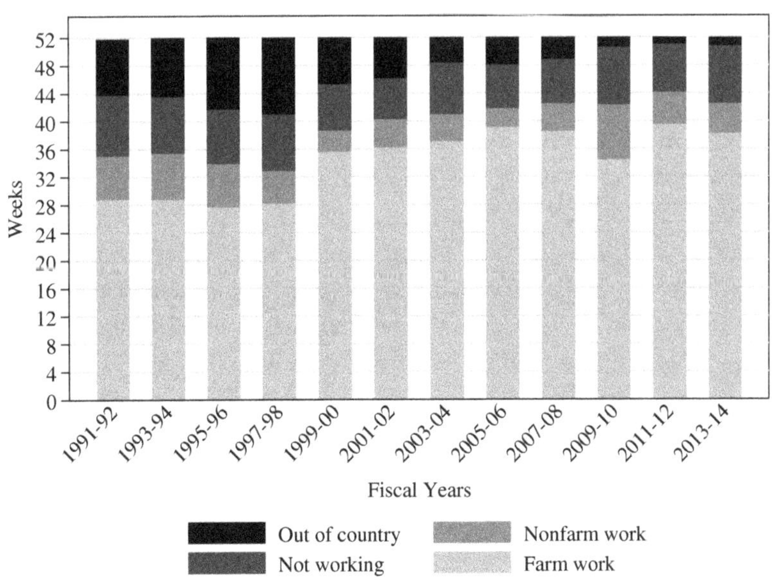

Fig. 14.5. Time allocation of unauthorized immigrant crop farmworkers.

Note: Omits immigrants arriving within past year.

Source: Author's analysis of data from Department of Labor, National Agricultural Workers Survey.

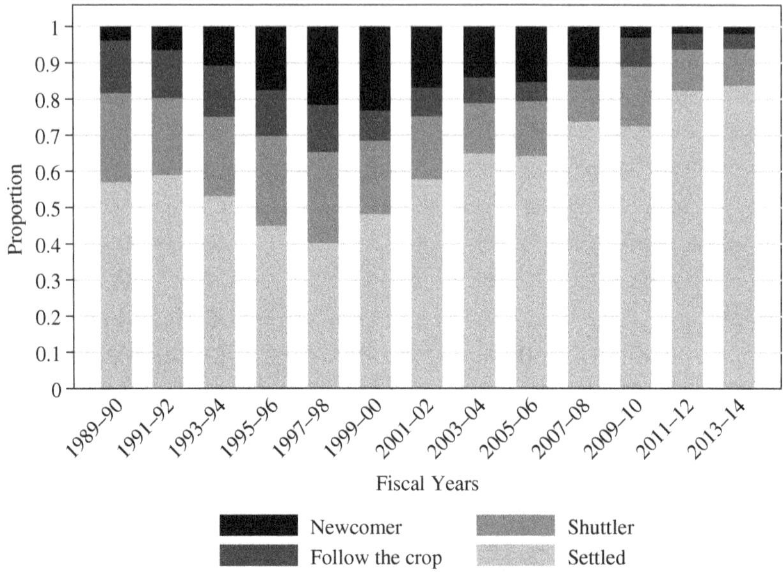

Fig. 14.6. Migration patterns of crop farmworkers.

Source: Author's analysis of data from Department of Labor, National Agricultural Workers Survey.

Farmworkers are also now less likely than in the past to travel long distances to work. As shown in Fig. 14.6, more than 80% of crop farmworkers are considered settled, meaning that they work at a single location within 75 miles of their home. This number is up from 40% in FY1997–1998. Among the remaining migrant workers, the largest group are "shuttlers", who work at a single farm location more than 75 miles from home and may (legally) cross an international border to get there. They made up about 10% of hired crop farmworkers in FY2013–2014, down from 25% in FY1997–1998. The "follow the crop" migrant farmworker, who moves from state to state working on different crops as the seasons advance, is now a relative rarity. These workers made up just 4% of crop farmworkers surveyed by the NAWS in FY2013–2014, down from a high of 14% in FY1989–1990.

The final category in Fig. 14.6 are the newcomers, recent immigrants whose migration patterns have not yet been established. The fact that they represent just 2% of the crop farm workforce, down from as much as

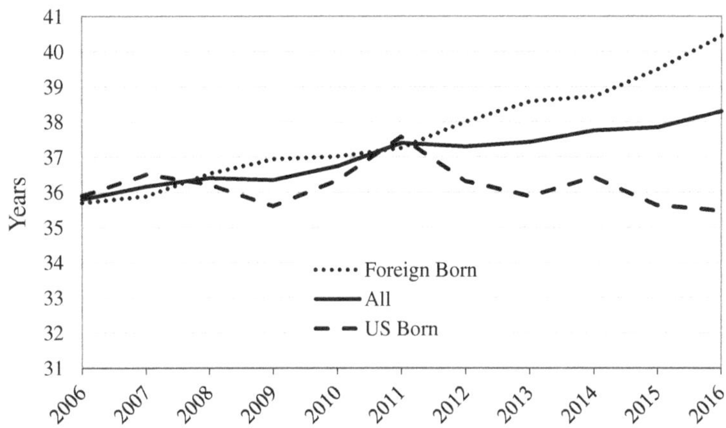

Fig. 14.7. Average age of manual laborers in agriculture.

Note: Included are Miscellaneous Agricultural Workers, and Graders and Sorters, in crops, livestock and agricultural support service industries.

Source: Author's analysis of data from Bureau of the Census, ACS.

23% in FY1999–2000, reflects the slowdown in net immigration from Mexico.

An immediate consequence of the slowdown in immigration is that the farm work force is aging. Using data on both crop and livestock workers found in the ACS, we can see that the average age of a manual farm laborer has risen from 36 to 38 since 2006, driven by the increase among the foreign-born segment of the labor force, whose average age has risen from 36 to 40.5 (Fig. 14.7).

14.4 Farmers are Adapting, and Labor Costs as a Share of Gross Cash Income Have Not Risen

Farmers are responding to the relative scarcity of farm labor in various ways. As we have seen, wages are rising, although the scope of wage increases is limited by the presence of competitive imports for many commodities. Some growers are offering one-time bonuses and non-wage inducements, including providing better training for field supervisors, whose poor relations with their work crews are a perennial source of conflict [Martin, 2017]. Second, growers are making greater use of mechanical aids, such as hydraulic platforms that replace ladders in the orchards and mobile conveyor belts that reduce the distance that heavy loads must be carried. These raise labor productivity, and permit older and female workers to perform some tasks previously done by younger men. Third, farmers are turning to newer technologies that fully mechanize portions of the production process. This is often an expensive proposition, both because of equipment costs and because mechanization usually requires replanting with new varieties that are suitable for mechanical harvest. Fourth, farmers are switching from some of the more labor-intensive fruit and vegetable crops to crops that are more readily harvested by machine. An example is the expansion of tree-nut acreage. This, too, is expensive, and requires a long time horizon. Recent concern over future water availability in California and elsewhere has heightened the uncertainty underlying this calculation. Lastly, farmers are making much greater use of the H-2A Temporary Agricultural Program, which provides a legal means to bring foreign-born workers to the United States to perform seasonal farm labor on a temporary basis. The program serves crop farmers and producers of livestock on the range (principally sheep and goats) but the restriction to seasonal labor has the effect of excluding other livestock producers, such as ranches, dairies, and hog and poultry operations, whose labor needs are year-round. This program has existed since the mid-1980s, but growers have long complained about its costs and administrative burden. Employers must demonstrate, and the US Department of Labor must certify, that efforts to recruit US workers were not successful. Employers must also pay a state-specific minimum wage, which is set at the prior year's regional average wage for all non-supervisory crop and livestock workers, as determined by the USDA's FLS, and is thus higher than the market wage for many lower-paid occupations. Growers also must provide housing at no cost, and pay for domestic and international transportation.

Despite these costs, Fig. 14.8 reveals that H-2A utilization has quintupled in the past 13 years, from just over 48,000 positions certified in FY2005 to 243,000 in FY2018, confirming that cheaper sources of immigrant labor are no longer adequate. Given that the average duration of an H-2A certification in 2017 was 5.4 months, the figure of 200,000

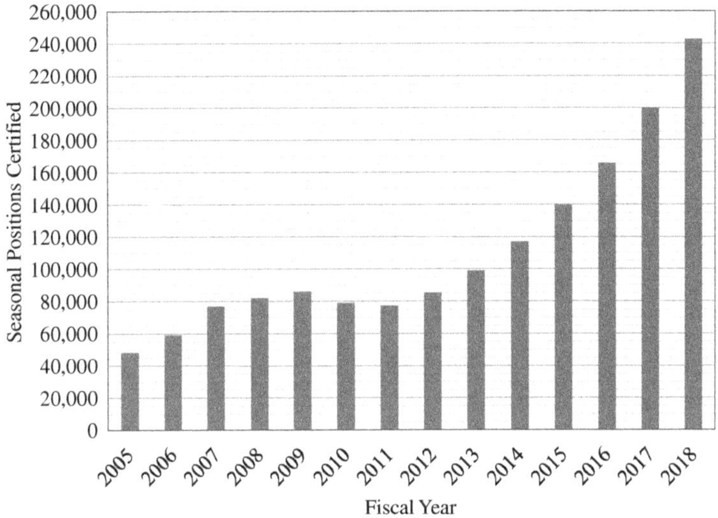

Fig. 14.8. H-2A certifications.

Source: Department of Labor, Office of Foreign Labor Certification.

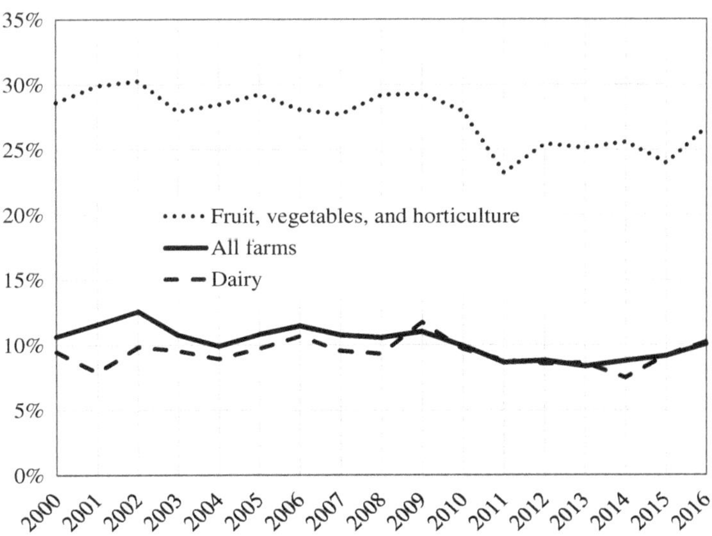

Fig. 14.9. Labor costs as a percentage of gross cash income.

Note: "Gross cash income" includes income from sales of commodities, other farm-related sales, and total direct government payments, all measured before expenses.

Source: US Department of Agriculture, NASS/ERS Agricultural Resource Management Surveys.

certified positions represents approximately 90,000 full-year equivalents, or about 7% of the 1.3 million jobs counted by the Bureau of Economic Analysis in 2017.

These various economic responses by growers appear so far to have contained total labor costs, which have held roughly steady as a share of cash expenses since 2000. Rising output prices for many fruits also have helped soften the impact of rising wage rates. As a result, labor costs as a share of gross cash income have not shown an upward trend since the turn of the century, although there was a statistically significant uptick in 2016 (see Fig. 14.9).

14.5 Discussion

The availability of an adequate supply of farm labor at economically viable wages is of perennial concern to growers of labor-intensive crops, and it might be argued that recent wage-growth rates are not unprecedented and are not evidence of an unusually severe labor shortage. However, several of the factors discussed above suggest that the current situation is indeed unusual. The decline in unauthorized immigration since 2007 is a novel development, and its impact on the crop farm workforce is clearly reflected in the declining share of recent immigrants and the rising age of those already here. Some of this decline appears to have been offset by the rapid growth of the H-2A program, which many growers had hitherto avoided due to its higher costs, and by the more intensive use of the existing labor force, with the result that overall employment has not fallen.

A recent proposal would revise the H-2A program to make it less expensive for growers, by lowering the applicable minimum wage from its current level of between $11 and $14 per hour, depending on the region, to 115% of the applicable state or federal minimum. In California, this would have lowered the 2018 wage rate for H-2A workers from $13.18 to $12.65, a decline of 4%, whereas in states such as Texas, with no state minimum wage, the H-2A wage rate would fall from $11.87 to $8.34, a 30% cut. The proposal would also eliminate the requirement to provide free housing and to pay worker transportation costs, and would restrict participating workers' access to legal services. In addition, the proposal would streamline the application process and expand eligibility to include year-round workers in livestock, food processing, aquaculture and forestry.

As of this writing, legislation including this proposal has failed to pass the US House of Representatives, despite having been modified several times in an attempt simultaneously to satisfy the various relevant interest groups. This political stalemate is arguably beneficial to current H-2A workers as well as to the nation's resident farmworkers, whose recent income growth would likely slow if the administratively-determined wage rate for the H-2A program were reduced. Moreover, because the current H-2A program is not subject to any numerical caps, it could in principle expand to cover a much larger share of the crop workforce. This expansion has already led to tensions between older, settled immigrant workers and younger H-2A recruits [Mines, 2018], tensions which would likely increase if policy changes accelerated H-2A adoption.

Some commentators [e.g. Taylor *et al.*, 2012] have argued that the long-run strategy for US farmers must be to reduce labor intensity yet further, rather than seek out expanded supplies of temporary immigrant workers. However, while Taylor *et al.* may be correct that over the long run, the number of Mexicans and Central Americans willing to work in agriculture are likely to fall, for the time being there appears to be no shortage of workers eager to participate in the H-2A program, which offers a ticket to a much higher wage than can be had south of the border. Moreover, if the length of the temporary visa is increased beyond its current 10-month limit, it could well become feasible to import labor from more distant countries. Ultimately, whether US agriculture pursues a lower-wage guest worker solution or a higher-wage more mechanized approach will likely be determined by political forces, as much as by economic or demographic trends.

References

Alden, E. (2017). Is border enforcement effective? What we know and what it means. *Journal on Migration and Human Security*, 5(2), pp. 481–490.

Charlton, D. and Taylor, J. E. (2016). A declining farm workforce: Analysis of panel data from rural Mexico. *American Journal of Agricultural Economics,* 98(4), pp. 1158–1180.

Cohn, D., Passel, J. S. and Gonzalez-Barrera, A. (2017). *Rise in U.S. Immigrants from El Salvador, Guatemala and Honduras Outpaces Growth from Elsewhere*. Pew Research Center, December.

Ifft, J. and Grout, T. (2017). State labor regulations and labor-intensive agriculture. *Farmdoc Daily*, (7): 111. Department of Agricultural and Consumer Economics, University of Illinois at Urbana-Champaign, June.

MacDonald, J. M., Hoppe, R. A. and Newton, D. (2018). *Three Decades of Consolidation in U.S. Agriculture*, United States Department of Agriculture, Economic Research Service, Economic Information Bulletin No. EIB-189, Washington, DC.

Martin, P. (2017). American agriculture at a crossroads between imports, machines and migrants. *The Hill*. December 25. http://thehill.com/opinion/immigration/366437-american-agriculture-at-a-crossroads-between-imports-machines-and (accessed 29 June 2018).

Mines, R. (2018). *Social Impact of the H-2A Program in the Salinas/Pajaro Valleys*. Conference presentation to conference titled "30 Years of NAWS Data", University of California, Davis, 12 April.

Passel, J. S. and Cohn, D. (2017). As Mexican share declined, US unauthorized immigrant population fell in 2015 below recession level. Pew Research Center, April.

Taylor, J. E., Charlton, D. and Yúnez-Naude, A. (2012). The end of farm labor abundance. *Applied Economics Perspectives and Policy*, 34(4), pp. 587–598.

Part E
Agri-food Chain

Chapter 15

Value Added and Employment Growth in EU Primary Agriculture and Food Processing

Trevor Donnellan* and Kevin Hanrahan

Agricultural Economics and Farm Survey Department, Teagasc, Athenry, Co. Galway, Ireland
**trevor.donnellan@teagasc.ie*

This chapter examines the relationship between agri-food's primary and processing sectors at the EU Member State (MS) level in this century. In terms of sector value added and employment, substantially different economic developments in the primary and processing sectors are evident across the MSs. This could mean that the agri-food sectors in individual MSs may continue to have differing capacities to generate income and employment, which is a concern for the design of future agri-food policy. The analysis indicates that the capacity of the agri-food sector to deliver economic growth is more limited in some MSs than in others, indicating a need for further investigation of the underlying causes.

15.1 Introduction

Agriculture and food processing remain important sectors, particularly in employment terms, in non-urban regions across the European Union (EU). Yet primary agriculture has long been perceived as a mature sector, consistent with the definition of a sunset industry [Radetzki, 2008]. However, this characterization of the sector has been revised by policy makers (and many economists) over the last decade, with the emergence of strong global food demand growth, driven largely by rising incomes and population growth in developing countries. This development led to a run-down of agricultural commodity stock levels, an overall tightening of agricultural commodity markets, and a 75% rise in real food commodity prices over the period 2003–2008 [Erten and Ocampo, 2013]. New demand for land, such as that required for the growth of biofuels, added to these pressures [Langeveld *et al.*, 2013]. While agricultural commodity markets went through a boom in the 2000s, a lack of economic growth and employment opportunities at the same time has been a source of inequality affecting rural areas [Fresco and Poppe, 2016].

In the "knowledge-based bio-economy" (KBBE) paradigm [European Council, 2000], new scientific knowledge and technological innovation are the driving forces behind sustainable wealth creation, but only if society adapts to these imperatives. In the KBBE era, a vibrant and growing food processing industry would be expected to make innovative and higher value added food products to satisfy rapidly growing numbers of increasingly sophisticated customers. Farmers would enjoy the benefits via "thriving rural livelihoods", which would be expected to flow from additional demands for agricultural output arising from developments in the KBBE. That at least is the narrative set out in official policy documents [e.g. European Commission, 2012]. If the KBBE agenda is not embraced, Birch *et al.* [2014] argue that Europe will fall behind globally in competitiveness and productivity gains.

The concept of the KBBE is not well defined, making it difficult to quantify statistically its existing scale, and impeding consideration of its existing or future economic benefits. However, the agri-food sector does have a recognized definition in published statistics. This provides a basis for the examination of the traditional agri-food component within the wider KBBE, looking at economic developments in the agri-food sector across the EU in the period since the turn of the 21st century. The term "agri-food" reflects the amalgamation of two distinct components, a primary farm sector based to a large extent on the production of raw materials, and a food-processing sector based around the transformation of those raw materials into edible products. Of course, the raw materials that are processed may originate within EU Member States (MSs) or they may be imported from elsewhere.

This chapter looks at observed growth in output, gross value added (GVA) and employment in the food processing industry to see whether this is reflected in growth in the volume, output value and GVA of primary agriculture, and whether there has been a common or heterogeneous experience across EU MSs. GVA includes both enterprise profits as well as the wages and salaries of employees, and contributes to GDP, but should not be conflated with income per worker.

15.2 Background

The 28 MSs of the EU are at different stages of economic development. This is reflected in the relative importance of more traditional sectors, such as agri-food, in overall economic activity at the MS level. Most of the countries of Western Europe enjoyed strong economic growth in the immediate decades after World War II, with manufacturing and services growing in economic importance relative to the agri-food sector. By contrast, in the post-war period, many of the countries of Central and Eastern Europe (CEE), were under central planning, which, among other things, led to a slower decline in the importance of agri-food in the overall economy.

The EU created the European Single Market in 1992, guaranteeing free movement of goods, services, capital and labor between MSs. Over the last 25 years, the EU has therefore become an increasingly integrated market for goods, services and labor. Enlargement of the EU to incorporate the CEE countries began in 2004, and was extended further in 2007 and again in 2013. As part of this enlargement, the CEE agri-food sector benefitted from the support of the Common Agricultural Policy (CAP), but, in joining the Single Market, it also faced competition from the agri-food sector of the EU MSs of Western Europe, the so-called EU-15.

Since the turn of the century, primary agriculture across individual EU MSs has continued to decline in importance in terms of contribution to GDP, and in terms of the absolute and relative share of total employment it provides. However, over the same period, it is less clear what trend should be expected, *a priori*, in terms of the food processing sector's contribution to GDP or the food processing sector's absolute and relative share of total employment at MS level. It is conceivable that growth in the food processing sector's value added would have contributed to stabilizing or increasing in output and employment in the overall agri-food sector.

The agriculture and food processing sectors of EU MSs are heterogeneous, and, depending on the country considered, there are differences in terms of the principal agri-food outputs produced. There are also differences in terms of the level of integration of the agri-food sector in MSs with that of neighboring countries. Both these factors lead us to assume that the relationship between the development of primary agriculture and food processing will not be consistent across the EU.

15.3 Analysis and Discussion

The analysis below relies primarily on an examination of the available Eurostat data at MS level. Such data has been converted to indices to facilitate the comparison of growth rates. The analysis explores whether there has been a common experience in terms of income or employment developments for the agriculture and food processing sectors, or whether there seems to be any relationship at all. Answering this question is important given that some policy makers are content to draw sweeping inferences about the economic health of farm incomes and farm employment solely from their interpretation of data on food production growth and/or food export growth performance.

The diversity in the contribution of agriculture to the economies of different EU MSs is evident in the importance of the sector in employment, output and GVA terms. Figure 15.1 illustrates the value of output (in nominal terms) generated in the Agriculture, Forestry and Fishing (AFF) sector and in the Food Processing, Beverages and Tobacco (FPBT) sector for the EU-28 over the period 2003–2014. It is evident that there has been an increase in the value of output in both sectors over the period, but that in percentage terms the growth in output value in the AFF sector has lagged behind the growth in output value in the FPBT sector. Over the period considered, the output value of the AFF sector of the EU-28 increased by 25%, whereas output growth in the EU-28 FPBT sector was 33%.

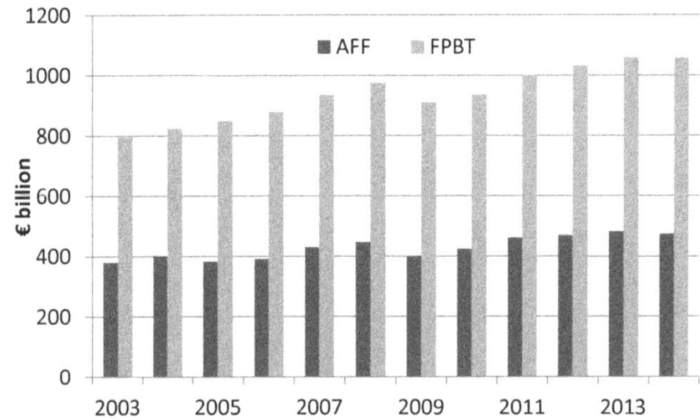

Fig. 15.1. EU-28 value of output of AFF, and FPBT.

Source: Eurostat.

GDP per capita by MS across the EU varies considerably, reflecting the different stages of economic development of the various MSs. Some economies have evolved to the point where GDP is dominated by the service sector, which has superseded manufacturing and primary agriculture as the driver of most economic activity in more developed economies. This dominance is particularly evident in urban areas and increasingly common even in rural areas. At the MS level, the joint GVA contribution of the combined AFF and FPBT sectors (hereafter the agri-food sector) to EU MS GDP is generally observed to be quite small, and may be expected to decrease in all MSs over time, as economies develop further.

Figure 15.2 shows the GDP share of the agri-food sector by MS in 2003 and 2013. Perhaps unsurprisingly, the contribution of the agri-food sector to GDP was highest in the two MSs with the lowest national GDP per capita, Bulgaria and Romania. In general terms, the GVA contribution of the agri-food sector to national GDP is found to be higher across the CEE countries than in Western Europe.

Across the EU-28, the GVA contribution of the agri-food sector has declined over the period 2003–2013, with a sharper rate of reduction in CEE MSs. Again, this might be expected given the different stages of economic development in Western Europe relative to CEE. In many EU MSs, the overall agri-food sector now represents less than 5% of GDP.

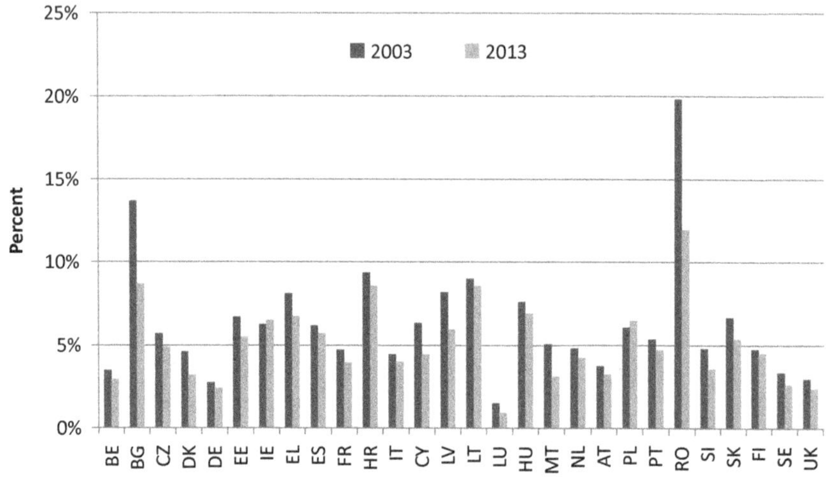

Fig. 15.2. GVA in AFF and FPBT as share of gross domestic product by EU MS, 2003 and 2013.

Source: Authors' elaboration based on Eurostat data.

Growth rates in employment in the AFF and FPBT sectors across the EU MSs over the period 2003–2013 are illustrated in Fig. 15.3.

In keeping with the declining trend in GVA contribution, there has been a general decrease in the absolute level of employment in these two sectors in many MSs. In several cases, AFF employment fell by between 20% and 55% between 2003 and 2013. However, there were some exceptions to this general downward trend: the data indicates that absolute AFF employment has increased, notably in Malta, Sweden and the UK.

Over the same period, FPBT sector employment fell in most EU MSs. The largest declines in employment were in Denmark and Slovakia, where employment declined by as much as 30%. More generally, the decline in the FPBT industry ranged from 10% to 20%. The level of FPBT employment remained stable in Greece and Spain, while in Italy, Cyprus, Luxembourg and particularly Poland employment in the FPBT industry increased.

Figure 15.4 illustrates the relative contributions of AFF and FPBT to overall GVA in the agri-food sector in 2013. The insights this measure can offer are useful but limited, in the sense that it points to differences

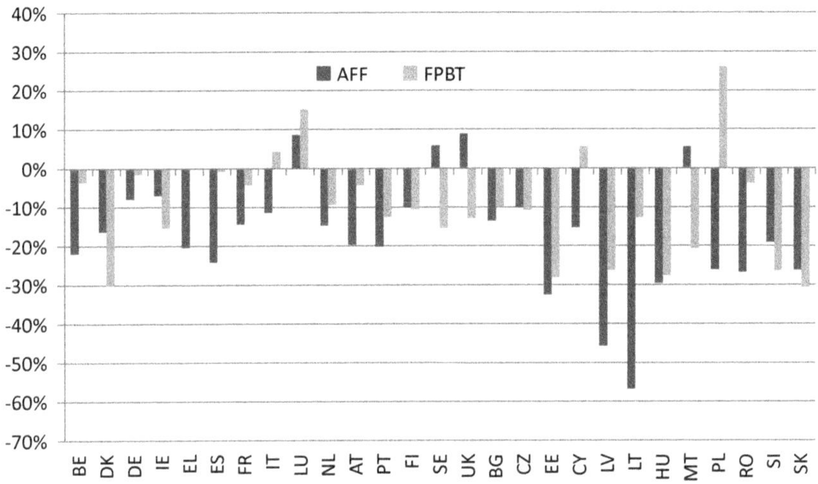

Fig. 15.3. Growth in employment 2003–2013 in AFF and in FPBT in EU MSs.

Source: Authors' elaboration based on Eurostat data.

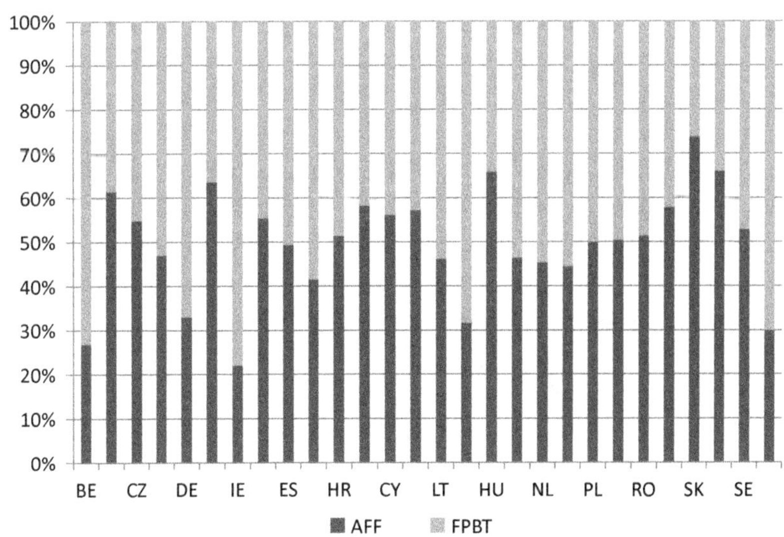

Fig. 15.4. Relative shares of GVA contributed by AFF and FPBT, by MS, 2013.

Source: Authors' elaboration based on Eurostat data.

between MSs in terms of the relative contribution of the primary and processing stages of production in the generation of value added — without revealing why such differences exist. The measure provides some indication of whether the FPBT sector in a given MS is adding value to the output of its primary production sector. An agri-food sector with a smaller share of its total aggregate GVA provided by the AFF sector would be adding more value to its primary production at the processing stage.

While the relative contribution to GVA of the primary and processing stage in Fig. 15.4 identifies, but does not explain, the observed differences across MSs, we can nevertheless posit some reasons for the observed differences.

First, the capacity to add value to primary production at the processing stage will depend to some degree on the nature of the primary production in a given MS. Where much agricultural production is composed of fresh produce, such as fruits and vegetables, the capacity to add value in the processing stage may be more limited than where a higher proportion of agricultural output is made up of livestock or livestock products, which tend to have a greater requirement and potential for conversion to higher value added processed food items.

Second, a high share of AFF GVA in total agri-food sector GVA may also indicate that a significant share of primary production is exported to other countries for further processing, with the value added accruing in the country to which the primary product has been exported. By contrast, a low share of AFF GVA in total agri-food GVA may indicate that the sector is adding considerable value to the country's primary production (or alternatively that the FPBT sector of the country is importing primary products for further processing). Ultimately, the reason why these differences exist across MSs requires much more detailed investigation that goes beyond the scope of this chapter.

The contribution of AFF to overall agri-food sector GVA varies significantly, ranging from as low as 22% in Ireland to as high as 74% in Slovakia, but there is no discernible dichotomy between the MSs in CEE and those in Western Europe. However, it is evident that MSs which have a substantial livestock sector tend to have a low share of AFF GVA within total agri-food GVA. For example, some of the lowest shares of AFF GVA are found in Ireland, Belgium, Denmark, France and the UK, all of which have substantial livestock sectors. In MSs, where crop, fruit and vegetable production are prevalent in agricultural output, AFF GVA tends to contribute more than half of overall agri-food GVA. This suggests that the dominance of particular agricultural activities in the agricultural sector output of an MS is a factor in determining the size and profitability of the food processing sector in different MSs relative to the size of the MS's primary agricultural sector. This apparent relationship between agricultural sector output composition and the size of the food processing sector may mean that the agri-food sector has less capacity to deliver additional output, employment and value added in some MSs as compared to others.

Figure 15.5 shows the nominal GVA per worker employed in the AFF and FPBT sectors across the MSs in 2013. The GVA contribution per worker in the AFF varies from as low as €3,000 per worker in Bulgaria and Romania to as high as €57,000 in the Netherlands. In general, the GVA per worker in AFF is around €40,000 in Western Europe and less than half that in CEE. There are exceptions to this general West/East divide, with a relatively high level of AFF GVA per worker in Slovakia, at

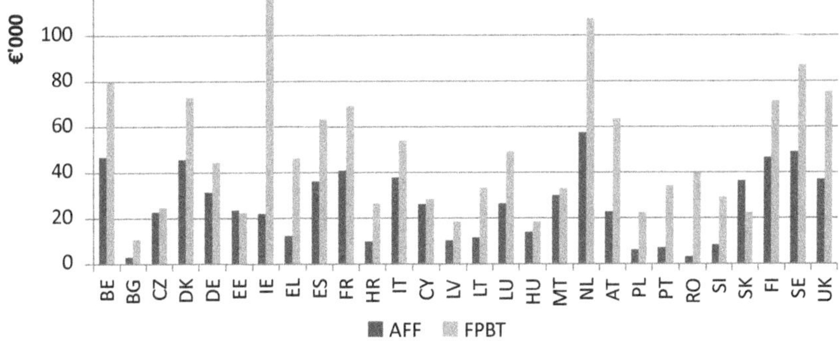

Fig. 15.5. GVA per worker in AFF and in FPBT, by MS, 2013.

Source: Authors' elaboration based on Eurostat data.

€36,000, and a comparatively low level of AFF GVA per worker in parts of the EU-15 such as Ireland, Austria, Greece and Portugal.

The range in GVA per worker in the FPBT sector across the MSs is vast: FPBT GVA per worker is highest in Ireland at €180,000, but lowest at just €11,000 in Bulgaria. In general, the level of this measure in Western Europe is around double that in CEE. With few exceptions, the GVA contribution per worker in the FPBT sector is higher than in the AFF sector. However, the ratio of GVA per worker in the FPBT relative to the AFF sector differs considerably, at over 8:1 in Ireland and as low as 1:2 in Slovakia.

Figure 15.6 presents a scatter plot of the growth in real GVA in AFF and FPBT over the period 2003–2013. MSs' AFF and FPBT industries are observed as either growing or contracting, and whether growth in the FPBT sector has in general been supportive or antagonistic to the growth in the AFF sector at the MS level.

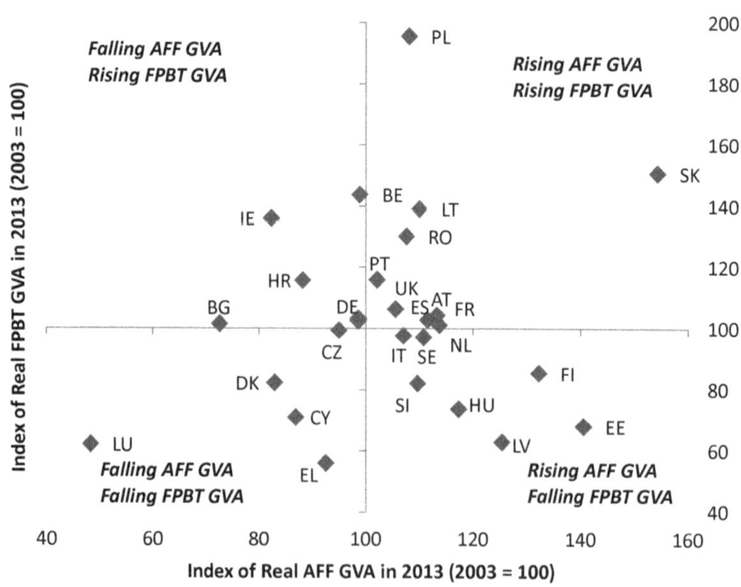

Fig. 15.6. Growth 2003–2013 in real GVA in AFF against that in FPBT.

Source: Authors' elaboration based on Eurostat data.

There is a cluster of countries with modest levels of growth in both AFF and FPBT GVA, but a number of MSs are dispersed some distance from this cluster. Poland is an outlier, with an increase of just 8% in real AFF GVA, but an increase of 95% in real FPBT GVA. This suggests that over the period 2003–2013 Poland's FPBT has either dramatically improved its capacity to add value to primary production, or alternatively that Poland increasingly imported primary products from elsewhere for further processing. Slovakia is also an outlier in that it shows an increase of over 50% in both real AFF GVA and real FPBT GVA, a much stronger rate of growth than observed across much of the EU. Greece, Cyprus and Denmark appear to have performed less well over the period, with appreciable contractions in both real AFF GVA and real FPBT GVA. Hungary, Latvia and Slovenia saw an increase in their real AFF GVA, but a contraction in their FPBT GVA. In geographic terms, these are small countries, and perhaps this development indicates that some agricultural raw materials and relatively unprocessed commodities were being exported to other MSs for further processing.

Figure 15.7 presents a scatter plot of the change in AFF and FPBT employment over the period from 2003 to 2013.

Fig. 15.7. Growth 2003–2013 in employment in AFF against that in FPBT.

Source: Authors' elaboration based on Eurostat data.

Unsurprisingly, most MSs are shown to have had declining levels of employment in both the AFF and FPBT sectors; most Western European MSs experienced a reduction in both AFF and FPBT employment of between 10% and 20%. The Baltic countries, as well as Hungary and Slovakia, experienced the largest percentage reductions in employment in both the AFF and FPBT sectors. Surprisingly, AFF employment increased in the UK, Sweden and Malta, but the FPBT sector in these countries continued to shed employment. Poland is again an outlier in that there was a considerable reduction in AFF employment, while employment in FPBT grew.

The focus of the analysis in this chapter has been quantitative, and confined to the MS level. No doubt there would be more to learn from further exploration at a more detailed spatial dimension. For example, this could reveal the extent to which both AFF and FPBT employment are spatially concentrated or dispersed within MSs.

Equally, a qualitative assessment would illustrate differences in the nature of the employment within, as well as between, the AFF and FPBT sectors. Taking an example within the AFF sector, the economic and social circumstances of small-scale farmers with off-farm employment opportunities are likely to differ from those of small-scale farmers in remote areas with limited or no such opportunities. Again, within the FPBT sector, it would be expected for that the average salaries and associated conditions of employment in a comparatively skilled subsector, such as brewing and distilling, would be superior to those observed in another subsector, such as meat processing where the necessary skills may be more limited. While job numbers are important, so is the nature of the associated employment.

15.4 Conclusions

The analysis in this chapter reveals that in the EU-28 the growth in output value and GVA of the FPBT sector has outpaced the growth in the AFF sector. In spite of this growth, there has been a general decline in the employment arising in both sectors in the EU-28, even in Central European countries where EU accession has meant higher levels of subsidy to agriculture.

The relative contribution of AFF GVA and FPBT GVA to overall agri-food GVA differs considerably across EU MSs. In Ireland, AFF GVA represents a little over 20% of overall agri-food GVA, whereas in Slovakia, AFF GVA represents over 70% of agri-food GVA, a striking degree of heterogeneity.

The analysis suggests that the FPBT sector in some MSs is particularly good at adding value to primary inputs and that the FPBT sector in other MSs is seemingly less able to do so. However, this conclusion ignores the possibility that EU enlargement may have facilitated greater trade in primary products, and this may have allowed the FPBT sectors in some MSs to import primary products from neighboring MSs for further processing. Purely in employment terms, it is easy to see how such a trade development could have positive and negative implications for the level of FPBT employment in the importing and exporting countries, respectively, engaged in such trade.

Considerable divergence across the EU is observed in terms of the growth rate in AFF GVA and FPBT GVA at EU MS level. In some countries, both sectors have grown over the last decade, while elsewhere both sectors have contracted, and there are even individual MSs, where the trend in AFF GVA and FPBT GVA growth is moving in opposite directions.

There are a number of possible explanations for the large variation in performance observed across MSs. One explanation is likely to lie in the extent to which trade in primary agricultural products between MSs has allowed GVA growth rates of individual MSs' FPBT sectors to diverge from those of the AFF sector. Another potential source of the divergence is growth in output value and GVA between the AFF and FPBT industries, in particular that some of FPBT growth is attributable to the intellectual property owned by food processing companies. To the extent that developments in the EU agri-food sector increase the share of high value added products in FPBT output, the link between growth in output and GVA in the AFF and FPBT may attenuate. Another influence may be the composition of primary agricultural output in some MSs — e.g. crops or livestock — and the associated strength of the related processing sectors.

Overall, this exploratory examination of the available data suggests that there has been a heterogeneous growth experience across the EU MSs over the last decade or so. Subsequent work could include an examination of intra-EU MS agri-food trade patterns, given that such trade is likely to be an important factor in explaining the divergence in growth rates between the AFF and FPBT sectors across individual MSs.

In summary, the evidence in this chapter suggests that, while agri-food may continue to contribute to economic activity, the sector is not an obvious engine for employment growth.

References

Birch, K., Levodow, L. and Papaioannou, T. (2014). Self-fulfilling prophecies of the European knowledge-based bio-economy: The discursive shaping of institutional and policy frameworks in the bio-pharmaceuticals sector. *Journal of the Knowledge Economy*, 5(1), pp. 1–18.

Erten, B. and Ocampo, J. A. (2013). Super cycles of commodity prices since the mid-nineteenth century. *World Development*, 44, pp. 14–30.

European Commission (2012). *Innovating for Sustainable Growth: A Bioeconomy for Europe*. Directorate-General for Research and Innovation Directorate E — Biotechnologies, Agriculture, Food Unit E.1, Brussels.

European Council (2000). *An Agenda of Economic and Social Renewal for Europe* (the "Lisbon agenda"), DOC/00/7, Brussels.

Fresco, L. O. and Poppe, K. J. (2016). *Towards a Common Agricultural and Food Policy*, Wageningen.

Langeveld, J. W. A., Dixon, J., Van Keulen, H. and Quist-Wessel, P. M. F. (2013). Analyzing the effect of biofuel expansion on land use in major producing countries: Evidence of increased multiple cropping. *Biofuels, Bioproducts and Biorefining*, 8(1), pp. 1–143.

Radetzki, M. (2008). *A Handbook of Primary Commodities in the Global Economy*. Cambridge University Press. ISBN 9780521880206.

Chapter 16

EU Food Quality Policy and Rural Employment*

L. Dries[†,§], J. Peerlings[†] and L. van de Pol[‡]

[†]*Agricultural Economics and Rural Policy Group, Wageningen University & Research, Hollandseweg 1, 6706KN Wageningen, The Netherlands*
[‡]*European Commission, DG Agri, Brussels, Belgium*
[§]*liesbeth.dries@wur.nl*

Changing consumer trends have stimulated the adoption of EU Food Quality Schemes that signal the link between the quality of a food product and its geographical origin. These Food Quality Schemes include the Protected Designation of Origin (PDO) and the Protected Geographical Indication (PGI). This chapter investigates the relationship between the use of the PDO/PGI scheme and rural development, in particular rural employment. The analysis is based on a comparison of the uptake of the PDO/PGI scheme in NUTS2 regions in the EU and regional employment indicators. The results show a positive link between PDO/PGI adoption and rural employment — for instance, because of lower unemployment or higher youth activity rates — in the Mediterranean area and Germany, but this finding cannot be generalized for the whole of the EU. Looking

*The research reported in this chapter received funding from the EU's Horizon 2020 research and innovation program under grant agreement No. 678024. A more extensive review of the regional uptake of Food Quality Schemes and their determinants is available at https://www.strength2food.eu/publications.

in particular at the EU's Less Favored Area regions, higher rates of unemployment and long-term unemployment are found in those regions that are more engaged in EU Food Quality Schemes. This counters the EU's claim that food quality policy can be an important tool to stimulate rural development in Less Favored Areas and in the more remote areas in Europe.

16.1 Introduction

With rising average incomes and more attention being paid to environmental and social characteristics of the agricultural food chain, the demand for qualitative, fresh and local food in Europe is increasing [EC, 2017a]. These drivers have also led to adaptations on the supply side. For example, over the recent years there has been a rapid increase in the number of local food systems and short food supply chains [Kneafsey *et al.*, 2013].

In line with these trends, the EU has introduced a number of Food Quality Schemes (Regulation 1151/2012): Protected Designation of Origin (PDO); Protected Geographical Indication (PGI); Traditional Speciality Guaranteed (TSG); and the organic label. Of these, the PDO and PGI labels are used to signal the specific link between the quality of a food product and its geographical origin. One of the EU's motivations is that this food quality policy can stimulate rural development in less favored areas (LFAs) (including mountain areas) and in the more remote areas in Europe [EC, 2012]. Due to demographic, infrastructural and geographical handicaps — such as low temperatures that induce shorter growth seasons, steep slopes that require more time to harvest, and poor accessibility which increases transportation costs [Santini *et al.*, 2015] — these marginal areas have higher production costs which make it more difficult to compete on price, and product differentiation may provide better opportunities [Barjolle *et al.*, 2005; Belletti and Marescotti, 2011].

While the Regulation does not guarantee premium prices for producers, it diminishes the risk of abuse of product names and ensures that production cannot be relocated to a different region. This may stimulate producers to invest in products with high value-added, and contribute to the viability of rural areas [Folkeson, 2005]. In addition, a study of several PDO and PGI cases has found that participation in these schemes can improve access to rural development support [Areté, 2013]. Access to measures concerning the support of farmers in food quality schemes and information and promotion activities of producer groups under food quality schemes are especially relevant here, but in some cases improved access to investment aids was also reported.

Turning to the issue of rural employment, several studies also claim that food quality schemes promote new job opportunities in agri-food production, processing and other related services [EC, 2007], and that food quality scheme production (at least at the farm level) requires a substantially higher labor input than the production of conventional agri-food products [van der Ploeg, 2002; de Roest and Menghi, 2000]. It can therefore be expected that there is a positive relationship between the regional uptake of PDO/PGI and rural employment.

This chapter links spatial distribution in the uptake of PDO and PGI in Europe to regional characteristics, in particular rural employment indicators. Previous studies that have analyzed the spread of PDO and PGI products in the EU have done so at the country level [e.g. London Economics, 2008]. Others have used case studies [London Economics, 2008; JRC, 2006; Marescotti, 2003; Belletti and Marescotti, 2002; Ackermann and Russo, 2010; Belletti and Marescotti, 2011; Santini *et al.*, 2015]. The analysis in this chapter is quantitative in nature, combining multiple datasets at NUTS-2 level [EC, 2017b; Eurostat, 2017], in order to investigate the relation between EU food quality policy and rural employment.

16.2 EU Food Quality Policy

Building on existing systems in France and other EU countries, the EU introduced its food quality policy in 1992 (Council Regulation (EEC) No 2081/92). EU food quality policy is based on signaling the geographical origin of agri-food products to consumers and protecting the name of the product against fraudulent use. Figure 16.1 shows the logos of the three quality schemes identified above. The distinction between the three schemes is as follows [EC, 2018]:

- **PDO:** This scheme identifies products that are produced, processed and prepared in a specific geographical area, using the recognised know-how of local producers and ingredients from the region concerned;

Label	PDO	PGI	TSG
Name	Protected Designation of Origin	Protected Geographical Indication	Traditional Speciality Guaranteed
Logo			

Fig. 16.1. EU Food Quality Scheme logos.
Source: EC [2018].

- **PGI:** This scheme identifies products whose quality or reputation is linked to the place or region where it is produced, processed or prepared, although the ingredients used need not necessarily come from that geographical area;
- **TSG:** This scheme identifies products of a traditional character, either in the composition or means of production, without a specific link to a particular geographical area.

As is clear from the definitions of the three schemes, the link with the region of production is strongest for PDO products, weaker for PGI products, and may be completely absent for TSG products. For this reason, the remainder of the chapter focuses on PDO and PGI products, and disregards TSG.

EU food quality policy offers several advantages to both consumers and producers. The PDO and PGI labels signal to consumers the authenticity of the food product and its quality [Dimara *et al.*, 2004; EC, 2012]. This allows consumers to make choices in line with their preferences, and lowers their transaction costs [Dogan and Gokovali, 2012; Verbeke *et al.*, 2012]. For PDO or PGI producers, the policy provides protection against fraud and others free-riding on their reputational capital. Without protection, imitations of high-quality PDO or PGI products might lead to the dissipation of premium prices and to the loss of rents for their producers [van Ittersum *et al.*, 2007]. In addition, PDO/PGI labels raise barriers to entry specific food markets [Dimara *et al.*, 2004] and provide competitive advantage to their producers [Fotopoulos and Krystallis, 2003].

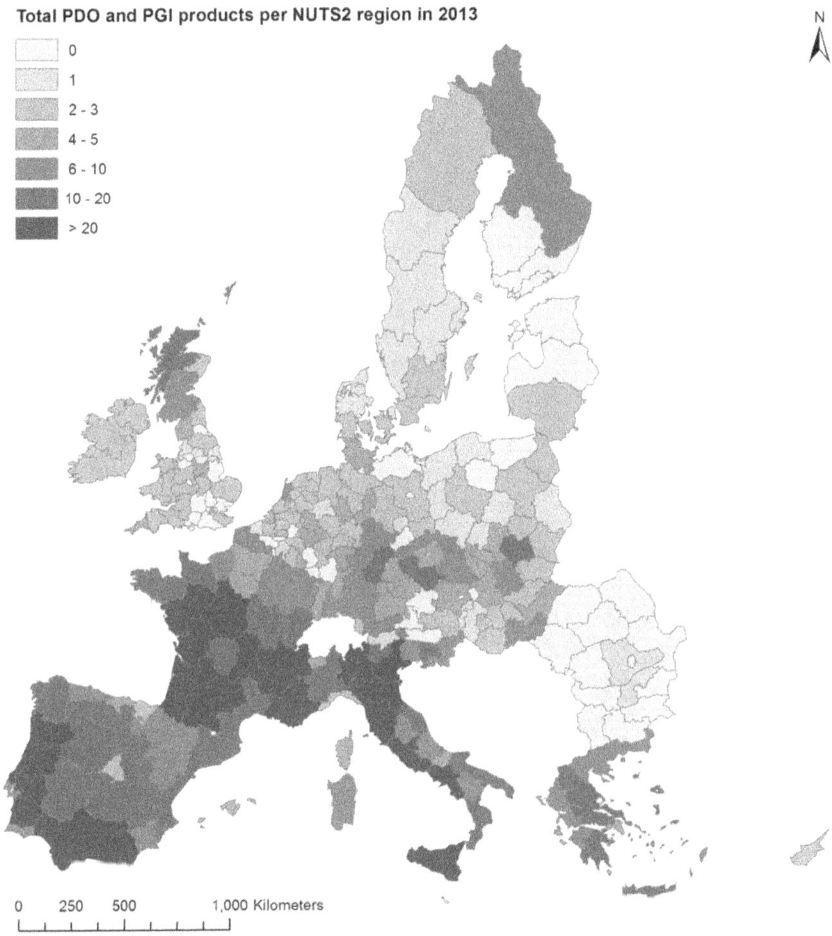

Fig. 16.2. Total number of PDO and PGI registrations per region (NUTS2).

Source: Own representation based on EC [2017b].

European Commission data may be used to give an overview of the registrations of PDO and PGI products for all NUTS2 regions in the EU.[a]

[a] NUTS2 regions refer to provinces, departments or the entire territory of a Member State [Eurostat, 2011]. Data was collected for all EU regions up to 2013, except where the necessary data was missing. The number of PDO and PGI products per region was derived from the Database of Origin & Registration (DOOR) [EC, 2017b]. Employment indicators and agricultural statistics were retrieved from Eurostat [2011, 2018].

Figure 16.2 indicates that the use of PDO and PGI labels is highest in the Mediterranean countries. With the exception of particular regions in Finland, Scotland, Czech Republic and Germany, the use of the EU food quality schemes is much less spread across Northern and Central European Member States (MSs).

Table 16.1 shows the PDO/PGI data underlying Figure 16.2, along with some regional indicators for economic activity and unemployment.

16.3 EU Food Quality Policy and Regional Employment

Out of the six EU countries with more than 100 registered PDO or PGI products, four are performing poorly in terms of employment indicators (Table 16.1). These are Portugal, Spain, Italy and Greece, which on average have higher shares of unemployment, youth unemployment and long-term unemployment than other EU member states. Also, Bulgaria and Romania, which acceded to the EU in 2007, show high levels of unemployment, especially for young people and for periods longer than 12 months. In these countries, as well as in many of the Member States that entered the EU in the 2004 accession wave, there is a larger agricultural labor force and a stronger reliance on subsistence farming than on average for the EU. On the other hand, the implementation of the EU food quality policy is relatively low in the New Member States (NMSs), the Czech Republic being a notable exception.

Table 16.2 shows correlation coefficients of PDO/PGI uptake and regional employment indicators for all EU NUTS2 regions (267 regions), for rural NUTS2 regions (120 regions), and for regions with an above-average share of LFAs (142 regions). In general, employment conditions are unfavorable in regions with the highest number of PDO or PGI registrations. Not distinguishing between rural and urban regions, the correlation is found to be positive and highly significant between PDO/PGI uptake and the regional unemployment rate, both in general, for young people and of long duration. Focusing on rural and LFA regions only, the coefficients for general unemployment remain strongly positive and significant, but the relationship between PDO/PGI and youth or long-term unemployment is weaker. There is a negative and highly significant correlation between the use of the EU food quality schemes and the

Table 16.1. PDO/PGI registrations and employment indicators for EU Member States.

	PDO/ PGI	Unempl. Rate (20–64 year)	Unempl. Rate (18–34 year)	Unempl. Rate (>12 months)	Share (%) of Agri-cultural labor	Share (%) of subsistence farming
EU	1581	10.6	17.0	47.1	—	—
FR	375	10.0	14.7	42.3	17.6	2.4
IT	310	11.9	29.1	56.4	20.9	13.1
ES	182	25.6	24.0	49.7	26.2	0.4
PT	144	16.5	18.8	56.4	47.2	18.9
DE	133	5.2	8.7	44.4	9.9	0.0
EL	120	27.3	28.2	67.1	65.4	18.0
UK	72	6.7	17.3	36.1	6.7	0.0
CZ	47	6.8	11.8	43.4	14.7	19.2
PL	36	10.2	16.4	42.5	75.2	37.7
NL	33	6.7	7.4	35.0	13.9	0.0
HU	24	10.0	20.1	48.6	65.2	64.4
SI	17	10.2	11.5	51.0	58.7	59.4
AT	16	5.1	9.0	24.6	19.7	0.0
BE	15	8.3	16.0	46.0	7.8	0.0
SK	14	13.9	17.8	70.2	13.1	51.4
SE	11	7.1	9.9	17.7	9.7	0.0
DK	9	6.6	8.1	25.5	14.7	0.0
FI	7	7.5	12.6	20.6	16.5	0.0
IE	5	13.3	20.4	57.9	53.6	0.0
LU	4	5.7	6.7	30.4	9.8	0.0
LT	3	11.9	15.2	42.9	73.0	56.3
CY	2	15.8	27.1	38.3	28.6	55.0
BG	1	12.7	25.9	57.3	65.9	33.2
RO	1	7.1	21.3	45.2	114.1	87.6
EE	0	8.6	14.5	44.5	25.3	31.4
LT	0	11.9	16.2	48.4	61.6	68.1
MT	0	5.7	10.1	45.7	15.6	32.3

Notes: PDO/PGI = Total number of PDO and PGI registered products produced in a Member State.
Source: Eurostat [2018].

Table 16.2. Correlation between PDO/PGI uptake and employment indicators, NUTS2, EU.

	All regions		Rural regions		LFA regions	
Indicator	Coefft.	Sig.	Coefft.	Sig.	Coefft.	Sig.
Rates/Shares of:						
Economic Activity	−0.173	***	−0.004		−0.099	
Unemployment Total (20–64 yr)	0.278	***	0.285	***	0.250	***
Employment Young (18–34 yr)	−0.268	***	−0.159	*	−0.225	**
Unemployment Young (18–34 yr) yr) t	0.225	***	0.056		0.191	**
Unemployment Long-term (>12m)	0.192	***	0.096		0.144	
Non-activity Long-term	0.234	***	0.211	**	0.158	*
Agric. labor in (15–64 yr) population	0.090		−0.019		0.158	*
Subsistence farming	−0.093		−0.247	***	−0.026	

Notes: (1) Population density was used to approximate remoteness and the degree of rurality of a region. Rural regions were identified as regions with an average population density equal to or lower than 150 inhabitants per square km. Less Favored Area (LFA) regions were identified as those for which the ratio of total hectares of LFA [Regulation (EC) 1257/1999] to total hectares of Utilized Agricultural Area was over 50%.
(2) Significance levels: ***1%; **5%; *10%.
Source: Own calculations.

occurrence of subsistence farming in rural regions. As stated earlier, this observation could be linked to the absence of PDO and PGI certifications in NMSs such as Bulgaria and Romania, where subsistence agriculture is still highly prevalent.

Table 16.3 takes a closer look at the countries that have registered the highest number of PDOs and PGIs, namely the Mediterranean countries and Germany. Again an assessment is made of the connection between the number of PDO/PGI registrations in a NUTS2 region and the main indicators of employment. The results provide a very different picture than that of Table 16.2. The correlation between PDO/PGI and unfavorable employment conditions is only weakly confirmed in the case of Spain.

Table 16.3. Correlations between PDO/PGI uptake and employment indicators, EU NUTS2, for Member States with over 100 PDO/PGI registrations.

	France		Germany		Greece		Italy		Portugal		Spain	
Indicator	Coefft.	Sig.	Coefft.	Sig.	Coefft.	Sig.	Coefft.	Sig.	Coefft.	Sig.	Coefft.	Sig.
Rates/Shares of:												
Economic Activity	0.608	***	0.313	*	0.158		–0.321		0.314		–0.318	
Unemployment Total (20–64 yr)	–0.611	***	–0.492	***	–0.020		0.086		–0.280		0.477	*
Employment Young (18–34 yr)	0.564	***	0.522	***	–0.126		–0.058		0.539		–0.320	
Unemployment Young (18–34 yr)	–0.490	**	–0.645	***	0.296		0.207		–0.525		0.455	*
Unemployment Long-term (>12m)	–0.629	***	–0.533	***	0.118		0.258		–0.314		0.180	
Non-activity Long-term	–0.599	***	–0.530	***	–0.002		0.127		–0.369		0.454	*
Agric. Labor in population (15–64 yr)	0.121		0.220		0.579	**	–0.484	**	0.519		0.449	*
Subsistence farming	—		—		–0.352		–0.293		–0.286		–0.081	

Note: Significance levels: ***1%; **5%; *10%.
Source: Own calculations.

For Greece, Portugal and Italy, none of the correlation coefficients are significant. In France and Germany, regions with a higher uptake of the EU food quality scheme certifications are even better off in terms of employment conditions: activity rates are higher and unemployment rates — general, youth and long-term — are significantly lower than in other regions. The results in terms of agricultural labor are mixed, with PDO/PGI regions in Italy showing lower shares of agricultural employment, while the opposite is true for Greece and Spain.

Analysis was also carried out for the Mediterranean MSs alone, where, as Figure 16.2 showed, PDO/PGI registrations were highest in the NUTS2 regions. Table 16.4 shows correlation coefficients for PDO/PGI uptake and employment conditions for all NUTS2 regions in these

Table 16.4. Correlation between PDO/PGI uptake and employment indicators, South-EU.

	South-EU		South-EU and Rural regions		South-EU and LFA regions	
Indicator	Coefft.	Sig.	Coefft.	Sig.	Coefft.	Sig.
Rates/Shares of:						
Economic Activity	0.078		0.311	**	0.199	
Unemployment Total (20–64 year)	–0.194		–0.075		–0.166	
Employment Young (18–34 year)	0.166		0.275	*	0.236	
Unemployment Young (18–34 year)	–0.080		–0.257		–0.185	
Unemployment Long-term (>12m)	–0.180		–0.191		–0.245	*
Non-activity Long-term	–0.234	**	–0.135		–0.250	*
Agric. Labor in popul. (15–64 year)	0.182		0.149		0.190	
Subsistence farming	0.012		–0.145		0.006	

Notes: (1) South-EU = France, Greece, Italy, Portugal, Spain. (2) Significance levels: ***1%; **5%; *10%.

Source: Own calculations.

"South-EU" MSs, and for their rural regions and for LFAs respectively. The positive correlation with adverse employment conditions that was found for the EU in general disappears and is even reversed for the Mediterranean area. Significantly, negative correlations are observed for long-term unemployment rates in the Mediterranean area as a whole, and for LFA regions within the area. Rural Mediterranean regions with high PDO/PGI uptake also display significantly higher economic activity rates and youth employment rates than regions with low use of the EU food quality schemes.

16.4 Discussion

EU food quality policy is intended to protect both consumers (from misinformation) and producers (from fraudulent use of their product name and hence, deterioration of local reputation and access to premium prices). However, its objective is broader, and aims to stimulate rural development and the viability of rural areas, especially for those with unfavorable local conditions [EC, 2012]. This positive link can result from the protection against relocation of production to more favorable regions (in the case of PDO/PGI products) or from improved access to rural development support [Areté, 2013; Folkeson, 2005]. Moreover, food quality schemes are claimed to promote new job opportunities in rural areas, which would lead to a positive relationship between the use of EU food quality schemes and rural employment.

Our results support this claim to some degree. More favorable employment conditions are found in regions that have a higher uptake of PDO/PGI quality schemes in the Mediterranean area. This observation was confirmed for the Mediterranean area as a whole, where long-term unemployment rates were significantly lower in the strong PDO/PGI regions, as well as for rural regions (significantly higher activity rates, also for young people) and regions with less favorable production conditions (lower long-term unemployment rates). The positive relationship between EU food quality schemes and employment is also confirmed for France and Germany, both countries which are major producers of PDO and PGI products. However, this positive message cannot be generalized for the EU as a whole. In particular, when all EU NUTS2 regions are taken together, a negative relationship is found between PDO/PGI uptake and regional employment conditions. The same holds for all EU rural regions and for all EU LFA regions, where higher engagement in EU food quality policy is associated with higher overall and long-term unemployment rates.

Some further points can be made. First, EU-wide analysis aggregates PDO/PGI favorable regions in the south of the EU with regions in the north and west of the EU, where the EU food quality policy is generally much less used as a differentiation tool in agri-food production. Some authors [e.g. Becker, 2009] even claim that this distinction relates to different perceptions of food quality in north-west and south EU Member States. In addition, EU Member States in the north and west of the EU generally score higher on indicators of economic development, including rural development and rural employment figures, than other Member States [Eurostat, 2017]. Taking these two observations together can at least partly explain why a negative relationship is found between EU food quality schemes and rural employment in the EU as a whole.

Another aspect that can influence results for the EU is the inclusion of new Member States. The most recent accession waves (excluding Croatia) involved countries that on average lagged behind the existing Member States in terms of rural development [Eurostat, 2017]. This was especially true for Bulgaria and Romania (accession in 2007). In turn, the New Member States have also had less time to familiarize themselves with EU food quality policy, as reflected in a low number of registrations of PDO or PGI products on average. In combination, the low use of EU food quality schemes and low levels of rural development, and hence rural employment opportunities, may be a driver of the negative relationship found for the EU as a whole.

Discussion of the caveats in the previous two paragraphs would suggest that the results that are found for the Mediterranean area are reasonable; in other words, a positive relation between the EU food quality policy and rural employment exists, at least for the Mediterranean area. However, a causal relationship between PDO/PGI registrations and rural employment cannot be claimed. Whether rural employment has improved as a result of EU food quality policy can only be proven based on an elaborate econometric analysis. Unfortunately, insufficient data was available for the current study to perform such an analysis.

16.5 Conclusions

One of the EU's explicit objectives for its food quality policy is to stimulate rural development, especially in marginal areas. Given the potential that the food quality schemes may have in creating employment opportunities in rural areas, this chapter ends with a few reflections on some of the policy aspects that require improvement in order to achieve the objectives and potential.

A first improvement concerns the application procedure for PDO or PGI registration. The process involves several steps, and requires approval from both the national competent authority and the European Commission, based on submitted documents. However, the current Regulation does not clearly delineate whether a product can be protected or not [Ackermann and Russo, 2010], and this leads to a certain degree of discretion available to the competent authority in accepting or rejecting an application. In some cases, this may allow for a bias toward national producers and the potential for collusion between governments and producers [Bowen, 2010]. Broude [2005] describes cases where producers "invented" traditions in order to market their products better. Certification authorities are also only able to scrutinize the materials that are delivered to them. Underlying reasons for applications, such as to restrict supply or to create a monopoly position, cannot be identified based on application forms.

A second improvement concerns the harmonization of the implementation of the regulation in different Member States [Gangjee, 2017]. Research by London Economics [2008] found that the authorities that are involved in the implementation of the regulation vary widely across Member States. For example, in Austria, Germany and the Czech Republic, applications are analyzed by an intellectual property rights agency instead of a government body as in other Member States. Also, some countries provide support during the registration process while others do not. Such differences in procedures and availability of support may have implications for the willingness to apply and the potential of local producers to be successful in obtaining PDO/PGI registration for their products. In addition, the frequency of inspections to prevent misuse of food quality schemes in the market differs widely between Member States. According to London Economics [2008], Luxembourg and Italy are the only Member States that employ dedicated agents to perform market place inspections.

The previous paragraph hints at the potential of exclusion of certain producers, in certain Member States, from the benefits of the policy. This aspect requires careful consideration of the Code of Rules which defines the territorial borders of the PDO, the production process, the characteristics of the product, etc. In some cases, the delineation of the geographic area in past applications has led to the exclusion of local producers from the use of the registered PDO/PGI name, although they were using the name for their products before the registration was approved. In other cases, local authorities have defined the geographic area of a PDO/PGI much more broadly in the Code of Rules than before, in the hope of expanding rural development benefits to a larger area [Belletti and Marescotti, 2011; Marescotti, 2003]. In addition, certain producers may be excluded from the benefits of EU food quality policy because of the investments required to adjust production processes as described in the Code of Rules [Belletti *et al.*, 2007]. To make EU food quality policy a real instrument that benefits rural development and employment, specifically in marginal areas, requires more attention to the barriers that marginalized capital-poor farmers in these regions face in participating in EU food quality schemes.

With the potential benefits of the EU food quality schemes deriving from the unique qualities of a PDO or PGI product and its territory of production, the current proliferation of these schemes in certain regions can be seen as another drawback [JRC, 2006]. With multiple registrations for similar products from the same region, the specific qualities of a product become less clear to consumers; hence, differentiation in the market deteriorates and premium prices can no longer be achieved. The expected positive effects for rural development and the creation of employment opportunities may then disappear. A current example of such overuse of the EU food quality policy is evident in the Spanish region of Andalusia, which hosts 14 registered PDOs for olive oil [JRC, 2006]. Related to this aspect is the limited consumer recognition of the EU food quality schemes and their labels. According to London Economics [2008], not only is recognition of the PDO and PGI label low among EU consumers, but also their knowledge about the meaning of the labels. This applies to consumers in the whole of the EU, as well as to those in the Mediterranean countries. In 2009, the EU made a first attempt at improving consumer recognition of the food quality schemes by making it compulsory to producers in the supply chain to use PDO and PGI logos on their product packaging.

Finally, this chapter has focused on the use of the PDO and PGI food quality schemes because of their specific link to a geographical production region. However, a third EU food quality scheme also exists, and may also hold potential for stimulating rural development and rural employment: the Traditional Speciality Guaranteed (TSG). The use of this label is so far limited: at the end of 2016, only 54 out of a total of 1374 registered products were registered as TSG [EC, 2017b]. Recent adjustments have been made to the regulation to better clarify the TSG scheme and to make it more attractive to potential users. However, Becker [2009] argues that the TSG scheme is bound to remain unsuccessful because it provides a lower degree of monopoly power to producers compared to the PDO and PGI schemes. Arfini *et al.* [2011] support this claim, and also argue that national authorities give more importance to the PDO and PGI schemes than to the TSG food quality scheme.

References

Ackermann, N. and Russo, F. (2010). *Adding Value to Traditional Products of Regional Origin: A Guide to Creating a Quality Consortium.* Vienna: United Nations Industrial Development Organization.

Areté (2013). *Study on Assessing the Added Value of PDO/PGI Products.* Executive Summary. https://ec.europa.eu/agriculture/sites/agriculture/files/external-studies/2013/added-value-pdo-pgi/exec-sum_en.pdf (accessed 8 October 2018).

Arfini, F., Albisu, L. and Giacomini, C. (2011). Current Situation and Potential Development of Geographical Indication in Europe. In E. Barham and B. Sylvander (eds.), *Labels of Origin for Food: Local Development, Global Recognition.* CABI, pp. 29–44.

Barjolle, D., Reviron, S. and Chappuis, J. M. (2005). Organization and Performance of the Origin Labelled Food Alliances. In A. R. Bellows, *Focus on Agricultural Economics.* New York, USA: Nova Science, pp. 91–126.

Becker, T. (2009). European Food Quality Policy: The Importance of Geographical Indications, Organic Certification and Food Quality Assurance Schemes in European Countries. *Estey Centre Journal of International Law and Trade Policy*, 10(1), 11–130.

Belletti, G. and Marescotti, A. (2011). Origin Products, Geographical Indication and Rural Development. In E. Barham and B. Sylvander (eds.), *Labels of Origin for Food: Local Development, Global Recognition*. CABI, pp. 75–91.

Belletti, G., Burgassi, T., Marescotti, A. and Scaramuzzi, S. (2007). The effects of certification costs on the succes of a PDO/PGI. In L. Theuvsen, A. Spiller, M. Peupert and G. Jahn (eds.), *Quality Management in Food Chains*. Wageningen Academic Publishers, Wageningen, the Netherlands, p. 512.

Bowen, S. (2010). Embedding local places in global spaces: Geographical indications as a territiorial development strategy. *Rural Sociology*, 75(2), pp. 209–243.

Broude, T. (2005). Taking “Trade and Culture” Seriously: Geographical Indications and Cultural Protection in WTO Law. *Journal of International Law*, 26(4), pp. 623–692.

Dimara, E., Petrou, A. and Skuras, D. (2004). Agricultural policy for quality and producers’ evaluations of quality marketing indicators: A Greek case study. *Food Policy*, 29, pp. 485–506.

Dogan, B. and Gokovali, U. (2012). Geographical indications: The aspects of rural developments and marketing through the traditional products. *Social and Behavioral Sciences*, 62, pp. 761–765.

European Commission (EC) (2007). *European Policy for Quality Agricultural Products*. Factsheet, https://ec.europa.eu/agriculture/publi/fact/quality/2007_en.pdf (accessed 8 October 2018).

European Commission (EC) (2012). Regulation (EU) No. 1151/2012 of the European Parliament and of the Council of 21 November 2012 on Quality Schemes for Agricultural Products and Foodstuffs.

European Commission (EC) (2017a, January 23). *Optional Quality Terms and Voluntary Certification Schemes*. https://ec.europa.eu/agriculture/quality/local-farming-direct-sales_en (accessed 8 October 2018).

European Commission (EC) (2017b). *Database of Origin and Registration (DOOR)*. http://ec.europa.eu/agriculture/quality/door/list.html?locale=en (accessed 8 October 2018).

European Commission (EC) (2018). *EU Agricultural Product Quality Policy*. http://ec.europa.eu/agriculture/quality_en (accessed 8 October 2018).

Eurostat (2011). *Regions in the European Union: Nomenclature of Territorial Units for Statistics NUTS 2010/EU-27*. Luxembourg: Publication Office of the European Union.

Eurostat (2017). *Statistics on Rural Areas: Labour Market*. http://ec.europa.eu/eurostat/statistics-explained/index.php/Statistics_on_rural_areas_in_the_EU#Labour_market (accessed 8 October 2018).

Eurostat (2018). *Eurostat Database*. http://ec.europa.eu/eurostat/data/database (accessed 8 October 2018).

Folkeson, C. (2005). *Geographical Indications and Rural Development in the EU*, School of Economics and Management, Lund University. https://lup.lub.lu.se/luur/download?func=downloadFile&recordOId=1334511&fileOId=1647280 (accessed 8 October 2018).

Fotopoulos, C. and Krystallis, A. (2003). Quality labels as a marketing advantage: The case of the "PDO Zagora" apples in the Greek market. *European Journal of Marketing*, 37(10), pp. 1350–1374.

Gangjee, D. (2017). Proving provenance? Geographical indications certification and its ambiguities. *World Development*, 98, pp. 12–24.

Ittersum, van K., Meulenberg, M., van Trijp, H. and Candel, J. (2007). Consumers' appreciation of regional certification labels: A Pan-European study. *Journal of Agricultural Economics*, 58(1), pp. 1–23.

Joint Research Centre (JRC) (2006). *Economics of Food Quality Assurance and Certification Schemes Managed within an Integrated Supply Chain*. Final Report.

Kneafsey, M., Venn, L., Schmutz, U., Balázs, B., Trenchard, L., Eyden-Wood, T. *et al*. (2013). *Short Food Supply Chains and Local Food Systems in the EU. A State of Play of Their Socio-economic Characteristics*. Luxembourg: Publications Office of the European Union, 2013.

London Economics (2008). *Evaluation of the CAP Policy on Protected Designations of Origin (PDO) and Protected Geographical Indications (PGI)*. Final Report.

Marescotti, A. (2003). Typical Products and Rural Development: Who Benefits from PDO/PGI Recognition? Paper presented to 83rd EAAE Seminar, *Food Quality Products in the Advent of the 21st Century: Production, Demand and Public Policy*, 4–7 September, Chania, Greece, pp. 1–18.

Ploeg, J. D. de (2002). High Quality Products and Regional Specialties: A promising trajectory for endogenous and sustainable development. Paper Presented at the International Conference, *The Future of Rural Policy*, OECD, Siena, Italy, 10–12 July.

Roest, C. de and A. Menghi (2000). Reconsidering 'traditional' food: The case of Parmigiano Reggiano cheese, *Sociologia. Ruralis*, 40(4), pp. 439–451.

Santini, F., Guri, F., Aubard, A. and Paloma, S. (2015). Geographical Indications and Territories with Specific Geographical Features in the EU: The Cases of Mountain and Island Areas. Paper for the 145th EAAE Seminar *Intellectual Property Rights for Geographical Indications: What is at Stake in the TTIP?* Parma, April 14–15.

Verbeke, W., Pieniak, Z., Guerrero, L., Hersleth, M. (2012). Consumers' awareness and attitudinal determinants of European union quality label use on traditional foods. *Bio-based and Applied Economics*, 1(2), pp. 213–229.

Chapter 17

Post-Farmgate Employment in the US

David Swenson

Department of Economics, Iowa State University, USA
dswenson@iastate.edu

Agricultural crops and animals are processed into foods, beverages, feeds, fuels, fibers, nutritional supplements and pharmaceuticals. Over time, as with all manufacturing sectors, there have been shifts in the prominence of different food processing subsectors, their labor needs, the locations of production facilities, technological reliance, and the structure of those industries in their relationships to suppliers (farms) and to buyers (ultimately, individual consumers). This chapter describes changes in the US food processing sectors over the past 50 years, focusing on three key dimensions: (1) trends and characteristics of the food sector's overall labor demand and supply; (2) selected structural and organizational changes in industries processing agricultural goods; and (3) the roles of selected technological change in terms of labor demanded and kinds of food and kindred goods produced.

17.1 Introduction

Food production in the United States involves a rich and intricate set of industrial activities, beginning with production agriculture and aquaculture; transportation and distribution intermediaries; processing by manufacturers of the original farm or fish commodities as delivered; the transformation of initial processing into consumer foods, beverages, animal feeds, or other goods; and ending with the distribution of manufactured products to wholesalers, food stores, restaurants and institutions.

The relationship between farm-produced goods and the nation's manufacturing sector is continually evolving to satisfy consumer food and convenience demands and to take advantage of other profitable, often non-food, production possibilities. For example, additional processing of grain and oilseed products yields a range of organic chemicals and byproducts that can be used to make paper, textiles, adhesives, plastics and solvents, to name a few.

Some agricultural commodities now have substantial non-food uses. Between 2000 and 2010, for example, there was a strong growth in the fraction of the US corn supply used to produce ethanol. The same can be said, but at lower quantities, about the conversion of oilseeds to biodiesel fuels. In 2017, ethanol production accounted for 30% of all uses of corn — up from 10.7% in 2004 [Economic Research Service (ERS), 2017], and biodiesel production used 33% of the nation's soybean oil in 2017 — up from less than 3% in 2004 [ERS, 2018].

There are functional distinctions regarding the relationships among agriculture, manufacturing, other economic sectors and consumers [Marion, 1986]. The bulk of farm-produced commodities is sold directly or through intermediaries to, typically, large and capital-intensive initial processors: for example, animal slaughtering facilities, grain millers, oilseed crushers, fluid milk facilities, vegetable and fruit canneries, and freezing operations. A sizeable share of these initially processed goods finds its way directly to consumers without further processing, as is the case with fluid milk or fresh, canned, or frozen fruits and vegetables, but a much larger share becomes inputs into subsequent manufacturing or service-providing industries like restaurants. Overall, most of the initial processing of farm commodities create *producer* goods. Producer goods are the ingredients used, after additional processing, to make finished *consumer* food and kindred products that are sold by food stores and by the food service industry.

A rudimentary comparison of the size of the food and kindred sectors that produce primarily as inputs suppliers to those that produce, ultimately, for household consumption can be gleaned from the 2016 Annual

Survey of Manufacturers in the US [Department of Commerce, 2017]. Manufacturers primarily engaged in the initial processing of raw agricultural commodities to be used as inputs into other food manufacturing activities had 35% of the value of manufacturing shipments and 35% of all employees in food, beverage and tobacco manufacturing. This initial processing is closer to the farm economy, so nearly two-thirds of the US food-related manufacturing sales and workers were at least one more step removed from the nation's agricultural sector. Moreover, while the consumer-oriented manufacturing component had 65% of both final sales and manufacturing workers, it commanded nearly 74% of the added value generated in the food processing sector. This higher value-added proportion is explained by higher wages paid in the sectors, producing primarily for consumer use and, secondarily, by higher profits.

17.2 Trends in Food Industry Employment

Employment in the US food, beverage and tobacco industries has varied over the years. Regional employment, too, has evolved. Early in the last century, major meatpacking facilities were located in large cities that were labor, transportation and animal supply hubs. The most famous example is Chicago, which dominated the nation in animal slaughter and the production of dressed, canned and packed meat products from the Civil War up to the Great Depression. As the western areas of the US developed, branch plants were subsequently located in Kansas City, Omaha, Sioux City, Sioux Falls, Wichita, Fort Worth and Denver, to name a few [Wade, 2005]. About 80 or so years later, comparatively little meatpacking activity is left in those historical centers. The industry decentralized in large part during the 1970s and 1980s, and moved to smaller cities that were closer to the pork, beef and poultry farms.

Examples of industrial concentration and redistribution abound in other areas of food production and processing. Sectors such as vegetable and fruit production were widely distributed historically, but became regionally concentrated as comparative production advantages were capitalized on over time. According to the 2012 Census of Agriculture, just 10 states accounted for 76% of US vegetable sales that year [ERS, 2015]. Many states supporting jobs in vegetable canneries or sustained regional fruit and berry production and processing cooperatives as late as the 1980s had lost many of those firms by the turn of the 21st century.

The food processing industry is ever-changing, but a constant factor is labor. Nearly all agricultural commodities require substantial processing labor before the crop or livestock becomes a food, feed, beverage, fiber or other good. Food production in general is classified broadly by government agencies as, *food and kindred* products manufacturing and as *beverage and tobacco* manufacturing. The majority of employment that processes agricultural grains, oil seeds, fruits, vegetables, melons, berries, and animals is found in those two subsectors of non-durable goods manufacturing. Ancillary and related employment is also found in sectors that manufacture pre-processed agricultural commodities, genetically engineered crops, or food production byproducts into "antibodies, vaccines, enzymes and other pharmaceutical proteins" [Graff and Moschini, 2004], as well as distilled into organic chemicals such as ethanol, which is used primarily as a motor fuel supplement.

Manufacturing jobs in the US have eroded over the decades, but food production jobs have remained somewhat more stable. In 1970, 9.6% of all manufacturing jobs were in food and kindred plus tobacco manufacturing. By 2016, that fraction had grown to 14.5% (Table 17.1). Though a larger and growing component of all manufacturing jobs, in 1970 just under 1 out of 50 US jobs was in food and related product processing, but by 2016 that ratio was 1 out of 100.

Total manufacturing jobs in the US were one-third smaller than in 1970, but food industry jobs were, in contrast, slightly larger than in 1970. Overall, due to population growth and food production efficiencies, the US had 923 food processing workers per 100,000 persons in 1970, but by 2010 that number was reduced to 545. Jobs in the industry have recovered somewhat this decade, and that ratio has grown to 589 jobs per 100,000 persons.

Growth in the number of food and related manufacturing establishments has also shown some interesting patterns of change (Table 17.2). Establishments producing food and animal feeds realized only modest growth between 1980 and 1990 but expanded greatly during the 1990s. Beverage manufacturing establishments declined during the 1980s,

Table 17.1. Characteristics of food and related manufacturing jobs, 1970–2016.

	1970	1990	2010	2016
As a percentage of all manufacturing jobs	9.6	8.8	13.9	14.5
As a percentage of all US jobs	2.1	1.2	1.0	1.0
Indexed job change (1970 = 100):				
All manufacturing	100.0	99.9	61.5	66.6
Food and related manufacturing	100.0	91.7	89.7	101.3
Jobs per 100,000 US population	923	691	545	589

Source: Regional Economic Accounts, US Bureau of Economic Analysis.

Table 17.2. Number of food establishments in the United States, 1980–2016.

	1980	1990	2000	2016
Food and animal feed	18,148	18,600	26,401	27,138
Beverages	2,641	2,035	2,748	8,319
Tobacco	194	143	121	146
Total	20,983	20,778	29,270	35,603

Source: County Business Patterns, US Department of Commerce, various years.

recovered in the 1990s, and then grew exponentially during the current decade. Tobacco manufacturers declined persistently through 2000 but have increased in the current decade.

As just noted, significant job growth this decade is found in the beverage industry. According to US Bureau of Labor Statistics compilations, employment in breweries doubled between 2010 and 2016, winery jobs grew by 48% and distillery jobs were up by 68%. Nearly all the growth was a result of the development of micro-breweries, small wineries and micro-distilleries.

Growth rates in the number of adult beverage manufacturing establishments were much greater than job growth, as Table 17.3 reveals. Winery establishments with payroll employees grew by 283%, breweries by 618% and distilleries by 923%. Sole proprietors and simple partnerships without employees are not counted in this compilation, so the actual expansion in these subsectors is even greater than indicated.

Table 17.3. Recent establishment growth in breweries, wineries and distilleries.

	2001 No.	2010 No.	2016 No.	Change 2001–2016 (%)
Breweries	396	527	2,843	618
Wineries	1,066	2,626	4,083	283
Distilleries	66	145	675	923

Source: Quarterly Census of Employment and Wages, US Bureau of Labor Statistics.

Table 17.4. Real wages and salaries per job in food and related manufacturing, 1970 through 2016: Selected industrial comparisons.

	1970	1990	2010	2016
	Wages & salaries in constant 2016 dollars			
All non-farm ($)	30,776	33,033	42,641	42,162
Manufacturing ($)	39,925	46,951	41,387	62,154
Food, beverage, & tobacco ($)	37,163	41,326	42,106	45,261
As a share of all manufacturing jobs (%)	93	88	102	73
As a share of all non-farm jobs (%)	121	125	99	107

Source: Regional Economic Accounts, Bureau of Labor Statistics. Wages deflated using the Bureau of Economic Analysis implicit price deflator for personal consumption expenditures.

Although employment in food processing sectors has been stable compared to all manufacturing, employee compensation among food processing workers has lost ground when compared to the average manufacturing worker and to the average non-farm jobholder. In 1970, the average food manufacturing worker made 93% of that of an average manufacturing worker annually and 121% of what an average non-farm worker made (Table 17.4). There were some ups and downs in those ratios over the decades, but by 2016 the relative earnings situation of food industry workers had deteriorated. They made per job 107% of the non-farm average and a much-reduced 73% of that of the typical manufacturing worker.

There have been real wage gains in the broader food manufacturing sector, but recently they have lagged other manufacturing sectors. Between 2010 and 2016, average real manufacturing worker pay grew by 50% compared with 7.5% for those in the food processing sector.

Table 17.5. Employment by region as percentages of all food and related manufacturing jobs, 1970–2016.

	1970	1990	2010	2016
New England	4.1	2.8	3.1	3.3
Mideast	19.9	14.4	12.5	12.1
Great Lakes	20.8	18.0	17.5	17.8
Plains	12.3	12.9	14.1	13.7
Southeast	20.2	24.2	25.8	24.5
Southwest	6.4	7.7	8.3	8.5
Rocky Mountain	2.9	3.5	3.4	3.9
Far West	13.5	16.4	15.3	16.2

Source: Regional Economic Accounts: State Annual Personal Income and Employment, Bureau of Economic Analysis.

It is instructive to look at the spatial shift in demand for food industry labor over time using the Bureau of Economic Analysis's eight regional designations (Table 17.5). Even though the region is growing in population, the Mideast saw its shares of food manufacturing jobs decline by over 7 percentage points comparing 2016 with a base year of 1970. The Southeast saw its shares grow by 4.3 percentage points, with slightly less growth in the Far West over that same time period. Meaningful growth also was realized in the Southwest, while substantial erosions in their employment shares also were found among the Great Lakes states.

17.3 Food and Related Industry Transformations

Farm product processing in the United States is ever-evolving. Technological advances continually change the manufacturing work environment and create new food-based production inputs and consumer products. Over time, too, dominant industrial processes change, radically altering the balance of market power in an industry, as was the case in the beef and pork packing industries in the 1970s and 1980s. Finally, due in part to the previous two factors, the role of organized labor in the food processing industries, as in nearly all manufacturing sectors, has waned.

The food production industry has a complex relationship with upstream farming and commodity origination sectors, as well as downstream relationships with distributors and retailers. Consequently, there are examples of vertical integration, as is the case in the poultry industry, where poultry processors have contracts with producers, or own or otherwise control the farm production of poultry [Vukina, 2001]. These types of processor–producer relationships became much more widespread in the pork industry in the 1990s and 2000s [Lawrence *et al.*, 1997]. Within similar industry types, there are also many instances of horizontal integration, as was the case in 2015 when Heinz and Kraft Foods merged into one dominant manufacturer of processed food products. The same is the case in beer manufacturing. Over time, AB InBev (which owns Budweiser) and MillerCoors acquired substantial market power and could claim three-quarters of all beer sales by 2011 [Howard and Ogilvie, 2011].

A good example of structural process and labor changes that radically altered a food manufacturing sector was the ascension and eventual dominance of Iowa Beef Processors (IBP) during the 1970s and the 1980s in the Midwest. Originally founded as Iowa Beef Packers, IBP created a production and marketing structure that upended the industry and, over a comparatively short period of time, drove many famous-name meatpacking companies into bankruptcy.

While it was a savvy, aggressive and even underhanded firm across a wide array of fronts, IBP gained prominence in the meatpacking industry through several key market-shaping features. Its initial innovation was to scale up the production of boxed beef and send those choice components to grocers, restaurants and other institutional users that then processed the meat for consumers. IBP was able to accomplish three things with its overall approach to meat processing: (1) it located plants amid animal supplies, thus allowing for higher bid prices than would have been possible for packers located at more distant regional processing centers like Omaha, Kansas City, Chicago, or Minneapolis; (2) it realized lower shipping costs because the boxed beef was significantly deboned and weighed less than shipping a whole carcass; and (3) it effectively "deskilled" the meatpacking labor process, which over time allowed IBP to drive down the price of labor [Fink, 1998].

Historically, much of the meatpacking industry labor was organized into the United Packinghouse Workers of America, which later became the United Food and Commercial Workers International Union. Most meatpackers were considered skilled butchers who could perform a range of processing activities as production required. All workers received the same level of compensation across all unionized firms under what was called a "master contract", and the compensation was considered competitive with that of other skilled manufacturing jobs. Packinghouse jobs were good jobs.

IBP, however, used a faster processing line that employed workers doing the same repetitive action on the line. They were not required to be butchers, but to be trainable to handle a specialized task. That is how the job of meatpacking was, in effect, deskilled. According to Lauck [1998], IBP boxed beef facilities paid workers about 17% less than workers in facilities with master contracts in 1981.

Over a comparatively short period of time, the IBP model, along with other factors, including changes in consumer meat preferences, resulted in significant reductions in the number of firms processing meat products. Between 1980 and 2000, the number of US beef slaughter plants went from 600 to 170, and the number of hog slaughter plants went from 500 to 180 [Barkema *et al.*, 2001].

The changes in the processes of meat product manufacturing and the prevailing pay also transformed the workforce of meatpacking. Meatpacking jobs have always been hard and dangerous, and historically those jobs were filled, especially in large cities like Chicago, by recent immigrants from Europe. As the industry regionalized after the first quarter of the 20th century, the jobs were filled by area residents who were predominantly white, often unionized, and socially and culturally mainstream.

The likelihood of union representation declined strongly during the 1980s, culminating dramatically in the Hormel strike in 1985 and 1986 in Austin, Minnesota. Local P-9 of the United Food and Commercial Workers union found itself clashing not only with Hormel but also with its parent union, which had adopted a much more conciliatory stance regarding pay, benefits and conditions of work negotiations during this time of widespread plant closings. Despite a long-term existing pay freeze at the pork processing plant, Hormel demanded reductions in hourly pay from $10.69 to $8.25 coupled with faster processing line requirements. The 10-month strike resulted in violence and the deployment of the Minnesota National Guard. When the local union refused to give in, the parent union placed the union into receivership and acceded to the company's demands [Brown, 2015].

As ultimately happened at Hormel, as it had in dozens of other plants across the Midwest and the Plains states, reduced hourly pay coupled with increased processing line speeds resulted in a decline in existing local residents' desire to work at the nation's meat processing facilities. Within a few years, the industry came to rely on Latino, Asian, East European, and later, African immigrants, many of whom were not authorized to be in the country [Barboza, 2001; Kandel and Parrado, 2005].

Using 2011–2015 data from the American Community Survey, a recent analysis concluded that 63% of butchers and other meat, poultry and fish processing jobholders in the US currently are foreign-born [New American Economy, 2017]. Further, as beef and pork processing plants relocated over the decades primarily to smaller communities closer to animal supplies, those communities had become more ethnically and culturally diverse, but many also attained economic resilience that other rural communities could not replicate [Cohen, 2017].

There are other notable transformations in the US food processing system. First, consumer preferences have altered household food demands. In the 1970s, beef was the dominant meat choice, followed by pork and chicken. By 1996 chicken had overtaken pork, and it had overtaken beef by 2010 [ERS, 2016]. This, of course, affects employment in both animal production and in processing. The sharp rise in chicken consumption aligns, therefore, with food processing employment growth in the US Southeast, where that industry is concentrated.

Further, there were significant changes in consumer demand over the decades for both fresh and processed food products based on: (1) nutritional awareness; (2) health and lifestyle changes, including many more women participating in the labor force, which in turn boosted the demand and the production of more ready-to-eat types of meals; and (3) demographic changes that affect where food production employment has shifted, both in terms of the nation's demographic makeup, as well as where the US is growing more rapidly [Barkema, 1991].

During the 2000s, the US corn ethanol industry expanded rapidly. The majority of that growth occurred in the Corn Belt and the nation's ethanol production capacity tripled between 2005 and 2010. While corn-based ethanol is denatured and not used as a beverage, the distilled grains resulting from the brewing process are valuable, high-protein animal feeds. As one-third of the corn mass used to produce ethanol results in animal feed, that industry's employment contribution to food and feed production is now substantial.

Nutritional supplements also are extracted from other corn and oilseed processing structures. The massive wet corn mills in the Midwest can produce sweeteners, starches, animal feeds and food supplements, such as amino acids.

Other comparatively recent innovations involve technologies that can extract more food products from conventional processing. Lean finely textured meat products for human consumption are now produced from the meat processing byproduct stream that conventionally went into animal feeds. Many of these processing advances and innovations mean that a different type of worker is needed in some aspects of food and nutritional products manufacturing — workers who are technologically trained in production systems that are highly automated instead of manual laborers.

17.4 Emerging Food Industry Labor Concerns

Two dimensions warrant scrutiny regarding the US food processing industries. The first is worker safety and the second is the overall labor supply.

According to the Bureau of Labor Statistics, the food manufacturing industry consistently accounts for the largest number of workplace fatalities, and that rate rose consistently through the 2000s. The likelihood of musculoskeletal disorders is high. These include back pain, sprains and strains, hernias, and carpal tunnel syndrome. The causes of these disorders are overexertion, repetitive motion and bending or other actions that stress joints and tissues [Bhushan, 2011].

There are frequent media reports about the inherent dangers of food processing employment [Lowe, 2016; GAO, 2005]. Among some sectors of the industry there are also problems with persistent high turnover. This high turnover results from stress, strain and injury, comparatively low pay, high output demands per worker, and the general working conditions that exist in some industries. Meat, poultry and seafood processing workers have higher turnover rates than workers in other food and feed producing industries, and retaining plant workforces is an ongoing problem [GAO, 2005].

These industries also have a much higher reliance on foreign-born workers who, in turn, may find themselves or their places of employment subject to immigration enforcement actions. As the US aggressively enforces immigration laws, farm workers, distribution and processing center workers, and food factory workers and their employers are subject to disruptions that could affect the flow of both agricultural products and manufactured food goods to consumers.

Finally, two general labor supply concerns confront the food manufacturing industry. The first is that younger workers are increasingly less willing to tolerate the pace and demands of factory jobs. This is a problem in several manufacturing subsectors, not just food and kindred manufacturing. Despite the comparatively higher pay received in manufacturing, including most food processing, many employers, especially in more rural areas, struggle to retain their workforces.

Part of this is a supply-demand mismatch caused by persistent rural outmigration to urban centers. Another factor is that a higher fraction of young people pursue post-secondary education degrees and certificates, so there is a much smaller pool of workers from which to draw. And part is due to the overall demographics of the country. The US population growth rate has slowed considerably since the early 1990s, mostly due to a declining birth rate. Exits of the Baby Boom generation from the labor force because of retirements are much greater than the entry of young replacement workers. Although the nation's population continues to expand, the ratio of the nation's workforce to its population is stagnant and considerably less than it was in the 2000s.

As in many industries, employers may try to boost compensation, may adopt new and labor-saving technologies, or may relocate facilities to or nearer larger population centers. Nonetheless, the US food producing industries have remained persistently resilient over the years in terms of employment. Their share of all manufacturing jobs has risen over the past 50 years, and overall employment trends have been mostly flat. However, labor and working condition concerns may affect that overall stability.

References

Barboza, D. (2001). Meatpackers' Profits Hinge on Pool of Immigrant Labor. *New York Times*. https://www.nytimes.com/2001/12/21/us/meatpackers-profits-hinge-on-pool-of-immigrant-labor.html (accessed 25 May 2018).

Barkema, A., Drabenstott, M. and Novack, N. (2001). The new US meat industry. *Federal Reserve Bank of Kansas City Economic Review*, 86(2), pp. 33–56.

Barkema, A., Drabenstott, M. and Welch, K. (1991). The quiet revolution in the US Food market. *Federal Reserve Bank of Kansas City Economic Review*, 76(3), pp. 25–41.

Bhushan, N. (2011). *Injuries, Illnesses, and Fatalities in Food Manufacturing, 2008*. Bureau of Labor Statistics. Washington, DC: US Department of Labor.

Brown, C. (2015). Hormel Strike August 1985 – June 1986: The Two-Front Labor War in Austin. *Star Tribune*. http://www.startribune.com/hormel-strike-aug-1985-june-1986the-two-front-labor-war-in-austin/313924351/ (accessed 25 May 2018).

Cohen, P. (2017). Immigrants Keep an Iowa Meatpacking Town Alive and Growing. *The New York Times*. https://www.nytimes.com/2017/05/29/business/economy/storm-lake-iowa-immigrant-workers.html (accessed 25 May 2018).

Economic Research Service (ERS) (2015). Vegetable Production, *2012 Census of Agriculture Highlights*. Washington, DC: USDA. https://www.agcensus.usda.gov/Publications/2012/Online_Resources/Highlights/Vegetable/Vegetable_Production_AgCensusHighlights.pdf (accessed 25 May 2018).

Economic Research Service (2016). *Food Availability and Consumption*. USDA, Washington, DC.

Economic Research Service (2017). *Feed Outlook FDS-17I*. USDA, Washington, DC.

Economic Research Service (2018). *Oil Crops Year Book*. USDA, Washington, DC.

Fink, D. (1998). *Cutting into the Meatpacking Line: Workers and Change in the Rural Midwest*. University of North Carolina Press, Chapel Hill, NC.

GAO (2005). Safety in the Meat and the Poultry Industry, while Improving, Could be Further Strengthened. *Report to the Ranking Minority Member, Committee on Health, Education, Labor and Pensions, U.S. Senate*. US Government Accountability Office, Washington, DC. https://www.gao.gov/new.items/d0596.pdf (accessed 25 May 2018).

Graff, G. and Moschini, G. (2004). Pharmaceuticals and industrial products in crops: Economic prospects and impacts on agriculture. *Iowa Agricultural Review*, 10(4), pp. 4–11.

Howard, P. and Ogilvie, G. (2011). Concentration in the US Beer Industry, Michigan State University. https://msu.edu/~howardp/beer.html (accessed 25 May 2018).

Kandel, W. and Parrado, E. A. (2005). Restructuring of the US meat processing industry and new hispanic migrant destinations. *Population and Development Review* 31(3), pp. 447–471.

Lauck, J. K. (1998). Competition in the grain belt meatpacking sector after World War II. *Annals of Iowa,* 57(2), pp.135–159.

Lawrence, J., Rhodes, V. J., Grimes, G. A. and Hayenga, M. L. (1997). Vertical coordination in the US pork industry: Status, motivations, and expectations. *Agribusiness*, 13(1), pp. 21–31.

Lowe, P. (2016). Working 'The Chain,' Slaughterhouse Workers Face Lifelong Injuries. *National Public Radio.* https://www.npr.org/sections/thesalt/2016/08/11/489468205/working-the-chain-slaughterhouse-workers-face-lifelong-injuries (accessed 25 May 2018).

Marion, B. W. (1986). *The Organization and Performance of the U.S. Food System.* D.C. Heath & Co., Lexington, MA.

New American Economy (2017). *Sea to Table: The Role of Foreign-Born Workers in the Seafood Processing Industry.* https://research.newamericaneconomy.org/report/sea-to-table-the-role-of-foreign-born-workers-in-seafood-processing-industry/ (accessed 25 May 2018).

US Census (2017). *2016 Annual Survey of Manufacturers,* US Department of Commerce, Washington, DC.

Vukina, T. (2001). Vertical integration and contracting in the US poultry sector. *J. Food Distrib. Res.,* July, pp. 29–38.

Wade, L. C. (2005). Meatpacking, *Encyclopedia of Chicago.* Chicago Historical Society.

Part F
Diversification

Chapter 18

Rural Diversification and Job Creation in the EU

Kenneth J. Thomson

University of Aberdeen and James Hutton Institute, UK
k.j.thomson@abdn.ac.uk

With the falling agricultural labor needs, economic diversification by farm and rural businesses — sometimes involving pluriactivity by farm household members — offers promise of alternative job creation to maintain populations and incomes in rural areas. In 2013 (the latest available data year), only 5.2% of all EU farms were diversified in terms of having income from a farm-based "other gainful activity" (OGA), such as agri-tourism, food processing or forestry, but those holdings generated 18.9% of all EU agricultural output. Farm diversification levels were low in, e.g. Italy, Poland, Bulgaria and Romania (all with many small farms), but high (over 30% by farm number) in Denmark, Austria, Germany, Finland and Sweden. In 2008, more than 20% of farms with more than 100 hectares (ha) had developed a diversification activity, against 10% of farms with less than 10 ha. OGAs were more common on livestock farms than on cropping farms, and more common in regions around cities, or with visitor attractions. Policy efforts to encourage diversification have been frequent, but not always backed with significant public expenditure compared to direct farm income support, even though the latter does little to stimulate new enterprises.

18.1 Introduction

As economic pressures lead to falling real incomes on farms and other small rural businesses, owners and managers naturally turn to business diversification as an alternative to either expansion (e.g. to exploit economies of scale) or selling up (e.g. by retiring). Within agriculture, efforts may be made to incorporate new enterprises, such as organic crops and livestock, or biomass production. However, there are obvious limits to these initiatives on a fixed area of land which technological advances may have made possible to manage with less labor. Moreover, employment may be sought for family members and local workers whose skills and interests are not necessarily agronomic.

This chapter focuses on the employment aspects of diversification types other than the above "agricultural diversification". Farm diversification in the EU shows a wide range of activities, which may be categorized as follows:

- agri-tourism, e.g. bed-and-breakfast, campsites, leisure enterprises;
- farm product processing and handicrafts;
- forestry, including small-scale wood processing;
- renewable energy, e.g. wind turbines, hydropower;
- others, e.g. contractual work such as landscape or gardening services.

Farm diversification can be distinguished from the rather different concept of "pluriactivity". Diversification refers to an economically OGA within the farm business, while pluriactivity refers to the farm producer (or another farm household member) who is employed on work unconnected with the farm business (although it may be located on the farm, in which case the definitions overlap). Diversification usually represents an allocation of farm household resources — labor, machinery, etc. — which promises to raise and perhaps stabilize total income, either to maintain household living standards, or to increase the farm's capital worth, thus enabling farm investment if needed.

More generally, rural diversification (of an economy, rather than individual enterprises) may be defined as regional economic development which involves more output and employment spread amongst a greater number of sectors (e.g. services) than in a single sector such as agriculture or extractive mining. This diversification may take the form of pluriactivity by farm household members, but more generally involves growth in non-farm enterprises, which may be large-scale (e.g. power stations, factories), or on a smaller scale and not greatly affected by the lack of agglomeration economies (the usual explanation for urban concentrations), e.g. household or consultancy services. Fusco *et al.* [2014] used measures of both diversification (of production) and pluriactivity (of work) as indicators for the sustainability of NUTS2 areas throughout the EU (and the equivalents in some other European countries), and found high levels of sustainability — partly explained by these indicators — in Germany, Austria and Switzerland, and low levels in some other countries with low indicators of diversification and pluriactivity.

According to Hill [2008], the international literature indicates that at the household level the main factors affecting change and adaptation, of which diversification forms a part, are human capital characteristics (e.g. age, experience, education, attitudes to risk), the nature of the farm and farm business, and the farm environment, e.g. its ease of access to markets, and IT facilities. He noted that much on-farm diversification can take place without policy assistance. However, both farm and rural diversification are frequently promoted for employment reasons, as offering alternative and better-paid jobs than traditional agriculture. In some cases, traditional skills may be revived to produce artisanal food and drink, or to introduce visitors to rural features of interest, such as wildlife or horse-riding. In other cases, new skills and capital (e.g. broadband, accommodation, services) must be acquired. In Europe, both these trends are readily observable.

18.2 EU Policies for Farm and Rural Diversification

The search for higher levels of employment and incomes in the rural areas of Europe goes back several centuries, certainly after industrialization, when a growing labor force began to be pulled/pushed into cities, or abroad. In some countries, slow farm structural and technical development, and domestic and border protectionism, reduced the pressures, but after the Second World War it began to become clear that traditional farming could no longer maintain rural populations. In response, policy makers found themselves facing a now-familiar dilemma: efforts to boost farm income through increased agricultural competitiveness, e.g. by farm consolidation, technological advance and farmer retirement, inevitably reduced farm and rural employment, while jobs in industry or services faced the greater efficiencies of operations centralized in towns and cities rather than dispersed over the countryside. Coloring these policy debates was the fact that, in nearly all countries, farming policy was in the hands of a Ministry of Agriculture (with farmer unions and cooperatives — both usually dominated by larger farm owners, not farm employees — as their natural constituents), while responsibility for rural affairs more generally diffused amongst ministries of industry, transport and others, as well as of agriculture. While all may have had employment as a general objective, farm ministries naturally focused more on food supplies and market support rather than jobs.

The formation of the European Economic Community (EEC) in the 1960s did not alter this situation, and indeed strengthened some aspects. The Common Agricultural Policy (CAP) represented a "foundation stone" of the new political entity, with an important Directorate-General of Agriculture (and later including Rural Development) in the European Commission, but there were no correspondingly strong DGs for Industry and Transport, and Member States (MSs) reserved most non-agricultural powers to themselves. However, Commission officials soon became aware of the growing problems of surplus farm labor and output. They began the slow creation of a common "structural policy" for the EEC, with rural employment often in mind. An early French suggestion of a separate agricultural structures fund was rejected in favor of the European Agricultural Guidance and Guarantee Fund (EAGGF, or FEOGA), with its two sections, of which "guidance" (i.e. for restructuring) was to receive a third of the total, though this proportion was never reached, nor a later financial ceiling threatened. Altogether, as Fennell [1997, p. 48] commented, "a very unsure and hesitant start".

The first steps in the EEC's agri-rural structural policy were taken in the wake of the refusal of the European Council, consisting of national Ministers, to accept the Commission's Mansholt Plan, which argued for halving of the farm labor force amongst the then six EEC members[a] over 10 years (i.e. by 1980). This would have involved finding alternative employment for about one million farmers and farm workers, and another 4 million becoming retired. One of the three 1972 Structural Directives mandated MS programs for socio-economic advice, including for alternative employment (i.e. diversification), but only France applied the measure to a significant extent, and even then only after many years of delay.

Parallel EEC policy developments at this time included the Less Favored Area (LFA) Directive 75/268, which directed CAP support to regions facing particular natural agricultural difficulties, such as mountainous land. However, this support took the form of direct income aids, with almost no attempt to diversify either the agricultural or the rural economy in such areas. A similar agro-centric approach was taken with the 1978–1979 "mediterranean package", which attempted to help the disadvantaged regions of France, Italy and Greece (the last a newly admitted MS). By contrast, the Integrated Development Programs (IDPs) implemented around 1980 in a few small areas in Scotland, France and Luxembourg addressed non-agricultural sectors such as fisheries, tourism and small-scale industry, but, in an era of scarce public funds, these schemes were not rolled out more widely, and did not displace support for farming prices and incomes.

The successor to the three 1972 Directives, Regulation 797/85 *on improving the efficiency of agricultural structures* (OJ L93, 30-3-85), maintained the agro-centric approach by offering aid to investments in tourist or craft industry projects, but only on LFA farms submitting "improvement plans". Its main innovations concerned aid to environmental land management and afforestation, not employment as such. Even the forward-looking "Perspectives Green Paper" [European Commission, 1985] looked only at the market situation for European farm products, rather than the wider rural economy.

However, other, non-agricultural, policy developments were beginning to come to bear, especially the reform of the Community's Structural Funds (Regional and Social, as well as FEOGA Guidance) with regional

[a]Belgium, France, West Germany, Italy, Luxembourg and the Netherlands. Denmark, Ireland and the United Kingdom joined the EEC in 1973.

targeting in mind in view of the enlargement of the Community in 1986 to include Spain and Portugal, and the signing in that year of the Single European Act with its 1992 goal of establishing a single market for goods, services, persons and capital — which might further disadvantage backward regions. The paper *The Future of Rural Society* [European Commission, 1988] took a similar broad view of the farming problem, and pointed to:

> the scope in many regions for the further diversification of rural economies [to be promoted by] the adjustment of the CAP, the reform of the structural funds, the reinforcement of other common policies (e.g. environmental policy), and … financial engineering (p. 67)

via support to small-scale and often isolated rural undertakings with limited financial and human resources. The result was the reform of the structural funds agreed in 1988, with greatly increased funds for:

> the development and structural adjustment of the regions whose development is lagging behind [(Objective 1) and for] the reform of the CAP (a) speeding up the adjustment of agricultural structures, and (b) promoting the development of rural areas (pp. 59–60).

Regulation 3808/89 encouraged the diversification of farm-based enterprises through tourism, craft activities, manufacture and sale of farm produce, and, importantly, eased — though only to a limited extent, and at MS discretion — the requirement that farming must be the main occupation before the farmer could qualify for Community investment aid. The First Cork Declaration on rural development [European Commission, 1996] was headed "Diversification", and urged support for investment, technical assistance, training, etc. for a more diversified rural economy; this was repeated in the Second Cork Declaration [European Union, 2016].

In its "Agenda 2000", which foreshadowed the EU's enlargement of 15 MSs (the EU-15) to include the post-socialist countries of Central Europe, the Commission argued that "Experience gained shows how rural diversification can be exploited in a flexible way as a necessary complement to farming". Within the EU itself, both farm and rural diversification became mainstream objectives of agricultural and structural strategy during the successive budgeting periods 2000–2006, 2007–2013 and 2014–2020, particularly within the third objective (Axis 3 until 2013) "improving the quality of life in rural areas and encouraging diversification of economic activity". The Rural Development Programs (RDPs) of the CAP's Pillar 2 included measures for "diversification into non-agricultural activities" by "a member of the farm household", with EAFRD contribution rates to public expenditure up to 50% (or 75% in less developed regions). After the financial crash of 2008, employment became a major objective, especially within the more recent "Europe 2020 growth strategy" for "a smart, sustainable and inclusive economy with high levels of employment".

Agenda 2000 also pointed out that, in Central Europe, "Restructuring can be expected to reduce the labor absorption capacity of agriculture, implying a need for diversification of their rural economies", and that, in these countries, farmers should not expect direct payments on the same basis as EU-15 farmers (who were receiving such payments to compensate for reduced price support), but were "in great need of structural improvement programs in agriculture and in the downstream sectors directly linked to it", in order to address the reduced labor absorption capacity of agriculture. A Special Accession Program for Agriculture and Rural Development (SAPARD) was launched in the ten potential MSs in Central and Eastern Europe (CEE) plus Malta and Cyprus in order to transpose to these countries a "Western European model of agricultural diversification" [Chaplin *et al.*, 2004].

However, it is notable that "Europe 2020" does not explicitly mention farm or rural diversification; instead, "a thriving, high quality agricultural sector" is to be achieved by "innovations" such as high-speed internet connections, and support for research and training. Within the recent (2017) "Future of Food and Farming" document, the European Commission argues that:

> Emerging sustainable rural value chains in areas such as bio-based industries, bio-energy and circular economy, as well as ecotourism offer opportunities for farmers and rural businesses to diversify their businesses, hedge risks and provide additional income: the policy should increasingly focus on supporting such efforts.

Current (2014–2020) EU rural development policy focuses on six main priorities, including Priority 6 "Promoting social inclusion, poverty reduction and economic development in rural areas", with a sub-priority "Facilitating diversification, creation of new small enterprises and job creation". The current Rural Development Regulation (RDR) does not provide for a measure specifically dedicated to farm diversification, but it does include a new measure (no. 6) "Farm and business development", which targets, among other beneficiaries, farmers or farm household members who diversify into non-agricultural activities. Two types of support are available. First, farms of all sizes located in rural areas are eligible for start-up aid for non-agricultural activities in rural areas up to a maximum of €70 000, paid in at least two instalments over a maximum period of five years and conditional on a business plan. Second, farmers branching out into new activities on their farm have access to investment support up to €200,000 to create and develop non-agricultural activities. Support for farm diversification can also be provided under the "bottom-up" Links between Actions for the Development of the Rural Economy (LEADER) initiative, and via more general RDR measures for knowledge transfer, advisory services and cooperation. Across the EU, MSs and regions have allocated 7.4% of total public expenditure (i.e. approximately €10.8 billion out of the total €161 billion) of EU and national RDP funds on Measure 6. Support for 'investments in non-agricultural activities' (which includes farm diversification) should be granted to 54,856 beneficiaries, many in Poland (16,550 beneficiaries), France (5,535), Finland (5,500) and Italy (3,391) [Augère-Granier, 2016], but rates of uptake, and outcomes, remain to be seen.

Further efforts to promote farm and rural diversification may be expected in future EU programming periods, especially as "innovation", as well as employment, rises up the policy agenda. However, these efforts will be subject to longstanding tensions as to the appropriate oversight of the relevant policy measures. Matthews [2007] has argued that:

> it would be wrong to give the impression that the apparent stability in the aims and objectives of this [EU rural development] policy over time means that this has been an uncontested concept. Rural policy in the EU was originally defined as a set of accompanying measures for farmers.

> There has been a continual tension between, on the one hand, what agriculture-based rural development involves (managed alongside the common agricultural policy) and, on the other hand, what economic and technological development in the countryside involves (managed under EU regional policy as part of the policy of territorial cohesion). The struggle to transform the policy from a sector-based to a territorial-based policy has been one of the defining themes in the evolution of the policy.

The European Commission (and national and regional governments in MSs) has exhibited these tensions for some time. Moreover, although the European Parliament — which has codecision powers over the EU budget and CAP — has always supported farm diversification, both in terms of general concern over the rural economy and the multifunctional role of farmers, and specifically to encourage women to play a more important role, its various Committees are subject to the same tensions.

18.3 Levels of Diversification and Pluriactivity

The triennial EU Farm Structure Surveys (FSSs) include questions on "other gainful activities" (OGAs) carried out on each agricultural holding in MSs. Unfortunately, there is often a long time gap between collecting this data and releasing it, and again until comprehensive analyses appear. Even at the time of writing (mid-2018), most official reports deal with OGA results up to 2010 or 2013, with 2016 FSS data still unavailable. The paragraphs below summarize some of the main findings from the available Eurostat reports.

In 2010,[b] around 5.2% of the 12 million farm holdings in the EU-27 had at least one other OGA ("OGA holdings"). However, this overall average was strongly influenced by the low proportion of OGA holdings in Italy, Poland and Romania, which together accounted for well over half

[b]Several countries raised the minimum threshold for holdings to be included in the 2010 FSS and this excluded many holdings previously included in the 2007 FSS, e.g. 46% in Slovakia, 40% in the Czech Republic, 27% in the UK and 26% in Poland [https://ec.europa.eu/agriculture/sites/agriculture/files/rural-area-economics/briefs/pdf/09_en.pdf].

(58.2%) of all EU-27 holdings. Many such OGA holdings were very small and employed less than a single full-time person. Amongst MSs, the OGA share ranged from less than 5% in Italy, Poland, Malta, Spain, Greece, Bulgaria, Romania, Cyprus and Lithuania (where it was under 1%) to more than one-third in Sweden, Austria and Denmark (where it reached 52%). When considered in terms of economic weight (based on standard farm output), OGA holdings were more important, as they generated 18.9% of EU-27 agricultural output in 2010. In some MSs, the relative importance of OGAs was even larger. For example, while only 1.1% of holdings in Bulgaria and Romania reported an OGA, they accounted for 13.5% and 9.6%, respectively, of total standard output [Eurostat, 2013]. Agricultural holdings that also offered tourism services accounted for 12.5% of the standard output of all OGA holdings in the EU-27, and other common OGAs included contractual work, forestry, the processing of farm products and renewable energy production. A total of 8.6% of all standard output was produced by holdings where OGAs generated at least 10% of turnover, among which 4% of all standard output was generated by holdings where OGAs generated more than half of turnover. As might be expected, managers of small farms tend to engage more in OGAs than managers of bigger farms, with over 60% of managers of farms with less than 5 ha Utilized Agricultural Area (UAA) UAA spending less than 25% of their working time on farming, while 70% of managers of farms with 100 ha or more working full time [EC, 2013]. On the other hand, farm holders with no OGA tended to be more common in the middle ranges of farm size (by area), with the holders of both very small (under 5 ha) and rather large (over 100 ha UAA) farms tending to have one or more OGAs alongside their agricultural work. Table 18.1 shows the proportions of smaller farms with OGAs.

In 2010, it was estimated that one in three EU-27 farmers undertook gainful activities other than farm work (i.e. were pluriactive), with 77% of these spending more time on these activities than on their own farm work. The share of pluriactive farm managers decreased with farm size (from 41.4% of the managers of farms between 0 and 2 ha, to 15.3% of managers of farms of 100 ha and above), whilst the share of managers of diversified farms increases with farm size, from 10.2 to 22.8%, respectively [Davidova and Thomson, 2014]. Pluriactivity tended to characterize

Table 18.1. Shares of farms in selected MSs with a main OGA by the holder–manager in the total number of farms by physical (ha) and economic (standard output) size, 2010 (%).

	Under 2 ha	Under 5 ha	Under €2,000	Under €8,000
Bulgaria	78	77	82	80
Slovenia	75	69	n.a.	n.a.
Czech Republic	52	48	54	49
Cyprus	48	47	49	48
Malta	43	43	44	45
Poland	43	41	46	40
Slovakia	41	42	n.a.	n.a.
Hungary	38	38	39	39
Latvia	35	34	35	34
Lithuania	31	31	33	32
Estonia	30	32	33	31
Portugal	25	25	25	25
Greece	25	22	26	23
Italy	23	22	24	23
Romania	21	20	21	20
Spain	17	18	21	20

Note: n.a. — Not available.
Source: Authors' calculations using Eurostat FSS 2010 database.

smaller farms, while diversification was more common on larger farms, and on animal husbandry farms rather than those specializing in field crops. Diversification was also more common around cities and in tourism areas, such as coasts and mountains with adequate infrastructure.

18.4 Diversification Policy Effects

Analysis of the effectiveness and efficiency of economic policy measures is generally made difficult by changing economic conditions (e.g. the global recession starting in 2008) and — as in the case of farm and rural diversification measures — by the simultaneous application of several related policy

Table 18.2. Support levels per beneficiaries per measure: Public expenditure divided by supported unit (€/unit).

RDP measure	Unit	Average	Minimum–Maximum
311: Diversification into non-agric. activities	Beneficiary	69,400	270–510,800
312: Business creation and development	Micro-enterprise	44,500	300–527,400
313: Encouragement of tourism activities	Activity	110,600	10–1,924,600

Source: ÖIR (2012, Table 9).

instruments with multiple objectives. Moreover, deadweight and displacement effects tend to reduce the outcome of policy measures. However, several efforts have been made to assess the impact of governmental attempts to stimulate and maintain employment via diversification support.

A study [ÖIR, 2012] of about 90 RDPs during 2007–2013 in all MSs showed the following levels of public expenditure on diversification and similar measures per "supported unit" (Table 18.2). About €2.5 billion, targeted at 80,000 beneficiaries, were programmed for Measure 311 "Diversification into non-agricultural activities", which was implemented by about three quarters of all RDPs studied. The actual average Measure 311 public spend of nearly Euro 70,000 per beneficiary was the fifth highest of the 18 measures analyzed (about the same as that for early retirement), but there were clearly high levels of variation from region to region, and those MSs reporting effectiveness usually combined several RDP measures, not distinguishing Measure 311. Only Austria, Flanders, the UK and some regions in Spain identified Measure 311 as creating or maintaining jobs, some of which were indirect or induced by re-spending.

According to a study of SAPARD in pre-accession MSs [Chaplin *et al.*, 2004], the success of diversification instruments, at least in Poland, Hungary and the Czech Republic, was very limited:

> "Overall less than 10% of farm households have pursued enterprise diversification and … [t]here is very little evidence of household farms generating significant numbers of new employment opportunities in these non-agricultural enterprises."

This was due, they argued, to poor infrastructure and low educational levels (which had also held back diversification during the 1990s), as well as the contrary influence of the anticipated high level of Pillar 1 support to farming.

More generally, Moreddu [2013] has argued that it is necessary to take into account possible obstacles to farm and rural diversification, such as land, labor and building regulations, and tax or social security systems. It is also necessary to consider how farmers may view diversification if its adoption might mean loss of eligibility for agricultural support.

Overall, the record of policy efforts to generate farm-based and rural employment via diversification support is mixed. As with other areas of policy, it seems that in regions where economic conditions are favorable, such as heavily urbanized areas, and in major tourist regions, policy support for diversification can be useful if not necessary, while in areas which are less accessible or which lack particular attractions, the scope for economic diversification is limited.

References

Augère-Granier, M.-L. (2016). *Farm Diversification in the EU*, European Parliamentary Research Service Briefing PE 581.978, April. http://www.europarl.europa.eu/RegData/etudes/BRIE/2016/581978/EPRS_BRI(2016)581978_EN.pdf (accessed 8 October 2018).

Chaplin, H., Davidova, S. and Gorton, M. (2004). Agricultural Adjustment and the Diversification of Farm Households and Corporate Farms in Central Europe. *Journal of Rural Studies*, 20(1), pp. 61–77.

Davidova, S. and Thomson, K. J. (2014). *Family Farming in Europe: Challenges and Prospects*, study prepared for the European Parliament Committee on Agriculture and Rural Development. http://www.europarl.europa.eu/RegData/etudes/note/join/2014/529047/IPOL-AGRI_NT(2014)529047_EN.pdf (accessed 8 October 2018).

European Commission (1985). *Perspectives for the Common Agricultural Policy*. Green Paper. COM (85) 333 final, 15 July.

European Commission (1988). *The Future of Rural Society*. Commission communication to the Council and to the European Parliament, 29 July. Bulletin of the European Communities, Supplement 4/88. COM(88)501. https://ec.europa.eu/agriculture/sites/agriculture/files/cap-history/crisis-years-1980s/com88-501_en.pdf (accessed 26 October 2018).

European Commission (1996). *Cork Declaration*. European Conference on Rural Development. Rural Europe — Future Perspectives, Cork, Ireland, 7–9 November. http://www.terport.hu/webfm_send/545 (accessed 26 October 2018).

European Union (2016). *A Better Life in Rural* Areas, Cork 2.0 Declaration. Luxembourg: Publications Office of the European Union. https://enrd.ec.europa.eu/sites/enrd/files/cork-declaration_en.pdf (accessed 26 October 2018).

European Commission (EC) (2013). *Structure and Dynamics of EU Farms: Changes, Trends and Policy Relevance*, EU Agricultural Economics Briefs No. 9, October 2013. https://ec.europa.eu/agriculture/sites/agriculture/files/rural-area-economics/briefs/pdf/09_en.pdf (accessed 8 October 2018).

Eurostat (2013). *Agriculture, Forestry and Fishery Statistics*. Pocketbook. https://ec.europa.eu/eurostat/web/products-pocketbooks/-/KS-FK-13-001 (accessed 27 October 2018).

Fennell, R. (1997). *The Common Agricultural Policy: Continuity and Change*. Oxford: Clarendon Press.

Fusco, D., Giordano, P., Greco, M. and Moretti, V. (2014). *Sustainable Agriculture in EU: a Method for a Synthetic Classification of the NUTS2 Areas*, Paper presented at EAAE Congress, 26–29 August, Ljubljana. https://ageconsearch.umn.edu/bitstream/182961/2/Sustainable_agriculture_in_EU_AegonSearch.pdf (accessed 20 August 2018).

Hill, B. (2008). *The Role of Agriculture and Farm Household Diversification in the Rural Economy of the United Kingdom*, Report to OECD Trade and Agriculture Directorate, Paris.

Matthews, A. (2007). *Rural Development in the European Union: Issues and Objectives*, paper presented at Conference "Public Policy and Rural Development: An EU/US Comparison" held at Wye College Campus, Imperial College London. http://citeseerx.ist.psu.edu/viewdoc/download?doi=10.1.1.629.1033&rep=rep1&type=pdf (accessed 22 February 2019).

Moreddu, C. (2013). *Factors and Policies to Favour Diversification of Rural Economy: OECD Experience*, Workshop on 'Policies to Enhance Agricultural Innovation and Productivity: Focus on China', Beijing, 24 October. https://www.oecd.org/agriculture/agricultural-policies/Moreddu-Session%20I%20Factors%20and%20Policies.pdf (accessed 20 August 2018).

Österreichisches Institut für Raumplanung (ÖIR) (2012). ÖAR-Regionalberatung, Polish Academy of Sciences, University of Gloucestershire and ECORYS. *Synthesis of Mid-Term Evaluations of Rural Development Programmes 2007–2013*: Final Report to European Commission. https://ec.europa.eu/agriculture/sites/agriculture/files/evaluation/rural-development-reports/2012/synthesis-mte-2007-2013/fulltext_en.pdf (accessed 26 August 2018).

Chapter 19

Special Study: The Role of CAP Rural Development Programs in Creating Rural Jobs in Poland

Katarzyna Zawalińska

Institute of Rural and Agricultural Development, Polish Academy of Sciences, (IRWiR PAN), Warsaw, Poland
kzawalinska@irwirpan.waw.pl

Poland accounts for almost a fifth of rural employment in the EU-28. It was also the largest beneficiary of 2007–2013 Rural Development Programs (RDPs) of all Member States (MSs) under the EU's Common Agricultural Policy (CAP). However, the Polish rural labor market suffers from many deficiencies, which, if not solved, may cause inefficient use of CAP funds or fail to reduce further emigration of the rural labor force abroad. The main goal of this chapter is to evaluate the impact of successive RDPs in Poland on employment, both in agriculture and other sectors of the economy. Both the direct impacts of the 2007–2013 RDP (i.e. effects explicitly related to beneficiary employment) and the indirect impacts caused by beneficiaries spending on goods and services in the economy are investigated. It is concluded that the RDP had an overall weak impact on employment because its measures created contradictory incentives on employment and delivered support through less productive types of subsidies. Although the RDP contributed to increased employment in industry and services, at the same time it hindered the outflow of labor from agriculture. The chapter concludes with some suggestions as to how Polish RDPs could be redesigned in order to achieve more desirable effects.

19.1 Introduction

Poland is one of the most agricultural countries in the EU-28, accounting for 18.9% of all persons working in agriculture in the EU-28 in 2016 [FDPA, 2018]. The share of the total population working in the national agricultural sector is also high (10.5% in 2016) and among the highest in the EU-28 after Romania (20.7%) and Greece (11.7%) [FDPA, 2018]. However, in Polish rural areas, the percentage of persons employed in agriculture fell from 42.5% in 2004 to 24.2% in 2016 [Labor Force Survey, 2018].

The first main problem related to employment in Polish rural areas is low labor productivity in agriculture, partly due to slow outflow of the labor force from this sector to more productive non-agricultural occupations [FDPA, 2018]. After Poland joined the EU in 2004, the share of persons employed in the primary sector (which is mainly agriculture) fell from 15.6% to 14.9%, and its contribution to national gross value added (GVA) shrank from 3.3% to 2.7% [GUS, 2017]. Labor productivity in the primary sector had increased by 16% by 2016,[a] but it declined relative to the rest of the economy, from 0.21 to 0.18, measured as a share in total GVA to share in total labor. For comparison, the secondary (industrial) sector increased its share of GVA from 25.2% to 26.5% and its labor share declined from 21.1% to 20.8%, so that its relative labor productivity increased from 1.19 to 1.27. Hence, the labor productivity gap between the primary and secondary sectors in Poland increased substantially over 12 years' membership of the EU, from 0.21 *vs.* 1.19 in 2004, to 0.18 *vs.* 1.27 in 2016. This indicates a large number of redundant workers, who constitute the so-called "hidden unemployment" in the agricultural sector.[b]

---

[a] Productivity is calculated as ratio of output to input: in 2004, primary sector output was 92,540 million zł and its labor was 2,139.5 thousand people, while in 2016 those numbers were 120,090 million zł and 2,385.5 thousand, respectively.

[b] In 2000, the redundant labor force in the agricultural sector was about 900,000 people [FDPA, 2000].

The second problem, which to a large extent explains the slow outflow of labor from agriculture, is lack of non-agricultural jobs in rural areas. The Labor Force Survey showed that in 2004 the unemployment rate in rural areas in Poland was on average 16.2%. However, that rate differed significantly between farmers (9.2%) and the landless population (26.2%) [FDPA, 2010, 2018]. Over the years 2004–2016, the unemployment rate in rural areas declined substantially to 6.1% (3.4% for farmers and 7.7% for the landless, respectively). However, much of that decline was due to the emigration of Polish rural citizens abroad, especially after it became legal to work in the EU. It is estimated that 600,000 rural citizens, accounting for 4% of the rural labor force, emigrated after Polish accession to the EU [FDPA, 2018]. However, over the years there has been a decline in the number of farmers among the emigrants.

The Common Agricultural Policy (CAP) has certainly contributed to developments in the Polish rural labor market. However, its many policy instruments created contradictory incentives for rural occupations. For example, under the 2007–2012 Rural Development Program (RDP), the "less favored area" (LFA) measure aimed at maintaining occupation in rural areas, while the "early retirement" measure encouraged the elderly population to give up farming activities.

Therefore, the main objective of the chapter is to estimate the impact of successive Polish RDPs on the creation of jobs over the period 2004–2015, when the funds of two full-period programs circulated in the economy (the current RDP in budgetary period 2014–2020 is not yet assessed as it is not finished). The chapter aims to estimate a net job effect, and so takes into account counterfactual as well as displacement and migration effects.

19.2 The Implementation of EU Rural Development Policy in Poland

From the beginning of its EU membership, Poland observed continuous growth in EU agricultural funds, from €297 million in 2004 to €5.3 billion in 2015 [FDPA, 2016]. In the first budgetary period 2004–2006 (when the EU-wide financial perspective 2000–2006 was already in progress), Polish rural areas were allocated €6.49 billion, of which €1.19 billion were devoted to the Sectoral Operational Program "Agri-food economy restructuring and modernization and rural development" (SOP Agriculture) financed by the EU Regional Policy, and €2.8 billion to regional RDPs financed by the CAP. Poland was then a beneficiary of the full seven-year budgetary period 2007–2013, in which rural policy was financed entirely through the European Agricultural Fund for Rural Development (EAFRD), and received €13.2 billion, the largest support among the Member States (MSs). Poland is currently receiving funds from the 2014–2020 budget (Table 19.1).

The priorities of rural policy differed between the two earlier periods. In the years 2004–2006, most budgetary support (62%) was allocated to measures related to the competitiveness of the agricultural sector (e.g. farm investments, support to young farmers, investments in the food processing sector). The second most important priority was environmental support (31%), and the third was support for rural areas and income diversification of farmers (7%), while a little was spent on "bottom-up" Links between Actions for the Development of the Rural Economy (LEADER) initiatives — see Figure 19.1. In the next period 2007–2013, those proportions changed: support for enhancement of competitiveness accounted for 45% of the RDP budget, environmental support was about the same (30%), but support for the rural economy was substantially increased (20%) and there was more LEADER support (5%).

Table 19.1. EU budget allocations for rural development in Poland for 2014–2020.

EU budgetary perspective	Structural funds and cohesion fund	Common agricultural policy
2000–2006 (at 2004 prices)	€12.8 bn, including SOP Agriculture 2004–2006 (€1.19 bn)	€5.3 bn, of which €2.8 bn for RDP 2004–2006, and €2.5 bn for direct payments
2007–2013 (at 2007 prices)	€67.2 bn	€28.2 bn, of which €13.2 bn for RDP 2007–2013, and €15 bn for direct payments
2014–2020 (at 2011 prices)	€72.6 bn	€32 bn, of which €10.9 bn for RDP 2014–2020, and €21.1 bn for direct payments

Source: Based on FDPA [2016], RDP [2004–2006] and RDP [2007–2013].

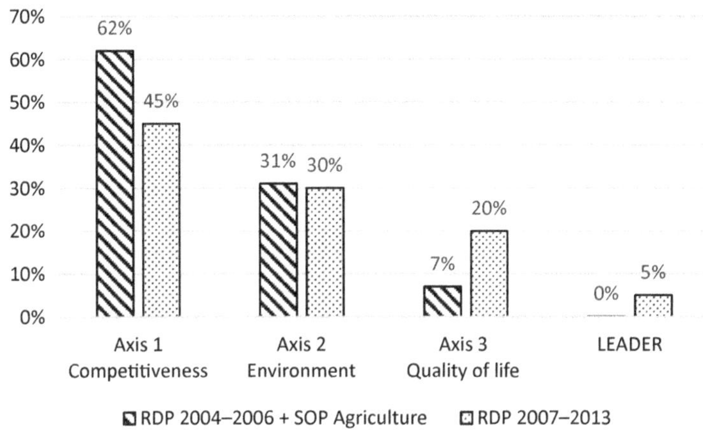

Fig. 19.1. Structure of spending on rural development priorities in two budgetary periods: 2004–2006 and 2007–2013.

Note: For the period 2004–2006, measures were allocated to 2007–2013 axes: There was no official division into axes, but the measures were similar.
Source: Own calculations and Zawalińska [2009].

Since EU aid under RDPs requires cofinancing from the state, the RDP 2007–2013 budget of €13.2 billion was increased by an additional €4 billion from the national Polish budget. By the end of 2015 (which was the last year of spending for this program), about €17.2 billion was distributed to almost 1.2 million beneficiaries who carried out 7.8 million various operations (i.e. single annual declarations of beneficiaries and completed investment projects of processing companies). Poland used 100% of its allocation from the EAFRD.

As for generation of jobs in rural areas, two measures within Axis 3 were in particular devoted to that goal: "diversification into non-agricultural activities" (accounting for 1.85% of the RDP budget) which supported new income sources for farmers, and "establishment and development of micro-enterprises" (3.53% of RDP) supporting new job generation in rural areas. Thus, overall, 5.38% of RDP 2007–2013 funds, or almost €1 billion, was spent on job generation (see Table 19.2). In the case of the latter measure (micro-enterprises), the beneficiaries received a subsidy of about €23,153 for each new job generated. The effects of this measure — 14.7 thousand completed projects and the

Table 19.2 RDP 2007–2013 implementation in Poland (as of 31.12.2015).

RDP and selected measures	Number of operations	Number of beneficiaries	Total amount (€ thousand)	Share in total payments (%)
Axis 1 Improving competitiveness, including:	945,431	355,672	7,726,123	44.92
Young farmers	38,858	38,858	732,759	4.26
Early retirement	557,093	73,470	2,363,290	13.74
Modernization	73,129	57,936	2,366,008	13.76
Axis 2 Improvement of environment and rural areas, including:	6,810,148	985,846	5,095,452	29.62
Less favored areas	5,847,357	925,224	2,521,627	14.66
Agri-environmental programs	833,348	169,351	2,216,415	12.89
Axis 3 Quality of life and diversification, including:	42,815	32,645	3,348,801	19.47
Diversification	15,718	15,277	318,576	1.85
Micro-enterprises	14,650	13,630	607,061	3.53
Axis 4 LEADER, including:	41,646	15,664	780,864	4.54
Local development strategies	40,167	15,327	651,245	3.79
Total	784,794	1,184,139	17,200,000	100

Source: Based on FDPA [2016].

disbursement of about €607 million of public aid — translated into the generation of 26.2 thousand rural jobs.

At the same time, over 15,000 farmers or household members diversified their sources of income from non-agricultural activities such as agritourism, services for agriculture and others, with public aid averaging about €20,000 each. In contrast to the micro-enterprises measure, this aid was provided without an obligation for beneficiary to generate a new job and maintain it for at least five years after completion of the project.

The number of new jobs directly generated by RDP support is certainly not sufficient to solve the problems of relatively low labor productivity, redundant employment in agricultural sector, or high unemployment among the landless population in rural areas. However, RDPs also affect employment through multiplier effects, i.e. employment in sectors where farmers spend their RDP funds. Such expenditure increases demand for investment and consumption goods and services which contribute to the expansion of such sectors in terms of employment.

19.3 Modeling the Impact of the 2007–2013 CAP on Jobs in Poland

In order to estimate the impact — *ceteris paribus* — of the 2007–2013 CAP, and in particular its RDP, on the Polish economy, the multi-regional CGE POLTERM model[c] for Poland based on Horridge *et al.* [2005][d] was applied. This model explicitly captures the behavior of industries, households, investors, government and exporters in the whole of Poland and its 16 voivodeships (NUTS2[e] regions), using a gravity (distance) formula [Wittwer, 2012] for interregional trade. It has all 10 NACE[f] sectors, designed to represent the main occupations in rural areas (see Figure 19.2). Three main production factors are included: land (LFA and non-LFA), labor and capital; and rural and urban households are distinguished. To estimate the impact of the 2007–2013 CAP, the model was run with and without the annual average expenditures.

The results summarized in Table 19.3 show that on average the 2007–2013 CAP had a rather weak impact on jobs — aggregate employment in Poland was 0.5% higher than it would have been without the policy. A slightly larger impact (0.3%) was due to direct payments than to the RDP (0.2%). However, the RDP had a more desirable impact as they encouraged outflow of rural labor from agriculture to non-agricultural occupations, as shown later.

---

[c] A CGE model consists of equations and data for several (sometimes many) economic sectors and the input–output relationships between them. It usually assumes "perfect" markets, profit-maximizing behavior by producers, and "utility"-maximizing behavior by consumers.

[d] The technical description and database specification of the model can be found in Zawalińska *et al.* [2013, 2017], while the approach to modeling the CAP and its measures is described in Zawalińska [2009], Törmä *et al.* [2010] and Zawalińska *et al.* [2016].

[e] According to the Eurostat Nomenclature of Territorial Units for Statistics (NUTS).

[f] Statistical Classification of Economic Activities (NACE) in the European Community.

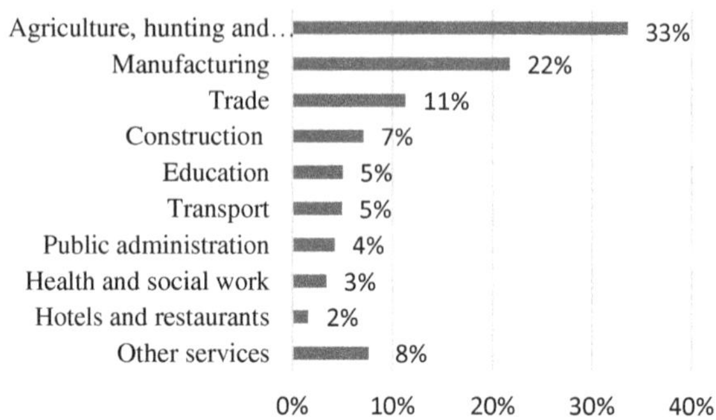

Fig. 19.2. Structure of employed persons in rural areas in Poland by NACE sections in 2007.

Source: Labor Force Survey [2009].

Table 19.3. CAP 2007–2013 impacts on jobs in Poland (% change).

	Total CAP	Direct payments	RDP
Aggregated employment effect	0.5	0.3	0.2
Primary sector	14.0	11.7	2.4
Industry	5.1	2.8	2.3
Services	0.9	0.4	0.5
Sectoral employment effects, including:			
1. Agriculture, hunting and fishing	14.0	11.7	2.4
2. Manufacturing, including:	−3.5	−1.8	−1.7
Food processing	6.6	3.6	3.0
3. Trade	0.5	0.2	0.2
4. Construction	0.6	0.3	0.3
5. Education	3.0	1.4	1.5
6. Transport	−1.1	−0.6	−0.5
7. Public administration	3.4	1.7	1.7
8. Health and social work	3.1	1.5	1.6
9. Hotels and restaurants	1.3	0.7	0.7
10. Other services	0.6	0.2	0.4

Source: Author's calculations based on POLTERM model.

Although CAP 2007–2013 in total hindered the outflow of employment from the agricultural sector, at the same time it contributed to job creation in non-agricultural sectors. In particular, direct payments created incentives for farmers to stay in the primary sector (employment 11.7% higher than otherwise), while much less (2.4%) was due to the RDP. That is because to a large extent RDP support was granted in the form of investment subsidies, while direct payments were linked to land, so that the former created incentives to replace labor by machines while the latter directly increased farmer revenues. At the same time, both aspects of the CAP contributed to higher employment in industry (by 2.8% and 2.3%, respectively) and services (by 0.4% and 0.5%, respectively). The RDP had a higher effect on job creation in services as its measures directly encouraged that type of occupation, i.e. vocational training, diversification into non-agricultural activities, establishment and development of micro-enterprises.

At the beginning of the analyzed period, in 2007, more people working in rural areas were employed in the primary sector (33%) than in manufacturing (22%), trade (11%), construction (7%) and services — e.g. public administration (4%), health and social services (3%), hotels and restaurants (2%): see Figure 19.2. That structure subsequently changed, partly due to the impact of CAP 2007–2013.

The 2007–2013 RDP increased employment in service sectors more than direct payments (0.33% *vs.* 0.27% in construction, 1.54% *vs.* 1.44% in education, 1.73% *vs.* 1.68% in public administration, 1.61% *vs.* 1.52% in health, and 0.69% *vs.* 0.66% in tourism), while the impact of direct payments was larger than of the RDP on industry sectors (3.56% *versus* 3.02% in food processing, and –1.84% *vs.* –1.67% in manufacturing[g]): see Table 19.3.

Non-agricultural employment increased due to CAP 2007–2013 most in the food processing sector (by 6.57%) but declined most in manufacturing (by –3.51%). So the CAP contributed to changes in the structure of employment in rural areas by lowering the importance of

[g]The impacts on non-food manufacturing are negative because labor moves from these sectors to CAP-supported food processing.

manufacturing (which accounted for 22% of rural employment and declined by 3.5%) and transport (which accounted for 5% of rural employment, and declined by 1.12%) but increased the importance of public services — education, administration and health (which accounted, respectively, for 5%, 4% and 3% of rural employment but due to CAP increased by 2.99%, 3.41% and 3.14%).

Individual RDP measures obviously had very little contribution to job creation, but it is interesting to compare their relative impact on employment. Three individual RDP 2007–2013 measures were analyzed: early retirement, granted in the form of direct income subsidies to farmers with no constraints on the way they spent the funds; modernization of agricultural holdings, granted as investment subsidies, lowering cost of capital for farmers, which had to be spent according to a business plan; and LFAs payments, granted in the form of land subsidies, paid per ha of agricultural land with no spending obligations.

The results show that investment support (the modernization measure) worked best for job creation. Almost the same amount was spent on that measure as on early retirement, and less than on LFAs, yet the aggregated employment effect was the highest (increase of 0.03% compared to 0.01% and 0.02%, respectively): see Table 19.4.

It is also important that investment support was the only measure which actually encouraged the outflow of people from agriculture (–0.18%) to other occupations, while LFA payments at best maintained farming occupations (0%), and early retirement even increased occupation in agriculture (by 0.08%) from what it would have been without that

Table 19.4. Impacts of selected RDP 2007–2013 measures on employment in Poland (% change).

Selected RDP 2007–2013 measures	Early retirement	Modernization	LFA
Aggregate	0.01	0.03	0.02
Agriculture, hunting and fishing	0.08	–0.18	0.00
Industry	0.01	0.33	0.08
Services	0.05	0.07	0.06
Share of funds in RDP 2007–2013 (%)	13.74	13.76	14.66

Source: Author's calculations based on POLTERM model.

measure. The modernization measure had many times higher impact on employment in industry than early retirement (increase of 0.33% vs. 0.01%). From the point of view of employment creation, investment subsidies work much better than income subsidies and land subsidies in that respect.

19.4 Conclusions

This chapter has focused on the evaluation of the impact of EU CAP funds, and of the RDPs in particular, on jobs in Poland in the period 2007–2013. It was found that the direct impact of the RDP on employment was very limited, first, because there are only a few measures which explicitly addressed employment (early retirement, diversification into non-agricultural services and establishment of micro-enterprises), and second, because some measures created opposite incentives on employment (e.g. LFA payments maintain agricultural occupations while early retirement encourages elderly farmers to leave). However, the RDP had indirect effects on employment through multiplier effects: RDP beneficiaries obtained a sudden, substantial and increasing amount of funds which they spent on goods and services in the form of investment and consumption. As these large amounts circulated in the Polish economy,[h] they created expansion in other sectors and hence also employment there.

The model results estimate that the 2007–2013 Polish RDP resulted in an increase in total national employment by only 0.23%. However, employment in agriculture was 2.39% higher than it would otherwise have been. In contrast, the impact of CAP direct payments on maintaining agricultural jobs was much larger: employment was 11.71% higher in this sector than it would otherwise have been.

RDP implementation slightly changed the occupational structure in rural areas. Agricultural employment still predominated, but employment in public services, initially rather small, increased the most, while employment in manufacturing (the second most important employing sector there) declined the most.

[h]This "circulation" increased over the years 2007–2013, as funds were released more freely, and it became better known how to apply for them.

It can be concluded that the 2007–2013 RDP measures granted in the form of investment subsidies were more effective in creating total employment than those granted in the form of land and income subsidies. At the same time, investment subsidies (such as the modernization measure) had the desirable effect of incentivizing outflow from agricultural occupations toward more productive occupations in industry and services. That is because they created incentives to buy machinery and invest in modernizing agricultural holdings, which led to the substitution of labor-intensive technologies by more capital-intensive ones.

The current (2014–2020) Polish RDP does not contain any new measures to address the problem of new jobs and is, therefore, unlikely to address any better the urgent problems in the rural Polish labor market of redundant labor, low agricultural labor productivity and insufficient numbers of non-agricultural jobs in rural areas. The creation of jobs was not an explicit RDP goal and so these Programs do not have proper instruments for that. However, if job creation becomes a RDP priority, there should be more measures with the explicit goal of creating new jobs (assured in the intervention logic), there should be more synergy between the measures (so that decrease in agricultural occupation is accompanied by creating non-agricultural rural jobs), more measures should be granted in the form of investment subsidies, and, last but not least, stricter *ex post* obligations should be imposed on beneficiaries as to the actual creation and maintenance of the jobs during the RDP and afterwards.

References

FDPA (2000). *Rural Poland 2000* (eds. Wilkin, J. and Nurzyńska, I.), Scholar Publishing, Warsaw, Poland.

FDPA (2010). *Rural Poland 2010* (eds. Wilkin, J. and Nurzyńska, I.), Scholar Publishing, Warsaw, Poland.

FDPA (2016). *Rural Poland 2016* (eds. Wilkin, J. and Nurzyńska, I.), Scholar Publishing, Warsaw, Poland.

FDPA (2018). *Rural Poland 2018* (eds. Wilkin, J. and Nurzyńska, I.), Scholar Publishing, Warsaw, Poland.

GUS (2017). *Statistical Yearbook of the Republic of Poland 2017*. Central Statistical Office, Warsaw, Poland.

Horridge, M., Madden, J. and Wittwer, G. (2005). The impact of the 2002–2003 drought on Australia. *Journal of Policy Modeling*, 27, 285–308.

Labor Force Survey (2009). *Labor Force Survey in Poland in the Years 2003–2007*. Central Statistical Office, Warsaw, Poland.

Labor Force Survey (2018). *Labor Force Survey in Poland 2018*. Central Statistical Office, Warsaw, Poland.

RDP (2004–2006). *Rural Development Program 2004–2006*. Ministry of Agriculture and Rural Affairs, Warsaw, Poland.

RDP (2007–2013). *Rural Development Program 2007–2013*. Ministry of Agriculture and Rural Affairs, Warsaw, Poland.

Törmä, H., Zawalińska, K., Blanco-Fonseca, M., Ferrari, E. and Jansson, T. (2010). *Regional CGE Model Layout with a Focus on Integration with the Partial Equilibrium Models and Modeling of RD Measures*, CAPRI-RD Deliverable 3.2.1, http://www.ilr.uni-bonn.de/agpo/rsrch/capri-rd/docs/d3.2.1.pdf (accessed 9 October 2018).

Wittwer G. (ed.) (2012). *Economic Modeling of Water: The Australian CGE Experience*. Springer, London.

Zawalińska, K. (2009). *Instruments and Effects of European Union Support for Regional Rural Development in Poland* (*in Polish*). Instytut Rozwoju Wsi i Rolnictwa Polskiej Akademii Nauk, Warsaw, Poland.

Zawalińska, K., Ciechomska, A. and Jendrzejewski, B. (2016). Challenges for modelling CAP 2014–2020 within CGE model framework. *Wieś i Rol.*, 4, 9–27.

Zawalińska, K., Giesecke, J. and Horridge, M. (2013). The consequences of Less Favoured Area support: A multi-regional CGE analysis for Poland LFA measure in Poland. *Agricultural and Food Science*, pp. 272–287.

Zawalińska, K., Tran, N. and Płoszaj, A. (2018). R&D in a post centrally-planned economy: The macroeconomic effects in Poland. *Journal of Policy Modeling*, 40 (2018), 37–59.

Chapter 20

The Role of Agriculture and Farm Household Diversification in the US Rural Economy

Thomas G. Johnson

3313 Memory Lane, Urbana IL, USA
johnsontg@missouri.edu

This chapter explores the consequences of US farm and farm family diversification strategies, including the consequences for their rural communities. The chapter first reviews recent changes in US agriculture and rural communities, with a focus on the changing role of non-farm and off-farm activities of farm families. The evidence is strong that diversification strategies produce benefits for the farms, the farm families, and the communities where they live. Diversification has allowed farm families to increase and stabilize their incomes, invest more in their farms, and connect to their communities. Communities benefit from stronger and more stable labor forces, stronger tax bases, increased range of services, enhanced recreational opportunities, and better access to quality food. As external pressures from globalization, demographic change and climate change continue to challenge rural economies, adaptation and diversification will continue to be an important strategy. Policymakers should explore policies to support and encourage diversification.

20.1 Introduction

Although production in agriculture, and in some cases the larger agri-food sector, accounts for a declining portion of developed nations' economies, agriculture still plays an important role in many regions. More importantly, it plays an evolving role in these regions, frequently affecting other sectors directly and indirectly. This chapter explores the myriad economic roles of the agricultural sectors and farm households in the US rural economy.

The US agricultural sector has been, and continues to be, at the forefront of technological change. The result has been continuous increase in the productivity of agricultural land and labor. Concomitant with this increasing productivity have been declines in the relative share of GDP that agriculture contributes. Meanwhile, traditional agricultural commodities are increasingly transformed into more convenient and higher-valued consumer products. Recently, the range of products manufactured from agricultural products has increased beyond food and fiber to include a variety of bio-based products, including biofuels. Furthermore, farms and farm households have diversified their products and activities to include agri-tourism, direct marketing, and environmental services such as watershed protection, wildlife habitat provision, carbon sequestration and wind power generation.

20.2 Role of Agriculture in Rural Areas

Farmland makes up just over 40% of the total land area of the US and has declined marginally over recent decades. Table 20.1 reports the number and size distribution of farms from the 2012 Census of Agriculture, the latest complete census available. The number of farms has declined slightly since 1997. Average farm size has remained relatively steady for many years. However, few are near the average size: most farms are much smaller, and much of the land is in much larger units. Over time, the amount of land controlled by farms smaller than 50 acres and larger than 2,000 acres has increased significantly (one acre equals to 0.405 ha).

Agriculture (crop and animal production), forestry, and fishing together account for less than 1% of total US GDP and less than 2% of employment in the US (see Table 20.2).

Table 20.1. US farms and farm size, 1997–2012.

	1997	2002	2007	2012
Farms	2,215,876	2,128,982	2,204,792	2,109,303
Land in farms (acres)	954,752,502	938,279,056	922,095,840	914,527,657
Average farm size (acres)	431	441	418	434
1–9 acres	205,390	179,346	232,849	223,634
10–49 acres	530,902	563,772	620,283	589,549
50–179 acres	694,489	658,705	660,530	634,047
180–499 acres	428,215	388,617	368,368	346,038
500–999 acres	179,447	161,552	149,713	142,555
1,000–1,999 acres	103,007	99,020	92,656	91,273
2,000 acres or more	74,426	77,970	80,393	82,207

Source: USDA, National Agricultural Statistics Service, Chapter 1, Table 1 [2014].

Table 20.2. Agriculture's contribution to US GDP, 2017.

	GDP 2017 ($ billion)	Share of GDP (%)	Employment 2016 (million)	Share of employment (%)
Agriculture, forestry, fishing, and hunting, including	173.4	0.89	3.5	1.9
Farm	131.4	0.68	2.6	1.4
Forestry, fishing, and related activities	42.1	0.22	0.9	0.5
Food, beverage and tobacco products	281.4	1.45	1.9	1.0
Textile, apparel and leather products	28.5	0.15	0.5	0.2
Food and beverage stores	166.9	0.86	3.2	1.7
Food services and drinking places	419.2	2.16	12.2	6.3
Total agric. & agriculture-related	1,249.2	6.41	24.8	13.0

Source: Bureau of Economic Analysis, GDP and Personal Income, Industry data, [2018]; USDA-ERS, Ag and Food Sectors and the Economy [2018].

Table 20.3. Total, rural and farm populations, US, 1980–2010.

	Total population (in '000)	Rural population (in '000)	Rural as percentage of total population	Farm population	Farm as percentage of total population	Farm as percentage of rural population
2010	308,746	50,428	16.3	n.a.	n.a.	n.a.
2000	281,422	59,061	21.0	2 987 531	1.1	5.1
1990	248,710	61,656	24.8	3 871 583	1.6	6.3
1980	226,542	59,495	26.3	6 051 000	2.7	10.2

Note: Farm population data were not collected after 2000; n.a. — not available.
Source: Statistics reported by the National Agricultural Statistics Service, USDA, and the US Census Bureau.

A report by the Economic Research Service (ERS) of the US Department of Agriculture (USDA) reveals agriculture's declining share of the American workforce. In 1900, 41% of the workforce was employed in agriculture, compared to less than 2% in 2000 [Dimitri *et al.*, 2005]. By 2016, that share had declined to 1.4%.

The farm population in the United States makes up a small portion of the total population and of the rural population. From 1980 to 2000, the percentage of the rural population residing on farms fell from 10.2% to 5.1% (Table 20.3). Statistics published by the USDA National Agricultural Statistics Service show that, in 1900, 39.2% of the total US population resided on farms, representing 65% of the rural population.

20.3 Role of Agriculture-related Industries in Rural Areas

Technological advances have led to enormous increases in labor productivity and overall efficiency in US agriculture. As a result, employment and value added (contribution to GDP) have declined as a share of US totals. For example, in the two decades between 1997 and 2017, farms' contribution to GDP fell from about 1.0% to 0.7%. At the same time, the employment and value added in agricultural-related industries along the supply chain have grown with the economy or increased in relative importance. The food, beverage and tobacco products sector, and food and

Table 20.4. Contribution to GDP by agriculture and agriculture-related sectors, 2017.

	US total ($ billion)	Percentage of US total
US Gross Domestic Product	19,390.6	100.00
Agriculture, forestry, fishing, and hunting	173.4	0.89
Farms	131.4	0.68
Forestry, fishing, and related activities	42.1	0.22
Food and beverage and tobacco products	281.4	1.45
Textile mills and textile product mills	18.9	0.10
Apparel and leather and allied products	9.6	0.05
Food and beverage stores	166.9	0.86
Food services and drinking places	419.2	2.16

Source: United States Department of Commerce, Bureau of Economic Analysis. 19 April 2018. GDP by Industry: Fourth Quarter and Annual [2017].

beverage stores have maintained their share of GDP. The food services and drinking places sector has expanded its share of the economy from 1.8% to 2.2% of GDP.

Table 20.4 presents the GDP in several agriculture-related industries in 2017. As the table shows, the contribution of farms to US GDP is a relatively small component (0.68% of GDP) of the total contribution of agriculture-related industries (5.51% of GDP).

A full assessment of agriculture's impact considers not only the size of the farm sector itself but also the farm inputs, processing and distribution sectors. This often involves the use of economic multipliers, which indicate the linkages among these sectors, but careful accounting avoids the double counting that can easily be introduced using this approach.

Many studies have been conducted to measure the economic impact or importance of the US agricultural sector, primarily at the state level. For these estimates to be meaningful, it is important to establish what is included in the definition of agriculture (farming, forestry, fishing, agricultural services, processing, retailing, etc.), the geographic area over which the estimates are made (community, country, state, or nation), and whether the impact of spending income earned in agriculture is included in the estimates.

20.4 Diversification of Activities by Farm Households in Rural Areas

The structure of US agriculture depends on off-farm employment, farm-related income and non-farm income of farm families. These sources of off-farm income are essential to most farm families, and the labor and services they provide are important to rural communities. Off-farm employment allows a larger number of families to live on their farms. This supports rural populations and in many rural communities is sufficient to sustain the communities. The supply of part-time labor in rural areas allows small businesses to remain competitive and rural local governments and schools to operate more efficiently. Off-farm income complements farm income and is a way that farm families, especially new farm families, manage the inherent risk and instability in farm income [Bubela, 2016].

In an analysis of 2007 Agricultural Resource Management Survey (ARMS) data, Vogel [2012] estimated that 29% of farms were involved in direct sales to consumers, 10% had agri-tourism enterprises and 10% produced value-added goods in addition to their farming operations. The average farm household involved in one of these complementary activities earned an extra $14,700 per year from on-farm diversification activities. Table 20.5 reports the farm-related income received by farm families over the 1997–2016 period. Farm-related income includes custom work,

Table 20.5. Sources of GCI of US farm families, 1997–2016.

	1997–2006 average ($ billion)	Percentage of GCI	2011 ($ billion)	Percentage of GCI	2016 ($ billion)	Percentage of GCI
Gross cash income	243.2	100	407.0	100	393.3	100
Cash receipts from crops and livestock	211.2	86.8	10.4	89.9	352.4	89.6
Government payments	16.9	6.9	30.8	2.6	13	3.3
Farm-related income*	15.1	6.2	113.6	7.6	27.9	7.1

Note: * Custom work, machine hire, recreational activities, forest products sales, and other farm sources.

Source: ERS, USDA, and Schnepf [2017].

Table 20.6. Average farm household income sources, US, 2017.

	Average farm household income ($)	Percentage of farm household income
Farm household income	118,980	100.0
Farm earnings	23,545	19.8
Off-farm income	95,435	80.2
Earned sources	67,222	56.5
Unearned income*	28,213	23.7

Note: * Interest income, dividend income, retirement and other transfer income, and other off-farm sources.
Source: ERS, USDA.

machine hire, recreational activities, forest product sales and other farm sources. Farm-related income has increased as a percentage of total gross cash farm income, while government subsidies have declined.

Table 20.6 shows the average income of farm households and the portion earned on and off the farm. As the table shows, farm earnings make up a small percentage of farm operator household income, with over 80% of income coming from off-farm sources. The majority of this off-farm income is from earnings, either through wages and salaries or from business income.

20.5 Factors Enhancing or Limiting Farm Household Diversification into Non-agricultural Activities

The discussion above indicates that off-farm employment is quite common among US farm households. The most recent data available from the USDA ERS survey shows that across all farm types, farm operator households earned 80.2% of their household income from off-farm sources [USDA ERS, Farm Household Income and Characteristics, 2018]. This percentage has increased over time, but off-farm work is not a new phenomenon — in the 1930s about 30% of operators reported off-farm work [Hoppe *et al.*, 2007]. Most off-farm income comes from earned sources.

In examining 2004 data, the ERS reports that although operator off-farm income varied across farm size, off-farm income earned by spouses was relatively stable across farm size [Fernandez-Cornejo *et al.*, 2007]. In 2004, 52% of farm operators and 45% of spouses worked off-farm. Off-farm wages and salaries provided 47% of farm household income in 2004, and farming income was only 17% of the household income [Covey *et al.*, 2005].

Off-farm income generally is seen as a means of smoothing out household income flow, which is often viewed as inadequate and/or unstable. Additionally, off-farm opportunities can provide fringe benefits such as health insurance and pensions [Fernandez-Cornejo *et al.*, 2007]. The main reason operators and spouses in the 2004 Agricultural Resource Management Survey offered for seeking off-farm work was to increase the household's income; other reasons included obtaining health insurance and personal satisfaction [Covey *et al.*, 2005]. The most important obstacle to farmers' ability to diversify their operations and to find off-farm employment is their degree of rurality (remoteness from urban areas and low density of population).

20.6 Agri-tourism and Direct-to-consumer Sales

Agri-tourism is a growing industry in the United States. Unfortunately, little data is available to allow us to quantify the extent to which this industry has developed nationally. Numerous studies have been conducted at the local and state level [Das and Rainey, 2010; Lobo *et al.*, 1999; Bernardo *et al.*, 2004; Schilling *et al.*, 2012]. According to ERS study estimates, about 52,000 farms (2.5% of US farms) participated in some form of agri-tourism and earned about $955 million in income from farm-based recreation in 2004. Types of agri-tourism activities included, outdoor recreation, such as fishing, hunting, wildlife study and horseback riding; education experiences, such as tours, cooking classes, wine tasting and museums; entertainment, such as festivals, barn dances and petting zoos; hospitality services, such as overnight farm stays and guided tours; and on-farm direct sales, such as "pick your own" operations, roadside stands and farmers' markets [Brown and Reeder, 2007].

Brown and Reeder described motivations for and limitations of agri-tourism. The benefits of agri-tourism included supplementing and diversifying farm income, utilizing assets and expanding employment opportunities, and the benefits to surrounding communities were higher income, land preservation, higher land values and an enhanced "sense of place". The limitations of agri-tourism discussed in this survey included legal liability issues, reduction in privacy, overuse of resources (e.g. overhunting and overfishing), local traffic congestion and conflicts over non-traditional land uses [Brown and Reeder, 2007].

The Brown and Reeder study examined characteristics of the farm operation, the farm operator, and the surrounding community and its proximity to larger urban centers. Results show that agri-tourism was most prevalent in counties with high population density but was more likely in counties farther from urban centers. Areas high in natural amenities also tended to have higher levels of agri-tourism. Farms with higher net worth were more likely to engage in and benefit from agri-tourism activities than farms with lower net worth [Brown and Reeder, 2007].

Several studies have examined the economics of agri-tourism or nature tourism in various states or regions of the US. Jolly and Reynolds [2005] discuss the potential of agricultural and nature tourism to increase farm revenues and provide an educational experience to non-farmers [Jolly and Reynolds, 2005]. Jolly and Reynolds [2005] surveyed residents in two California counties and showed a high interest and participation rate in agriculture and nature tourism. Motivating factors included direct purchasing of fresh products, experiencing nature, and vacation and relaxation. Also included in the survey were questions regarding on-site spending during trips, which averaged between $5 and $40 per trip, illustrating the potential for farm revenue from tourism activities.

Rademaker *et al.* [2007] surveyed farmers and ranchers who were engaged in or planning tourism or recreation businesses [Rademaker *et al.*, 2007]. The most frequently selected businesses were Fish, Wildlife and Parks (FWP) block management, fee hunting and fishing, guesthouse/cabin rentals, outfitter guide businesses and working farm/ranch vacations. The most important reasons cited for operating a recreation business were to generate additional income, to offset fluctuations in agricultural income, and to fully utilize the farm resources. The most restrictive obstacles were legal liability issues, regulations and legal constraints, and lack of time on the operator's part.

Kuehn and Hilchey [2001] surveyed agri-tourism industry in New York and found that agri-tourism activities included farm produce stands, Christmas trees, pick-your-own operations, maple production, greenhouses, wineries, livestock breeding, and bed-and-breakfast establishments. The study reports that the primary motivation for engaging in tourism activities was to increase the farm business' profitability. Other reasons included the desire to work directly with people, the opportunity to provide an educational service and employment for family members. The main concerns business owners noted were legal liability and the high cost of liability insurance. Other concerns included costs of marketing and advertising, labor costs, government regulations, taxes, the need to attract customers, weather, and effects on production concerns.

In Hawaii, the value of agri-tourism in 2006 ($38.8 million) increased by 14% compared to 2003 ($33.9 million). Specific agri-tourism activities include on-farm sales directly to farm visitors, other retail sales, outdoor recreation, accommodations, education and entertainment [National Agricultural Statistics Service, 2008]. In Vermont, income from agri-tourism was $19.5 million in 2002, and more than one-third of farms in the state participated in some agri-tourism activity. The most common source of agri-tourism income was direct sales of farm commodities. Other agri-tourism activities included accommodations, outdoor recreation, education, and entertainment [New England Agricultural Statistics Service, 2004].

Local and regional food systems in the US have grown dramatically over the last 25 years. Just one indicator of this growth is the number of farmers' markets (see Table 20.7), which, over this period, increased five-fold. Low *et al.* [2015] found that most of the local food farms are small (85% of these farms have sales of $75,000 or less), but most of the sales are by large farms (Table 20.8). Local food farms with gross cash farm income above $350,000 accounted for 5% of local food farms but 67% of sales. Another indicator of the magnitude of the local and regional food systems movement comes from the 2015 Farm to School Census. The census found that 42% of schools surveyed were involved in farm-to-school activities.

Table 20.7. US farmers' markets.

Year	Number of farmers' markets
1994	1,755
1996	2,410
1998	2,746
2000	2,863
2002	3,137
2004	3,706
2006	4,385
2008	4,685
2010	6,132
2012	7,864
2014	8,268
2016	8,669

Source: USDA, Agricultural Marketing Service [2018].

Table 20.8. Number of direct-to-consumer farms and sales, US, 2002–2012.

	2002	2007	2012
All farms reporting direct-to-consumer sales	116,733	136,817	144,530
Percentage of all farms	5.5	6.2	6.9
Direct-to-consumer sales ($ million)	812	1,211	1,310
Percentage of all farm sales	0.4	0.4	0.3

Source: Low *et al.* [2015].

20.7 Conclusions

The US agricultural sector and the farm families that manage work and live on these farms continue to adapt to changing technology, macroeconomic conditions and changing societal demands. Diversification has been one of these adaptive responses. The circumstances and trends described in this chapter reveal several realities about farms, farm households and rural regions in general.

Rural is not synonymous with agriculture. In fact, only a small percentage of US workers (at the national and the non-metropolitan levels) are employed directly in production agriculture. Policies that focus on support for conventional crop and animal agriculture provide limited benefits for the broader rural population and places. In fact, many of these policies have little relevance to large numbers of smaller farms. In contrast, policies that help farms and farm families diversify support a broader spectrum of farm families and rural residents.

Conventional crop and livestock farming is rarely the major source of employment or income for farm families. Most farms rely heavily on off-farm employment and income. In fact, in 2017, more than 80% of total farm household income was from off-farm sources, and, on 91% of farms, the operator, spouse, or both worked off the farm.

The evidence is strong that diversification strategies for farms and farm family livelihood produces benefits for the farms, the families and the communities where they live. Diversification has allowed farm families to increase and stabilize their incomes, invest more in their farms, and connect to their communities. Communities benefit from stronger and more stable labor forces, stronger tax bases, increased range of services, recreational opportunities and quality of food.

As external pressures from globalization, demographic change and climate change continue to challenge rural economies, adaptation and diversification will continue to be an important strategy. Policymakers should explore policies to support and encourage diversification.

References

Bernardo, D., Valentin, L. and Leatherman, J. (2004). *Agritourism: If We Build it, Will They Come?* Risk and Profit Conference, Manhattan, Kansas, pp. 19–20. http://www.uvm.edu/tourismresearch/agtour/publications/Kansas%20State%20Study.pdf (accessed 27 October 2018).

Brown, D. M. and Reeder, R. J. (2007). *Farm-Based Recreation: A Statistical Profile*. Economic Research Report Number 53, USDA, Economic Research Service.

Bubela, H. J. (2016). Off-farm Income: Managing Risk in Young and Beginning Farmer Households, *Choices*. Q3. http://www.choicesmagazine.org/

choices-magazine/submitted-articles/off-farm-income-managing-risk-in-young-and-beginning-farmer-households (accessed 9 October 2018).

Covey, T., Green, R., Jones, C., Johnson, J., Morehart, M., Williams, R., McGath, C., Mishra, A. and Strickland, R. (2005). *Agricultural Income and Finance Outlook*. AIS-83, United States Department of Agriculture, Economic Research Service.

Das, B. R. and Rainey, D. V. (2010). Agritourism in the Arkansas Delta Byways: Assessing the economic impacts. *International Journal of Tourism Research*, 12(3), pp. 265–280.

Dimitri, C., Effland, A. and Conklin, N. (2005). *The 20th Century Transformation of U.S. Agriculture and Farm Policy*. Economic Information Bulletin Number 3, United States Department of Agriculture, Economic Research Service.

Fernandez-Cornejo, J., Mishra, A., Nehring, R., Hendricks, C., Southern, M. and Gregory, A. (2007). *Off-Farm Income, Production Decisions and Farm Economic Performance*. Economic Research Report Number 36, United States Department of Agriculture, Economic Research Service.

Hoppe, R. A., Korb, P., O'Donoghue, E. J. and Banker, D. E. (2007). *Structure and Finances of US Farms: Family Farm Report, 2007 Edition*. Economic Information Bulletin Number 24, United States Department of Agriculture, Economic Research Service.

Jolly, D.A. and Reynolds, K. A. (2005). *Consumer Demand for Agricultural and On-Farm Nature Tourism*. Research Brief 2005-01, University of California Small Farm Center.

Kuehn, D. and Hilchey, D. (2001). *Agritourism in New York: Management and Operations*. Fact Sheet, New York Sea Grant, State University of New York at Oswego.

Lobo, R., Goldman, G., Jolly, D., Wallace, B., Schrader, W. L. and Parker, S. (1999). Agritourism benefits agriculture in San Diego county. *California Agriculture*, 53(6), 20–24.

Low, S. A., Adalja, A., Beaulieu, E., Key, N., Martinez, S., Melton, A., Perez, A., Ralston, K., Stewart, H., Suttles, S., Vogel, S. and Jablonski, B. B. R. (2015). *Trends in U.S. Local and Regional Food Systems* (AP-068). US Department of Agriculture, Economic Research Service. http://scholarship.sha.cornell.edu/articles/1058 (accessed 9 October 2018).

Rademaker, L., Nickerson, N. P. and Garu, K. (2007). *Montana's Agritourism and Recreation Business: Ten Years Later. Research Report* 2007–4, Institute for Tourism & Recreation Research, College of Forestry and Conservation, University of Montana.

Schilling, B. J., Sullivan, K. P. and Komar, S. J. (2012). Examining the economic benefits of agritourism: The case of New Jersey. *Journal of Agriculture, Food Systems and Community Development*, 3(1), p. 199.

Schnepf, R. (2017). U*S Farm Income Outlook for* 2017, Congressional Research Service. https://fas.org/sgp/crs/misc/R40152.pdf (accessed 9 October 2018).

United States Census Bureau (various years). Population and housing unit estimates.

United States Department of Agriculture, Agricultural Marketing Service (2018). National Count of Farmers Market Directory Listings Graph: 1994–2017. https://www.ams.usda.gov/sites/default/files/media/NationalCountofFM Directory17.JPG (accessed 9 October 2018).

United States Department of Agriculture, Census of Agriculture (1987, 1992, 1997, 2002, 2007, 2012). http://www.agcensus.usda.gov (accessed 9 October 2018).

United States Department of Agricultural, National Agriculture Statistics Service. *Census of Agriculture Data.* http://www.nass.usda.gov (accessed 9 October 2018).

United States Department of Agriculture, National Agricultural Statistics Service (2008). *Hawaii Agricultural Statistics.* https://www.nass.usda.gov/Statistics_by_State/Hawaii/Publications/Miscellaneous/agtour.pdf (accessed 9 October 2018).

United States Department of Agriculture, New England Agricultural Statistics Service (2004). *Vermont Agri-Tourism 2002.* http://www.uvm.edu/tourism-research/agritourism/publications/VT%20Agritourism%202002%20 Fact%20Sheet.pdf (accessed 10 October 10 2018).

United States Department of Agriculture, Economic Research Service (2018). *Ag and Food Sectors and the Economy.* https://www.ers.usda.gov/data-products/ag-and-food-statistics-charting-the-essentials/ag-and-food-sectors-and-the-economy (accessed 9 October 2018).

United States Department of Agriculture, Economic Research Service (2018). *Farm Household Income and Characteristics.* https://www.ers.usda.gov/data-products/farm-household-income-and-characteristics (accessed 9 October 2018).

United States Department of Agriculture (2018). *Farm to School Census.* https://farmtoschoolcensus.fns.usda.gov (accessed 9 October 2018).

United States Department of Agriculture, National Agricultural Statistics Service (2018). *United States Summary and State Data: Geographic Area Series.* Volume 1, Part 51, AC-12-A-51. https://www.agcensus.usda.gov/Publications/2012/Full_Report/Volume_1,_Chapter_1_US/usv1.pdf (accessed 9 October 2018).

United States Department of Agriculture, National Agricultural Statistics Service (2018). *Farms and Land in Farms 2017 Summary* (February). http://usda.mannlib.cornell.edu/usda/current/FarmLandIn/FarmLandIn-02-16-2018.pdf (accessed 9 October 2018).

United States Department of Commerce, Bureau of Economic Analysis. April 19 (2018). *Gross Domestic Product by Industry: Fourth Quarter and Annual 2017*. https://www.bea.gov/system/files/2018-04/gdpind417.pdf (accessed 11 October 2018).

United States Department of Commerce, Bureau of Economic Analysis. *Regional Economic Accounts*. http://www.bea.gov/regional (accessed 9 October 2018).

Vogel, S. J. (2012). Multi-enterprising farm households: The importance of their alternative business ventures in the rural economy. *USDA-ERS Economic Information Bulletin*, (101).

Part G
Rural Recreation

Chapter 21

Rural Tourism and Recreation in the EU

Bill Slee

The James Hutton Institute, Aberdeen, UK
bill.slee@hutton.ac.uk

Rural tourism and recreation have emerged as significant parts of the rural economy in the European Union. This diverse sector is highly variable in character, and its employment importance varies greatly over space, with farm household members sometimes highly engaged and sometimes rather disengaged from the provision of the associated services. The regional social, cultural and economic benefits depend on the type of tourism and the structure of regional economy. Where interesting cultural landscapes are juxtaposed with low-intensity farming and strong local food cultures, there is often a strong agri-tourism sector. Rural tourism and recreation are not without controversy: the sector may be overhyped as a development strategy in remote areas, and some forms of tourism such as second homes can disrupt local housing markets and exacerbate social tensions. However, in general, rural tourism and recreation can be seen as positive contributors to European rural economies, and they contribute significantly to rural employment.

21.1 Introduction

Over the last 50 years, while there has been an attritional and significant decline in the farm sector's contribution to regional and national economic output in Europe, the contribution of the "tertiary" service sector has grown dramatically. In the more developed parts of rural Western Europe, services account for over 70% of employment and GDP; and the sector is generally growing at the expense of primary (e.g. farming) and secondary (e.g. manufacturing) sectors. The composition of the highly diverse service sector varies greatly over space, but tourism and recreation have emerged as major components in many areas. The rural tourism sector is itself highly varied in character, and farm tourism is but one component. Often, but by no means always, the relatively agriculturally disadvantaged areas have developed strong tourism-related service sectors, but in other areas of high landscape quality in peri-urban areas, the residential economy[a] has penetrated the farmed countryside, with hobby farming and the equine industry often a significant presence and with rural land in demand for formal and informal recreation by commuters and nearby residents.

Tourism and recreation are closely connected. Recreational activity is part of how the tourist spends his/her time and money, visiting attractions, and engaging in passive viewing or in more athletic recreation. Such activities are undertaken by both local residents and tourists; and where the residential economy is strong, recreational activity may arise more from local residents than tourists. Both groups often use the same facilities, although some activities, such as equestrian activities, take distinctive forms in different areas, with trekking more common in touristic areas and livery in peri-urban areas.

This shift in economic emphasis in the countryside from a place of production to a place where consumption of its leisure attributes assumes considerable importance is a general feature of developed western economies [Slee, 2005]. A process of commodification of countryside has occurred [Butler *et al.*, 1997; Kneafsey, 2001] which seeks to "marketize" these new relationships. Although some areas still retain a strong primary production role, over large areas of Europe the economic importance of

---

[a]From the French term *économie résidentielle.*

the countryside as a place of amenity consumption in its widest sense has far surpassed its importance in primary production. In contrast, in North America, the farmed landscape seems rather less important as an amenity resource, with designated federal and state lands the primary magnets of attraction and the natural resource base seen as the key attraction [English *et al.*, 2000; Butler and Clark, 1992]. This may reflect demand differences and both the time depth of European cultural landscapes and the extensive areas of attractive non-agricultural rural land in North America.

Because of its diverse structure, its embeddedness in regional economies (rather than in specifically rural economies) and poor sectoral data in comparison to the farm sector, the exact size of the rural tourism sector is often uncertain. Part of the problem of estimating the size is definitional. Rural tourism and recreation embrace the accommodation sector, day visitor attractions and a panoply of services, including food, food service and retailing that are major recipients of tourist and recreation spending. The tourism sector arguably includes second homes, about which opinion is divided as to their contribution to rural economies [Gallent *et al.*, 2005]. But expenditure in tourist destinations also includes that of local residents, so careful attribution is needed to determine the size of the industry in terms of its contribution to GDP and employment.

The identity and attributes of a destination can emphasize the natural environment and ecotourism [Kaupilla and Karjalainen, 2012], the historic built environment [Silva and Leal, 2015; Eusebio *et al.*, 2017], activity tourism, health and wellbeing tourism [Pesonen *et al.*, 2011], the farmed environment or cultural tourism. The farm sector's engagement with tourism and recreation is highly variable over space. Sometimes, as in parts of the Alps, the UK's Lake District or Scandinavian montane areas, there is wholesale engagement, but in other areas where intensive farming prevails, tourism is often present in a much more limited way.

Farming and land use more generally provide a green infrastructure which generates what are now termed ecosystem services, including landscapes, rural cultures, farmland biodiversity and traditional buildings. These public goods underpin a significant amount of rural tourism, but unless marketized through farm household engagement in tourist services, they remain as positive externalities which are captured by the visitor or tourism businesses but for which the provider is generally unrewarded.

It can also be argued that the negative externalities from agriculture, generally most pronounced in intensive farming areas, are likely to suppress the demand for rural tourism and recreational services. Garrod *et al.* [2006] make a case for better connecting rural tourism development with the provision of "countryside capital" — the bundle of assets, including public goods — that provide the green infrastructure in which tourism takes place.

The tourism industry necessarily generates socio-economic impacts, many of which are positive, but some of which are negative. Its presence creates an injection of investment and outside income, which can either ripple through local economies or leak out, depending on the nature of the enterprise and its connections. Its growth can be haphazard, chaotic and market-driven, or policy-driven with an eye to generating a more solid platform for regional development [Komilis, 1994]. It can be embedded in a wider regional economy or operated as an enclave. Its sustainability has become a hot topic [Stabler, 1997], not least because the wealth it brings can result in environmental pressures on water supplies, sewage systems and infrastructures. It involves travel, increasingly air travel, which leaves a high environmental footprint. Indeed, Lenzen *et al.* [2018] suggest that tourism may be responsible for around 8% of all global anthropogenic GHG emissions.

For a variety of reasons, primarily relating to food security and farm income support, the farm sector has been singled out for sectoral policy support in most western developed economies. As pressure has grown from the WTO and, in particular, from food-exporting countries to reduce farm support, the policy aims for the farm sector have morphed from an exclusive emphasis on food security and stable prices to the protection of public goods and the avoidance of public bads, and toward rural economic diversification. Part of this reorientation of rural policy has also been a movement away from agricultural exceptionalism toward more integrated rural policy and the promotion of place-based rural development. As well as being promoted actively by the OECD as a "territorial" model of rural development, this reorientation has been partially accomplished by support for integrated rural development in the EU through its Structural and Investment Funds (ESIFs) generally and through the application of the principle of Community Led Local Development (CLLD). Tourism and recreation are often integral to place-based territorial development and their promotion has often been part of such policies.

In this chapter, the diverse nature of the tourism and recreational sector is explored, the size of the sector is considered, and the actual and potential contribution of the farm sector is examined. The contribution of policy to the development of the sector is considered before some conclusions are drawn together about the importance and impact of the sector.

21.2 The Nature of Rural Tourism and Recreation

Although the rural tourism sector has grown dramatically in recent decades, largely as a result of the increase in free-moving tourists associated with enhanced personal mobility, the roots of rural recreation are much older. Religious pilgrimage has been taking place in Europe since the Middle Ages and remains a powerful force. Murray [1997] asserts that the *Camino de Santiago* along Northern Spain attracted as many as 500,000 pilgrims a year in the 13th century. By 2018, over 300,000 visitors completed the *Camino* and received certificates out of a total of 2.5 million visiting Santiago de Compostela.[b] Health tourism has an equally long history, initially involving the movement of people to inland places with "healthy" spa waters and later to the coast where marine water assumed a similar status. The nobility often left the cities in summer months to avoid the heightened risk of disease, and to find better air quality and alternative leisure pursuits in country retreats. The Grand Tour of Europe was very much part of an aristocratic upbringing from the 15th century onwards. From the mid-19th century, there is evidence of wealthy urban people taking summer lodgings both in the farmed countryside of places such as Devon [Torr, 1921] and in mountain areas. Arguably, the romantic idealization of nature from the early 1800s created new sensibilities which led to the opening up of mountain areas as destinations, sometimes, as in the Scottish Highlands, nurtured by the depictions of novelists such as Sir Walter Scott.

---

[b] See https://www.ultreyatours.com/blog/what-is-the-camino-de-santiago (accessed 9 October 2018).

Currently, rural tourism and recreation have highly divergent characteristics in different parts of Europe. There are three major types of rural region where holiday tourism and recreation assume greater significance: the mountain areas, especially those with potential for both winter and summer sport and recreation; the coastal areas and their immediate hinterlands; and the areas of high landscape value, often associated with less intensive farming systems, where both cultural and biophysical elements provide enhanced attractiveness. In all of these areas, ecotourism has assumed increased salience as the environment is increasingly packaged and commodified. In Eastern, Central and Northern Europe, hunting and fishing are often a significant attraction. Writing about Northern Finland, Kaupilla and Karjalainen [2012] assert that: "tourism in rural areas is based on nature and nature-based activities", not even mentioning farmed landscapes as an attractant: a conception similar to that in North America. And, over and above holiday tourism, the use of farms as a provider of business tourism (i.e. visitors for work purposes rather than holiday tourists) should also be recognized as a possibility.

Rural areas are widely presented as repositories of national and regional identities, as places of repose and peace in a post-modern world. The emergence of neo-endogenous development as a framing of contemporary rural development practice [Ray, 2006] describes the space in which new local food and drink products are developed and in which old local products can be revitalized. These characteristics can be exploited by the tourism sector. Their differentness from everyday urban life emerges as a major reason for their attractiveness.

21.3 The Economic Size of the Tourism and Recreation Sector

The principal drivers of increased demand for rural tourism have been income growth, increased available time for recreation (especially for retired people), much-enhanced private mobility and much-enhanced technology, from weatherproof clothing and mountain bikes to the internet for booking. Whereas early tourism depended on paddle boat or railways, the emancipation of private mobility has spread the demand for rural tourism and recreation over a far wider range of places. As mass tourism has stagnated, so the demand for authenticity and variety has created new possibilities for rural tourism, where the pursuit of distinctiveness has become central to many tourists' desires. Further, many households now take several holidays, often including short breaks.

The supply side of the tourism experience is the accommodation sector and the day visitor attraction sector, and the retail and restaurant offer that straddles both residential and tourist needs. Hotels, guest houses and self-catering accommodation dominate the provision of bed-spaces. In some places, holiday villages and other purpose-built structures assume importance. In most cases, the farm sector is only a minor player in the direct supply of tourism and recreational services. Forest owners and larger estate owners have often provided hunting facilities for paying guests or friends, and this has often led to the provision of a wider accommodation offer, either in the aristocratic houses of the estate owners or in nearby hotels.

There is a diverse geography of farm household engagement. It is sometimes asserted that very small farms lack the resource base to engage in tourism and that large agribusinesses have such a productivist orientation that there is no space in their business model for tourism. But in practice, provision of tourism and recreational goods and services can be found from peasant farm to aristocratic grand houses, always more likely where landscape or nearby facilities and attractions contribute to a wider tourism offer. Even in rather poor post socialist countries, agro-tourism has emerged as a livelihood strategy to complement farming activity, but it tends to be concentrated in certain areas, especially the mountains, and adjacent to other cultural attractions, such as the painted churches of Romanian Moldova [Iorio and Corsale, 2010].

Although there has been widespread recognition of the growth of rural tourism, it was a major event in the farmed livestock sector in the United Kingdom — the severe 2001 outbreak of Foot and Mouth Disease — which paradoxically revealed the scale of the tourism and recreation sector's contribution to the economy of rural Britain. The weighty economic analysis of this epidemic [NAO, 2005] revealed that the impact of the shutdown of the non-farm rural economy on the tourism sector was significantly greater than the impact on the farming and food sector. The report concluded that:

> in the private sector, the areas most affected by the outbreak were agriculture, the food chain and supporting services, which incurred net costs of £0.6 billion; and tourism and supporting industries, which lost revenues of between £4.5 billion and £5.4 billion.

Public compensation to the farm sector amounted to nearly £1.6 billion, but these data showed for the first time the enormous contribution of tourism to rural economy — at least double farming's contribution — a fact never before quantified in a comparable way to the farm sector's contribution to rural wellbeing. Indeed, Scott *et al.* [2004, p. 1] concluded that:

> the unanticipated magnitude of effect of the outbreak should direct more attention to the nature of the space shared as a public good by agriculture and rural tourism.

The paucity of national level statistics for rural and farm tourism in other countries should therefore not be taken as an indication of the sector's small size so much as the challenge of accurate estimation caused by definitional problems. It would be entirely reasonable to assert that over large swathes of rural Europe, the tourism and recreation sector contributes far more to rural GDP than does the farm sector, regardless of the engagement of the farm sector in that activity.

The accurate estimation of tourism employment is made difficult by the nature of the sector and by the large number of self-employed businesses in many rural areas, which means that the workforce is not found in official employee data sources. Errington (1990) found that a high proportion of self-employment was found in the tourism services sector in a range of UK locations. He also found that in three out of four different investigated rural regions of England, tourism employment significantly exceeded that of the agricultural sector.

Because of its diverse composition, the contribution of rural tourism and recreation to employment in the rural economy is not especially easy to evidence, even though as a service industry it is relatively employment-intensive [Snowdon and Thomson, 1998]. It contrasts sharply with

Table 21.1. Share of bed-spaces at EU level by type of region (millions).

Type of area	2012	2015
City	6.3	7.0
Towns and suburbs	9.3	9.7
Rural	14.1	14.4

Source: http://ec.europa.eu/eurostat/statistics-explained/index.php/Tourism_industries_-_economic_analysis (accessed 9 October 2018).

farming which has become much more capital intensive in recent decades. As a proxy of the distribution of tourism employment in rural areas, the share of rural tourism by bed-spaces at EU level can be considered. Occupancy rates tend to be higher in city locations where seasonality is less marked than in more rural areas, so it is likely that the number of jobs in urban areas is proportionately higher but, as almost 50% of bed-spaces are rural, this suggests a very significant source of rural employment. European tourism employs a high percentage of women and a high proportion of young adults, and thus contributes to a more inclusive rural workforce (see Table 21.1).

There is good evidence that tourism employment multipliers are higher for smaller-scale tourism providers than for larger-scale enterprises. Slee *et al.* [1997] used detailed survey data for rural Scotland which showed that leakage of tourism benefits out of local economies was much higher for large-scale tourism businesses than for small embedded rural tourism businesses. This explains the frequent desire to position "soft" tourism[c] as a key part of many strategies for sustainable development in rural areas [Roberts and Hall, 2001].

Tourism in the EU has grown in importance in recent years. The EU database reveals that:

> tourism industries (mainly and partially) showed a stronger growth than the total economy for all indicators concerned. Looking at those

[c] Soft tourism is characterized by small enterprise size, local ownership, embeddedness in existing infrastructures and low environmental impact.

industries that are 'mainly tourism' the value added recorded a growth of +24% between 2012 and 2015, the number of enterprises grew by +14%, the turnover by +11% and the number of persons employed by +6% (for the total economy the corresponding growth rates were +14%, +5%, +5% and +3% respectively. *Source*: http://ec.europa.eu/eurostat/statistics-explained/index.php/Tourism_industries_-_economic_analysis#Key_economic_indicators (accessed 9 October 2018).

Obtaining good tourism data represents a challenge. Batista e Silva *et al.* [2018] have recently reviewed the possibilities of using big data to supplement official tourism data and build a better picture of its geographical concentration and seasonality. The authors note that in 2016 over 10% of Europe's GDP was derived from tourism, with the figure in excess of 20% in some countries. The greatest numbers are found in key destination cities, but the highest levels of tourism dependency are in rural, coastal and mountain regions. However, the authors do not provide any clear indication of the data sources to elicit employment creation arising from tourism.

In total, it seems likely that just under 10% of the European Union workforce is engaged in tourism as narrowly defined by accommodation catering, transport and travel agency sectors. Given that tourist spend impacts heavily on some other services, the real contribution of the tourism industry and its associated employment is considerably greater. Of course, the distribution of the employment is highly uneven, but a very substantial proportion of bed-spaces are in rural areas, and in some regional economies, such as South-West and North-West England, Brittany, the Alps, Tuscany, and Spanish and Greek islands, rural tourism is a major part of total economic activity.

21.4 The Nature and Diversity of Farm Tourism

Farms and other land-based businesses in rural areas have been providers of tourism accommodation for a long time. The roots of farm tourism go back at least to the mid-19th century. By mid-20th century, the typical tourist provider offered "bed and breakfast", often in more remote areas with an evening meal as an option. From the 1950s onwards, there was a shift toward the provision of self-catering accommodation, in part of the farmhouse or in converted outbuildings and barns, in new-build chalets, or in static caravans. Self-catering is less onerous on the provider and means the farm family is relatively distanced from the visitor, or at least can engage on their own terms. Some farms also offer campsites and stances for mobile caravans and motor homes.

There has been a long-running debate about precisely what constitutes a farm tourist enterprise. The farming community has often sought to protect the identity of the working farm as a distinctive attribute of the tourism offer, especially when urban dwellers have tended to buy farmhouses and farm buildings and run tourist enterprises without any intention of becoming real farmers [Flanigan *et al.*, 2014; Streifeneder, 2016]. In many European countries, farm tourism associations exist to try to certificate the farm tourism product, and in some cases there is legislative reinforcement of the definition of the product.

The scale of farm tourism varies greatly from region to region. In Italy, where there are legal regulations defining agro-tourism, there are currently nearly 3,000 providers in South Tyrol and over 4,000 in Tuscany. In Austria, 6% of all tourist beds are on farms, and 14% of all tourist nights in Bavaria are on registered farm premises [Streifeneder, 2016].

Farm tourism is a highly gendered activity and is often seen as a supplementary income source for farm women. It can be disparaged by productivist farmers.[d] Garcia Ramon *et al.* [1995, p. 269] assert that "the work of women in rural tourism is fundamental and indispensable within the context of family-based agrarian activity." Indeed, it is apparent when examining farm tourism that it frequently provides a household adjustment strategy for farm families and, in many cases, cross-subsidizes more economically fragile and less profitable farming enterprises.

The product mix on some farms connects strongly to regional food and drink specialties. Food tourism is not exclusively a farm activity but small-scale artisanal production of food and drink is often a distinguishing feature of Southern and Central European farms and provides a compelling narrative for a population seeking distinctiveness of tourism

[d]Over 30 years ago, I recall asking a Devon farmer if his farm had diversified into other income sources. His reply: *No, I'm not diversified, but the missus (the farmer's wife) is* reflects that mentality.

experience. It is less a feature of North-West European farm tourist provision where the penetration of the industrial food system has been greater, but even in the UK, food tourism is seen an important part of regional identity-building [Everett and Aitchison, 2008].

As well as the traditional product mix, there are also many providers on farms of more specialized farm holidays. For many years, organic farms have offered working holidays. A movement that began as Working Weekends on Organic Farms has become "wwoofing": there are 650 such farms in the UK, and well over 300 in Austria, 265 in Spain and 85 in the Netherlands [https://wwoofinternational.org, accessed 9 October 2018]. The practice of volunteering on traditional farms is also found in South Tyrol, Italy [Streifeneder, 2016].

Farm recreation and tourism merge with horse-related tourism, and in many peri-urban and upland areas horse-related leisure and recreation are major land-using activities. However, many riding establishments would fail the authenticity tests of some countries' regulations on farm tourism. The nature and diversity of the horse industry makes it extremely hard to delimit as horses have morphed from being draught animals to recreational animals. As well as farms that have become wholly devoted to horses for recreation, there are many farms where ponies and horses graze alongside farm livestock. While many horse-related establishments are an expensive hobby, others offer a highly profitable diversified enterprise for farmers, far outperforming what any agricultural enterprise could provide [Slee, 1987].

The distinctiveness and traditional nature of rural tourism is seen as a major selling point [Sanagustin *et al.*, 2011]. However, the extent to which the farm tourist is consuming an authentic by-product of traditional farming or a consciously constructed pastiche has been questioned, especially in relation to some mountain farming regions [Daugstad and Kirchengast, 2013]. A conscious connecting of farm and land-based traditional crafts and foods to specific regions is part of both a natural and policy-induced strategy, in which rural development agencies and LEADER[e] groups have exploited the cultural economy as a tourism development strategy.

---

[e] The acronym LEADER stands for *Liaisons Entre Actions pour le Developpement de l'Economie Rurale*. These schemes are funded by Pillar 2 of the CAP, and are a key part of the European Union's strategy for Community-Led Local Development (CLLD).

The development of rural tourism is thus caught between the need for authenticity and distinctiveness which entails embeddedness in regional identity, and the understanding of the market background from which most tourists emanate. Consequently, it is frequently incomers who may be more sensitive to urban-based demands that are best able to capture the rural tourists spend.

21.5 The Policy Context

The extent to which rural tourism development is framed by farm or regional policy is often a decisive influence on what is supported by public policy. Where the framing of policy need is in the context of Pillar 2 of the CAP, the framing is likely to be much more agro-centric. In contrast, where the public policy focus is on regional development, there is less likely to be a focus on rural areas and farms in particular, and more on the wider tourism industry including attractions and visitor centers.

In the European Union, the suite of measures that contributes to rural and regional development comprises five funds, collectively known as European Structural and Investment Funds but most often referred to as Structural Funds: the guidance element of the CAP, the European Fund for Rural Development (EAFRD); the European Regional Development Fund (ERDF); the European Social Fund (ESF); the Cohesion Fund (operational only in less developed Member States); and the European Maritime and Fisheries Fund (EMFF). As early as the 1990s, Structural Funds were deployed in various countries to try to build regional capacity for rural tourism, although, with reference to Denmark, Hjalager [1996] argues for institutional innovation as a necessary precursor to effective development.

Four examples from Scotland indicate the kind of projects supported by European funds. In the 2007–2014 Rural Development Program (RDP), LEADER funded the development and business plan for a forest mountain bike enterprise, which led to a cash injection into the Borders economy of Southern Scotland of about £11 million a year. The 2007–2014 ERDF funded the "Mountains for People" project to improve mountain paths in three major walking destinations of Scotland. Over the same period, the ESF funded a social enterprise academy which supported nearly 300 social enterprises, including several with links to outdoor activities for disadvantaged and difficult-to-employ young people. A community business on the small Hebridean island of Tiree was funded under the EMFF to develop moorings to increase the number of tourist boats visiting the island.

The way in which Pillar 2 of the CAP is operationalized varies considerably from country to country. Sometimes within LEADER much of the expenditure is channeled into farm businesses, including into farm diversification such as tourism. Where LEADER funds comprise a larger component of the total Pillar 2 funds, the commitment to non-farm rural development is likely to be greater, though in some Member States LEADER funding is still targeted primarily at farms rather than wider rural development.

In some countries such as Finland and Spain, national governments have developed LEADER-like entities as local development vehicles. Especially in Spain, with a government policy to spread the benefits of tourism more widely into rural Spain, LEADER has been an important policy in nurturing rural tourism. For example, many communities along the Camino de Santiago routes have used LEADER funding to provide touristic services.

21.6 Conclusions

Rural tourism is a highly diverse component of the rural economy, and differs in scale and character from one place to another. Its differentiated character generates different consequences for economy, society and environment in different places. Where it is embedded in rural communities and strongly connected to local food and culture, it can reinvigorate social, cultural and economic life, and be environmentally benign. Where it is based on externally owned enclave developments, leakage out of local economies is rapid, it is culturally disruptive, and it tends to have a high carbon footprint. Between these two stereotypical extremes there is an enormous variety of practice.

Tourism peripheries are in danger of being exploited for urban cores in ways that do not maximize beneficial impacts [Salvatore *et al.*, 2018], although there are some examples of the strategic embedding of tourism in local development strategies [Lopez and Garcia, 2006]. Collaborative effort among multiple and diverse stakeholders is seen as essential as improving the tourism offer, enhancing competitiveness in marginal areas and reducing leakage of benefits out of local economies. In developing countries, engagement of the rural poor is more likely through migration to resorts for seasonal work than through use of the peasant farm as a tourism product [Biddulph, 2015].

Employment in tourism is often criticized because it is seasonal and low paid. However, this scarcely distinguishes it from many jobs in agriculture and the food processing sector. Certain types of rural tourism can be strongly linked to other parts of the local economy, and have high income and employment multiplier effects. However, in some tourism destinations, a high proportion of the workforce is non-local. This will reduce local multipliers but may well enable remittances to be sent back to remote rural areas and subsequently invested in local development elsewhere.

The farm tourist sector is a subset of the wider rural tourism system. In some areas it has developed into a significant part of the farm household economy; in others it is almost invisible. This reflects the geography of opportunity, with farmed countryside with traditional farming systems seen as attractants and areas dominated by industrial farming having a modest agro-tourism presence. It provides a highly gendered opportunity for farm women and diversifies the farm household income stream. It combines well with artisanal food and drink enterprises, and can provide a highly distinctive and sought-after tourism product.

There are some contentious issues surrounding rural tourism, including its sustainability, its economic impacts and its impacts on society and culture. In most cases, the balance of benefit over cost gives it a positive contribution to rural economy, society and environment, but the sector lacks the protective backstop of farm income support and is driven by the rigors of the market place. This should enhance its competitiveness. Nonetheless, given the importance of public goods and the need for regulation in the sector, the rigors of the market need counterbalancing by a planning and policy framework that ensures the sector's coordinated and effective development.

References

Batista e Silva, F., Marín Herrera, M. A., Rosina, K., Ribeiro Barranco, R., Freire, S. and Schiavina, M. (2018). Analysing spatiotemporal patterns of tourism in Europe at high-resolution with conventional and big data sources. *Tourism Management*, 68, 101–115.

Biddulph, R. (2015). Limits to mass tourism's effects in rural peripheries. *Annals of Tourism Research*, 50, pp. 98–112.

Butler, R., Hall, C. M. and Jenkins, J. (eds.) (1997). *Tourism and Recreation in Rural Areas*, Wiley, Chichester.

Butler, R. and Clark, G. (1992). Tourism in rural areas: Canada and the UK, in I. Bowler, C. Bryant and M. Nellis (eds.) *Contemporary Rural Systems in Transition* Volume 2: Economy and Society, CAB International, Wallingford.

Daugstad, K. and Kirchengast, C. (2013). Authenticity and the pseudo-backstage of agritourism. *Annals of Tourism Research*, 43, pp. 170–191.

English, D. B. K., Marcouiller, D. W. and Cordell, H. K. (2000). Tourism dependence in rural America: Estimates and effects. *Society and Natural Resources*, 13, pp. 185–202.

Eusebio, C., da Silva D. S., Carneiro, M. J., Kastenholz, E. and Figue, E. (2017). Who is consuming the countryside? An activity-based segmentation analysis of the domestic rural tourism market in Portugal. *Journal of Hospitality and Tourism Management*, 31, pp. 197–210.

Everett, S. and Aitchison, C. (2008). The role of food tourism in sustaining regional identity: A case study of Cornwall, South West England. *Journal of Sustainable Tourism*, 16(2), pp. 150–167.

Flanigan, S., Blackstock, K. and Hunter, C. (2014). Agritourism from the perspective of providers and visitors: A typology-based study. *Tourism Management*, 40, pp. 394–405.

Gallent, N., Mace, A. and Twdwr-Jones, M. (2005). *Second Homes: European Perspectives and UK Policies.* Routledge, London.

Garcia Ramon, M. D., Canoves, G. and Valdovinos, N. (1995). Farm tourism, gender and the environment in Spain. *Annals of Tourism Research*, 22(2), pp. 267–282.

Garrod, B., Wornell, R. and Youell, R. (2006). Re-conceptualising rural resources as countryside capital: The case of rural tourism. *Journal of Rural Studies*, 22, pp. 117–128.

Hjalager, A.-M. (1996). Agricultural diversification into tourism: Evidence of a European Community development programme. *Tourism Management*, 17(2), pp. 103–111.

Iorio, M. and Corsale, A. (2010). Rural tourism and livelihood strategies in Romania. *Journal of Rural Studies*, 26, pp. 152–162.

Kaupilla, P. and Karjalainen, T. P. (2012). A process model to assess the regional economics of fishing tourism: A case study in northern Finland, *Fisheries Research*, 127/8, pp. 88–97.

Kneafsey, M. (2001). Rural cultural economy: Tourism and social relations. *Annals of Tourism Research*, 28(3), pp. 762–783.

Komilis, P. (1994). Tourism and sustainable regional development. In Seaton A.V. *et al.* (eds), *Tourism the State of the Art*, Chapter 7. Wiley, Chichester.

Lenzen, M., Sun, Y.-Y., Faturay, F., Ting, Y.-P., Geschke, A. and Malik, A. (2018). The carbon footprint of global tourism, *Nature Climate Change*.

Lopez, E. P. and Garcia, F. J. C. (2006). Agrotourism, sustainable tourism and ultra-peripheral areas: The case of Canary Islands. *Pasos*, 4(1), pp. 85–97.

Murray, M. (1997). Exploring the dialectics of route-based tourism: The Camino de Santiago. *Tourism Management*, 18(8), pp. 513–524.

National Audit Office (NAO) (2005). *Foot and Mouth Disease: Applying the Lessons*, DEFRA, Report by the Comptroller and Auditor General, HC 184 Session 2004–2005.

Pesonen, J., Laukkanen, T. and Komppula, R. (2011). Benefit segmentation of potential wellbeing tourists. *Journal of Vacation Marketing*, 17(4), pp. 303–314.

Ray, C. (2006). Neo-endogenous rural development in the EU. In Cloke, P., Marsden, T. and Mooney, P. (eds.), *The Handbook of Rural Studies*. Sage Publications, London.

Roberts, L. and Hall, D. (2001). *Rural Tourism and Recreation: Principles to Practice*. CABI, Wallingford, pp. 278–291.

Salvatore, R., Chiodo, E. and Fantini, A. (2018). Tourism transition in peripheral rural areas: Theories, issues and strategies. *Annals of Tourism Research*, 68, pp. 41–51.

Sanagustin, M. V., Mosene, J. A. and Gomez y Patino, M. (2011). Rural tourism: A sustainable alternative. *Applied Energy*, 88, pp. 551–557.

Scott, A., Christie, M. and Midmore, P. (2004). Impact of the 2001 foot-and-mouth disease outbreak in Britain: Implications for rural studies. *Journal of Rural Studies*, 20, pp. 1–14.

Silva, L. and Leal, J. (2015). Rural tourism and national identity building in contemporary Europe: Evidence from Portugal. *Journal of Rural Studies*, 38, pp. 109–119.

Slee, R. W. (1987). *Alternative Farm Enterprises*. Farming Press, Ipswich.

Slee, R. W. (2005). From countrysides of production to countrysides of consumption? *Journal of Agricultural Science*, 143(4), pp. 255–265.

Slee, R. W., Farr, H. and Snowdon, P. (1997). The economic impact of alternative types of rural tourism. *Journal of Agricultural Economics*, 48(2), pp. 179–192.

Stabler, M. J. (ed.) (1997). *Tourism Sustainability: Principles to Practice*, CAB Books, Wallingford.

Streifeneder, T. (2016). Agriculture first: Assessing European policies and scientific typologies to define authentic agritourism and differentiate it from countryside tourism. *Tourism Management Perspectives*, 20, pp. 251–264.

Snowdon, P. J. and Thomson, K. J. (1998). Tourism in the Scottish Economy. In MacLellan, R. and Smith, R. (eds.), *Tourism in Scotland*. Thomson, London, pp. 70–92.

Torr, C. (1921). *Small Talk at Wreyland*, Cambridge University Press, Cambridge.

Chapter 22

Agri-tourism and Rural Outdoor Recreation in the US: A Framework for Understanding Economic and Employment Dynamics*

Dawn Thilmany[†,||], Rebecca Hill[†], Michelle Haefele[†], Anders van Sandt[†], Catherine Cullinane Thomas[‡], Martha Sullins[†] and Sarah A. Low[¶]

[†]*Colorado State University, Colorado, USA*
[‡]*US Geological Survey, USA*
[¶]*University of Missouri Extension, USA*
[||]*Dawn.Thilmany@ColoState.edu*

Agri-tourism and rural outdoor recreation are positioned at an important intersection between agricultural, natural resource, economic development and rural issues. This chapter summarizes some of the important dynamics of these sectors, including the role of land use, regional drivers, motivations for farmers and travelers, and economic impacts. As a means to illustrate several key points, highlights of several

*The views expressed here are those of the authors and may not be attributed to the University of Missouri, US Geological Survey, or Colorado State University.

case studies, papers and reports about rural outdoor and agricultural tourism are summarized. To conclude, a research agenda for those interested in the role of tourism to rural economies is framed.

22.1 Introduction

Agri-tourism, commonly defined as "farming-related activities carried out on a working farm or other agricultural settings for entertainment or education purposes" [Arroyo *et al.*, 2013], is a relatively new area of discovery for rural policy, economic development and employment. However, the boundaries and characteristics of agri-tourism are ill-defined, leading one study to develop a conceptual framework that incorporates five categories of activities including direct sales, education, hospitality, outdoor recreation and entertainment [Chase *et al.*, 2018]. It suggested that it may also be useful to include peripheral tiers, including other community-based food, agriculture and natural resource-based activities. For this reason, agri-tourism and rural outdoor recreation are worth considering jointly as they both leverage the natural assets (land, natural resources), human capital (skills, family members) and cultural heritage of rural places. Moreover, there is evidence both subsectors are important economic drivers for rural areas. In the US, agri-tourism and outdoor recreation have connections to larger rural policy issues including land use and conservation, emerging public interest in reconnecting with their food system, and leveraging the diverse heritage and histories of rural communities across America to create entrepreneurial and economic opportunities.

While the growth and success of agri-tourism varies across regions and farm/ranch types, the number of agri-tourism farms and ranches in the contiguous US grew by roughly 64% between 2002 and 2012 according to the 2012 USDA Census of Agriculture, the most recent available data (USDA collects such data only for activities directly occurring on the farm). In 2012, 33,161 farms reported $704 million in revenues from agri-tourism and recreational services; however, the total percentage of farms and ranches with agri-tourism in the US is still relatively low at 1.6%, and accounts for only 0.2% of gross farm revenues. It is important to recognize, however, that agri-tourism revenues collected by farms are just the start: economic inflows to surrounding communities may be significantly more when one considers visitors' spending on lodging, dining, retail, and additional recreational enterprises while visiting the area — increasing the economic impact of agri-tourism to a host community.

Given the size, growth and potential linkages to rural development, this chapter will provide context for agri-tourism's role in linking a wide array of public issues to economic development in the rural US. First, we examine the supply-side factors associated with US agri-tourism, including regional assets most associated with agri-tourism. We then discuss factors associated with visitor demand for agri-tourism. Finally, we examine the nexus between agri-tourism and the rural economy; its spillovers, relevant policies, and impacts.

22.2 The Potential Supply of Agri-tourism in the US

22.2.1 *Patterns of landownership and outdoor recreation in rural America*

The settlement of the US territory in North America was often motivated by the prospect of owning land. Today, rural land ownership in the US is a mixture of public and private lands. Such a mix creates a complex narrative for the rural outdoor recreation and tourism sector that may host activities on private, local, state or federal lands. The US federal government owns 640 million acres of land, about 28% of the nation's total land area [Vincent *et al.*, 2017]. Federal land ownership varies drastically between the East and West regions of the US: the majority of federal lands are located in the West (Figure 22.1). Specifically, federal land ownership as a proportion of land ownership in the US varies from less than 1% for several states in the East to almost 85% of the land area in the Western state of Nevada.

The supply of outdoor recreation opportunities mirrors Federal land ownership, with a large portion of recreation opportunities occurring on publicly owned Western lands. Figure 22.2 shows the distribution of publicly owned (including federal, state and locally owned) outdoor recreation lands (Figure 22.2(a)) and privately owned outdoor recreation lands (Figure 22.2(b)).

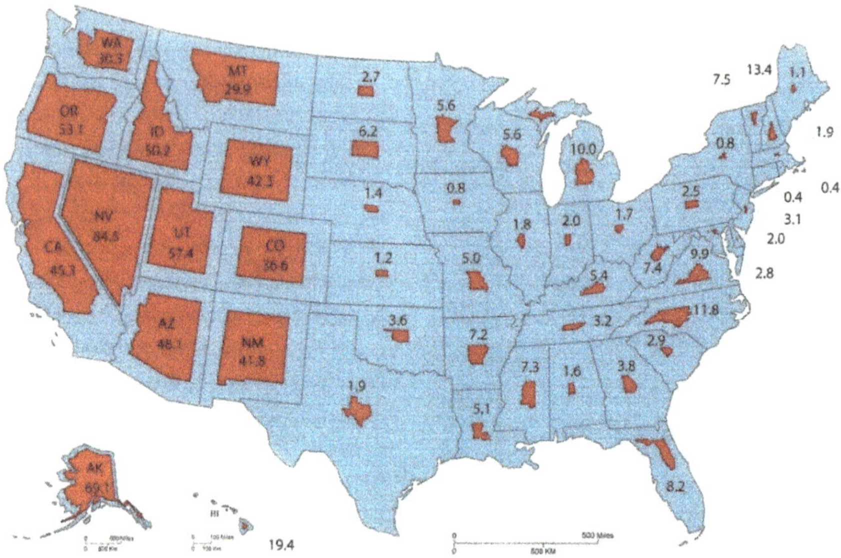

Data source: U.S. General Services Administration, *Federal Real Property Profile 2004*, excludes trust properties.

Fig. 22.1. Federal land as a percentage of total state land area (map courtesy of the Bill Lane Center for the American West, Stanford University).

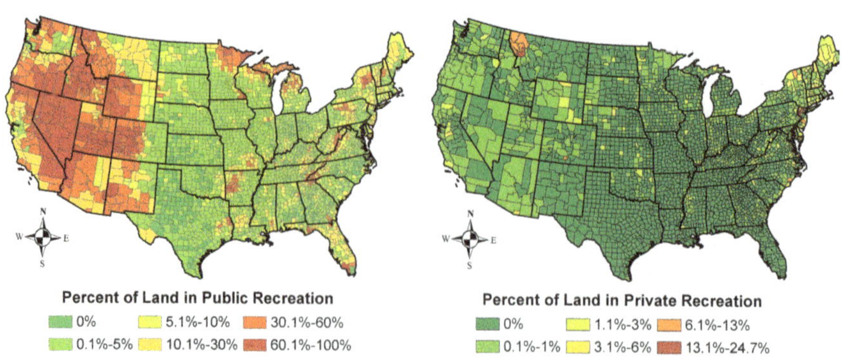

(a) (b)

Fig. 22.2. Public (a) and private (b) outdoor recreation as a share of total county area.

Note: See text for variable definitions.

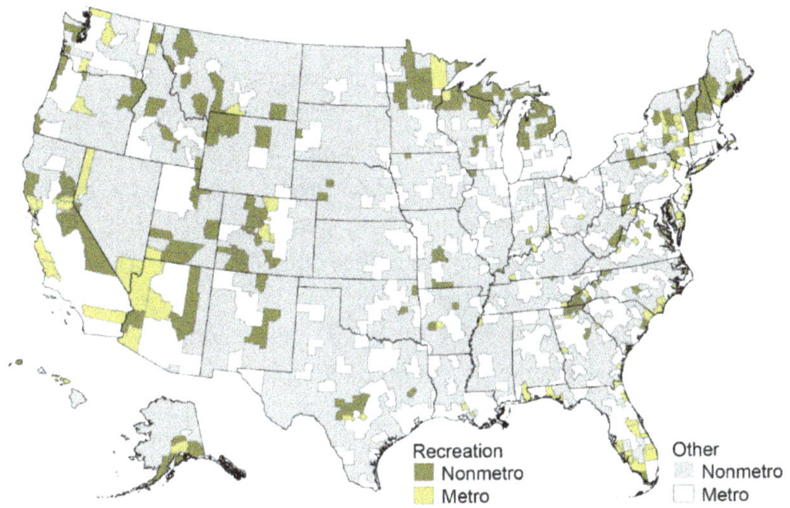

Fig. 22.3. Recreation counties in the US, 2015.

Public outdoor recreation lands are defined as any land that is owned by a government entity and open to the public for recreational use, while private outdoor recreation land is similarly defined with private land ownership. The variables were created using the 2010 Protected Areas Database of the United States (PADUS) geodatabase which represents public land ownership and conservation lands, including voluntarily provided privately protected areas.

Although a large portion of recreation lands occurs in the West, counties with recreation-dependent economies are distributed across the nation (Figure 22.3).

The US Department of Agriculture (USDA) Economic Research Service (ERS) classifies 333 counties in 43 US States as recreational. These recreation counties are determined by a weighted index of (1) jobs; (2) earnings in entertainment, recreation, accommodations, eating/drinking places and real estate; and (3) the share of vacant housing units intended for seasonal/occasional use. Counties with a score more than one standard deviation above the mean are defined as recreational.

22.2.2 *Agri-tourism and the rural economy*

Rural economies have substantial economic development challenges. Many rural areas of the US are losing population (Figure 22.4), which presents challenges for rural leaders seeking to maintain the people and tax base necessary to support key public services (health care, education, cultural programs). Population loss also generates challenges for local businesses, whose markets diminish unless other (urban or otherwise non-local) consumers can be attracted.

Due to relatively high rates of economic growth, rural recreation counties are often presented as rural success stories. Indeed, research suggests that recreation and tourism can help diversify the local economy. A diverse rural economy is less vulnerable to the boom and bust cycles of natural resource extraction and traditional farming enterprises, and recreation and tourism activities can provide additional income to farm households [Reeder and Brown, 2005]. Rural well-being varies

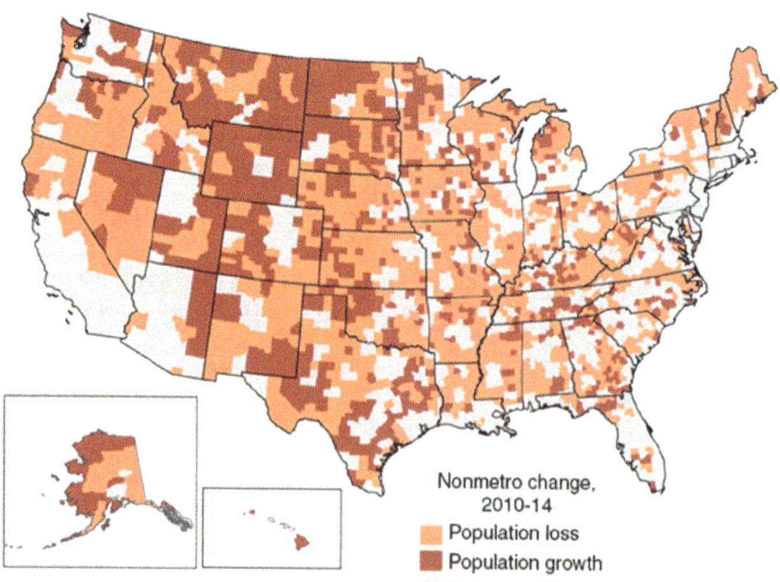

Fig. 22.4. Non-metro population loss widespread in all Eastern States, 2010–2014.
Source: USDA, Economic Research Service, using data from US Census Bureau.

across space, often with the natural assets or industrial composition of a region. Specifically, rural areas with recreation-based economies tended to outperform other rural areas in several measures including median household income and poverty rates (Figure 22.5), and educational attainment, population growth and increased health outcomes [Reeder and Brown, 2005].

22.2.3 *Location and operational factors associated with farms participating in agri-tourism*

Demand for outdoor recreation is increasing, but government-provided outdoor recreation opportunities are remaining constant, creating a gap between government supply and the demand from the public. This gap in outdoor recreation supply is increasingly being filled by private landowners who create opportunities for public outdoor recreation on their land as they see opportunities to attract visitors [Goldbach, 2012].

As with outdoor recreation in general, there are complex community and enterprise-specific regional and spatial patterns in agri-tourism provision across the US. Van Sandt *et al.* [2018] find that travel infrastructure, region and rurality, characteristics of the local economy and proximity to outdoor attractions are all significantly associated with agri-tourism provision.

The diversity of farm, cultural, and community assets make it important to understand the differences in tourism strategies that may be best suited to development of the recreational sector. Larger farms and ranches that produce specialty livestock, horses, and grapes/wine tend to generate more agri-tourism revenue than smaller farms. It is also more common to have larger operations offering experience-based agri-tourism activities such as organized events, entertainment and outdoor recreational activities [Van Sandt *et al.*, 2018]. Grapes, and associated wine production, represents one of the largest drivers of higher agri-tourism economic activity, likely reflecting the longstanding popularity of wine-based agri-tourism. Smaller farms and ranches (grossing under $350,000 per year) tend to attract more agri-tourism business through fruit and nut production, perhaps offered through U-pick operations or sales at farm stands offering unprocessed or value-added products.

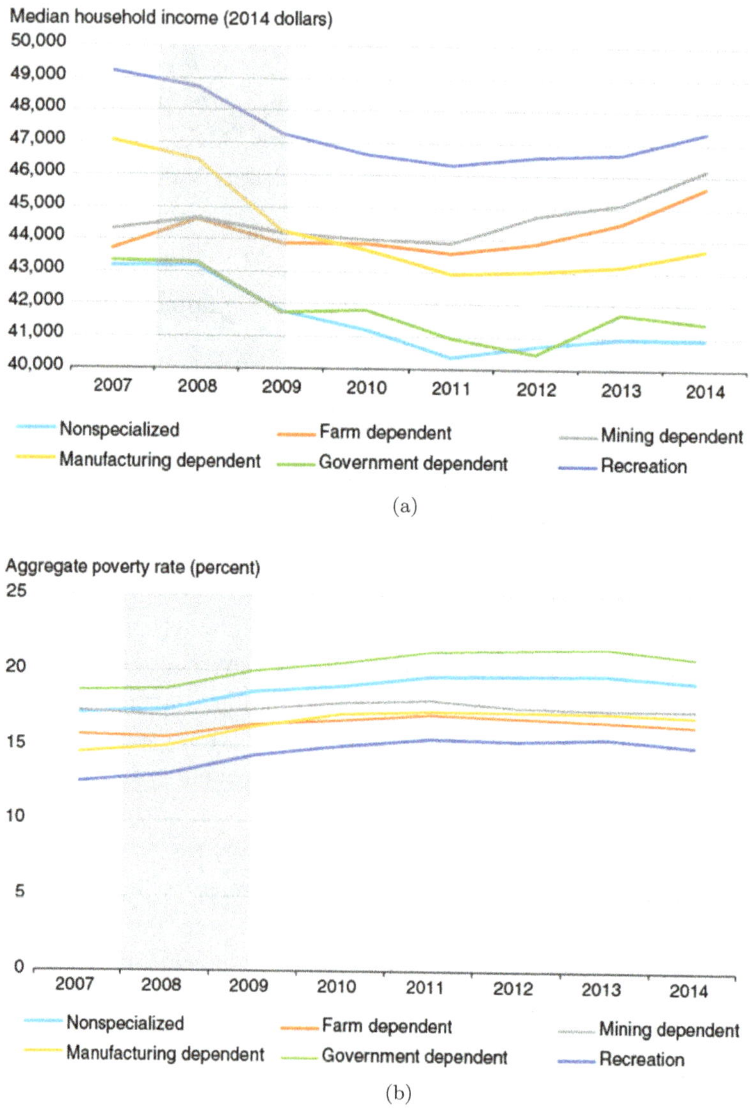

Fig. 22.5. Rural recreation counties fare better than many other rural counties in median household income (a) and poverty rates (b).

Note: Medians show that half of those who live in a type of county are in a county with a lower median household income, and the other half are in a county with a higher median household income. Values are in constant 2015 dollars deflated by the Consumer Price Index.

Source: USDA, Economic Research Service estimates based on Small Area Income and Poverty Estimates datasets.

In general, Van Sandt *et al.* [2018] conclude that agritourists are drawn toward experiences with unique types of agricultural production, especially those that are more conducive to human interactions (e.g. horses and fruit *vs.* sheep or bees). In addition, agritourists tend to place higher values on agri-tourism activities that take advantage of the region's history, culture, or natural assets. For example, agritourists place higher values on horseback-riding activities in the West, compared to those in the Midwest, most likely due to the region's rich cowboy culture and many scenic areas under both private and public land management [Hill *et al.*, 2017].

22.2.4 *The motivation to pursue agri-tourism on-farm*

Many studies have reviewed the motivations driving individual farm and ranch operators to offer agri-tourism or recreation opportunities. While many have suggested employment, particularly of family members, as a motivation, recent research suggests that other factors, such as connecting to customers and enhancing quality of life, may be more important drivers.

The motivations to pursue agri-tourism likely vary by operation and are complex. Barbieri [2008] found that US agri-tourism business owners, when compared to non-agri-tourism farm businesses, were more likely to be driven by firm profitability, report agriculture as their primary occupation and have adult children living at home. Based on these factors, the author suggests that agri-tourism may be creating on-farm/ranch employment for family members. In a study of Canadian agri-tourism businesses, Barbieri [2010] examined 19 goals related to agri-tourism development in Canada and found a complex set of market-based and non-market-based goals (such as continuing to farm and enhancing quality of life) were ranked highest, while generating employment for family members was ranked lowest among a subset of family-related goals.

McGehee [2007] points out that motivations may change as the business evolves and ages, and finds that agri-tourism job creation may have a limited impact at the farm level, averaging four part-time employees for each agri-tourism enterprise. McGehee and Kim [2004] looked at a continuum of motivations and outcomes for agri-tourism entrepreneurs and their businesses, finding that generating additional income was ranked higher by respondents than creating jobs for family members. Similarly, a 2015 study of Colorado agri-tourism business owners reported that creating jobs for family members was ranked lowest of all desired outcomes, while connecting the farm/ranch to its customers (of agricultural product enterprises) was ranked the highest [Hill *et al.*, 2017; Van Sandt and Thilmany, 2016].

Perhaps these motivations could also be considered in the context of the size of farm and community. From other research reported here, small farms near urban areas seem less concerned about job creation, and instead focus on building a loyal customer base to capture the food dollars of nearby residents. And, in contrast, larger operations may view agri-tourism as a means to diversify their income stream. But still, given their seasonal agricultural labor needs and fewer alternative employment options during off-season in their surrounding rural communities, it may help to fully utilize workers they already employ in peak season, and even if they're just able to hire a handful of workers, for small towns, that may be a relatively important impact.

22.3 Exploring Varying Demand for Agri-tourism Across the US

Given the diverse set of agri-tourism opportunities in the US, it is no surprise that demand for agri-tourism varies with visitor demographics and traveler type. As a whole, US agritourists do not look different from the rest of the population. According to a 2014 survey of 1,000 agritourists who had participated in agri-tourism in the Western US, agritourists differ from the general population in that they are slightly more likely to be female (55%), be from slightly higher-earning households (median household income: $62,500), and are generally younger (median age: 34) than the US population [Hill *et al.*, 2017].

Farms and ranches proximate to metro areas are able to take advantage of demand from nearby visitors. As with most travel, US agritourists prefer destinations closer to their residence. So, even though agri-tourism farms and ranches that are relatively small (with less than $350,000 in sales) generally report less revenues, those near population centers capture relatively higher agri-tourism revenue than their peers. In contrast, larger-scale farms and ranches benefit from the demand created by "a getaway effect," a term Van Sandt *et al.* [2018] termed for being remote from major travel corridors and high-density urban areas. As such, larger operations offering experiences and access to uncongested natural resources appear successful at drawing tourists to more rural locations and collecting a greater level of revenues from such long-term visits [Van Sandt *et al.*, 2018].

The decision to participate in agri-tourism seems evenly distributed across the population, yet the types of agri-tourism that draw such visitors does vary, not only across consumers with varying demographic characteristics, but also across traveler types. A recent survey of agritourists found that agri-tourism destinations are often a primary draw, with 72% of respondents listing their visit to an agri-tourism site as the primary purpose for their trip [Hill *et al.*, 2017]. For the other 28% of respondents, agri-tourism represented a complementary excursion from their main trip. A significant portion of these secondary agri-tourism visitors (19%) listed a state or national park, beach, or forest as their primary destination, suggesting that proximity to outdoor recreation destinations may provide opportunities for agri-tourism. Van Sandt *et al.* [2018] also find evidence of a higher share of farms report revenues from offering when they are located along scenic byways. That finding, together with travelers reporting numerous multi-destination trips, may signal that there is potential to attract more visitors to consider stopping at an agri-tourism site as a pit stop while on road trips through these scenic byways.

Knowing that travelers bundle multiple destinations/activities within a single trip to maximize their experiences (and utility) relative to their travel costs, we can surmise that the surrounding community and locational characteristics play important roles in travelers' demand for agri-tourism experiences. Van Sandt *et al.* [2018] find that agri-tourism sites earn more revenue when they are surrounded by a cluster of other agri-tourism sites, so competitive forces appear to be outweighed by the agglomeration benefits of a variety of attractions to draw visitors to an area. In short, cooperation among recreational providers should trump concerns about competition.

Beyond the idea that visitors are attracted by the choice of multiple activities within a small travel radius, on the supply side, agri-tourism firms may simply benefit from efficiency gains from joint promotion, programming and information-sharing. One example of coordination of joint promotion and programming is illustrated in an agri-tourism case study of Butte County, California [Hill *et al.*, 2017]. Butte County is a 90-minute drive from the nearest large metro area — a challenge for those potential urban visitors who find that drive to be too far for a weekend. To strengthen and promote agri-tourism as a regional visitor draw, a network of county, municipal, tourism industry and hospitality industry agencies are working with local agri-tourism operators to develop coordinated plans.

22.4 Economic Impacts of Agri-tourism

In order to consider the broader benefits of agri-tourism to communities and regional economies, researchers commonly frame and estimate economic impacts in a variety of ways [Bauman and Thilmany, 2017]. Given the differences in the operational models and nature of visitors (locals *vs.* out-of-area visitors) for agri-tourism, careful consideration must be taken when modeling economic impacts. The direct effects (monies brought into the community, particularly by non-local visitors) may have positive income-diversification and cash-flow implications for farm operators. But also, there is interest in how those additional revenues may circulate through the economy as the farm owner or its employees spend their earnings, creating indirect effects. Whether benefits accrue to farms directly or to their broader community, it is important to understand as broader economic spillovers may help to bolster community support for operations attracting visitors to the area.

The nature of agri-tourism, in part, makes measuring the distribution and type of employment created difficult — both on-farm and in the wider community. For example, agri-tourism itself is broadly defined — from on-farm sales, to children's camps, to hunting and much more. In addition, the labor needs of each enterprise type are different. High-visitation, customer-service-oriented agri-tourism requires a lot more staff on-site than does a farm store. Furthermore, the spillover and competition effects of agri-tourism on the community will depend on the presence of community-based assets (i.e. natural amenities), infrastructure to support visitation (i.e. lodging, restaurants, other retail stores), as well as other activities that compete with agri-tourism for visitor dollars.

Several studies have estimated employment creation related to agri-tourism at a local, regional or state level. A 1998 study of a single agri-tourism operation in populous San Diego County found that the operation generated 69 full- and part-time jobs in the city of Carlsbad alone [Lobo *et al.*, 1999], and that for every $1 million spent by visitors in Carlsbad, 33 jobs in the retail food sector and 37 jobs in the recreation sector were created. A 2005 economic impact study for Maine found that agri-tourism in the state supported a total of 1,762 full- and part-time jobs, including 39% of all hired farm workers; indirect employment was estimated at 165 part- and full-time jobs in other sectors [Allen *et al.*, 2006]. Thilmany *et al.* [2007] used visitor data from the Colorado Tourism Office and a 2006 traveler expenditure survey to model the economic contributions of agri-tourism. The study found that agri-tourism generated an estimated 14,665 direct and indirect jobs in the Colorado economy, equivalent to 7% of all the state's jobs in tourism. These jobs depended primarily on out-of-state visitor expenditures (80% of agri-tourism's impact in Colorado was attributed to out-of-state travelers).

In the Delta Byway region of Arkansas, a primarily agricultural area, researchers estimated a baseline economic impact of agri-tourism using visitor and expenditure data from the Arkansas Parks and Tourism Department [Das and Rainey, 2008]. Based on several agri-tourism growth scenarios, the study predicted that growth in employment would occur primarily in low-paying hourly jobs in the retail sector (e.g. hunting supply retail), followed by accommodations and food service. Overall, the study found that the greatest employment impacts were within non-agricultural businesses in the Delta Byway communities, such as retail, lodging and food services businesses. Marcouiller [2007] stresses that while tourism jobs are often entry-level, the industry itself may create incentives for entrepreneurial endeavors; indeed, rural areas in the United States have a higher proportion of both farm and non-farm proprietor employment [Bureau of Economic Analysis, 2017]. So, beyond employment gains, some of the positive economic benefits from tourism may be masked if the services and goods on which travelers spend money are provided by non-employer entrepreneurs who open for business if they perceive unmet demand from out-of-area visitors.

22.4.1 *Federal lands and policy affect the economic impacts of outdoor recreation and agri-tourism*

Land available for outdoor recreation, whether publicly or privately owned, provides natural areas and open spaces, which numerous studies have found to have significant economic values [McConnell and Walls, 2005; Bolitzer and Netusil, 2000; Shultz and King, 2001; Riddel, 2001], and connections with rural employment growth [McGranahan *et al.*, 2010]. Marcouiller and Hoogasian [2014] explore the specific role that recreation on public lands plays in rural development, noting that public lands — federal, state, and local — contribute to an area's natural amenities, which have been linked to more robust economic development [McGranahan, 1999].

Recent research shows that rural counties with a higher proportion of federal lands have faster population, income and employment growth than counties with less federal land [Kovacs *et al.*, 2017; Rasker *et al.*, 2013; McGranahan, 2008; Thompson *et al.*, 2006; Shumway and Otterstrom, 2001]. Goldbach [2012] found that the provision of new private outdoor recreation may be coupled with existing public outdoor recreation. Federally designated National Parks are an important driver of nearby agri-tourism ventures. Tourism spillovers provided by proximity to national parks are important to the many rural communities serving as gateways to national parks, forests, and seashores. According to 2017 data from the National Park Service, 331 million people visited US national parks and spent an estimated $18.2 billion in gateway regions across the US. Visitor spending in gateway communities include accommodations, food and retail expenditures, along with spending in recreational industries, which may include agri-tourism spending. A breakdown of this spending can be seen in Figure 22.6 [Cullinane Thomas *et al.*, 2018].

Research offers clear evidence of the positive impacts of national parks and monuments to their surrounding communities. One such study looked at the economies surrounding the 17 national monuments that were

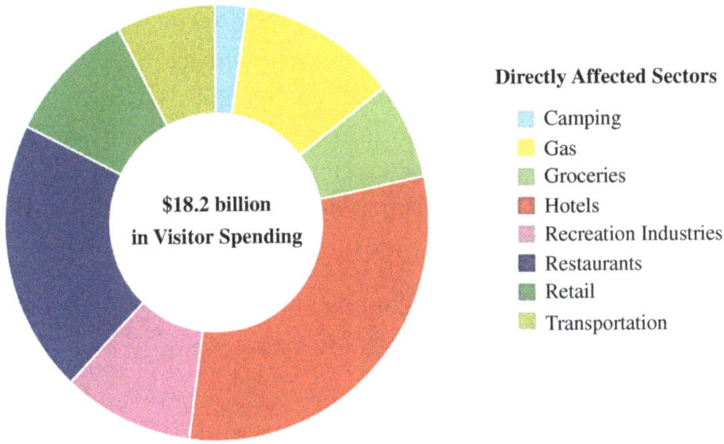

Fig. 22.6. Visitor spending in gateways to National Parks, 2017.

created between the years of 1982 and 2001. In each instance, they found that the local economies surrounding the monument expanded following the creation of the new monument [Headwaters Economics, 2017]. Another study found that for each 100,000 acres of wilderness, National Park or National Monument in a county, the per capita income of their residents increased by $4,360 [Rasker *et al.*, 2013].

Marcouiller and Hoogasian [2014] describe several important federal programs that promote outdoor recreation as a rural development tool. Some of these programs seek to increase participation in outdoor recreation generally (e.g. the National Park Service's *Outdoor Nation* and the Bureau of Land Management's *Wilderness Inquiry*). Other programs stimulate the growth and use of both private and non-federal supply of recreation lands by facilitating infrastructure and training (e.g. the *Community Forest and Open Space Program* (US Forest Service) and the *Land and Water Conservation Fund* (National Park Service)). Other policies encourage or facilitate recreation on private lands. For example, the Natural Resources Conservation Service (NRCS) provides incentives to landowners to allow temporary access for recreation on farmland through the *Voluntary Public Access and Habitat Incentive Program.* Similarly, the US Forest Service's *Forest Legacy Program* provides funding to preserve private forest lands that can be used for recreation.

Another federal policy affecting recreation on private lands is the Conservation Reserve Program (CRP). Administered by the USDA NRCS, CRP pays farmers to remove environmentally sensitive land from agricultural production in order to reestablish native plant species, improve water quality, prevent soil erosion, and reduce the loss of wildlife habitat. Some private land owners permit hunting on CRP (see Box 22.1).

Box 22.1: An example of the economic impacts of the Conservation Reserve Program on agri-tourism

Loomis *et al.* [2015] surveyed deer, waterfowl, and upland game bird hunters in North and South Dakota to estimate the proportion of hunting that takes place on private land enrolled in the Conservation Reserve Program (CRP). Survey results were used to estimate the economic impact that CRP land used by out-of-state hunters had on the two states' economies. Results showed the relative importance of CRP land to hunting-tourism.

Over half of upland game bird hunting took place on CRP land, 42% of deer hunting in North Dakota and 23% in South Dakota took place on CRP lands, and 23% of waterfowl hunters in North Dakota, and 21% in South Dakota used CRP lands (Table 1). This agri-tourism activity generated over 1,000 jobs and millions in economic impact in these two states. In addition to the expenditures from out-of-state hunters, in-state resident hunting on CRP lands also generated spending in rural areas amounting to an additional contribution of $42 million in the two states.

Table 1. Economic impacts and jobs from hunting on conservation reserve lands in North Dakota and South Dakota.

	Deer hunting		Water hunting		Upland game bird hunting	
	North Dakota	South Dakota	North Dakota	South Dakota	North Dakota	South Dakota
Proportion of total hunting on CRP lands	42%	23%	23%	21%	69%	56%
Impacts (millions of 2014 dollars)	$0.13	$0.66	$3.57	$1.40	$15.87	$35.45
Jobs	3	12	68	29	276	730

Source: Loomis *et al.* [2015].

22.5 Informing a Future Research Agenda on Agri-tourism and Rural Economies

Despite its potential as a farm diversification and rural development tool, agri-tourism is not a magic bullet. However, recent growth in the broader tourism sector, the number of farms reporting recreational enterprises, and the longstanding goal of the US to strengthen rural economies, all lead one to believe that agri-tourism is worthy of future study. The diversity of interests that travelers revealed in past research indicates that farms of all scales and geographic locations have opportunities to attract visitors. The businesses that are most likely to benefit from agri-tourism are those that can jointly offer and promote traveler experiences that are customized to the traveler base already coming to their area (particularly for small operations without the resources to promote and recruit travelers themselves). But, in the case of sizable operations with large landholdings, they may be better positioned to integrate their natural capital and leverage the draw of other outdoor recreation assets in their regions. Since there is already research focused on agri-tourism and its travelers, and parallel work on national parks and public lands, perhaps it is time to consider whether further integrating such research projects could result in richer findings.

Inherent in this call for more integrated research is the longstanding issue of how to measure the economic contribution of tourism and outdoor recreation in an economy. There are several government classifications and sectors that are commonly used to measure the travel sector (lodging and segments of retail, transportation and recreation), but there is not currently a formally structured industrial code for tourism or for outdoor recreation. The US Bureau of Economic Analysis (BEA) produces a travel and tourism satellite account that measures the contribution of travel and tourism-related economic activity to the US gross domestic product; and the BEA is currently prototyping an outdoor recreation satellite account to measure the size of the outdoor recreation economy (which includes agri-tourism activities among a broad range of outdoor recreation activities) [Highfill *et al.*, 2018]. These satellite accounts provide economy-wide estimates of economic activity, and therefore their primary usefulness is in helping to understand nationwide trends and patterns. Given the small and fragmented nature of agri-tourism and rural recreation [Chase *et al.*, 2018], data and tools that would enable finer geographic measures of the tourism and outdoor recreation industries would facilitate future research on agri-tourism's economic development implications.

The economic opportunities associated with agri-tourism include both on-farm jobs and income, as well as increased business activities in support sectors, such as lodging, retail and food services. Economic contributions flowing from these opportunities may increase farm income and may provide new employment or entrepreneurial opportunities in rural areas; however, many new jobs may be in lower-paying hospitality and retail services sectors. We conclude that, although understanding the economic contributions of the recreation and tourism sectors to the economy is important, it is even more important to understand who benefits and to what degree.

Finally, to fully translate this research to farm stakeholders, there should be more information on how local and state policies and programming also align with their operational goals. In order to successfully assess and navigate the development of more agri-tourism and outdoor recreation, technical assistance providers and local governments should make the policy environment for such enterprises transparent. Both Colorado State University and Rutgers University have developed materials to guide producers in their states and regions (http://agri-tourism.rutgers.edu/training, https://agri-tourism.localfoodeconomics.com, both accessed 9 October 2018). As another example, the American Planning Association has recognized that need, and has compiled a collection of useful articles (https://www.planning.org/knowledgebase/agri-tourism/, accessed 9 October 2018). Continued efforts to provide such guidance, and if possible, harmonization on various issues such as zoning, on-farm lodging (e.g. AirBnB) and hiring contractors to guide outdoor experiences, would lessen perceived barriers to potential agri-tourism and outdoor recreation operators.

References

Allen, T. G., Gabe, T. M. and McConnon, J. C. (2006). *The Economic Contribution of Agri-tourism to the Maine Economy*, University of Maine, Department of Resource Economics and Policy, REP Staff Paper #563.

Arroyo, C. G., Barbieri, C. and Rich, S. R. (2013). Defining agri-tourism: A comparative study of stakeholders' perceptions in Missouri and North Carolina. *Tour. Manag.*, 37, pp. 39–47.

Barbieri, C. (2008). A comparison of agri-tourism and other farm entrepreneurs: Implications for future tourism and sociological research on agri-tourism. *Proc. 2008 Northeastern Recreation Research Symposium*, GTR-NRS-P-42.

Barbieri, C. (2010). An importance-performance analysis of the motivations behind agri-tourism and other farm enterprise developments in Canada. *Journal of Rural and Community Development*, 5, pp. 1–20.

Bauman, A. and Thilmany, D. (2017). Exploring localized economic dynamics: Methods driven case studies of transformation and growth in agricultural and food markets. *Econ. Devt. Quart.*, 31(3), pp. 244–254.

Bolitzer, B. and Netusil, R. (2000). The impact of open spaces on property values in Portland, Oregon. *Journal of Environmental Management*, 59(3), pp. 185–193.

Chase, L. C., Stewart, M., Schilling, B., Smith, B. and Walk, M. (2018). Agritourism: Toward a conceptual framework for industry analysis. *Journal of Agriculture, Food Systems, and Community Development*, 8(1), pp. 13–19.

Cullinane Thomas, C., Koontz, L. and Cornachione, E. (2018). 2017 *National Park Visitor Spending Effects: Economic Contributions to Local Communities, States, and the Nation*. Natural Resource Report NPS/NRSS/EQD/NRR—2018/1616. National Park Service, Fort Collins, Colorado.

Das, B. R. and Rainey, D. V. (2008). *Distributional Impacts of Agri-tourism in the Arkansas Delta Byways Region*. Selected paper 2008 American Agricultural Economics Association Annual Meetings, Orlando, FL.

Goldbach, R. (2012). *Spatial Dimensions of Natural Resource Decisions: Private Responses to Public Resource Decisions*, Colorado State University PhD dissertation, ProQuest Dissertation Publishing.

Headwaters Economics. (2017). *Updated Summary: The Economic Importance of National Monuments to Local Communities*. Headwaters Economics. https://headwaterseconomics.org/wp-content/uploads/monuments-summary.pdf (accessed 9 October 2018).

Hill, R., Thilmany, D., Sullins, M., Van Sandt, A., Hardesty, S. and Snyder, C. (2017). *Agri-tourism in the West: Outreach Approaches and Strategies that Work for Producers and Communities Exploring New and Expanded Efforts*. Organized symposium for the WAEA Annual Meetings. Lake Tahoe, CA. https://agri-tourism.localfoodeconomics.com (accessed 9 October 2018).

Highfill, T., Franks, C., Georgi, P. S. and Howells, III, T. F. (2018). Introducing the outdoor recreation satellite account. *Bureau of Economic Analysis Survey of Current Business*, 98(3).

Kovacs, K., Haight, R. G. and West, G. (2017). Protected area designation, natural amenities and rural development in forested counties in the continental United States. *Growth and Change*, 48(4), pp. 611–639.

Lobo, R. E., Goldman, G. E., Jolly, D. A., Wallace, B. D., Schrader, W. L. and Parker, S. A. (1999). Agri-tourism benefits agriculture in San Diego county. *California Agriculture*, 53(6), pp. 20–24.

Loomis, J. (2002). *Integrated Public Land Management: Principles and Applications to National Forest, Parks, Wildlife Refuges, and BLM lands*, 2nd edition. Columbia University Press: New York, NY.

Loomis, J., Haefele, M., Hill, R. and Miller, M. (2015). *Economic Contribution, Impacts, and Economic Benefits of Deer, Waterfowl and Upland Game Bird Hunting in North and South Dakota: Relationship to CRP Lands.* Report to the USDA Farm Services Agency. https://www.fsa.usda.gov/Assets/USDA-FSA-Public/usdafiles/EPAS/PDF/Loomis_EtAl_SD_ND_HUNTING_Economic_Study_Final_9-19-2015.pdf (accessed 9 October 2018).

Marcouiller, D. (2007). "Boosting" tourism as a rural public policy: Panacea or Pandora's box? *Journal of Regression Analysis and Policy*, 37(1), pp. 28–31.

Marcouiller, D. W. and Hoogasian, A. (2014). The role of public outdoor recreation providers in supporting rural development. In Payson, Steven (ed.). *Public Economics in the United States: How the Federal Government Analyzes and Influences the Economy*. ABC-CLIO: Santa Barbara, CA.

McConnell, V. and Walls, M. (2005). *The Value of Open Space: Evidence from Studies of Non-Market Benefits*. Resources for the Future. January.

McGehee, N. G. (2007). An Agri-tourism systems model: A Weberian perspective. *Journal of Sustainable Tourism*, 15(2), pp. 111–124.

McGehee, N. G. and Kim, K. (2004). Motivation for agri-tourism entrepreneurship. *Journal of Travel Research*, 43, pp. 161–170.

McGranahan, D. A. (1999). *Natural Amenities Drive Rural Population Change*. Food and Rural Economics Division, Economic Research Service, US Department of Agriculture. Agricultural Economics Report No. 781.

McGranahan, D. A. (2008). Landscape influence on recent rural migration in the US. *Landscape and Urban Planning*, 85, pp. 228–240.

McGranahan, D., Wojan, T. and Lambert, D. (2010). The rural growth Trifecta: Outdoor amenities, creative class and entrepreneurial context. *Journal of*

Economic Geography, 11(3), pp. 529–557. https://doi.org/10.1093/jeg/lbq007 (accessed 9 October 2018).

Rasker, R., Gude, P. and Delorey, M. (2013). The effect of protected federal lands on economic prosperity in the non-metropolitan west. *Journal of Regional Analysis and Policy*, 43(2), pp. 110–122.

Reeder, R. and Brown, D. (2005). *Recreation, Tourism and Rural Well Being*. Economic Research Report Number 7.

Riddel, M. (2001). A Dynamic Approach to Estimating hedonic prices for environmental goods: An application to open source purchase. *Land Econ.*, 77(4), pp. 494–512.

Shultz, S. and King, D. (2001). The use of census data for hedonic price estimates of open space amenities and land use. *The Journal of Real Estate Finance and Economics*, 22, pp. 239–252.

Shumway, J. M. and Otterstrom, S. M. (2001). Spatial patterns of migration and income change in the mountain west: the dominance of service-based amenity-rich counties. *The Professional Geographer*, 53(4), pp. 492–502.

Thilmany, D., Sullins, M. and Ansteth, A. (2007). *The 2006 Economic Contribution of Agri-tourism to Colorado: Estimates from a Survey of Colorado Tourists*. Colorado State University, Department of Agricultural and Resource Economics, EDR 07-24.

Thompson, E., Hammond, G. and Weiler, S. (2006). *Amenities, Local Conditions, and Fiscal Determinants of Factor Growth in Rural America*. The Federal Reserve Bank of Kansas City, Economic Research Department. Research Working Paper, RWP 06-08.

US Bureau of Economic Analysis, Regional Data. https://www.bea.gov/iTable/index_regional.cfm (accessed 30 November 2017).

US Bureau of Labor Statistics, Quarterly Census of Wages and Employment. https://www.bls.gov/data/ (accessed 30 November 2017).

US Census Bureau, American Community Survey (2016). https://www.census.gov/library/visualizations/2016/comm/acs-rural-urban.html (accessed 9 October 2018).

US Department of the Interior (2012). Chapter 5: Public Conservation Lands and Rural Economic Growth, in: *The Department of the Interior's Economic Contribution*, FY 2011. 214 pp.

US Travel Association (2017). *Domestic Travel Factsheet*. February. https://www.ustravel.org/system/files/media_root/document/Research_Fact-Sheet_Domestic-Travel.pdf (accessed 9 October 2018).

Van Sandt, A. and Thilmany, D. (2016). Diversification through Agri-tourism in a Changing US Farmscape. *Western Economics Forum*, (15): 52–58. Fall.

Van Sandt, A., Low, S. and Thilmany, D. (2018). A Spatial Analysis of Agri-tourism in the US: What's Driving Clusters of Enterprises? *Agricultural and Resource Economics Review*. https://doi.org/10.1017/age.2017.36 (accessed 9 October 2018).

Vincent, C. H., Hanson, L. A. and Argueta, C. N. (2017). *Federal Land Ownership: Overview and Data*. Congressional Research Service. 7-5700, R42346.

Chapter 23

Special Study: Agri-tourism as a Strategy for Farm Economic Development in New Jersey, USA: Opportunities and Cautions for Farmers

Brian J. Schilling*, Michelle Infante-Casella, Stephen J. Komar and William J. Bamka

Rutgers, The State University of New Jersey, NJ, USA
**brischi@njaes.rutgers.edu*

The expansion of agri-tourism has been a notable trend in the United States in recent decades. Inviting the public onto farms for recreational enjoyment offers the opportunity for farm economic development, particularly in the Northeastern region of the country where urban expansion and exurban growth pose significant challenges to farming. For many urban-influenced farms, agri-tourism synergizes with direct-to-consumer marketing of farm products and capitalizes on strong consumer interest in "local food". At the same time, agri-tourism is often an entirely new business paradigm for traditional production-wholesale farms, and brings new business challenges and risks. This chapter summarizes recent statistics on the prevalence and significance of agri-tourism in the US, with a focus on this sector's prominence in the Northeast region. Drawing from experiences in New Jersey, a leading agri-tourism state, important business risk factors associated with agri-tourism are discussed.

23.1 Introduction

Financial pressures force many American family farms to seek farm revenue expansion through various forms of entrepreneurship, including product or market diversification [Vogel, 2012]. Agri-tourism is an increasingly popular form of alternative agricultural enterprise development in many regions of the country, particularly in the relatively more urbanized Northeast. Agri-tourism is defined generally as the invitation of the public onto working farms for educational and recreational purposes, and is inclusive of a wide range of innovative on-farm direct-to-consumer marketing activities (e.g. farm retail stands, pick-your-own enterprises, etc.) that blend the sale of agricultural farm products with farm experiences.

Federal statistics show that farm income from agri-tourism activities exceeded $2 billion in 2012 (Table 23.1).[a] Agri-tourism has emerged as a particularly important economic adaptation strategy for small farms (<$250,000 in gross sales). Small farms account for 88% of US farms and operate 451 million acres of farmland — nearly half of the US agricultural land base. As such, they are a dominant characteristic of the American agricultural landscape, and define the economy and social fabric of countless rural communities. Small farms, especially those operating in urban-influenced areas where farmers can capitalize on proximity to dense consumer markets, are more inclined to engage in agri-tourism activities as a strategy to mitigate high operating and land access costs, scale inefficiencies, challenges accessing consolidating retail channels, urbanization pressures, and difficulties competing in markets reorganizing at a global scale [Schilling *et al.*, 2014]. Federal data are telling — small farms account for 63% of aggregate agri-tourism income, but generate only 11% of the value of farm products sold.

Federal statistics demonstrate the significance of agri-tourism as a farm and rural community development strategy in the United States.

---

[a]This revenue estimate is conservative. The National Agricultural Statistics Service enumerates agri-tourism income and direct marketing sales separately. The latter is defined to include only the sale of farm products sold "directly to individual consumers for human consumption", and thus it excludes a range of ornamental products (for example, nursery stock, flowers, Christmas trees) and other non-consumables.

Table 23.1. Small farms' reliance on agri-tourism.

		Farms with gross sales of		Percent of total	
	All farms	<$250,000	≥$250,000	<$250,000	≥$250,000
Number of farms	2,109,303	1,860,053	249,250	88.2	11.8
Land in farms (million acres)*	914.5	451.1	463.4	49.3	50.7
Value of farm products sold ($ billion)	394.6	44.0	350.7	11.1	88.9
Income from agri-tourism ($ billion)	2.0	1.3	0.7	63.3	36.7

Note: "Agri-tourism" data in this table and chapter reflect the sum of the "value of agricultural products sold directly to individuals for human consumption" and "income from agri-tourism and recreational services", reported in the 2012 Census of Agriculture.

* One acre equals to 0.405 ha.

Source: Data compiled from the 2012 Census of Agriculture [USDA-NASS, 2014].

This chapter provides a localized perspective on the importance of agri-tourism in New Jersey, a highly urbanized state in the Northeastern part of the country that is simultaneously a leader in agri-tourism. A chronology of efforts to support agri-tourism development in the state is presented. Examples of key business challenges and risk factors associated with agri-tourism development are highlighted.

23.2 Agri-tourism and Economic Development in New Jersey Agriculture

A high concentration of agri-tourism activity lies within the nine Northeastern US states, an area of the country where agriculture often exists at an urban fringe [Schilling *et al.*, 2012]. Data from the most recent federal Census of Agriculture show that the region generates only 4.2% of all US farm gross sales, but 23.9% of combined direct marketing and agri-tourism income [USDA-NASS, 2014]. Further, growth in the

Northeast's agri-tourism revenues outpaced national growth in this sector by more than 63% between 2007 and 2012.

New Jersey, nestled between the large urban centers of New York City and Philadelphia in the southernmost portion of the Northeast, is the most densely populated state in the US and is also the most urbanized. More than 30 million people — roughly one-tenth of the US population — with an aggregate personal income in excess of $1 trillion live within 100 miles of the central part of the state. Steady transitions to high-returns-per-acre crops such as fruits, vegetables, ornamentals and nursery stock reflect an important farmer adaptation strategy to urbanization pressures on agriculture.[b] Further, these types of farm production are a mainstay at the state's many direct-to-consumer market venues. A statewide survey of agri-tourism conducted in 2006 found that 21% of New Jersey's farms offered some form of agri-tourism, and that these activities contributed $57.5 million to aggregate farm income [Schilling *et al.*, 2012].[c] The breakdown of agri-tourism income was as follows:

- 70.5% from on-farm direct marketing (e.g. pick-your own, U-cut Christmas trees, farm markets);
- 16.0% from outdoor recreational activities (e.g. hunting, fishing, bird watching, horse riding);
- 9.4% from entertainment (e.g. hay rides, corn mazes, petting zoos, haunted attractions);
- 3.3% from educational tourism (e.g. school groups, winery tours, farm work experiences);
- 0.9% from on-farm accommodations (e.g. bed and breakfasts, picnicking, birthday parties).

[b]Census of Agriculture data show that sales of nursery/greenhouse/floriculture/sod products, fruits and berries, and vegetables accounted for 73% of New Jersey's farm revenue in 2012. In 1982, these same sectors accounted for only 58% of the state's farm industry revenue. High land values and labor costs contributed significantly to these transitions.

[c]The survey did not capture farms that offered agri-tourism activities without a fee (e.g. free farm tours).

The authors' experiences with agri-tourism operators during field-based Rutgers Cooperative Extension[d] programming suggest that the wide-ranging types of on-farm entertainment and educational activities offered by New Jersey farmers most frequently serve to increase customer traffic to existing on-farm retail enterprises (e.g. farm stores, roadside markets, pick-your-own operations). Amid a growing number of competitors (e.g. other farms, garden centers, supermarkets and "big-box" retailers) and constantly evolving consumer preferences, the most successful agri-tourism operators exhibit a perpetual cycle of adaptive behavior. Examples of innovations in farm marketing include new value-added product development (e.g. wine, artisanal foods), crafts, production tailored to meet local customer needs (e.g. nursery stock acclimated to local growing environments), and food items that satisfy consumer food values (e.g. free-range eggs, organic produce) or evolving ethnic and cultural preferences. These types of farm adaptations capitalize on the increasingly broad base of consumer interest in the benefits perceived in local food systems.

While direct-to-consumer marketing of farm products has a long history in New Jersey, the inclusion of recreational and educational activities into farms' product mixes has surged in the past two decades in response to economic pressures and the market environment (i.e. rapid suburban development in agricultural areas, low-cost social media marketing options). Farm-level benefits of agri-tourism enterprise development include the expansion or diversification of revenue streams, stabilization of household income amid seasonal fluctuations in farm earnings and higher unit prices for products [Schilling *et al.*, 2006; Schilling *et al.*, 2014; Barbieri, 2013; Nickerson *et al.*, 2001]. Many

---

[d]Cooperative Extension refers to a national system of non-formal education delivery, most commonly through partnerships between the nation's land grant universities, and state and county governments. Central to the mission of Extension is the targeted dissemination of science-based information to various stakeholders. Agriculture has long been a traditional focus for Extension programming. Cooperative Extension was established federally in 1914 with the passage of the Smith-Lever Act. Federal funding for Cooperative Extension is managed by the United States Department of Agriculture's (USDA) National Institute of Food and Agriculture.

agri-tourism activities allow producers to expand financial returns from existing farm assets with little new capital investment.

The cultivation of the next generation of American farmers is an often-cited policy objective as the ownership of a substantial proportion of the nation's farmland resources will change hands in the near future due to farmer retirements [Bigelow *et al.*, 2016]. Over the past decade, Rutgers Cooperative Extension faculty have observed the growing importance of agri-tourism as a strategy adopted by multigenerational farms to support the livelihoods of younger family members or allow a phased transition of land and business ownership to the next generation of operators. Agri-tourism is also an important industry entrance strategy employed by beginning farmers to overcome challenges related to land and wholesale market access, limited capital availability and credit access, or scale inefficiencies.

For some New Jersey farms, agri-tourism activities remain ancillary in nature and supplement traditional farm income through limited seasonal events (e.g. a farm "open house" or pick-your-own activities). In other cases, agri-tourism generates substantial farm income during peak seasonal windows (e.g. festivals and hayrides during the autumn harvest or corn mazes and "haunted" barns in the weeks preceding Halloween). In yet others, agri-tourism is the central element of the farm business model. Customer volumes at agri-tourism farms are commensurately variable. One of the state's largest agri-tourism farms is a year-round destination centered on a vibrant farm market offering educational programs for children, farm tours, pick-your-own activities, and value-added farm products. The owners report an annual customer volume in the 700,000–800,000 range. In recent years the owners have developed a farm winery to further expand product offerings and enable their adult children to remain engaged in the farm, creating a multigenerational business and a pathway for business succession.

Some New Jersey agri-tourism farms have evolved incrementally over time from "traditional" production-wholesale operations. For example, a fruit farm in southern New Jersey began direct marketing produce from a small wagon in the mid-1990s. As the direct marketing business grew, a permanent retail market was constructed. The farm began growing wine grapes in the late 1990s and established a winery soon after. With the return of two adult sons to the business, the farm today offers wine tastings, farm festivals and a range of other activities to engage customers and the broader public.

Other farms' transitions to agri-tourism have occurred more rapidly, within the span of a few years. As an example, a dairy farm facing sustained depressed milk prices diversified production to include fruits, vegetables, sweet corn, pumpkins and other products sold at a produce stand built on the farm. The farm owners continued to innovate and diversify their product offerings with the addition of a pick-your-own pumpkin patch, a corn maze and hayrides. The farm most recently established itself as a popular destination for Halloween-themed events, including haunted farm attractions.

The benefits of agri-tourism extend beyond the farm gate. Schilling *et al.* [2011] find that agri-tourism activities on New Jersey farms stimulated an additional $33.3 million in economic activity in other business sectors (e.g. suppliers, service providers). In addition to expanding and diversifying local economic bases, agri-tourism contributes to a community's quality of life by expanding recreational opportunities, providing access to fresh farm products, and contributing to the retention of the open space and cultural amenities conferred by agricultural lands. Agri-tourism can also foster positive interactions between farmers and non-farmers that increase awareness of food production, agrarian heritage, resource stewardship and agricultural issues. These interactions may also raise public support for farm retention and development policies, or reduce community conflicts stemming from undesirable by-products (e.g. noise, dust, odors) of agricultural production.

23.3 Efforts to Support the Development of New Jersey's Agri-tourism Industry

Agri-tourism as an economic development strategy for New Jersey's farm industry began gaining traction in the early to mid-1990s during an industry-wide strategic planning initiative known as the FARMS Commission. Research supporting the planning effort found that 43% of farmers participating in a comprehensive statewide survey conducted in 1993 by the USDA's National Agricultural Statistics Service offered educational or recreational on-farm activities to the public, most often in the form of hunting and fishing or farm tours offered without fee [Schilling *et al.*, 2006]. In fact, less than one-quarter of farms reporting agri-tourism charged a fee for those activities.

More formal recognition of agri-tourism as a potentially important economic development strategy began emerging in the mid-2000s. In 2004, New Jersey's State Board of Agriculture endorsed agri-tourism as a statewide economic development strategy for the farm sector. The following year, New Jersey Secretary of Agriculture Charles M. Kuperus empaneled the New Jersey Agri-tourism Industry Advisory Council to better define the scope of agri-tourism in the state, identify the needs of agri-tourism operators and advance strategies to support the sector's growth. The task force commissioned researchers at the New Jersey Agricultural Experiment Station (Rutgers University) to examine these issues. However, agri-tourism and innovative farm direct marketing strategies were already in place on many farms. Research sponsored by the State Department of Agriculture documented that, among 48 established agri-tourism operators, 47% had been offering such activities since at least the 1970s [Schilling *et al.*, 2006].

Rutgers Cooperative Extension programming began coalescing in 2012 with the organization of three regional agri-tourism educational conferences in New Jersey that were attended by nearly 300 farmers, agricultural service providers and government officials. Participant feedback resulted in the creation of an agri-tourism working group at Rutgers University to coordinate and deliver extension programming in this area and to lead a multistate project in the Northeast aimed at identifying and responding to the needs of farmers engaged in, or contemplating the development of, agri-tourism enterprises. Today, the working group conducts farm assessments to assist agri-tourism operators with enterprise risk management.

23.4 Challenges Facing New Jersey Agri-tourism Operators

Agri-tourism presents significant opportunities for many New Jersey farmers. At the same time, agri-tourism is an entirely new business model for agricultural producers transitioning from a production-wholesale business or an enterprise engaged in only limited direct marketing. It follows that an agri-tourism-centric operation will face new operational challenges, such as different staffing demands and employee skill set requirements (e.g. customer service and hospitality skills) or the need to employ different marketing approaches.

The development of an agri-tourism enterprise also raises new risk management considerations. An especially important concern lies in the fact that opening a farm to the public elevates safety concerns and introduces additional liability exposures. Inviting people onto the farm for agri-tourism is a "numbers game". As the volume of visitors rises, so too does the likelihood of an injury. A farm owner has the legal obligation to take necessary precautions for protecting the safety and welfare of farm visitors. Accidents, however, happen. In some cases, an unscrupulous visitor may fraudulently claim an injury occurred on a farm and seek compensatory or punitive damages. Agri-tourism operators therefore need to take measures to manage legal liability, and to protect their personal and business assets in the event that a visitor is injured.

Another emerging challenge in New Jersey is linked to the pace of innovation in the sector and, subsequently, uncertainty in terms of its boundaries — fundamentally, what is "agri-tourism", and what is not? Clearly and consistently defining the industry remains a fundamental need [Chase *et al.*, 2018]. It is requisite for measuring the industry's growth and performance, which in turn has implications for justifying the allocation of Cooperative Extension and other agricultural service provider resources to support its development. More pertinently, ambiguity in the definition and scope of agri-tourism leads to difficulties determining coverage under, or compliance with, certain agricultural laws and regulations that may discourage business expansion or create unforeseen obstacles for farmers.

23.4.1 *Farm safety and liability*

Welcoming visitors to the farm to purchase agricultural products or to engage in educational and recreational purposes, while a promising business opportunity, presents additional legal liabilities to farm operators due to the exposure of guests to safety risks inherent on working farms. It is important to consider, for example, that most farms have evolved over time to maximize agricultural production efficiency. The incorporation of agri-tourism requires safe and efficient movement of visitors into and within the farm, including people with limited mobility or disabilities. This raises issues of establishing proper ingress and egress capable of accommodating anticipated visitor volumes and adequate parking, including overflow areas needed during times of peak customer volumes. Several large "destination" farms in New Jersey generate traffic levels that pose safety issues or create localized road congestion that raise neighbor complaints and tax local police resources.

Farm safety considerations are wide-ranging, particularly when receiving visitors who lack familiarity with the realities of a working farm. Safety risks inherent in many farms include trip and fall hazards (e.g. uneven terrain, stumps in a Christmas tree field), exposure to noxious plants or insects, and adverse weather conditions. There are also risks associated with visitors accessing farm equipment and machinery, or assembling in barns or other farm structures (e.g. fire). Farms with livestock or seasonal animal attractions face the risks of a farm guest being injured by an animal or exposed to zoonotic diseases.

Agri-tourism accidents have resulted in deaths. In 2013, several people were sickened by exposure to *E. coli* 0157:H7 while visiting a Minnesota farm's pumpkin patch. One child developed hemolytic uremic syndrome, which caused severe kidney damage. During subsequent court proceedings, it was determined that the illnesses resulted when visitors were allowed to pet and feed the farm's cows through a feedlot gate. It was further found that the farm owners did not implement proper sanitation measures (e.g. manure was present on the animals and gate, and no handwashing facilities were present) nor were visitors warned about possible biosecurity hazards. In 2016, a jury awarded the child a $7.55 million verdict.

In 2017, an undisclosed settlement was reached in a lawsuit filed after a teenage girl was killed in a haunted hayride accident that occurred in 2014 after the vehicle pulling the wagon lost its brakes. Other passengers were injured. In 2014, a teenager working as a zombie at an Idaho corn maze was killed when he was struck by a bus being used as part of a zombie paintball Halloween attraction. The farm was fined by the US Occupational Health and Safety Administration; a wrongful death lawsuit is pending.

Farm-based safety risks and associated legal liabilities can never be eliminated. However, they can be managed through a comprehensive approach to farm safety and risk management. Rutgers Cooperative Extension programming developed for New Jersey farmers by the authors [see Schilling *et al.*, 2017] advises that agri-tourism operators should:

- Conduct routine farm inspections to identify and mitigate hazards, and pay particular attention to "attractive nuisances", or activities that might reasonably be expected to attract the interest of visitors, especially children (examples: irrigation ponds, tractors, farm animals).
- Designate and monitor areas that are off-limits to visitors (e.g. storage areas, irrigation ponds).
- Develop plans of operation for farm activities (i.e. a hayride or petting zoo) that identify safety risks, and outline specific protocols and rules for safely managing the attraction for guests.
- Establish emergency response protocols.
- Schedule a site walk-through with local emergency responders so that they develop familiarity with the operation.
- Create an incident response form to detail and document accidents that occur on the farm.
- Train employees to understand farm safety concerns and implement safety procedures, plans of operations for specific farm activities, as well as emergency response procedures.
- Install proper signage with farm rules and warnings against known hazards.
- Consider the use of liability waivers or other indemnification measures.
- Understand and comply with applicable laws, regulations and codes.
- Maintain records on accidents, farm inspections, employee training, hazard mitigation efforts and other details that demonstrate efforts to maintain a safe farm environment for visitors.
- Discuss the agri-tourism enterprise with legal, insurance and other qualified professionals to identify liability management strategies.

23.4.2 *Regulatory issues and compliance*

Consistent and reliable data on agri-tourism tend to be limited due to variability in terminology and the definitions employed [Chase *et al.*, 2018; Schilling *et al.*, 2012]. Terminology is yet to be standardized in the academic literature, practitioner publications and policy [Phillip *et al.*, 2010]. There exists a variety of terms used to denote "agri-tourism", including farm tourism, agritainment, farm recreation, and rural tourism. Similarly, the definition of agri-tourism and the activities included therein lack consistency. Does agri-tourism have to occur on a working farm, or does it include off-farm venues such as agricultural fairs and community farmers' markets? Does income need to be generated, or can agri-tourism encompass recreational and educational activities that are offered without fees (e.g. a free farm tour)? For an activity to be considered agri-tourism, does there need to be a clear and direct nexus between that activity and the production or marketing of agricultural products (as opposed to a farm simply serving as the venue for an event such as hot-air ballooning, a catered wedding, or a monster truck exhibition)? The latter question is particularly important in the context of regulatory and policy discourse within New Jersey agriculture.

Two examples emerge from current agricultural policy discourse in New Jersey. The state's Right to Farm Act protects commercial farms engaging in normal agricultural activities and practices from nuisance complaints or overly restrictive regulation. Similar laws exist in all 50 US states. As an example, a commercial farm may create dust while tilling a field that is perceived as a nuisance by a residential neighbor who, in turn, may take legal action to stop the offending agricultural activity. The state's Right to Farm Act provides an affirmative defense to the farm, meaning that the nuisance complaint would be dismissed even if the claim of dust and noise generation is indeed factual.

Among the activities protected under the New Jersey statute are "agriculture-related educational and farm-based recreational activities *provided that the activities are related to marketing the agricultural or horticultural output of the commercial farm*". Charging visitors a fee for a hayride to a U-pick pumpkin patch or offering a corn maze to generate additional customer traffic at an on-farm retail market during the harvest season is generally viewed as an activity subject to right-to-farm protection because there is a clear nexus between the activity and product marketing. Nuisance complaints from neighbors inconvenienced by noise or additional road traffic would therefore by nullified. But what about activities that "push the envelope" and call into question whether the required nexus to marketing the farm's agricultural or horticultural output is sufficient, or exists at all? Consider a farm-to-table dinner that features the farm's own beef and produce *versus* a catered wedding at a winery that generates only nominal wine sales. What about a farm with haunted corn maze and barn attractions during the Halloween season that, while occurring in an agricultural setting, generate no agricultural product sales during the events?

Right-to-farm protections afforded to commercial farms under New Jersey statute are a powerful defense against nuisance suits and may even pre-empt local regulations deemed to be overly restrictive to farming. Being deemed ineligible for right-to-farm protection does not mean that an activity is impermissible; it simply means that a commercial farm does not have an affirmative defense to engage in it unfettered by neighbor complaints or local government ordinances. Current policy discussions in the state center on concerns over overextending the statutory protections to activities falling outside of the legislative intent to protect against the disruption of customary farming practices.

The Agriculture Retention and Development Act, passed concurrently in 1983 with the Right to Farm Act, established New Jersey's farmland preservation program. To date, more than 227,000 acres of farmland (32% of the state's remaining farmland base) have been permanently preserved under the program. Properties protected under the program are subject to a deed of easement that specifies that the enrolled lands are "retained for agricultural use and production".

> The deed of easement expressly prohibits the use or development of enrolled lands for non-agricultural purposes. A provision in the easement terms allows an owner of preserved farmland to "derive income from certain recreational activities such as hunting, fishing, cross-country skiing and ecological tours, only if such activities do not interfere with the actual use of the land for agricultural production and that the activities only utilize the [p]remises in its existing condition.

Unlike right to farm, deed-of-easement compliance is about permissibility; an activity is allowable on a preserved farm, or it is not. Generally, the construction of a farm retail stand, storage barn, or structure to house farm labor will be allowed under the deed of easement (sometimes with required prior approval from the easement holder). On the other hand, the use of a farm field and wooded area for paintball or the construction of a new building solely for use as a haunted attraction or corporate retreat facility will be deemed impermissible. Then there are gray areas, such as farm-to-table dinners or weddings, the permissibility of which may hinge on the extent to which such activities are (or are not) linked to the marketing and sale of the farm's products.

Right to farm and farmland preservation are cornerstone agricultural retention and development policies in New Jersey. In both instances, agri-tourism is contemplated as either a protected (right to farm) or permissible (farmland preservation) activity under certain conditions; however, the blurred and ever-shifting boundaries of agri-tourism present significant challenges to program administrators and uncertainty to farmers. The state agency charged with administering these programs has empaneled subcommittees to examine agri-tourism in the context of the current regulatory framework and statutory authority underlying both programs. The subcommittees are charged with making recommendations to better define the range of agri-tourism activities protected/permitted under right to farm/farmland preservation and providing necessary regulatory clarity to farmers engaged in agri-tourism.

23.5 Concluding Thoughts

Agri-tourism in the United States is significant, growing and evolving, particularly in the Northeastern region where many farms face challenges associated with scale of operation and urbanization pressures. Academic research has shown that agri-tourism can enhance farm profitability and confer additional financial, as well as non-pecuniary benefits to farms and their communities. While technological innovations in agriculture often have roots in the scientific and academic communities (frequently in partnership with farmers), we observe that agricultural marketing innovations tend to evolve more organically within the farming community. It follows that agricultural service providers, including Cooperative Extension, often need to play "catch up" with farmers to first understand the nature and efficacy of evolving innovative marketing strategies before being in a position to generalize best practices or provide guidance. The same holds true in the legislative and regulatory arena. While challenging, such effort is warranted.

References

Barbieri, C. (2013). Assessing the sustainability of agri-tourism in the US: A comparison between agri-tourism and other farm entrepreneurial ventures. *Journal of Sustainable Tourism*, 21(2), pp. 252–270.

Bigelow, D., Borchers, A. and Hubbs, T. (2016). *US Farmland Ownership, Tenure, and Transfer*. Economic Information Bulletin 161, US Department of Agriculture, Economic Research Service, Washington, DC.

Chase, L., Stewart, M., Schilling, B., Smith, B. and Walk, M. (2018). Agri-tourism: Toward a conceptual framework for industry analysis. *Journal of Agriculture, Food Systems, and Community Development*, 8(1), pp. 13–19.

Nickerson, N., Black, R. and McCool, S. (2001). Agri-tourism: Motivations behind farm/ranch business diversification. *Journal of Travel Research*, 40(1), pp. 19–26.

Phillip, S., Hunter, C. and Blackstock, K. (2010). A typology for defining agri-tourism. *Tourism Management*, 31(6), pp. 754–758.

Schilling, B., Attavanich, W. and Jin, Y. (2014). Does agri-tourism enhance farm profitability? *Journal of Agricultural and Resource Economics*, 39(1), pp. 69–87.

Schilling, B., Sullivan, K. and Komar, S. (2012). Examining the economic benefits of agri-tourism: The case of New Jersey. *Journal of Agriculture, Food Systems, and Community Development*, 3(1), pp. 199–214.

Schilling, B., Komar, S., Bamka, W. and Infante-Casella, M. (2017). *Managing Liability on Agri-tourism Farms*. Rutgers Cooperative Extension Fact Sheet FS1265.

Schilling, B., Marxen, L., Heinrich, H. and Brooks, F. (2006). *The Opportunity for Agri-tourism Industry Development in New Jersey*. Food Policy Institute Report No. RR-0706-010. Rutgers Food Policy Institute, New Brunswick, NJ.

Schilling, B., Sullivan, K. and Komar, S. and Marxen, L. (2011). *The Economics of Agri-tourism in New Jersey*. Rutgers Cooperative Extension Fact Sheet E333.

United States Department of Agriculture, National Agricultural Statistics Service (2014). *2012 Census of Agriculture, US Summary and State Reports*. USDA-NASS, Washington, DC.

Vogel, S. (2012). *Multi-Enterprising Farm Households: The Importance of Their Alternative Business Ventures in the Rural Economy*. Economic Information Bulletin 101, US Department of Agriculture, Economic Research Service, Washington, DC.

Index

J

L

M

N

O

P

R

CPSIA information can be obtained
at www.ICGtesting.com
Printed in the USA
BVHW061350270619
552080BV00001B/2/P

9 781786 347084